Palm Springs Confidential

Playground of the Stars!

Palm Springs Confidential

Playground of the Stars!

★ HOWARD JOHNS ★

BARRICADE BOOKS

FORT LEE, NEW JERSEY

Published by Barricade Books Inc.
185 Bridge Plaza North
Suite 308-A
Fort Lee, NJ 07024
www.barricadebooks.com

Library of Congress Cataloging-in-Publication Data
A copy of this book's Library of Congress Cataloging-in-Publication record can be obtained from the Library of Congress

First Printing
Manufactured in the United States of America

For Craig in heartfelt appreciation of his special friendship

Author's Note:
While I've tried to identify any house that has been razed or rebuilt, a few of the homes mentioned no longer exist.

Contents

Acknowledgments

The genesis of *Palm Springs Confidential* was in 1999 when I began compiling a locator guide to movie star homes. I had already written extensively for *Palm Springs Life* and other magazines about desert celebrities, several of whom had died, and their homes, which were listed for sale.

Los Angeles Magazine, among other publications, contacted me for help in identifying some of these addresses. Curiously, no reputable handbook existed other than erroneous tourist maps which had scant regard for historical accuracy. I took it upon myself to correct that glaring oversight and started researching this absorbing topic. Then an idea occurred to me.

I remembered bicycling through the different neighborhoods five years earlier after my arrival in the desert, fresh from my world travels and eager to learn about this humbling life, talking with retired actors such as Desert Museum benefactor George Montgomery, Diana "Mousie" Powell, and Donald Woods, among others, who befriended me.

I rang their doorbells again, we talked, and they unwittingly began my search for the truth that eventually became a personal mission. Their extensive knowledge, stretching back more than seventy years, proved to be a guiding light, though by no means were they the only ones that encouraged me in my quest. It was fortunate that I arrived in the desert when I did because the curtain was about to come down on the end of a truly magnificent era, which is how I met Bob Hope, Sonny Bono, Frank Sinatra, Ginger Rogers, Phil Harris, Alice Faye, Charles "Buddy" Rogers, and other celebrity homeowners who graciously shared their thoughts with me. I was introduced to Frank Bogert, John Conte, Gloria Greer, and others, all of whom had interesting stories and in one way or another helped to further my understanding of the desert's complex social hierarchy.

As an editor-at-large for *Palm Springs Life*, I was doubly fortunate to meet and interview the surviving architects of midcentury modern homes such as Albert Frey, E. Stewart Williams, and Donald Wexler, who shared their memories of working with the stars and other enlightening tidbits. Their conversations were vital and informative, and they spurred me onward to seek out more people, some of them now departed, whose names appear in these pages. All of the above individuals and many others that I met in passing at cocktail parties and business functions, added to this wonderful learning experience. Memories are one thing, however; facts are another.

While the task of researching and writing this book has been a labor of love, it has not been easy because of the noticeable lack of reliable documentation on this subject. Consequently, I have spent many hundreds of hours over the last three years putting together the confusing pieces of the puzzle that make up this compelling timeline in American history.

From the outset, it was a test of skill that proved both challenging and complicated. I did not want to repeat the mistakes of other writers, even though I respected their opinions. So I dug deeper, longer, and harder to find the truth. This exacting method set a high standard for me, and it was not without its own set of problems. After all, people derive pleasure from a good story. They don't want to be bored with tedious explanation or unnecessary detail. So, instead of contradicting every unfounded rumor or allegation, except where it is transparently false, I have tried to give various elements renewed perspective so that each story remains as enjoyable to read as it is, I am hopeful, correct. The result is an unprecedented number of celebrity homes, numbering more than five hundred confirmed residences and their corresponding addresses, that have been thoroughly researched by myself and authenticated through extensive interviews, private research, and public documents.

This daunting task could not have been accomplished without the kind assistance of numerous people who assisted my research on many and different levels. This interweaving cooperation, spread out across days, months, and years, helped me unlock some of the mysteries that have been kept buried in the sand of this magical desert.

Of tremendous assistance to me throughout the book's long gestation was the professional and courteous staff at Palm Springs City Library, in particular, reference librarians Nancy Robinson (retired), Shelly Thacker, Tom Lutgen, and Jon Fletcher, as well as reference coordinator Sastri Madugula. Their immaculate files proved most helpful in confirming dates, times, and places.

My sincere appreciation to Ray Kelley at First American Title Company, Riverside, whose official records verified the existence of many celebrity homes that were previously unidentified or whose ownership was a matter of contention. Without his help, this book would still be unfinished.

I owe a debt of gratitude to Sally McManus, director, Palm Springs Historical Society, for her kindness in helping me to choose rare photographs from its extensive archives. I also learned a great deal about Indian tribal customs from Agua Caliente Cultural Museum.

Other valuable assistance came directly and indirectly from celebrities, many of them homeowners at one time or another, who I interviewed during my residence and others I knew or met socially in Palm Springs and/or Hollywood. They include John Agar, Chris Alcaide, Jerry Antes, Jay Bernstein, Susan Bernard, Paul Burke, Jean Carson, Michael Childers, Linda Christian, Susie Coelho, Tony Curtis, Roy Dean, Edward Dmytryk, Yolande Donlan, Anne Douglas, Kirk Douglas, Billie Dove, James Galanos, Paul Gregory, Val Guest, Alan Hamel, George Hamilton, Richard Harrison, Jerry Herman, Betty Hutton, Jack Jones, Morgana King, Karen Kramer, Marc Lawrence, Francis Lederer, Ruta Lee, Patrick Macnee, Tony Martin, Terry Moore, George Nader, Andrew Neiderman, Stefanie Powers, Maria Riva, Harold Robbins, Keely Smith, Suzanne Somers, Robert Stack, Rod Taylor, Loretta Young, and Frank Zane.

Many desert residents were equally forthcoming about their own homes or recollections about famous neighbors, friends, and relatives, which assisted my investigation: John Baldwin, Jay Benoist, Jim Bertram, Russell Chappell, Linda Christiansen, Terri Cohn, Tracy Conrad, Craig Corbett, Ray Corliss, James Greenbaum, Mel Haber, Rosalie Hearst, Stefan Hemming, Hugh Kaptur, Bernice Korshak, Cliff Lambert, Ben Lane, Nelda Linsk, Andy Linsky, Arthur Lyons, Bob MacDonald, Wendy Maree, Francis Markley, Rose Mihata, Mark Miller, David Norton, Faye Otto, Hal Polaire, Ken Rosemeyer, Marc Sanders, Don Shaevel, Paul Shepard, Lew Sherrell, and Mary Sorrentino. The Riverside County Sheriff coroner supplied official reports of the murder of Tom Neal's wife, and Alan Ladd's often-misconstrued death.

Robert Henning, curator of collections at Santa Barbara Museum of Art, gave me a keen insight into the life of Wright S. Ludington. Dan Cuddy, chairman of First National Bank, Alaska, described his close friendship with Henry J. Emard. Several widely known individuals chose to speak to me only on the condition of anonymity.

Other helpful information was obtained throught the City of Palm Springs, *The Desert Sun, The Hollywood Reporter*, Los Angeles City Library, *Los Angeles Times*, the Margaret Herrick Library of the Academy of Motion Picture Arts and Sciences, *New York Times, Palm Springs Life*, and *Variety*.

Additional photographs were supplied by Backlot Books & Movie Posters, Cinema Collectors, *Desert Homes*, Steve Kiefer, Wayne Knight, Larry Edmunds Bookshop, and Anthony Petkovich.

Finally, I wish to acknowledge my publisher, Barricade Books, which provided this worthwhile project with the support and encouragement it needed. To all of the above people who assisted in my endeavors, and especially the galaxy of stars, large and small, that have made the desert shine so brightly, I thank you.

—Howard Johns
Palm Springs, October 2003

Preface

The electric windmills stand like rows of armed sentinels 110 miles east of Los Angeles on Interstate 10. Their polished blades spin in fifty-mile-per-hour gusts of wind that continuously buffet eight lanes of speeding traffic pushing against the forces of nature to reach journey's end. *Whoosh!* A metallic sign looms overhead, its white arrow pointing in the direction of prehistoric rocks that have been piled high along the roadside as if by an unseen giant hand.

Then, as abruptly as a tumbleweed rolling into view, four words spell the end of the lengthy pilgrimage across the parched desert landscape. And, magically, it is green everywhere. Welcome To Palm Springs.

This is one of America's winter playgrounds, the golfing capital of the world. Two million tourists visit the sun-drenched California city each year. Forty-four-thousand full-time residents live within its borders. They own luxury homes, drive expensive cars, and swim in five thousand sapphire pools.

The average year-round temperature of this fountain of youth is eighty-one degrees—the same age as many of its older residents, who luxuriate in air-conditioned health spas, pop mouthfuls of vitamin pills, and work out with their personal trainers at the gym. It's become a standing joke among comedians to call Palm Springs "God's Waiting Room" or "the Gay Nineties" because its aging population is either gay or ninety. Sometimes the humor is less funny, more caustic: "the land of Sodom and Gonorrhea," or as Larry Gelbart put it, "the Happy Humping Grounds, the place to take it off and get it on."

Not everyone who lives in this promiscuous land of sun and sex is super rich. Not all of them are famous. But they share a common bond: *the cult of celebrity*. For here, in this protected Garden of Eden dwell numerous citizens whose names are as familiar to the general public as items in a Sears' catalog.

From Marilyn Monroe's bedroom antics to the booze-filled revelry of the Rat Pack to thousands of horny teenagers on spring break and Robert Downey Jr.'s headline-making hotel drug bust, supermarket tabloids and reality TV shows cannot get enough of exceptional people doing ludicrous things to each other or committing heinous crimes here.

"Palm Springs has long observed with tolerant eyes the peccadilloes of Hollywood celebrities who enjoyed unwinding and sometimes misbehaving in the desert," said Associated Press entertainment writer Bob Thomas, who might have added Beverly Hills plastic surgeons, trial lawyers, and nefarious characters in dark glasses to that list. A picture rapidly emerges of consumption so conspicuous as to make an outsider gag on his cup of Starbucks coffee.

"Nowhere in America is the Mafia's presence more blatant than in this resort," claimed best-selling author Kitty Kelley, who called Palm Springs "a citadel of organized crime" overrun with New York crime bosses and Chicago gangsters accompanied by their bodyguards.

Who knew? Yet, 115 years ago when stagecoaches stopped in Banning, twenty-five miles to the west, to change horses and take on water, the area of today's Palm Springs was a proposed agricultural development named Palm Valley where mineral springs soothed the sore feet of Cahuilla Indians and a handful of white townsfolk sold provisions at the general store. So utterly remote was this chalky promontory of the Sonoran desert that prior to its discovery no less than five separate expeditions searching for water on their way from Mexico to the California coast between 1772 and 1846 failed to find any trace of this mythologized settlement known since earliest civilized times by native Indians and Mexicans as *Palma de la mano de Dios*—or "palm of God's hand." Not until 1853 when a U.S. railroad engineer encountered the bubbling sulfur baths, which he called Agua Caliente, did the area achieve a modicum of recognition and acquire the name by which it is known today: Palm Springs.

As nice a name as that was, in actuality, the only palm trees were at the base of nearby Mount San Jacinto in the jagged canyons that offered shade and protection from the blistering summer heat. This was the natural habitat of bighorn sheep and predatory mountain lions. Man was a stranger here.

"When I was a boy," remembered American baritone Lawrence Tibbett, a native of Bakersfield, "the mountain I climbed most was San Jacinto, eleven thousand feet high."

Before the introduction of electricity and automobiles, the sleepy community (population: three hundred) below San Jacinto catered mostly to terminal sufferers of asthma and tuberculosis. Nobody could have predicted that one day this hamlet of sanitariums would take root as a world-class tourist resort and blossom into a bustling residential city.

It took a handful of Hollywood moviemakers seeking desolate locations—vampish Theda Bara as *Salome*, Rudolph Valentino galloping over the dunes in *The Sheik*—to nurture Palm Springs from infancy to adulthood. The sandy hills and barren landscape were ideally suited for exterior filming, and in the intervening years, scores of film companies descended on the region, taking full advantage of the unusual topography that contained a great range of scenery from spiny Joshua trees and barrel cactus to lush waterfalls and tepid streams. The influx of strange people wearing derbies and spats must have shocked the local horse-and-buggy crowd who were unaccustomed to such wealth. The impoverished Indians, busily picking berries and harvesting wild corn, were probably scared out of their wits by the alien sight of jodhpur-wearing directors with megaphones yelling instructions at crowds of costumed extras.

Within a short time "the Springs," as it was nicknamed, became the ideal place for carloads of movie stars to rest—its relative isolation helping satisfy their increasingly obsessive need for privacy. They stayed at swank, rococo-themed plaster palaces such as El Mirador and the Desert Inn; went horseback riding at timber-framed Smoke Tree Ranch; and played tennis at the ranch-style Racquet Club. Thus began a trend of actors, agents, writers, directors, producers, and composers fleeing the confines of big-city living for the wide open spaces where, as a result of the Great Depression and the Second World War, they encountered displaced socialites, aristocrats, and dethroned royalty whose lives had been disrupted by the war and were now on permanent vacation. They all, patricians and producers alike, frequented the desert's cheap lodgings, frolicked in the crystal clear pools, and made uninhibited love under the stars.

Whenever Hollywood came to town, Palm Springs waited like a smiling concierge ready to cater to the demands of these and other high-profile visitors. At first it was fun, then it became a social obligation arranging a daily itinerary of tennis luncheons, hotel luaus, barbecues, costume parties, and formal dinners. Eventually it turned into a lucrative business with cooks, gardeners, chauffeurs, and maids working hard to keep the stars well fed and looking good.

The price that everyone paid, of course, was their silence in maintaining a visage as neat and unspoiled as the hotel bed linen that was laundered and pressed daily. Which brings us to the subject of the stars and their homes.

These perfectly constructed, immaculately trimmed compounds were built for their owners, most of whom paid cash, as a refuge from the world's intrusions, though in a bizarre paradox, these homes and the people who occupied them gradually became the focus of increased scrutiny. It came in the form of society photographers and gossip columnists, fans, and favor seekers. The stars responded with a generosity of spirit, lending their presence to sporting events and charities. They did this to reciprocate the generous hospitality they enjoyed, as well as in hopes that their occasional indiscretions and improprieties would be concealed. But mostly, it was to thank others for a good time.

And what a time it was. For seventy-five years, Palm Springs has been the privileged domain of a large contingent of American show business icons, people like Bing Crosby, Lucille Ball, William Holden, Dinah Shore, and Cary Grant, onward to Elvis Presley, Liberace, Suzanne Somers, Barry Manilow, Lily Tomlin, and Merv Griffin. Here, like migrating exotic birds, they made their secondary homes, unwound from the daily pressures of work, or otherwise enjoyed undisturbed liaisons.

Many of Hollywood's domineering moguls also went to ground in Palm Springs: Samuel Goldwyn, Jack Warner, Darryl Zanuck, and Walt Disney, along with directors John Ford, William Wyler, and Howard Hawks. In Hollywood, these cigar-chomping bullies were considered to be giants. Among the sagebrush, cactus, and verbena, they shrunk to the size of everyday neighbors. The studio bosses and their overworked minions weren't the only ones to partake in the desert's pleasures.

"At weekends, a stream of besotted lovers, transients, and misfits streamed to Palm Springs, where a colony of drunks and fornicators had by now been founded," affirmed the blustering actor Patrick Macnee.

Not all lost souls who moved here were bent on self-destruction. Great strides were made in the field of architecture, the link between art and commerce, commerce that got up a head of steam when the Southern Pacific Railroad decided to lay down tracks at the end of the nineteenth century, bringing the first wave of sightseers to the city's front door.

The Springs is also the final resting place of a select group of cinematic pioneers, including *Thin Man* actor William Powell, Racquet Club founder Charles Farrell, and dynamic entertainers Frank Sinatra and Sonny Bono, each of whom helped promote Palm Springs to the world at large.

And it's where unsurpassed presidential court jester Bob Hope, one of the desert's staunchest advocates, lived until his death at age one hundred in 2003. Hope, perhaps more than any other person, symbolized the languid pace and friendly manner of Palm Springs—once a bucolic community of slip rails and horse corrals, now widely urbanized, its growing infrastructure dissected with four-lane highways and concrete sidewalks.

The time that these VIPs spent here is the stuff of desert folklore, tales told and stories spread about the pampered lives of the rich and famous: where they stayed, dined, and slept—and with whom they did it. Sure, these famous faces laughed, cried, and loved; but where *exactly* did it all take place? Let's take an up-close and personal look at Palm Springs confidential.

In Palm Springs, as even the casual observer knows, several main streets are dedicated to well-known movie stars and celebrities. There's Farrell Drive named after Charles Farrell, and to the north, a nod to the screen's earliest singing cowboy, Gene Autry Trail. Bogert Trail honoring civic leader Frank Bogert is to the south. Thrown in is a smattering of smaller star-studded streets such as Bellamy, Powell, Wayne, and Simms roads, Wyman Drive, and Davis Way.

But before the stars arrived, the first homes, most of them poorly improvised huts called "tent houses," were made of canvas and wood. The pioneering families, gathered in small clusters, struggled to provide food and shelter despite fierce windstorms and flash floods. Only the main street, renamed Palm Canyon Boulevard was paved. From 1930, the town's roads, originally identified simply as North, South, East, and West, underwent significant name changes that were part municipal expansion and part recognition of the region's centuries-old Indian settlements and later Spanish colonization. What followed was an inevitable jumble of ethnic names—Alessandro, Belardo, Ortega, Prieto, Caballeros, Amado, Escoba, Ramon, Saturnino, Tachevah, Baristo, Alvarado, and Tahquitz. Indian Avenue, the longest street, bisected the reservation line.

The majority of today's non-Indian inhabitants probably couldn't distinguish one appellation from another. How many people, for example, know that Alejo Patencio, the name of two major thoroughfares, was once headman of the Agua Caliente tribe, or that Marcus Belardo, whose name occupies two city streets, was Alejo's assistant? Lee Arenas, whose surname graces yet another road, was the tribe's secular leader, guide, and interpreter, while Ramon Manuel, Pedro Chino, John Andreas, Calistro Lugo, and Clemente Segundo, all of whose names are now on street signs, were highly respected ranchers, who tended gardens of corn, squash, and melons. Man lived in harmony with nature. Plants and animals were sacred. This strong Indian heritage gives Palm Springs much of its mystical allure, as if protecting the populace from unseen forces according to ancient folklore, while reproaching them, when necessary, for their misdeeds.

Of course, none of these people could even remotely be considered a celebrity. Neither were the early European settlers: Nellie Coffman, Raymond Cree, Katherine Finchy, Ruth Hardy, John McCallum, Welwood Murray, and Prescott Stevens, whose accomplishments earned them nameplates on city roads, parks, and schools.

It fell to others more experienced at glad-handing to lay claim to the celebrity distinction. In the interim, three brave men publicized the desert's unspoiled charms: the bearded environmentalist and Sierra Club founder John Muir, naturalist writer-poet J. Smeaton Chase, and scenic photographer Stephen Willard. They scaled mountains and hiked canyons long before pleasure-seeking capitalists flew over them. Among the desert's earliest celebrity inhabitants, though they surely did not intend it when they put down tentative roots at the beginning of the last century, were German-born illustrator Carl Eytel, whose sketches and paintings adorned many books and periodicals; *National Geographic* color photographer Fred Payne Clatworthy; and syndicated cartoonist for the Hearst Corporation James Swinnerton, known to millions of readers as "Swin."

It's interesting to note that except for when Frank Sinatra actually lived on Frank Sinatra Drive in Rancho Mirage, the stars did not reside on these eponymous avenues. Instead, they made their homes in and around the city's flourishing nightclubs, bars, and restaurants. Eventually, many stars leased private houses or built their own castles. In subsequent years, these various abodes, some of them humble, others more extravagant, have taken on renewed importance as an integral part of the desert's social history. It was at these palm-fronded, bougainvillea-scattered homes, mansions, and estates that a good deal, if not all, of the legendary sex, all those wild parties, and even the occasional murder took place.

Without Hollywood, it can be argued, there would be no Palm Springs as we know it today. To prove it, the stars left behind telltale reminders of their staggering wealth and rampant hedonism: piano-shaped swimming pools, cement handprints, and monogrammed wrought-iron gates. Certainly without the allure, glamour, and fairy dust of these silver-screen memories, real estate values in the desert would be considerably diminished.

And for that special privilege, many movie-star aficionados from around the world are willing to pay top dollar for the chance to own a bona-fide celebrity home so they can sit in their favorite chair and contemplate the miracle of star power.

Chapter 1

Racquet Club Rendezvous

The ritzy neighborhood known as the Racquet Club sits at the north gateway of Palm Springs within a rifle shot of the old Pony Express route. It runs west toward the mountain, east off Palm Canyon Drive, and south from San Rafael Road to Vista Chino. This historic section of Palm Springs homes takes its name from the Racquet Club, the raucous hotel resort founded by **Charles Farrell** and **Ralph Bellamy**. At one time it housed, wined, and dined more stars than there were in heaven. *Seventh Heaven*, to be exact.

That was the first motion picture to star Farrell and cherubic newcomer **Janet Gaynor**, his frequent screen partner and longtime friend. The pair was frequently seen at village dances. This winsome couple costarred in twelve films together, including *Street Angel, Sunny Side Up, Delicious,* and *Change of Heart,* and they were jointly responsible for much of Palm Springs' early allure.

Before Charlie Farrell became a marquee name on movie theaters, the soft-spoken actor with the Cape Cod accent came to the desert to alleviate his hay fever. His second career as owner of the **Racquet Club** at 2743 North Indian Canyon Drive put Palm Springs on the map and wads of cash in Charlie's pocket. They sold Coca-Cola, but the *beer* was on the house, Farrell claimed, since nobody had a liquor license when the club first opened.

Contrary to popular belief, it was not the result of German cinema star Marlene Dietrich's demand that nonmembers Farrell and Ralph Bellamy be thrown off El Mirador's tennis courts that led Farrell to build his own club. Rather, Farrell said, it was the idea of running a sportsmen's lodge that appealed to Bellamy and him.

Top: Charlie Farrell feigns amusement at Marilyn Monroe (Courtesy of Palm Springs Historical Society). *Left:* Ralph Bellamy (Backlot Books & Movie Posters). *Right:* Racquet Club main entrance (Courtesy of the Racquet Club). *Bottom:* Janet Gaynor and friend at a costume party (Courtesy of Palm Springs Historical Society).

1

According to Bellamy, he was horseback riding with Farrell along Indian Avenue (now Indian Canyon Drive) on a warm day in 1933 near Leaning Rock, a sacred vertical stone slab that beckons departing visitors to return, when they came upon a sign protruding like a man's upraised hand on the roadside:

53 ACRES FOR SALE
SEE ALVAH HICKS

"How much?" they asked the seller. "Thirty-five hundred dollars," Hicks replied. Farrell and Bellamy couldn't believe their good fortune. *Sold!* Another less-told version is that Farrell stopped by the Desert Inn one weekend to see his Oscar-winning costar Janet Gaynor and her mother, Laura. When Farrell told them he was thinking about buying rural property at Lake Arrowhead to open a tennis club, the ever-practical Gaynor furrowed her girlish brow and replied, "For goodness sake, Charlie, why don't you find something here?"

Farrell took her advice, and he and Bellamy bought several acres of land at the furthest end of town. If you believe in Indian mythology, Farrell's heart was invested with *Um Naw*, the great Indian spirit that protects all within its holy reach and ensures each recipient safe passage to the afterlife for their good deeds.

Whichever story is true, the following year, amid much star-studded fanfare, the Racquet Club, complete with two new tennis courts and Olympic-size swimming pool, opened for business on December 15, 1934. After a slow start, it quickly became a magnet for Hollywood's elite, two hundred of whom gladly paid $650 apiece for annual membership to sip chilled martinis and dance to Rudy Vallee's orchestra on Saturday nights.

The club's first four members, Bellamy stated for the record, were Frank Morgan, Charles Butterworth, Reginald Owen, and Paul Lukas.

"We gave Charlie Butterworth and Paul Lukas each a piece of property adjoining the club on which to build houses. When the houses were completed," Bellamy said, "we had an offer to sell forty of the fifty-three acres for $4,000."

The buyer was real estate investor and future Desert Museum donor Walter Marks, who built a residential development (now homes and condominiums). However, it wasn't just a place for Hollywood types waiting for their big break. Tennis champions Bill Tilden, Don Budge, Gene Mako, Alice Marble, and Lew Hoad played tennis there, helping to foster the club's sporty image.

Bellamy soon felt overwhelmed by the hotel chores and sold his interest to Charlie, who continued happily running the club with his actress-wife, Virginia Valli. Valli may be best remembered as the lesbian heroine of Alfred Hitchcock's first film, *The Pleasure Garden*. She retired when she wed Farrell. A relieved Bellamy wasted no time in resuming his acting career and was nominated for an Oscar for his efforts in 1937's *The Awful Truth*, but didn't take home the award until he was presented an honorary Oscar in 1986. Although the crinkly-haired actor received high praise for his portrayal of President Franklin Roosevelt on the stage and screen in *Sunrise at Campobello*, he is probably best remembered for his scene-stealing roles as cantankerous business tycoons in *Trading Places* and *Pretty Woman*. Bellamy died from a lung ailment in 1991.

★   ★   ★

Never shy about beating its own drum, the Racquet Club showed the way for all future Palm Springs clubs and restaurants by selling its well-earned reputation to the world.

"Swim in the same Olympic-size pool where Marilyn Monroe was discovered."

"Sip a Bloody Mary at the Bamboo Lounge (where it was created)."

Although debate has swirled around this last claim, the christening of the spicy tomato and vodka drink, first called the Folding Farrell, was authenticated by one star who was present, though not of legal age, at the time: Farrell's demitasse costar Shirley Temple.

What cannot be denied are the origins of the bar's tropical décor, which was designed by Mitchell Leisen, an Oscar nominee for best art direction for 1929's *Dynamite*. Although mocked for his clubfoot, Leisen was in steady demand as a painter, sculptor, and dressmaker. The same year Leisen put the burnished touches to the Racquet Club, this all-round achiever directed the trio of Carole Lombard, Fred MacMurray, and Ralph Bellamy in *Hands Across the Table*—his sixth feature film, solidifying Leisen's growing reputation for romantic comedy.

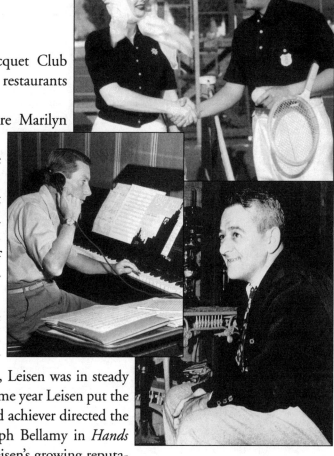

Top: Lucille Ball and Desi Arnaz on the tennis court (Cinema Collectors). *Left:* Hoagy Carmichael composing at the piano (Wayne Knight Collection). *Bottom:* William Wyler in good humor (Courtesy of the Wyler family).

Hoagy Carmichael, who composed "Stardust," "Ole' Buttermilk Sky," and "Georgia on My Mind," among hundreds of well-worn pieces of sheet music, spent the Christmas holidays at the Racquet Club in 1937. Carmichael found the place so laid back that he later became a resident of Rancho Mirage, alternating songwriting and acting in such films as *To Have and Have Not*, *The Best Years of Our Lives*, and *Young Man With A Horn*, while living here.

In 1938, **William Wyler**, who directed his lover Bette Davis in her second Oscar-winning role as the Southern temptress *Jezebel*, broke off the affair when he married Texas-born actress Margaret Tallichet at the home of actor Walter Huston in Running Springs, located in the San Bernardino National Forest. The newlyweds then honeymooned at the Racquet Club. On Thanksgiving Day 1949, their three-year-old son, named William Wyler Jr., mysteriously took ill in Palm Springs and died in Desert Hospital.

A whole decade before they became America's favorite husband-and-wife television stars, **Lucille Ball** and **Desi Arnaz**, who had fallen in love on the set of RKO's musical

Top: Audrey Hepburn and Mel Ferrer (Courtesy of Palm Springs Historical Society). *Bottom:* Doris Day with Marty Melcher (Courtesy of Palm Springs Historical Society).

comedy *Too Many Girls*, gave in to each other's charms at the Racquet Club. In August 1940, according to Lucy's biographer Kathleen Brady "the two sped in the summer heat to Palm Springs with their suitcases filled with her frilly nightgowns and his silk pajamas and vivid Mandarin dressing gowns."

Gutsy woman's director **Vincent Sherman**, whom Bette Davis fell for when he directed her in *Old Acquaintance* and *Mr. Skeffington*, shared connecting rooms with rival star Joan Crawford at the Racquet Club during location filming for *The Damned Don't* Cry, based on the life of gangster Bugsy Siegel's mistress, Virginia Hill. According to Sherman, Crawford forced him to have sexual intercourse with her, once in the darkened screening room at Warner Brothers and another time under the spraying bathroom shower of her Brentwood home.

Others found the club's quarters equally convivial. Doris Day and manager-husband Marty Melcher (previously married to Patti Andrews of the Andrews Sisters), spent time there. Melcher wed the twenty-seven-year old, freckle-faced singer in 1951. He received producing credits on nineteen films in which she was romantically paired with Rock Hudson, Cary Grant, Rod Taylor, and James Garner, over the next seventeen years.

War and Peace husband-and-wife costars Audrey Hepburn and Mel Ferrer, who directed her in *Green Mansions* and later produced *Wait Until Dark*, were guests, as were cultivated actress Jean Simmons and her second husband, Richard Brooks, who directed her in *Elmer Gantry*.

The Racquet Club was happy to oblige celebrities who wished to keep their names out of gossip columns.

Spencer Tracy and **Katharine Hepburn**, who were secret lovers for twenty-five years, fell into that category. They maintained a cloak of invisibility whenever they stayed at the club. According to George Cukor, who directed the odd couple in *Keeper of the Flame, Adam's Rib*, and *Pat and Mike*, "they had an apartment converted for them in the old servants' quarters, and no one ever saw them."

Club employees tolerated the two's eccentric behavior and were well tipped not to reveal details of Tracy and Hepburn's adulterous affair. The club's management especially didn't want tidbits leaked to Hollywood's rival "snoop sisters" Hedda Hopper and Louella Parsons. Hedda in her silly hats and Louella with crimson lipstick smudged across her face were Cinderella's worst nightmare come to life: two old bags with nothing better to do than spread malicious gossip, which made Farrell's job that much harder.

No one was safe. Parsons had news-gathering spies planted all over the desert where Hopper, a former actress, had once supplemented her income by selling real estate. Louella's biggest peeve was Orson Welles, whom she excommunicated over *Citizen Kane*. Hopper's bête noire was Charlie Chaplin, and she frequently crossed swords with Humphrey Bogart and Marlon Brando, whom she castigated for their bad manners. Such were the pitfalls of stardom. The pratfalls were much more fun.

Bing Crosby's trademark prank was taking a bottle of Glenlivet Scotch from bartender George "Tex" Gregg and filling up customers' half-empty glasses—regardless of what they were drinking. Another time, Lupe Velez took off her brassiere and panties and went skinny-dipping. Then there was the time that bug-eyed actor Peter Lorre got pushed into the pool by Gilbert Roland. "I beg your pardon, amigo," Roland apologized, extending his bronzed arm. Lorre smiled, gripped the actor's outstretched hand, and yanked him into the water.

The strain of running a private hotel, indulging stars' whims, and catering to their puffed-up egos could not have been easy for Farrell, who was at the beck and call of club guests twenty-four hours a day. Nevertheless, his constant promotion of the city earned him the sobriquet "Mr. Palm Springs."

The charm of the club was not lost on **Kirk Douglas**, who recuperated there after a bout of pneumonia in 1952. Douglas and happily-wed actors George Montgomery, Dinah Shore, Desi Arnaz, Lucille Ball, William Holden, and Brenda Marshall played in regular celebrity tournaments. Clark Gable and Spencer Tracy deliberated over chess games on the club lawn, decorated by a set of two-foot-high chessmen.

Douglas played a part in one real-life drama that started for him with a call to the club in October 1949. It was from the Los Angeles Police Department. Douglas, who was spending the weekend entwined in the pool with actress Evelyn Keyes, was a suspect in the disappearance of Hollywood showgirl Jean Spangler. The raven-haired beauty had been an extra on *Young Man With a Horn*, in which Douglas played a struggling musician based on the life of cornetist Bix Beiderbecke.

One day, Spangler supposedly went to meet a man called "Kirk" and was never seen again. The testy actor, whose name was partially scribbled on a piece of paper in the girl's handbag found near a gate in Griffith Park, told LAPD officers that he did not remember meeting Spangler or making a date with her to go out on the town. The police believed him and let him go. Spangler's disappearance was never solved, although it has been suggested that foul play or a possible botched abortion led to her body being unceremoniously buried in the outlying desert.

Thereafter, a relieved Douglas exercised better judgment over his extramarital affairs with the likes of Gene Tierney, Marlene Dietrich, and the waiflike Italian actress Pier Angeli, to whom he was briefly engaged. He even found time for a hot and heavy romance with socialite Irene Wrightsman, the free-spirited daughter of Palm Beach, Florida, millionaire Charles Wrightsman, whom he met at the club one weekend. "For two days, we hardly left the room," bragged Douglas.

Robert Evans dining with Joan Collins (Larry Edmunds Bookshop).

Discretion or the lack of it, however, didn't stop the rush of girls who threw themselves at producers' feet and into their king-size beds, none more so than the loquacious New York huckster, **Robert Evans**. The slick salesmanship of the former partner in clothing company Evan-Picone put women into pants when "ladies" only wore skirts and dresses. It's commonly believed that Norma Shearer got into *his* after the MGM grande dame spied him poolside at the Beverly Hills Hotel.

Evans was signed to play Shearer's long-dead husband, producer Irving Thalberg, in the Lon Chaney biopic, *Man of a Thousand Face*s. Next, with a fake tan and a stuffed crotch, Evans was cast as a Spanish matador in Ernest Hemingway's tale of lost love *The Sun Also Rises*—the role that brought him the greatest ridicule. The five-times married Evans went on to become Charles Bludhorn's Wonder Boy at Paramount Pictures, where he produced the box-office trifecta *Rosemary's Baby*, *Love Story*, and *The Godfather*, and mined such box-office gold as *Chinatown*, *Marathon Man*, and *Black Sunday* before his luck ran out on *Urban Cowboy*, *Popeye*, and *The Cotton Club*, which almost landed him in jail for his dubious association with murdered film investor Roy Radin.

Weep not for Evans, he's a survivor. He regained career momentum in 1992, after beating a near-fatal cocaine addiction, when he got Sharon Stone to sign on to *Sliver*. Evans called Joe Eszterhas's script, "the best fuckin' screenplay I'd read in a decade." Critics didn't have the same assessment. Still Evans soldiers on. The master of reinvention became a movie art-house attraction ten years later when he narrated the film version of his autobiography, *The Kid Stays in the Picture*.

★　　★　　★

If the term "star maker" truly can be applied to any one person, it is **Johnny Hyde**, the dwarfish but dynamic William Morris agent, who represented two of that era's biggest pinups: pouty-lipped, bad girl Lana Turner and rosy-cheeked, flamenco dancer Rita Hayworth. It was said that Hyde "signed more starlets with his dick than most guys did with their fountain pens," according to business writer Frank Rose.

Hyde's charm was not his diminutive appearance, though he was delicately handsome, said Rose, "like a toy person." Rather, Hyde's strength lay in his genius in spotting raw talent and molding his discoveries into moneymaking commodites. Such was the case with Norma Jeane Dougherty, a shy photographer's model (first snapped on a crisp black-and-white negative by the club's photographer-in-residence, Bruno Bernard) whom Hyde repackaged when no one else knew what to do with her and launched her as the ultimate fifties sex bomb: Marilyn Monroe. True, she probably would have become a star without him, but she became a legend because of him.

Their professional and personal relationship began in 1949 when she gave Hyde a mighty blow job. He was so appreciative that he got her bit parts in *Love Happy* and *The*

Asphalt Jungle; then came *All About Eve* and the offer of a 20th Century-Fox seven-year contract. While Monroe's career was finally on the ascent, Hyde's health was on the decline. He had a diseased heart and was constantly taking nitroglycerin tablets to ease the pain of angina attacks.

After a brief stay in Cedars of Lebanon Hospital, a rejuvenated Hyde begged Monroe to spend Christmas 1950 with him at the Racquet Club, as they had the previous year. Now, on the brink of stardom, she refused his offer. On December 17, two days after Hyde's arrival, while pining for Monroe, his ticker gave out. A speeding ambulance took Hyde back to Los Angeles where he died the next day at age fifty-five.

Farrell, meanwhile, was elected the mayor of Palm Springs, in recognition of his hostelry accomplishments. Then, producer Hal Roach Jr. coaxed Farrell out of semiretirement to play Gale Storm's silver-haired father in the 1952 sitcom, *My Little Margie*. These two key events brought an avalanche of media coverage to the village—and heaps more stars.

Racquet Club guests liked to play musical bedrooms: Marie McDonald and Harry Karl. Harry Karl and Debbie Reynolds. Debbie Reynolds and Eddie Fisher. Eddie Fisher and Elizabeth Taylor. Ginger Rogers married her fourth husband, Jacques Bergerac, in a private ceremony there in 1953. Rock Hudson and Phyllis Gates (the secretary of Hudson's gay agent Henry Willson) marked time at the bar while waiting to say their arranged "I Do's." Dewy-eyed young lovers Robert Wagner and Natalie Wood strolled hand in hand through the grounds. Foxy newlyweds Shelley Winters and Anthony Franciosa sucked each other's toes by the pool.

Tony Curtis and Janet Leigh made whoopee and a daughter, Jamie Lee, there between pictures in 1958, the same year that blond-haired actor Gene Raymond and his wife, Jeanette MacDonald, rested at the club after the operatic actress underwent appendix surgery and contracted hepatitis.

Whatever the mutual attraction, murder investigation, or medical ailment, Racquet Club guests were treated like twenty-four-carat royalty—and deservedly so. After all, where else could a person have so much enjoyment with so little concern? A typical day,

Top: Robert Wagner makes a splash (Howard Johns Collection). *Left:* Ginger Rogers dances cheek-to-cheek with Jacques Bergerac (Courtesy of Palm Springs Historical Society).

for example, began with a hearty poolside breakfast followed by a tennis lesson and lunch. Later, guests showered and changed into evening clothes for dinner and dancing.

Farrell's love of showmanship resulted in a million bucks' worth of free publicity for the club, which was often mentioned on weekly radio shows hosted by the unmistakable voices of Bob Hope, Jack Benny, and Fred Allen. Farrell eagerly sought commercial endorsements, made frequent TV guest-shot appearances, and even filmed his short-lived TV series, *The Charlie Farrell Show*, there. No wonder Farrell's pride and joy, which he sold for a mint in 1959, carried a $1.2 million price tag.

Eventually, the club's conservative attitude, the rise of golf's popularity, combined with stars' eagerness to own their own homes at newer country-club developments such as Thunderbird, Tamarisk, and El Dorado, caused the Racquet Club to fall out of favor. In 1999, Los Angeles businessman Bernard Rosenson, the president of Sign of the Dove, a company that owned eight assisted-living facilities in California, became the latest in a long line of starry-eyed entrepreneurs who took over the history-laden hotel and promised to return it to its glory days.

Invoking the rage of former guests, Rosenson announced he was going to convert the eleven-acre property into a gay and lesbian retirement community—complete with same-sex commitment ceremonies and catered wedding parties—with rents ranging from $2,700 to $5,000. The idea didn't go over well. On June 1, 2003, after spending three years and several millions remodeling the club's restaurant and forty-two bungalows, Rosenson threw in the towel, and the Racquet Club closed without fanfare. But during its heyday, it was the first choice of Hollywood at play. Actor George Hamilton, who is never lost for words, summed it up best. "You could play tennis, eat a great meal, swim, go home and change, come back, have a drink at the bar, lead into dinner, go dancing, and meet interesting people."

★   ★   ★

Gregson Bautzer, the hotshot Hollywood lawyer, tennis player, and popular male escort who represented a Rolodex of flashy clients, lived next door to the Racquet Club at 154 West San Marco Way. Built in 1947, this cozy four-bedroom bungalow—which had been May Company owners Tom and Anita May's first desert home—is where the lascivious Bautzer, who deflowered Lana Turner, fondled Ginger Rogers, serviced Joan Crawford, and tied the knot with British actress Dana Wynter, lived on and off until the 1970s.

"Greg was a real Beau Brummel and an incorrigible flirt," said Bautzer's ex-girlfriend Dorothy Lamour. The high-priced legal eagle first made headlines as Ingrid Bergman's divorce attorney during the scandalous Roberto Rossellini-*Stromboli* affair, which produced an illegitimate son, Robertino. Then, accepting his clients' thankful kisses, Bautzer moved on to practice corporate law for the likes of Diners Club president Alfred Bloomingdale, kooky billionaire Howard Hughes, and MGM hotel owner Kirk Kerkorian until a fatal heart attack in 1987 put the secret-coded "walking weenie" six feet under.

★   ★   ★

Mervyn LeRoy, the esteemed producer of the timeless children's classic *The Wizard of Oz*, lived behind the club at 166 West San Marco Way. It was a sentimental choice of address. LeRoy, a Best Director Oscar nominee for *Random Harvest*, and his second wife, Kitty Spiegel, honeymooned at the club back in 1946. When not producing films, LeRoy directed them with all the boundless energy of a beagle at a foxhunt. His credits include *Little Caesar, I Am a Fugitive From a Chain Gang, Anthony Adverse, Blossoms in the Dust,* and *Little Women.*

Inside this unpretentious tile-and-stucco home, LeRoy held production meetings for three weeks on the Roman epic *Quo Vadis?* He read scripts for many of his forthcoming films. He conferred with writer Leonard Spigelgass on *A Majority of One* and spent six weeks preproduction on *Mary, Mary.* Another time, LeRoy and Irving Wallace, the writer of portentous historical tomes, such as *Lust For Life* and *The Agony and the Ecstasy*, wrote an unproduced screen treatment for *The Helen Morgan Story.*

"It wasn't all work," LeRoy, a prominent racehorse owner and president of Hollywood Park for twenty-two years, admitted. "There were times I played tennis and times I went off on trips with my friends."

One of those trips took LeRoy, Jack Warner, Darryl Zanuck, and Bryan Foy (a low-budget film director who started out life in the vaudeville act of Eddie Foy and the Seven Little Foys) duck hunting in Mexicali.

While living in this house, LeRoy, the recipient of two special Academy Awards, was shocked when a mouse jumped out of a kitchen cabinet and bit his face. Afterwards, his friend and neighbor, William Powell, who couldn't pass up such a sublime moment, gave LeRoy a cocktail shaker inscribed: "From The Champion Worrier Of All Times To The Runner-Up."

In 1974, another of LeRoy's friends, former UCLA All-American football hero and Columbia Pictures head of production **Mike "M. J." Frankovich** (the adopted son of comedian Joe E. Brown), moved into the pest-free home with his decorous actress-wife, **Binnie Barnes**. Barnes played romantic leads as Catherine Howard in *The Private Life of Henry VIII* and Lady De Winter in 1939's *The Three Musketeers.* She died in 1998, six years after her husband, who had suffered from Alzheimer's disease. LeRoy died in 1987.

Armand Deutsch, whose family founded the Sears, Roebuck and Company department store chain, moved into 153 Santa Clara Way in 1948. The independently wealthy Deutsch, described by fellow resident Stanley Kramer as "the first person who seemed to take me seriously as a producer," invested in what was to be the socially concerned filmmaker's first picture, *This Side of Innocence.* The film was never made. Instead, Kramer used the money to form his own company and went on to make the highly praised ciné-ma vérité works *So This Is New York, Champion,* and *Home of the Brave.* Deutsch, meanwhile, was installed as a producer at MGM, where he became noted for his delicate treat-

ment of unconventional subject matter, many of these films directed by John Sturges, including *Right Cross, The Magnificent Yankee,* and *Saddle the Wind.*

★ ★ ★

Owl-faced comedy director **Alexander Hall**, who made the original versions of *Little Miss Marker, Here Comes Mr. Jordan* (remade as *Heaven Can Wait* with Warren Beatty), and *My Sister Eileen,* owned the house at 165 Santa Clara Way in 1952. Hall's crazy humor was a perfect antidote for the Depression-era blues, notably in *Goin' to Town* starring Mae West, for whom Hall wrote the saucy line "I'm a good woman for a bad man," and later the offbeat *Once Upon a Time,* featuring Cary Grant as the ingenious owner of a dancing caterpillar.

Top and bottom left: "The Sunset" at 2905 La Puerta del Sol (Photos by John Waggaman). *Right:* Charles Butterworth (Larry Edmunds Bookshop).

But things went downhill for Hall (formerly Lucille Ball's lover) soon after his third wife, Marjorie Franklin, divorced him and married the sneering, evil-eyed character actor Jack Lambert in 1959. For some reason, Hall never worked again. In 1968, Marjorie Lambert was found dead in the Santa Clara Way home, which she had received from Hall in the divorce settlement, the same day that Jack Lambert, who played psychopathic villains in *The Killers, Kiss Me Deadly* and *Machine-Gun Kelly,* served her with divorce papers. Lambert told police he discovered his wife's body sprawled across the covers of their king-size bed. He had given her the kiss of life, he said, in an attempt to revive her, though many people suspected it was the kiss of death. The coroner was unable to reach a decision, and no charges were filed. Four months later, a heartbroken Alexander Hall died at age seventy-four.

★ ★ ★

Around the corner at 2905 La Puerta del Sol, surrounded by fifty palm and tamarisk trees, is "The Sunset," a noble-looking Spanish Colonial *casa,* once owned by spindly, horse-faced comedic actor **Charles Butterworth**, whose specialty was playing balding bachelors with a roving eye. Butterworth's timid appearance belied his reputation as an ardent lover who was more than anatomically equipped to play the part.

In *Every Day's a Holiday,* he uttered the immortal and much-imitated line, "Why don't you get out of those wet clothes and into a dry martini"—the favorite invitation of this inebriated actor, who spent twelve years imbibing various spirits while living it up in Palm Springs.

After his divorce from Ethel Kenyon, who subsequently married *Modern Screen* and *True Story* magazine publisher Ernest Heyn, Butterworth was briefly engaged to fruity-voiced Broadway star and future *Gilligan's Island* actress Natalie Schafer and dated New York fashion model Ruth "Dusty" Anderson. (Anderson later married stage and film director Jean Negulesco.)

A seasoned journalist prior to entering films, Butterworth ran with a hard-drinking showbiz crowd that included writers-at-large Marc Connelly, Dorothy Parker, Robert Benchley, and S. J. Perelman. The group indulged in much good-natured ribbing and other tomfoolery as residents-in-common of the famed Garden of Allah, where F. Scott Fitzgerald, creator and alter ego of *The Great Gatsby*, suffered a fatal heart attack in Sheila Graham's apartment on December 21, 1940. Eight days later, Fitzgerald's heir apparent, Nathanael West, author of the allegorical Hollywood novel, *The Day of the Locust*, and West's wife were killed returning from Mexico by car on Highway 111 between Calexico and El Centro.

The deaths hit Butterworth hard. He sunk into a haze of alcoholic debauchery, and his career slowly slipped away. Inconsolable but for his ever-present bottle of rye, there are some who believe Butterworth committed suicide. According to Sheila Graham, it's more likely that a completely soused Butterworth lost control of his French-made automobile in mid-1946 and crashed into a North Crescent Heights lamppost in Beverly Hills, not far from the treacherous spot where Benchley always feared he would be mowed down by oncoming traffic and where Paramount publicity man Terry de Lapp was killed while crossing the street.

Five years after Butterworth's death, his beneficiary, Lois Earl, sold the house to **Robert Hornstein**, Texan heir to the Puss 'n Boots cat food fortune. Hornstein was a marvelous host, and, by all accounts, a rapacious homosexual, who restocked the bar and printed up party invitations. Among Hornstein's anointed guests were MCA agent **Jennings Lang**, the future producer of three star-studded *Airport* movies, as well as the Clint Eastwood thriller *Play Misty For Me* and the box-office shaker *Earthquake*.

Lang rented the house shortly before he was ambushed in a Los Angeles parking lot in Christmas 1951 and shot in the groin by producer Walter Wanger, who suspected him of having an affair with his actress-wife Joan Bennett. When police arrived on the scene, Wanger screamed, "I've just shot the sonofabitch who tried to break up my home!"

Wanger pleaded not guilty by reason of temporary insanity and spent four months in jail for the crime.

Lang's friend and Oscar-winning *Johnny Belinda* actress **Jane Wyman** leased the house from Hornstein on the rebound from her failed marriage to Ronald Reagan after she miscarried their third child in 1951. That same year Wyman received a third Oscar nomination, this time for *The Blue Veil*, and was snapped by a photographer running around town with her handsome date and future husband, bandleader Fred Karger.

Two years later, **Joan Crawford**, a Best Actress Oscar home wrecker for *Mildred Pierce*, was Hornstein's feted houseguest prior to strapping on a set of six-shooters in

Jane Wyman covers up (Howard Johns Collection).

Nicholas Ray's Western catfight, *Johnny Guitar*. One night, while dining with Hornstein at the Doll House restaurant, Crawford, having downed her fourth vodka, tied an apron around her trim waist and went from table to table, taking people's orders—delighting some customers and confusing others who insisted that she wasn't Joan Crawford.

In 1959, Bob Hornstein sold the Sunset. He moved to Europe and settled on the bohemian island of Capri, throwing *dolce vita* parties, where he handed out silk scarves to the likes of Jacqueline Kennedy Onassis and Elizabeth Taylor, when not luring beach boys and young sailors into his home for oral sex.

"Hornstein was a tall, blonde Adonis," recalled Jane Easton, a shapely RKO starlet who attended a party given by Hornstein for Joan Crawford and her fourth husband, Pepsi-Cola chairman Alfred Steele, in 1955. "His villa was fabulous," she told *Vanity Fair*. "The party was a sit-down dinner with many guests, a large orchestra, and dancing." It was later alleged that Hornstein, in a fit of alcoholic sexual dalliance, bit off a boy's penis. To avoid a scandal, he reportedly bought the boy's parents a villa and quietly disappeared from the island.

Paul Lukas, man-about-town (Steve Kiefer Collection).

Suave Hungarian leading man **Paul Lukas** became Hollywood's primo "Continental-in-residence" after spending several years working in Europe, notably as the star of Alfred Hitchcock's British-made thriller *The Lady Vanishes*. He lived next door to Butterworth and Hornstein at 2965 La Puerta del Sol. Lukas and his wife, Grizella Benes, were among the first stars to move to the desert. He indulged his fondness for sports as a charter member of the Racquet Club where Lukas built a two-bedroom cottage on this site, costing $4,750 in 1935.

Later, he reprised his Broadway role as the defiant German father who resists the Nazis in Lillian Hellman's anti-Fascist play *Watch on the Rhine* to win an Oscar as Best Actor of 1943, beating out Humphrey Bogart, Gary Cooper, Mickey Rooney, and Walter Pidgeon.

Aside from having proved his acting chops, Lukas is credited with inventing (or at least popularizing) men's tassel loafers. In 1948, he took a worn pair of Oxfords to Alden shoemakers and asked them to create a newer, more comfortable design—the result was a slip-on leather shoe with topside lacing and tassels. The stylish new shoe made its debut at the Lefcourt and Morris stores in 1950 and was soon available in a variety of colors. The well-shod Lukas wore these shoes until his death from a heart attack, age ninety-four, vacationing in Tangier, Morocco, in 1971.

Producer **Samuel Briskin**, who cofounded Liberty Films with his longtime friend Frank Capra, moved to 133 West San Carlos Road one year after their company, which made *It's a Wonderful Life*, was dissolved in 1951. Briskin signed on at Paramount, where he went on to produce two of his most compelling films, James Stewart in *Strategic Air Command* and Frank Sinatra in *The Joker is Wild*. Capra, meanwhile, settled in La Quinta.

★   ★   ★

Because the Racquet Club section is located so far north, almost out of sight of the city's law enforcement, this film-loving neighborhood has had its fair share of troubles—assaults, rapes, and burglaries.

On the evening of March 21, 1984, police were called to the poolside apartment of Jake Ehrlich and video porn star **Shauna Grant** in the Sands Spa Hotel, at 496 West Dominguez Road (between Los Felices Road and Paseo de Anza) behind Tuscany Plaza.

Grant, christened Colleen Applegate, was the prototypical "girl next door" whose specialty was giving two-fingered blow jobs, which she did efficiently in more than fifty X-rated movies, winning six Erotica Film Awards. The frizzy-haired blonde possessed "the most perfect, all natural perky breasts ever to see the light of a camera," panted one male fan captivated by her innocent schoolgirl look.

Top: Porn star Shauna Grant (Bill Margold Collection). *Bottom:* Sands Spa Hotel where Shauna Grant killed herself (Photo by Howard Johns).

During Grant's busiest year, 1982, she had consensual sex with at least thirty partners, underwent an abortion, and contracted herpes. She also appeared nude in dozens of men's magazine centerfolds, among them *Penthouse* and *Hustler*. Grant was sexy, but she wasn't smart. The lip-glossed oral expert could have become a cult "crossover" movie star like Ginger Lynn Allen and Traci Lords if she hadn't developed a deadly taste for nose candy that used up most of her income from porn—an estimated $100,000. It turned her into a nervous wreck, and she resorted to stealing money to feed her coke habit.

Just when Grant thought things couldn't get any worse, she was arrested in downtown Palm Springs for driving without a license. Her boyfriend, Jake Ehrlich, the owner of Pelle, a downtown leather goods store, had earlier been busted for selling drugs. Their lives were a mess; she was broke and unemployed.

At twenty, it seemed as if her life was finished. When the day of reckoning arrived, rather than have her unsavory past revealed in court, Grant freaked out. She locked herself in Ehrlich's bedroom, put his .22-caliber rifle against her head, and pulled the trigger. According to newspaper reports, the bullet passed through her brain and embedded itself in the blood-spattered wall.

Paramedics rushed her comatose body to Desert Hospital where she was placed on life support. Two days later at the request of her sobbing parents, Phillip and Karen Applegate of Farmington, Minnesota, the plug was pulled. Grant's appalling story inspired the TV movie *Shattered Innocence*, and she was the subject of a Frontline documentary, *Death of a Porn Queen*, which aired on PBS.

★   ★   ★

Mostly, though, the Racquet Club and its interweaving streets are still associated with the stars and those who dallied there.

Tunesmith, licensed pilot, and crack golfer **Jimmy Van Heusen** (real name: Edward Chester Babcock) occupied the leafy Spanish hacienda at 333 West Cabrillo Road from 1948 to 1951. This vintage two-bedroom cottage, next to the Racquet Club Garden Villas manager's office, looks like a small hotel where movie extras waiting patiently to read the next day's call sheets might have stayed. No such luck. But Van Heusen did have luck in this first of four desert homes he owned. In fact, he got a lot of his divine inspiration, he said, "noodling" by the pool in the hot afternoon sun with a pencil in one hand and a highball in the other.

The highly productive Van Heusen, who took his nom de plume from the popular men's shirt label, received fourteen Oscar nominations and won four of them for his songwriting prowess on "Swinging on a Star," "All the Way," "High Hopes," and "Call Me Irresponsible."

★   ★   ★

The **Racquet Club Colony** is a maze of one- and two-bedroom garden villas that were designed with modernistic aplomb by pioneer desert architect William F. Cody and constructed in 1964 by father-and-son contractors George and Robert Alexander. The Racquet Club Colony is situated southwest of the hotel tennis courts and parking lot.

Jazz-influenced pop stylist **Morgana King**, who played Marlon Brando's loving wife, Mama Corleone, in *The Godfather* and its 1974 sequel, *The Godfather Part II*, owned a condominium there in 1999. King's first LP, "A Taste of Honey," made the creamy-voiced singer a New York nightclub favorite.

Top: Jimmy Van Heusen with his awards (Courtesy of Palm Springs Historical Society). *Bottom:* Linda Christian and Tyrone Power in 1953 (Courtesy of Linda Christian).

★   ★   ★

Currently residing in her own poolside villa is jet-setting actress **Linda Christian**, the second wife of raffish Hollywood leading man Tyrone Power. The couple had two daughters, Romina and Taryn. The marriage reportedly fell apart after the liberated Christian, who appeared seminude in *Tarzan and the Mermaids* and wore a revealing décolletage in *Slaves of Babylon*, found Power cheating on her. She later wed British actor Edmund Purdom.

Christian's choice of locale is no accident. Born Blanca Rosa Welter, this green-eyed, olive-skinned beauty with a classical face that inspired New York sculptor Jacob Epstein and Mexican painter Diego Rivera was discovered and renamed by Racquet Club member Errol Flynn.

Her headline-making divorce from Power netted Christian a reported $1 million. When he died in 1958, she showed up at the funeral uninvited and unannounced, causing a media frenzy. The publicity led to roles in *The V.I.P.s*, *The Beauty Jungle*, and *The Moment of Truth*. But Linda's acting career never attracted as much attention as her love life, which was always the subject of hot gossip: a $100,000 gift of jewelry from playboy Robert Schlesinger (which caused a stir when Van Cleef & Arpels insisted upon payment); a Hong Kong shopping spree with Brazilian millionaire "Baby" Pignatari; wild flings with the Marquis de Portago, tycoon Dirceu Fontoura; and a reputed roll in the hay with heroic Spanish bullfighter Luis Dominguin.

Christian's later years have been spent on less-taxing activities such as traveling and painting. In 1994, her name made the news again when Ylenia Carrisi, the twenty-five-year-old daughter of Romina Power and Italian singer Al Bano, vanished without a trace in the French Quarter of New Orleans. Theories abound as to what happened to her: she was abducted; she changed her identity; she jumped in the river. A somber Christian visited the city to search for her missing granddaughter, but returned empty-handed. What happened to Carrisi has yet to be determined.

Following in the beefy biceps of Steve Reeves, Gordon Mitchell, and Peter Lupus is physique model-turned-actor **Richard Harrison**, a native of Salt Lake City, who wound his way west like so many others before him in search of fame and fortune on the oil-slathered sands of Muscle Beach, California. After a short-lived stint in Hollywood playing bit roles as pilots and soldiers, this garrulous, blond-topped club resident bought an airline ticket to Europe with high hopes of being discovered by the likes of Rossellini, Federico Fellini, or perhaps Luchino Visconti. It didn't happen.

But Harrison did make the acquaintance of director Sergio Leone. He humored the director's sexual advances, but did not accept the director's offer to play the poncho-clad man-with-no-name in *A Fistful of Dollars*, which turned Clint Eastwood into a star. Not one to fret over lost opportunities, Harrison gritted his teeth and bared his chest in a string of Italian sword-and-sandal epics that paid him many thousands of lira and plastered his face on billboards across Europe as the toga-wearing hero in *Invincible Gladiator*, *Avenger of the Seven Seas,* and *Gladiators 7*. He also starred in a string of spaghetti Westerns, imitating Eastwood's squinty-eyed gunman. Upon retiring, Harrison moved to Palm Springs and unsuccessfully ran for mayor in 1995 and 1999.

The recent accolades bestowed on various midcentury architects for their advanced building designs are nothing new. As early as 1937, for example, the house that **Richard Neutra** designed for **Grace Lewis Miller** at 2311 North Indian Avenue (south of Via Escuela) won its creator the *House Beautiful* competition. The home's solid concrete floors, large glass paneling, and sheet-metal exterior were typical of the Bauhaus minimalist style. Bauhaus founder Walter Gropius, like his prize-winning student Neutra, insisted that metal stresses and tensions be substituted for concrete and wood-supporting beams in all his designs.

Miller's unusual home was noteworthy for another more-pragmatic reason: It was where this physical fitness instructor, actress, and amateur historian wrote an unproduced screenplay about Missouri River explorers Meriwether Lewis and William Clark. She became a leading authority on the subject of Lewis and Clark's famous expedition to the Pacific coast. (Charles Farrell later owned her home, which was subsequently snapped up by a cheap buyer for $70,000 in 1979.)

Built in 1959, Racquet Club Road Estates, the Alexander family's third planned development after Twin Palms and Vista Las Palmas, was comprised of approximately sixty homes in the northeast area. Monuments of great architecture they are not! These were cheap and expendable buildings, which meant that architects and contractors could reap substantial profits without investing large amounts of time and money in their construction.

The misconception that people demanded thin walls, no insulation, and flimsy carports instead of secure garages is a falsehood perpetuated by cashed-up developers and architectural revisionists. It is not an opinion generally shared by individual homeowners who time and again found themselves the unwitting victims of construction defects and sundry concerns often associated with these houses. But they do look good.

Even Raymond Chandler, the paragon of American detective fiction, was impressed. "The bungalows with their wide roofs were set close to the drive so that there was room for the pool in back, and the patio, which represented the ultimate advancement of civilization in the desert," he wrote in *Poodle Springs*.

Beverly Hills couturier **Sy DeVore** was the designer of elegant tuxedo and sharkskin suits with narrow lapels and cuffless pants that were all the rage with fashion conscious male dressers such as Frank Sinatra, Bing Crosby, Bob Hope, George Burns, Dean Martin, and Jerry Lewis. DeVore owned the estate at 2808 Sunny View Drive (between San Rafael and Racquet Club Drive, just off Indian Canyon Drive).

It was the spastic comedian Lewis who set up the former New York clothing store salesman as Hollywood's leading tailor with a shop on Vine Street. "In 1949 alone," Lewis boasted, "I bought 100 suits from him at $250 apiece, also 135 cardigan sweaters, and more pairs of slacks than I could count." Alas, DeVore, to the consternation of his tailor-made clients, died in 1966. His home sold for a modest sum in 1997. DeVore's tombstone inscription fittingly reads "Beloved by all."

★   ★   ★

Unfortunately, the same could not be said for the Racquet Club, which by the 1980s was a mere ghost of its former self. Successive changes of ownership further undermined its already sullied reputation, the result of an influx of hustlers and call girls, and the club was soon closed more than it was open. Ten years after the club premises and surrounding bungalows had fallen into shabby disrepair, *GQ* creative director **Jim Moore**, while on a trip from New York, stumbled onto the historic neighborhood unfairly referred to as the "north end" and believed it deserved a second chance.

In 1993 Moore plunked down $110,000 on a steel-framed home, designed by architect Donald Wexler, at 3100 North Sunnyview Drive where, twenty-five years earlier, autonomous filmmaker **Stanley Kramer**, a nine-time Oscar nominee, lived with his second wife, actress Karen Sharpe, daughters Katharine, Jennifer, Casey, and son Larry. Kramer produced President Bill Clinton's favorite film *High Noon* and directed such heavy-handed "message" pictures as *The Defiant Ones, Inherit the Wind*, and *Guess Who's Coming to Dinner?* In 1977 Kramer left Hollywood and moved to Seattle. He died in 2001.

★   ★   ★

Stanley Kramer and wife Karen Sharpe (Courtesy of Karen Kramer).

In 1995, **Douglas Keeve**, the director of *Unzipped*, a documentary about New York fashion designer Isaac Mizrahi, paid $85,000 for a similar steel-framed house, also designed by Wexler, at 3165 Sunnyview Drive. Then in 1997, Los Angeles artist **Jim Isermann**, whose modular wall designs are a combination of modernism and garish pop art, followed suit and purchased another Wexler home at 330 East Molino Road. The Palm Springs renaissance had begun.

This unexpected rebirth came about as a result of the 1987 stock market crash, which sent the real estate market into a tailspin, causing inevitable short sales and foreclosures—a trend that continued to hurt the local business sector for another ten years until the inevitable turnover in property sales began pushing prices back up again.

★　★　★

John Payne contemplating middle age (Backlot Books & Movie Posters).

Leading man **John Payne**, who was equally adept at wartime flagwavers such as *To the Shores of Tripoli*; tune-filled period musicals, *Hello, Frisco, Hello*; and teary-eyed romantic dramas, *Miracle on 34th Street*, lifted barbells each morning at 407 Laurel Circle, where he lived during his retirement from films in 1961. Although best known as a singing actor, after he turned forty, Payne sought to change his image and carved out a comfortable niche playing "wronged men" in a series of cheaply made Westerns and crime melodramas. Payne made an early grab for the rights to Ian Fleming's novel *Moonraker* in 1955. When he was unable to secure all the books in the series, he gave up his one-year option— a costly mistake as the James Bond monopoly, which would have made Payne a rich man, is now worth hundreds of millions, if not billions.

★　★　★

Short, bespectacled producer **Alex Gottlieb**, who oversaw ten films with knockabout comedians Bud Abbott and Lou Costello, two of them—*Jack and the Beanstalk* and *Abbott & Costello Meet Captain Kidd*—in garish Super Cinecolor, took the weekends off with his wife, Polly Rose, sister of Tin Pan Alley songwriter and showman Billy Rose (played by James Caan in *Funny Lady*), at 581 Laurel Circle.

★　★　★

Slick-haired character actor **Milburn Stone**, who played town physician "Doc" Adams on CBS-TV's *Gunsmoke* for twenty years, resided with his wife, Jane Garrison, at 2839 North Davis Way in 1959.

★　★　★

Warner Brothers contract player **Russell Arms**, who portrayed sensitive young men in *The Man Who Came to Dinner*, *Captains of the Clouds*, and *By the Light of the Silvery Moon* and was a regular guest performer on *Your Hit Parade*, still lives at 2918 North Davis Way.

The first desert home of MGM child star **Jackie Cooper**, a Best Actor Oscar nominee at the tender age of nine for 1931's *Skippy* and made people weep as the plucky son of hard-drinking boxer Wallace Beery in *The Champ*, can be found at 2981 North Davis Way, where Cooper lived in 1960.

Also in 1960, crusty actor **Darren McGavin**, who played Frank Sinatra's dope pusher in *The Man With the Golden Arm*, purchased the Alexander home at 511 Desert Willow Circle. It is is now owned by Dodie Frasier, the first wife of *Little House on the Prairie* actor Michael Landon. When McGavin lived in this small house, however, the vampire-chasing star of *Kolchak: The Night Stalker* was still a lanky young man on the verge of network stardom plying his trade as crime-busting *Mike Hammer* and the ferry captain in *Riverboat*—light years away from his Emmy-winning turn as Candice Bergen's grouchy dad on *Murphy Brown* and Agent Arthur Dales in the paranormal cable hit, *The X-Files*.

Fifties disc jockey **Alan Freed**, the man credited with coining the phrase "rock 'n' roll," who was discredited for accepting bribes in the record industry's huge payola scandal (filmed as *American Hot Wax* starring Tim McIntire as Freed), died penniless at 309 Desert Holly Circle, off Starr Road, in 1965, a victim of kidney disease. Freed's injured reputation was partly restored when his ashes were interred in the Rock and Roll Hall of Fame in his hometown of Cleveland in 2002.

Top: Darren McGavin looks surprised (Cinema Collectors). *Bottom:* Ruta Lee, Mary Martin, and Debbie Reynolds (Courtesy of Ruta Lee).

Sparkling musical comedy performer **Ruta Lee**, who showed her flair in *Seven Brides for Seven Brothers* and *Funny Face*, launching the Canadian-born actress on a long film and television career, resided for more than eighteen years at 315 Desert Holly Circle, which she purchased in 1960.

Phil Feldman, producer of Sam Peckinpah's ultraviolent Western, *The Wild Bunch*, and its tongue-in-cheek follow-up *The Ballad of Cable Hogue*, preplanned both films at 2788 North Starr Road, where he lived in 1968.

German-born actor **Udo Kier**, who played campy monsters in Andy Warhol's *Flesh for Frankenstein* and *Blood for Dracula*, currently owns the property at 2555 North Via Miraleste, for which he paid $300,000 in 2002.

Hollywood producer and agent **Milton H. Bren**, who showcased Broadway musical star Alfred Drake in his one-and-only top-billed film, *Tars and Spars*, and directed Gloria Swanson in the disastrous screwball comedy, *Three for Bedroom C* (derailing the actress' highly publicized *Sunset Boulevard* comeback), weekended at 215 West Racquet Club Road during the 1939-40 season.

Bren was the former business partner of agent-brothers Victor and Frank Orsatti, who negotiated the sale of Frank Baum's book, *The Wizard of Oz*, to MGM for their client Judy Garland. They also brought triple gold-winning Olympic Games' figure skater Sonja Henie to Hollywood. Bren later married Oscar-winning *Key Largo* actress Claire Trevor. He died of a brain tumor in 1979.

Former talent agent **Edward Small**, whose sturdy independent productions of *I Cover the Waterfront*, *Palooka*, and *The Count of Monte Cristo* put him on the moviemaking map, formed his own production company while living at 251 West Racquet Road in 1938. He then embarked on lavish cinematic versions of the literary classics *The Last of the Mohicans*, *The Man in the Iron Mask*, and *The Corsican Brothers*.

American tennis champion **Frank Shields** was ranked the nation's number one player in 1933. He parlayed his fame into a short-lived movie career as a second lead in Samuel Goldwyn's *Dead End* and the Ritz Brothers trifle, *The Goldwyn Follies*. Shields lived at 283 West Racquet Club in 1938. *Suddenly Susan* actress Brooke Shields is his granddaughter.

Nearby at Jack Roberts' whitewashed Spanish hacienda at 287 West Racquet Club Road, which he bought for $350,000 in 2002, legend has it that Swedish-born superstar **Greta Garbo**, nicknamed "the Sphinx" because of her frozen expression, recovered behind closed drapes from a traumatic breakup with her emoting *Flesh and the Devil* and *Queen Christina* costar John Gilbert. However, there is no proof to support the claim that she ever stayed here.

Greta Garbo alone and happy (Larry Edmunds Bookshop).

Garbo did spend much time elsewhere in the desert. In 1939, she stayed at the home of nutritionist Gaylord Hauser, and in 1948, she visited the home of Frank Sinatra, located one mile away. In 1967, her brother, Sven Gustafson, died in Desert Hospital from a heart attack, age sixty-eight. Following her much-publicized early retirement, Garbo traveled extensively throughout America and Europe, using the alias Harriet Brown. Several of these visits brought her westward again, where the reclusive actress and health fanatic indulged her favorite pursuits of swimming, walking, and visiting churchyards.

★　★　★

Moon-faced character actor **Albert Salmi**, a brawny exponent of Stanislavsky's Method, tapped his volatile emotions to play some of the screen's nastiest gunmen, sheriffs, and prison wardens. In 1965, Salmi lived at 412 East Racquet Club Road with his second wife, Roberta Pollock. The chameleonlike Salmi relished changing faces in movies like *Wild River*, *The Outrage*, *Brubaker*, and *Dragonslayer*. Unfortunately, his mean-guy persona went beyond his screen roles. In 1990, he shot his wife at his home in Spokane, Washington, then turned the gun on himself.

★　★　★

In 1963, **Debbie Reynolds**, who won a beauty contest at sixteen impersonating Betty Hutton, bought the Alexander house with the concrete block wall at 757 East Racquet Club Road. Her ex-husband, Harry Karl, occupied it in 1973, and her parents then lived there for ten years until the death of her father, Ray Reynolds, in 1986. Debbie Reynolds sold the house for $79,500 in 1987.

★　★　★

Jackie Coogan broke people's hearts as a cute child star in Charlie Chaplin's silent film *The Kid*, then made worldwide headlines when he was cheated out of a $4-million fortune by his greedy parents, and finally became a star all over again playing ghoulish Uncle Fester in TV's *The Addams Family*. Coogan lived at 1050 East Racquet Club Road from 1975 onward, where fans of the classic sitcom remember seeing him waiting for taxis outside the house.

On March 1, 1984, the four-times married Coogan died from a heart attack while visiting his daughter, Leslie, in Santa Monica. (Her son is straight-to-video actor Keith Coogan.) Six years later, Jackie Coogan's youngest son, Christopher, who worked as a

Top: Albert Salmi on the rampage (Larry Edmunds Bookshop). *Bottom:* Jackie Coogan as Uncle Fester (Steve Kiefer Collection).

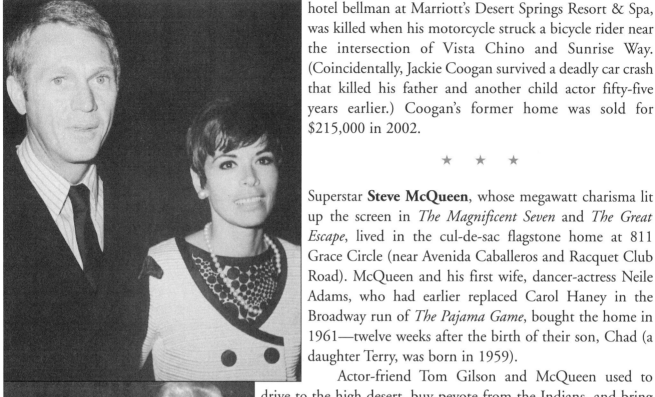

hotel bellman at Marriott's Desert Springs Resort & Spa, was killed when his motorcycle struck a bicycle rider near the intersection of Vista Chino and Sunrise Way. (Coincidentally, Jackie Coogan survived a deadly car crash that killed his father and another child actor fifty-five years earlier.) Coogan's former home was sold for $215,000 in 2002.

★　　★　　★

Superstar **Steve McQueen**, whose megawatt charisma lit up the screen in *The Magnificent Seven* and *The Great Escape*, lived in the cul-de-sac flagstone home at 811 Grace Circle (near Avenida Caballeros and Racquet Club Road). McQueen and his first wife, dancer-actress Neile Adams, who had earlier replaced Carol Haney in the Broadway run of *The Pajama Game*, bought the home in 1961—twelve weeks after the birth of their son, Chad (a daughter Terry, was born in 1959).

Actor-friend Tom Gilson and McQueen used to drive to the high desert, buy peyote from the Indians, and bring it home. Then they'd cook it in boiling water, eat the leaves, and get stoned. They also smoked marijuana, took LSD, and snorted cocaine, according to Adams.

McQueen's family witnessed his metamorphosis from a working actor in *Hell is for Heroes* and *Soldier in the Rain* to the bristling powerhouse star of *The Cincinnati Kid* and *Nevada Smith*, capped by his Oscar nomination as Best Actor in *The Sand Pebbles*.

"We were in Palm Springs when we were notified," remembered Adams. "Steve was pouring concrete in the garage when I handed him the telephone. It was an exciting moment."

The unconventional McQueen, who owned 135 motorcycles and 35 cars, including a burgundy Ferrari and a Jaguar XKSS, roared down to Sambo's restaurant and celebrated by ordering giant hamburgers and chocolate milkshakes with vanilla ice cream.

Top: Steve McQueen and Neile Adams (Cinema Collectors). *Bottom:* Paul Burke and Lyn Peters (Courtesy of Lyn Burke).

★　　★　　★

Chiseled TV star **Paul Burke**, who played police detective Adam Flint in *The Naked City* and Colonel Joe Gallagher on *Twelve O'Clock High*, has lived undisturbed at 2217 Avenida Caballeros for more than forty years, leaving home only when his agent called him for guest-starring roles on such top-rated drama series as *Magnum P.I.*, *Hotel*, *Dynasty*, and *Columbo*. The earnest-looking Burke played wealthy patriarch "C. C." Capwell for eight years on the NBC daytime drama, *Santa Barbara*. He quit acting in 1994. Burke's father, New Orleans boxer Marty Burke, who fought Jack Dempsey and Gene Tunney, died here, age eighty-one, in 1978. Burke's wife, Lyn Peters, whom he married in 1979, now runs a successful catering business.

Meanwhile, a completely different kind of actor, **Mr. Blackwell**, (real name: Richard Selzer), the preening fashion critic/author of the laugh-out-loud Annual Worst Dressed List, and his partner, Beverly Hills hairstylist Robert Spencer, once cohabited the house at 715 Spencer Drive. This was one of three homes that Spencer (the son of a contractor), built on the same street, which is named after him, in 1960.

Lest you think Blackwell's tart observations were uttered out of jealousy, he was also a successful fashion designer, creator of the strapless pink-and-white floral evening gown worn by Lily Pons for her grand entrance on *The Eddie Fisher Show*, as well as the elaborately beaded costumes worn by Jane Russell, Connie Haines, and Beryl Davis during their Riviera Hotel engagement in Las Vegas.

Some memorable highlights from Blackwell's worst dressed lists: Shelley Winters (a rag doll), Elizabeth Taylor (a chain of link sausages), Lena Horne (a plucked chicken), Barbra Streisand (Ringo Starr in drag), Debbie Reynolds (a Christmas tree), Carol Channing (a bird of paradise), Ann-Margret (Marlon Brando in a G-string), Liza Minnelli (a fried egg), Ali MacGraw (Pocahontas), and Cher (a cockatoo).

Director **Henry Levin** captured the pained expressions of Clifton Webb at his sardonic best in *Mr. Scoutmaster* and *The Remarkable Mr. Pennypacker*, thrust Ivy League singer Pat Boone to the front ranks of beefcake stardom in *Bernardine* and *April Love*, and gave Dean Martin his greatest makeover as bed-hopping secret agent Matt Helm in *Murderers' Row* and *The Ambushers*. Levin scrutinized the script for his most-complicated undertaking, the special effects-laden Cinerama fairy tale, *The Wonderful World of the Brothers Grimm*, starring Laurence Harvey and Karl Boehm, while living at 888 Spencer Drive in 1961. Eleven years later, Levin found himself in Hong Kong directing black superstar Fred Williamson in *That Man Bolt*. He died in 1980.

Veteran cameraman **Arthur E. Arling**, who operated the heavy three-strip Technicolor blimps that recorded the burning of Atlanta in *Gone With The Wind* and the precious wildlife of Florida's everglades in *The Yearling*, helping to win both films Oscars for Best Color Cinematography, retired to 352 North Glen Circle in 1970. Arling was Betty Grable's favorite cameraman on half a dozen song-and-dance flicks, among them *My Blue*

Heaven and *Call Me Mister.*

In 1955, "Art" earned his own Oscar nomination for the gleaming black-and-white cinematography that documented Susan Hayward's hellish performance in *I'll Cry Tomorrow.* Arling is also credited with devising the "gauze look" that softened Doris Day's blotchy complexion, making her seem younger than her actual age on *Love Me or Leave Me, Pillow Talk,* and *Lover Come Back.*

★ ★ ★

Yet another unsung motion picture artist was **Leo Tover**, one of the greatest cinematographers of Hollywood's Golden Age, who lived at 2294 Starr Road. Tover photographed 120 films, including the first (silent) version of *The Great Gatsby,* followed by *The Vagabond Lover, The Big Broadcast of 1936, Bluebeard's Eighth Wife,* and *The Major and the Minor*—second of three standout collaborations with writer-director Billy Wilder.

Tover received Oscar nominations for the Wilder-scripted *Hold Back the Dawn* and William Wyler's *The Heiress.* He also created startling photography for the masterful science fiction tale, *The Day the Earth Stood Still,* in addition to lensing Elvis Presley's screen debut in *Love Me Tender,* Jules Verne's subterranean *Journey to the Center of the Earth* (directed by his neighbor, Henry Levin), and Marilyn Monroe's last film, the unfinished *Something's Got To Give.*

Tover died on the last day of 1964. The home's next resident was fellow cinematographer **Clifford Stine**, who handled special-effects photography on the science fiction classics *It Came from Outer Space, This Island Earth, Tarantula,* and *The Incredible Shrinking Man.*

★ ★ ★

Top: Stubby Kaye (Backlot Books & Movie Posters) *Bottom:* Billy and Pierrette Daniels (Backlot Books & Movie Posters).

Stage and film actor-comedian **Stubby Kaye**, who as "Nicely-Nicely Johnson" sang "Sit Down, You're Rockin' the Boat" in both the Broadway and film versions of Frank Loesser's musical *Guys and Dolls,* lived at 2108 George Drive (at the corner of Via Escuela). Kaye, who also played Marryin' Sam in *Lil' Abner,* Herman in *Sweet Charity,* and Marvin Acme in *Who Framed Roger Rabbit?,* moved to the Colony in Rancho Mirage, where he died of undisclosed causes on December 14, 1997.

★ ★ ★

Smoky-voiced nightclub vocalist **Billy Daniels** aka "Mr. Black Magic," the father of six children including the late Chicago radio personality Yvonne Daniels, lived at 2126 George Drive from 1960 to 1965. Daniels' soulful renderings of "That Old Black Magic,"

"Them There Eyes," and "Love Is a Many-Splendored Thing" kept his name on pop music charts, though his questionable association with underworld figures led him to being stabbed in one widely publicized incident and charged with a shooting in another. Towards the end of his life, Daniels, who drove a white Rolls Royce, suffered ill health and twice underwent heart bypass surgery. He died in 1988. (Son Billy Daniels Jr., lived two blocks south from his famous father at 980 East Garden Road.)

★　★　★

Ivan Tors, the aquatically inclined producer of *Sea Hunt* and *Flipper*, owned the house at 1866 Jacques Road, where he lived with sons Steven, Peter, and David in 1964. Tors, who also produced *Daktari* and *Gentle Ben*, was among the first filmmakers to embrace ecological themes. He later set up Africa USA, a 260-acre Southern California wildlife preserve, to help protect endangered species. He filmed several of his animal TV shows there with actor-friend Marshall Thompson.

★　★　★

Fifties fashion trendsetter **Don Loper**, who created form-fitting gowns for singers Peggy Lee and Connie Francis and was Ella Fitzgerald's personal designer, owned the estate at 2101 Milben Circle (off Via Escuela), where he shed his trademark black silk Edwardian suits in favor of tropical shirts and cabana shorts.

A former musical child prodigy and choreographer (he danced with Ginger Rogers in *Lady in the Dark*, worked as Arthur Freed's assistant, and was a close friend of Vincente Minnelli), Loper toiled long and hard over dressmaking patterns until he became the head of a $25-million international company, manufacturing women's and men's wear collections, ranging from apparel and handkerchiefs to jewelry and toiletries.

In 1955, Loper guest-starred as himself in a memorable episode of *I Love Lucy*, titled "The Fashion Show," where Lucille Ball goes shopping for an expensive $100 dress. The show featured many Palm Springs actors' wives: Sue Carol (Alan) Ladd, Brenda (William Holden) Marshall, Frances (Van) Heflin, Marilyn (Forrest) Tucker, Jeanne (Dean) Martin, Sheila (Gordon) MacRae, and Mona (Richard) Carlson. He later caused howls of laughter when he put frumpy *Valley of the Dolls* novelist Jacqueline Susann in hot pants.

On August 24, 1972, in a freakish accident, Loper fell from a ladder at his Bel Air home, puncturing a lung. He slipped into a coma and died three months later, age sixty-five.

★　★　★

Return south to Vista Chino and go east until you come to Avenida Caballeros.

★　★　★

Hal Polaire, who worked in film production for four decades, lived at 1165 Louise Drive (off East Vista Chino and North Avenida Caballeros) in 1996. Polaire earned his film-making stripes as an assistant director on Billy Wilder's *Some Like It Hot, The Apartment,* and *Irma la Douce.* He later served as production assistant on *Who's Afraid of Virginia Woolf?,* graduating to associate producer on Robert De Niro's boxing tour de force, *Raging Bull.* Polaire was the executive producer on *Betrayed* and *The Music Box.* Polaire died in 1999, age eighty-one. His son, Michael Polaire, co-produced David Lynch's *Mulholland Drive* and Steven Soderbergh's *Solaris.*

Character actor **Don Barclay**, who lived at 2110 North Deborah Road (off Sunrise Way and Via Escuela), played bulbous-nosed drunks, piano players, and coach drivers in more than eighty films, including *Kid Galahad, Honky Tonk, This Gun For Hire,* and *My Darling Clementine.* Barclay's expressive voice was also heard in Walt Disney's *Cinderella, Alice in Wonderland, Peter Pan,* and *101 Dalmatians,* culminating in his live-action role as Mr. Binnacle in *Mary Poppins.* He died in 1975.

Cheryl Crane first came to the public's attention nearly half a century ago when the troubled teenage daughter of Beverly Hills restaurateur Stephen Crane, owner of the Luau, and his actress-wife, Lana Turner, star of *The Postman Always Rings Twice,* and *The Bad and the Beautiful,* fatally stabbed her mother's lover and small-time hood, Johnny Stompanato, with a butcher knife after he threatened to kill the "Sweater Girl" in the upstairs bedroom of their Beverly Hills home on Good Friday, April 4, 1958.

Stompanato had developed an uncontrollable hard-on for the shimmering sex symbol, sending flowers and candies to Turner in an effort to marry her or at least get her into bed. A sucker in more ways than one for well-hung Latin men, Lana fell hook, line, and sinker for Johnny's bullshit until she realized too late that her boyfriend worked for gangster Mickey Cohen.

When she tried to break off the affair, Stompanato told her it was a bad idea. They repeatedly came to blows until that fateful night when Cheryl, fearful for her mom's safety, ran upstairs with the knife and banged on the bedroom door. Arrested by police and sent to Juvenile Hall, Crane went on trial for murder in one of Tinseltown's most-sensational trials.

The prosecution's exaggerated accusations of Turner-Stompanato beatings, incest, and a ménage à trois, which drew a shocked response, flew thick and fast in the packed courtroom until fast-talking defense attorney Jerry Geisler, an expert jury swayer, called his star witness.

People sat riveted to their seats as the seconds ticked by. When a weepy, duck-tailed Turner, whose scandalous film *Peyton Place* was still playing in theaters, took the stand, she

Lana Turner cracks a smile (Backlot Books & Movie Posters).

Cheeta the chimp preparing for his next art show (Courtesy of Dan Westfall).

delivered a fainting performance captured by newsreel photographers that merited a second Oscar nomination. The heated courtroom proceedings—broadcast live on TV stations and splashed across newspaper front pages around the world—helped ensure the record-breaking success of her next film, *Imitation of Life,* the title of which was an apt metaphor for the star's bouts with alcoholism and seven failed marriages. Turner's "tissues-and-tears" emoting had its desired effect, persuading jurors of her lover's abusive behavior and his deserving punishment. Sensing vindication, Geisler moved for a dismissal of the charges. Eventually, Turner's daughter was acquitted of justifiable homicide and set free.

But the acquittal did not end the soap opera. For years, unsubstantiated rumors circulated that Turner did the deed and that fourteen-year-old Cheryl, who was made a ward of the court and placed in her grandmother's custody, took the rap. (Harold Robbins used the same mother-daughter premise for his novel, *Where Love Has Gone.*) Even Turner, who was crowned queen of the 28th Palm Springs Mounted Police Rodeo in 1968, seemingly warmed to the idea.

"I'd kill the son of a bitch again," the silver-haired actress allegedly told her Hemet hairdresser-friend, Eric Root.

Not so, according to Crane's compelling autobiography *Detour,* in which she recounted her all-too-sordid childhood, including, she maintained, being raped and molested for three years by her stepfather, Lex "Tarzan" Barker. Why didn't she tell her mother? Cheryl said Barker threatened to send her to Juvenile Hall. Of course, that's exactly where she ended up after Stompanato's death, and by that time, Barker was long gone.

It's no small wonder that Crane, who suffered recurring nightmares, gradually lost interest in men. Eventually, she found lasting happiness with bisexual fashion model Joyce LeRoy, setting up house together in San Francisco. Today, they live in a luxury villa they purchased in 1996 in the Sundance Resort at 2926 Sundance Circle West, located off San Rafael Road and Avenida Caballeros—seven months after Turner's death at age seventy-five.

One celebrity neighbor, meanwhile, doesn't speak any language except his own, which might be just as well considering Cheryl Crane's understandable disdain for the male species. **Cheeta**, the scene-stealing, face-contorting, hand-clapping chimpanzee, who upstaged three monosyllabic *Tarzan* actors and outlived them all, is very much alive, well, and hooting at visitors from his cage at "Casa de Cheeta" at 1033 East Francis Road. Now an agile seventy-one, Cheeta (real name: Jiggs), who also milked applause as Ronald Reagan's bottle-feeding experiment in *Bedtime for Bonzo,* now spends his days grooming, eating bananas, and painting "ape-stract" art that his human owner, Daniel Westfall, who cares for eight other simians, sells to the public.

★   ★   ★

Further east, bald comedy foil **Sid Tomack**, who played wisecracking waiters and guileful con artists in scores of movies, including Bob Hope's *Sorrowful Jones*, *The Lemon Drop Kid*, and *That Certain Feeling*, resided at 2153 North Cerritos Road (between North Sunrise Way and Farrell Drive) until his death from a heart ailment on November 12, 1962. A scene-stealing actor whose bark was worse than his bite, Tomack repeatedly threatened George Reeves on TV's *The Adventures of Superman*. He also played Al, the boyfriend of Marie Wilson on *My Friend Irma*, as well as Knobby Walsh on the *Joe Palooka* show.

★   ★   ★

And, for four years, until his death in 1993, **Sergio Galindo**, the Mexican abstract author of thirteen novels, among them *A Mexican Masquerade* and the prize-winning *Otilia's Body*, lived at 3099 North Greg Circle, overlooking Palm Springs Country Club, 2500 North Whitewater Club Drive.

The eighteen-hole championship public golf course was originally named Whitewater Country Club when it opened in 1961. Rita Hayworth was photographed practicing her golf swing in 1963, two years after divorcing fifth husband James Hill. The two met during the filming of *Separate Tables*, which Hill co-produced.

More recently, novice filmmaker Randy Pike tried unsuccessfully to raise investment capital while at the club. He had paid $50,000 for a one-year option to use James Dean's name and likeness in a movie he hoped to produce about the actor's troubled life.

Pike was one of several gullible people duped into handing over large sums of cash in return for bogus distribution contracts offered by fly-by-night Hollywood con man Jon Emr, who was killed by a barrage of gunfire in a Culver City drive-by shooting in 1991.

Given the predisposition of such unsavory persons to make a dishonest extra buck, it should come as no surprise to learn that Future Homes Incorporated property developer, Milton Wershow, who subdivided much of this windy neighborhood, had as his partner Beverly Hills loan broker Al Yarbrow, known for his shady dealings with Teamsters Union lawyer and reputed mob go-between Morris Shenker.

It was the conservative, well-dressed Yarbrow, who was charged by authorities with diverting funds from Bradley Mortgage Company's impound accounts of four hundred homeowners for other business ventures in the get-rich-quick savings and loan banking scandal of the 1980s. Actress Debra Winger named Yarbrow as a defendant in her 1997 lawsuit against Cinefin Corporation after it refused to honor her $1.5 million pay-or-play contract when the company halted shooting of her feature film, *Divine Rapture*, after two weeks.

Chapter 2

Trouble In
Little Tuscany

Immediately to the west of the Racquet Club is Little Tuscany Estates—a small rocky outcrop of custom-built homes in and around Chino Canyon, the former summer home of Indian tribal shaman Pedro Chino and his family. Named after the hilly region of northern Italy favored by painters and poets since the fourteenth century, this protected enclave was first subdivided and offered for sale in 1935 by Rufus Chapman, a local realtor. Some homes are small bungalows, while others are huge, multilevel constructions with unobstructed views.

Beware! This holy place brings good luck to people who respect the ancient gods. But if you offend them, it is said, dire consequences will follow.

Former Actor Tom Neal Booked in Slaying of Wife at Palm Springs

Top: Newspaper headline of Gail Neal's murder (Howard Johns Collection).
Left: Tom Neal's home at 2481 Cardillo Avenue (Photo by Howard Johns).
Right: Tom and Gail Neal (Howard Johns Collection).

★ ★ ★

April Fool's Day 1965 was no joke for pugnacious actor **Tom Neal**. That was the day he shot and killed his twenty-nine-year-old wife, Gail Evatt, in the front living room of their rented home at 2481 Cardillo Avenue. (Peculiarly, the family of Gloria Swanson—no relation to the silent screen actress—that owned this ramshackle, four-bedroom house also ran Sands Spa Hotel where Shauna Grant died, which gives them the dubious distinction of owning *two* infamous celebrity homes.)

According to police reports, Neal wanted to have sexual intercourse that night, but Gail, a pretty brunette receptionist from the Palm Springs Tennis Club, wasn't in the mood. Rather than continue the fight, Gail, who planned to seek a divorce, grabbed a bedspread and prepared a makeshift bed on the living-room sofa. The crackle of flames in the gas fireplace must have made her drowsy. Police believe she was drifting off to sleep when a jealous Neal, who suspected his wife of infidelity, entered the room and demanded sex. When she refused, Neal purportedly tugged at her sweater and green pedal pushers until he broke the zipper. Neal then took aim at his wife's head with a .45 caliber pistol and pulled the trigger.

When the police arrived at dawn the next day, they found Gail Neal lying face up on three bloodstained sofa pillows with a dark red hole in the left side of her head. Her legs were akimbo, white underpants pulled halfway down her waist. Neal, a coat slung over his hunched shoulders, stood silently outside the house with his attorney. It was the beginning of the end of his life.

A former prizefighter whose quick fists made him the Mickey Rourke of his day, Neal had starred in a bunch of B movies in which he frowned and fretted and flexed his biceps: *Flying Tigers, China Girl, Air Force, First Yank in Tokyo,* and *Detour*—a grim tale of murder that hung over him like a black cloud. In it, he played a doomed pianist who falls in love with a young woman and strangles her with his bare hands. Neal, it seemed, had difficulty separating fantasy from reality and in moments of intense emotional stress, he became that same character: a man cursed by his inner demons.

In 1951, fate tempted him in the bewitching figure of Barbara Payton, a bottle-blonde movie starlet, who was so turned on by Neal's lovemaking, she said, that it "sent red hot peppers down my thighs." But when Payton announced she was dumping him for callow actor Franchot Tone, Neal beat his competitor to a bloody pulp, sending him to the hospital for ten days with a concussion and broken nose.

Neal threw a knockout punch, but it was Tone who emerged the sympathetic winner, and Payton was so overjoyed, she married him. When his movie roles dried up, Neal retreated to Palm Springs where Ethel Strebe offered the persona-non-grata actor the temporary job of dinner host at her restaurant, the Doll House.

How it must have infuriated Neal to take reservations from fellow costars like George Montgomery (*Ten Gentlemen From West Point*) and Alan Ladd (*Beyond Glory*). So he turned to landscaping, which people snickered was the only thing he could do without hurting somebody.

Neal was charged with first-degree murder in the death of his wife. His twenty-day trial in Indio Court was the longest and most-publicized legal case in that city's history. Barbara Payton, whose own career ended in oblivion when she was arrested for prostitution, drunkenness, and passing bad checks, was a spectator. A jury of nine women and three men listened to evidence from twenty-one witnesses before convicting Neal of involuntary manslaughter. Instead of going to the gas chamber as he deserved, Neal was sentenced to ten years in state prison. He died in 1972, eight months after being paroled for good behavior. Neal was fifty-eight.

Although film and stage actor **Gar Moore** starred in Roberto Rossellini's neorealistic

Italian war film *Paisan*, he is mostly remembered for less-challenging roles in Universal-International's *Illegal Entry*, *Johnny Stool Pigeon*, and *Abbott & Costello Meet the Killer* which he made while married to pint-sized comedy actress Nancy Walker. Moore resided at 160 Via Olivera in 1959.

Gravel-voiced, pockmarked, Hollywood gangster actor **Marc Lawrence**, who shot up the screen in *This Gun For Hire*, *Dillinger*, *Key Largo*, and *The Asphalt Jungle*, now hides out with his favorite companion, Nicky, a toy poodle with a diamanté collar, in the pink stucco home he built for himself at 2200 Vista Grande Avenue (between Via Olivera and Via Escuela).

The film noir star, who made a lucrative career for more than sixty years playing hoodlums, hit men, and Italian *capos* in three hundred films and TV shows, has lived in this nondescript house surrounded by piles of Etruscan art and filled with yellowing movie posters since 1977. His daughter, Toni, an actress-sculptor, and his artist-son, Michael, pay him obligatory visits twice a year.

To date, the irascible actor has survived the McCarthy communist witch hunts, the death of his screenwriter wife Fanya Foss, and a near-fatal car crash. (Rescuers had to cut him out of his crushed Lexus.) Most recently, the hardy nonagenarian was seen in *From Dusk Till Dawn* and *Gotti*, as well as the Arnold Schwarzenegger apocalyptic thriller, *End of Days*. Lawrence's own end, however, seems nowhere in sight. He still works occasionally and pops up frequently on the celebrity book-signing circuit to promote his bitter memoir, *Long Time No See*.

Marc Lawrence feeling Britt Ekland's thigh (Courtesy of Marc Lawrence).

Rough-and-tumble actor **Don Castle**, who was groomed for stardom in MGM's *Dr. Kildare*, *Andy Hardy* and *Nick Carter* film series, but never quite caught on with movie audiences despite his close resemblance to Clark Gable, lived at 447 West Via Escuela. Castle also played minor roles in *The Big Land* and *Gunfight at the OK Corral*, and served as associate producer for the *Lassie* TV series. Castle died from a medication overdose following a traffic accident in 1966.

★   ★   ★

Australian-born actor **Tristan Rogers**, the insolent Robert Scorpio for ten years on the long-

Soap opera star Tristan Rogers (Steve Kiefer Collection).

running daytime soap opera *General Hospital,* has been a resident at 483 West Via Escuela (originally Chino Mesa Estates) since 1997. A familiar TV face for three decades, Rogers is also in demand as the weathered voice of Outback Steakhouse, in addition to many cartoon characters.

Rogers was arrested and convicted of his second drunk-driving offense in 1993 and placed on three-year's probation. His desert move was intended to keep him sober and away from temptation, which is why he prefers to stay home with second wife Teresa Parkerson and their two kids.

But it hasn't deterred him from enjoying the local nightlife, including a visit to Toucan's, a gay bar, where patrons spotted Rogers drinking a Yuletide toast with a male buddy on Christmas Eve 2001.

Rogers is not the only cast member from *General Hospital* who calls the desert home. Stage-trained actor **Ron Hale**, who plays Dr. Mike Corbin in the same medical series as well as its spin-off *Port Charles,* is a nearby city resident.

★   ★   ★

Steve Broidy, the kindly president of Monogram Pictures, later Allied Artists, which produced the *Bowery Boys, Mr. Wong,* and *Charlie Chan* series, owned the house at 535 Via Escuela from 1951 to 1966. (Note: Actor Robert Young is often misidentified as the home's former owner, but he did not live here.)

The no-frills equivalent of Miramax, Broidy's company released such prestige pictures as William Wyler's *Friendly Persuasion* and Billy Wilder's *Love in the Afternoon.* He backed William (*The Exorcist*) Friedkin's first film *Good Times* starring Sonny and Cher. In 1972, Broidy quietly bankrolled *The Poseidon Adventure* for producer-friend Irwin Allen when a cash-strapped 20th Century-Fox was unable to come up with all the money. The film grossed $42 million and kicked off the movie stars-in-jeopardy film cycle that has remained a ticket-buying staple for thirty years.

Broidy performed many philanthropic endeavors and was a recipient of the Jean Hersholt Humanitarian Award. He crafted the merger of Cedars of Lebanon and Mount Sinai Hospitals into Cedars-Sinai Medical Center, of which he was president, served as a director of Union Bank, and was a benefactor of such schools as Loyola University in Los Angeles and Marymount and Claremont colleges. A longtime baseball fan, Broidy suffered a fatal heart attack, age eighty-six, doing what he loved best: munching on a hot dog while watching a ball game at Dodgers Stadium on April 28, 1991.

★   ★   ★

In 1967, rugged leading man **Rod Taylor,** who followed Errol Flynn across the Pacific

Ocean from Australia to Hollywood, where he battled savage morlocks in *The Time Machine* and defended a coastal town against attacking gulls in *The Birds*, owned the house at 444 West Mariscal Road. Taylor vacated the home when he divorced his second wife, Mary Helim, in 1969.

★   ★   ★

Singing Irish leprechaun **Dennis Day**, a regular on Jack Benny's radio program as the naive teenager ("Gee, Mr. Benny!") and was the butt of his cheap jokes in the film *Buck Benny Rides Again*, lived at 485 West Santa Elena Road, one block north of Chino Canyon Road. The crooner of a tearful version of "Danny Boy" spent his retirement drinking Coors, eating Pepperchinis, and watching *The Benny Hill Show* on TV. He died from Lou Gehrig's disease in 1988.

★   ★   ★

Local tour guides insist that **Zsa Zsa Gabor** once lived in regal splendor at 595 West Chino Canyon Road. Gabor has made a career out of playing the matrimonial merry-go-round and has become the brunt of jokes for her single-minded attraction to aristocratic husbands who can afford her wild spending sprees on excessive makeup, diamonds, and furs. The most-frequently wed and parodied of Hungary's three famous gold-digging sisters, Gabor's choice of acting roles sound less like films and more like perfumed pages from her own diary: *Lovely to Look At, We're Not Married,* and *The Story of Three Loves,* among many others.

Top: Irish singer Dennis Day (Backlot Books & Movie Posters). *Bottom:* Zsa Zsa Gabor in her feline prime (Larry Edmunds Bookshop).

The fact that this house, which was owned by Los Angeles interior designer Hamilton Garland, was not built until 1968 and Zsa Zsa never officially purchased it, hasn't stopped the avalanche of frosty anecdotes about her matrimonial activities that were supposed to have taken place here.

Whatever the naked truth, Zsa Zsa's nine mates have included hotel-chain owner Conrad Hilton, whom she married in 1942, and the silver-tongued, Russian-born actor George Sanders, her dutiful husband from 1949 to 1957. (Sanders took over as star of RKO's long-running series *The Saint* from actor Louis Hayward, a resident of the Mesa.) Gabor first fell for Sander's roguish charm in *The Moon and Sixpence,* which she saw at a New York movie theater in 1942. During one scene, Sanders violently beat Hedy Lamarr.

"This is the man for me," Zsa Zsa excitedly told her mother, Jolie Gabor (pronounced *Show-ly*), who was seated next to her. *Zap!* Gabor got her wish, beatings and all.

Right: Elvis Presley live in concert (Steve Kiefer Collection). *Below:* Elvis Presley's home at 845 West Chino Canyon Road (Photo by Howard Johns).

"George had wanted a *hausfrau*, and that's what my glamorous daughter became," complained Mama Gabor. "When Zsa Zsa heard his car, she would run to the bar and prepare his vodka then drop to her knees, and he'd pat her head like a dog and say, 'Are you a good girl?'"

Apparently, she was not. The end of their marriage came shortly after Sanders's star-making performance as the waspish theater critic, Addison DeWitt, in *All About Eve*. Friends said that Sanders became convinced that he was a great dramatic actor and embarked on a very busy trans-Atlantic film career. Left alone, Zsa Zsa began an affair with equine-endowed Dominican playboy Porfirio Rubirosa, who was twice as much fun as George. Although they were briefly reunited in the weirdly prophetic *Death of a Scoundrel* about a foreigner who cons American women out of their money, the Sanders-Gabor marriage was over.

Prolific Austrian composer **Ernst Krenek,** whose more than 240 compositions include music for orchestras, string trios and quartets, piano sonatas, operas, and choral works, moved to Palm Springs in 1966. "Der Sprung uber den Schatten," "Johnny spielt auf," "Das Leben des Orest," and "Der Goldene Bock" are just some of Krenek's operas using the versatile twelve-tone technique devised by Arnold Schoenberg. There are currently twenty-one recordings of Krenek's work available on CD.

Gladys Krenek, honorary president of the Ernst Krenek Institute in Vienna, still resides at 623 West Chino Canyon Road. Her late husband, who died in 1991, was honored with a special one-hundreth-birthday celebration by the Ernst Krenek Society in Palm Springs and Vienna, where he is buried. Krenek's personal archive is housed at the University of California, San Diego.

Elvis Presley owned two homes in his all-too-brief lifetime: the two-story limestone Graceland mansion in Memphis, Tennessee, where he died from cardiac arrhythmia caused by a deadly cocktail of pills—codeine, Quaaludes, Valium, pentobarbital, butabarbital, and Phenobarbital—while sitting on the john; and the secluded Palm Springs wrought-iron manse, located high on the south side of West Chino Canyon Road, which he enjoyed from 1970 until his death in 1977.

Presley bought the five-thousand-square-foot Spanish-style contemporary home (number 845) from Richard "Dick" McDonald, co-founder of the worldwide hamburger chain—who undoubtedly appreciated Elvis's insatiable appetite for his starchy products, even if he didn't like the singer's mawkish music.

Between concert tours, the king of rock 'n' roll and lover of junk food lived it up behind the gates of this four-bedroom love shack, which first caught his attention when driving through the neighborhood while he was renting another house at 372 Camino Norte. Elvis enjoyed different modes of transport, mostly Cadillacs courtesy of Plaza

Motors, and watched multiple television sets from Hallmark TV, surrounded by walls of gold records and trophies, whenever he stayed in the desert. But superstardom had its downside.

"All we do now after an engagement is fly back to Graceland to be locked up there for a couple of weeks, till we get bored and back to L.A., then to Palm Springs to be a recluse in the desert," Presley confided to comedian Sammy Shore.

Presley's "arranged" marriage to twenty-one-year-old army brat Priscilla Beaulieu, who was fourteen when they first met, consisted of pills, Polaroids, and play-acting, but no fully consummated sex, Beaulieu protested, following the birth of their only child, Lisa Marie. After Elvis and Priscilla's highly publicized divorce in 1973, Presley remodeled this home, adding a large black-and-white-tiled recreation room and a new master bedroom suite.

But the remodeling didn't stop there. According to friends, Elvis didn't like the long hours at RCA recording studios, so he remodeled the living room's vaulted ceilings with acoustical tiles and recorded two songs "Are You Sincere?" and "I Miss You" there.

In 1979, pop singer **Frankie Valli**, whose title song from the movie *Grease* became a number one hit, arranged to buy Presley's home and some of its contents. A promissory note held by Marjorie McDonald, wife of the home's prior owner, prevented the sale. Ricky Nelson's personal manager and Sun Studios concert promoter Gregory McDonald (no relation) acquired Presley's home in 1986. It is now used as a corporate retreat. Prices range from $1,000 per night to $10,000 a month.

If you've ever sipped a Coke, smoked a Lucky Strike, or nibbled a Premium cracker, then you've tasted the fertile imagination of commercial industrial designer **Raymond Loewy**, one of the one hundred most-influential Americans of the twentieth century. The French-born Loewy's highly influential design work includes the shapely Coca-Cola bottle, red Lucky Strike cigarette pack, and the silver Greyhound bus. He also designed the experimental Studebaker Avanti (the only automobile exhibited in the Louvre), as well as logos for Exxon, Shell, and Air Force One, plus the interiors for NASA's Skylab and Space Shuttle.

"Tierra Caliente," Loewy's former home at 600 Panorama Road, which he built in 1946, has undergone extensive restoration by metalware manufacturers Jim Gaudineer and Tony Padilla. Renowned Swiss architect Albert Frey designed the original house, famous for its kidney-shaped swimming pool that stretches from outside the home into the living room where, at a cocktail party, William Powell and singer Tony Martin took a wrong step backward and fell in.

Patricia Hearst, the bank-robbing hostage/victim of the Symbionese Liberation Army, whose reign of urban terror ended when police raided a Compton, California, house and killed five members in a hail of gunfire, is said to have recuperated from her nineteen-month ordeal in the palatial home of her late uncle, George Randolph Hearst, the eldest son of American publishing tycoon William Randolph Hearst, at 701 Panorama Road. Rosalie Wynn Hearst, his widow, later sold the house to Harvey and Lori Sarner for $1,650,000. Two decades after Patty Hearst's kidnap ordeal, offbeat film director John Waters gave her acting roles in *Cry Baby, Serial Mom, Pecker,* and *Cecil B. DeMented.*

★　★　★

Austrian-born composer **Frederick Loewe** lived nearby at 815 Panorama Road for twenty-eight years. A classically trained concert pianist with a large head, pale complexion, and deep-set eyes, "Fritz" Loewe and his writing partner, lyricist Alan Jay Lerner, collaborated on the hugely successful Broadway musicals *Brigadoon, Paint Your Wagon, My Fair Lady,* and *Camelot.* These and other evergreen works would probably never have been written if the two men had not met by chance in the men's room of the New York City Lambs Club.

Loewe's gentle disposition contrasted with Lerner's imperiousness, creating sparks that resulted in the team's best songs: "Almost Like Being in Love," "On The Street Where You Live," "I Could Have Danced All Night," "Thank Heaven For Little Girls," and many more.

The team's growing bankroll allowed them to enjoy the trappings of success. They each owned a penthouse apartment in New York, villas on the French Riviera, a seventy-five-foot yacht, and two Rolls Royce convertibles (blue for Lerner, gray for Loewe). Both had a taste for the good life and beautiful women. Yet they were the oddest of showbiz couples: Loewe writing melodies in his undershorts; Lerner nervously chain-smoking on a nearby couch, a worn copy of Roget's Thesaurus sitting next to a half-empty decanter of whisky. That's how "The Rain in Spain," one of their best-known songs, was written.

Lerner, pacing back and forth in their office, suggested the title. "Good," nodded Fritz, "I'll write a tango." Ten minutes later, they had finished it.

But the pressure of turning out hit songs threatened Loewe's fragile health (he was sidelined midcareer by a massive heart attack), and Lerner, who suffered from depression, became addicted to amphetamines, bringing their eighteen-year "marriage" to an end. They ceased working together, but remained friends.

Top: George Randolph Hearst's home at 701 Panorama Road (Photo by Howard Johns). *Center:* Good neighbors (*l to r*): Frederick Loewe, Viola Loewy, and Raymond Loewy (Courtesy of Palm Springs Historical Society). *Bottom:* Frederick Loewe's home with "Camelot" crest at 815 Panorama Road (Photo by Howard Johns).

After Loewe moved to the desert in 1960, his daily routine consisted of horseback riding and pruning the rose garden on his thirteen-acre chaparral described by *Time* magazine as "an airy glass pleasure dome" complete with a bar, library, and fireplace. Singer Marion Bell, the second of Lerner's eight wives, noticed that her husband's ex-partner had a framed check for $1 million prominently displayed on the living room wall.

"The bed turns on turntable," the *New York Herald-Tribune* rhapsodized of Loewe's hilly abode, "so that if he gets sick of one view he can select another." He also selected nubile young women to keep him company at dinner parties, for which he cooked gourmet meals and played the piano for Raymond Loewy, Mary Martin, Greta Garbo, Red Skelton, and Frank Sinatra—which he named his collection of goldfish!

Loewe, whom his neighbor Mel Haber later accused of being "mentally incompetent," died on Valentine's Day 1988 after being admitted to Desert Hospital with chest pains. He was eighty-six. His estate and musical royalties were left to various medical institutions and to friends such as Franchine Greshler and Kitty Carlisle Hart.

★   ★   ★

Top: Magda Gabor's home at 1090 Cielo Drive (Courtesy of Fernando Ruiz). *Bottom:* George Sanders up to no good (Backlot Books & Movie Posters).

Business tycoon **William Edris**, who took control of Seattle's famed Olympic Hotel in 1943, owned two houses at the top of Chino Canyon in 1954: one at 1860 Vista Drive, the other at 1030 Cielo Drive, which was designed by E. Stewart Williams with a flat, asymmetrical V-shaped roof. Edris's hotel tenure coincided with the Second World War when young servicemen massed in University Street, dubbed Victory Square, and Seattle theatergoers packed into the Metropolitan Theater next door.

Every U.S. president since Herbert Hoover has stayed at the hotel, which also welcomed John Wayne, Bob Hope, Bing Crosby, Joan Crawford, John Glenn, Jimmy Hoffa, and Elvis Presley. In 1955, Edris sold the hotel for $3.5 million. He died in 1969. Twenty-two years later, Edris's Cielo Drive home was purchased for $1,200,000.

★   ★   ★

Despite Zsa Zsa's dubious local pedigree, her older and better-behaved sister, **Magda Gabor**, most definitely lived at 1090 Cielo Drive in a contemporary-style house with a spacious kitchen. (The house took eighteen months to remodel after she bought it.) Strangely, Magda was also married to George Sanders, establishing what may be a matrimonial record: cuddly George was Magda's fifth husband and Zsa Zsa's third. Apparently

Sanders had a thing for the family's "look"—though it was more likely this scoundrel was after their money.

It was no secret that, by the time of his marriage to Magda, George was washed-up and virtually broke. The real surprise was that Magda, who was left a wealthy widow after the death of her contractor-husband Tony Gallucci in 1967, fell for Sanders's ploy. A heavy smoker, Magda had given up acting to become a hostess, but she suffered a stroke in 1966 and was unable to speak. Her right arm was useless, so she did everything with her left.

Magda's doting fiancé was actor and neighbor Gar Moore, who made a delicious strawberry trifle for her parties—but had no idea he was about to be left standing at the altar. On December 4, 1970, Sanders, lonely and despondent after the death of his fourth wife, actress Benita Hume, called Magda and asked her to marry him. Although she couldn't speak, she murmured "y-y-yes." Delighted, Sanders drove to the desert where Magda, smiling from ear to ear, met him at the front door of her house dressed in a hostess gown, holding a tin of caviar and a bottle of vodka.

Sanders put on a red velvet dinner jacket, and they sped off down the hill to get a blood test and buy a wedding ring while family and friends hastily dressed for the ceremony. The couple's wedding took place several hours later in Indio, and a reception was held afterwards at the Racquet Club. Six weeks later, Magda discovered the cruel deception and ended their marriage. A new man, gay artist John Morris, who called her "Magpie," then entered Gabor's life.

Depressed and still broke, Sanders retreated into a haze of booze and pills.

"George was a bitter, mixed-up man," observed the ever-wise Jolie Gabor, noting he was "cold as an icebox"—like the villainous Mr. Freeze, that he played on TV's *Batman*. Grimly, the man who began his career as the hero's best friend in *Foreign Correspondent* and was nominated for an Oscar in *All About Eve* ended his days playing assassins and pedophiles in cut-rate melodramas like *The Candy Man* and *Psychomania*.

In 1972, Sanders committed suicide in a hotel in Barcelona, Spain, leaving behind a note complaining of boredom. An increasingly reclusive Magda Gabor, who never left the Cielo Drive house except to lunch with her mom and sisters at Le Vallauris, died two months after the death of her mother in 1997. Magda's home sold for $440,000 in 1998.

Chapter 3

Las Palmas Payback

The true home of Palm Springs royalty is fashionable Las Palmas Estates, nestled beneath the cracked granite escarpment known as Dry Falls or Tachevah (pronounced *Ta-che-va*), meaning plain view. This pristine subdivision, which is situated northwest of Palm Canyon Drive and boasts the largest number of celebrity homes, dates from the mid-1920s when it was first developed by New York builder Alvah Hicks and his son, Harold Hicks.

The leafy neighborhood comprises two distinct sections: Old Las Palmas, which stretches southward from Vista Chino and ends at Alejo Road; and Vista Las Palmas, which extends west of Via Monte Vista. Many of these buildings are historically important not only because of the owners' bloodlines, but also because of their style of architecture, which ranges from early Californian to classic desert midcentury modernism—that low, glassy, horizontal, sleek look that's become so popular with magazine photographers and fashion editors.

At the northernmost tip of the neighborhood, we begin with the home of fabled penny-pinching radio and TV personality **Jack Benny** at 424 West Vista Chino, which the publicly parsimoniously inclined, but privately generous star of *Man About Town*, *To Be Or Not To Be*, and *George Washington Slept Here* shared with his actress-wife, **Mary Livingstone**.

His quintessential Las Palmas home, designed by William Cody and built in 1952 by George Alexander for May Company owners Tom and Anita May, is one of the foremost examples of post-and-beam desert construction. A few years later, May decided on a makeover, wanting to make it different than other houses in the area. He hired Samuel Marx, a beaux-arts-style architect long admired for his stripped-down interior designs of

Top: Jack Benny's home at 424 West Vista Chino (Courtesy of Andrew Linsky). *Bottom:* Jack Benny and Mary Livingstone (Courtesy of Palm Springs Historical Society).

Top: Barry Manilow at the keyboard (Wayne Knight Collection). *Bottom:* Richard Neutra designed the house at 470 West Vista Chino (Courtesy of Nelda Linsk).

hotels and department stores (he created the May Company's modernistic gold tower) using rectilinear limestone, granite and marble slabs, to redesign the house in contemporary steel and glass, which Marx, who resided at this address, completed shortly before his death in 1964.

The Bennys, who were close friends of the May family (Mary Benny once worked for them as a lingerie salesgirl), moved here in 1965. It was their third desert home.

"I've probably been coming here longer than anyone," Benny said at the time. "I just don't stay like Bob Hope, Bing Crosby and Red Skelton."

But whenever he did visit, Benny was an entirely different person. "In Palm Springs, daddy played golf every day, read books and magazines, even enjoyed a Scotch and soda before dinner—something he rarely if ever did at home," said his daughter, Joan Benny, who grew up here and in Beverly Hills.

According to corner store druggist Don Shaevel, Benny used to stroll down to Germain Brothers to buy groceries and chat with customers. The deadpan comedian broadcast many of his radio shows, which were heard by more than thirty million listeners every Sunday night, from the American Legion and historic Plaza Theatre, where a small street appropriately called Jack Benny Plaza was later named in his honor.

And what sweet memories: Benny's theme song *Love In Bloom*; the lopsided walk; that frozen-faced stare; an annoyed pause . . . "Oh, Rochester!" The eternally thirty-nine-year-old fusspot died from pancreatic cancer in 1974. He probably would have fainted at the home's record-breaking selling price if he were still alive in 2001: $1,775,000 paid by Michael Kilroy of Redondo Beach. Kilroy bought it from Andrew Linsky, who paid $700,000 for the house in 1995. Benny's astonished reply? "*W-e-l-l!*"

★　　★　　★

A near-perfect example of postwar modernism, circa 1946, which has become one of the most-photographed homes in Palm Springs, thanks to the explosion of modernist architecture's popularity, sits at 470 West Vista Chino. It is the former digs of Grammy- Tony- and Emmy-winning singer-songwriter **Barry Manilow**. Richard Neutra, whose own association with movieland stretches back to the flickering silent movies and the Hollywood Garden Apartments, which he designed in 1927, designed this Vista Chino home for

Pittsburgh retailer Edgar Kaufmann. Earlier Kaufmann had commissioned Frank Lloyd Wright to build Fallingwater, his tranquil home-on-a-river in rural Pennsylvania.

"Motion pictures have undoubtedly confused architectural tastes," bemoaned Neutra, a harsh critic of the growing penchant for English peasant cottages, Arabian minarets, and Georgian mansions, that became the rage in Hollywood, which may explain his adherence to minimalist Bauhaus philosophy.

Throughout the time Manilow, who scored his first number-one hit single "Mandy" in 1973, lived here, however, the protection of modernism took a backseat to climate.

"The weather in Palm Springs is glorious in January," said Manilow, a longtime winter resident. "While the rest of the country freezes and catches colds, it's usually eighty degrees there."

While living in this glass-and-steel house, Manilow, a restless native of the Big Apple, who wrote twenty-five consecutive Top 40 hits then suffered a creative dry spell and underwent psychotherapy to cure him of depression, became rejuvenated.

Top: Frances Bergen, Dina Merrill, and Edgar Bergen (Backlot Books & Movie Posters). *Bottom:* The Bergens' home at 1575 North Via Norte (Photo by Howard Johns).

"I found myself sleeping late," he said. "I caught up on books I had wanted to read, and sometimes I'd even go to the piano and try to write."

Manilow was too busy enjoying the home's comforts, however, to consider repairing it, and by 1993, he had moved on. The sun-bleached dwelling, looking slightly worse for its many years of constant wear, was sold that same year to savvy Newport Beach couple Brent and Beth Harris for $982,500. The Harrises, who are architectural historians, faithfully restored Neutra's original work, winning raves from preservationists nationwide.

Oscar-winning ventriloquist **Edgar Bergen**, one of the top radio and film performers of the 1930s, whose knuckleheaded creations Charlie McCarthy and Mortimer Snerd entertained three generations of children on *The Charlie McCarthy Show*, lived in this pink-colored house, named "Casa de Capricorn," at 1575 North Via Norte (on the corner of Via Sol) from 1947 through 1951.

Bergen, who became a millionaire from real estate, owned a block on Sunset

Jascha Heifetz and his violin (Wayne Knight Collection).

Boulevard where his magic shop was located. Former John Robert Powers fashion model Frances Westcott was his wife. Their daughter, Candy, who lived here as a five-year old toddler with her parents, grew up to become actress Candice Bergen, the headstrong TV anchorwoman on the long-running CBS sitcom, *Murphy Brown*, and a dedicated animal rights activist.

In 1975, former silent screen actress **Ruth Taylor**, who played Lorelei Lee in the first film version of *Gentlemen Prefer Blondes*, lived in this house. Her son is screenwriter-actor Buck Henry, who shared Oscar nominations with Calder Willingham for their screenplay of *The Graduate*. Taylor died in 1984.

★   ★   ★

Emmy-winning Los Angeles KNBC-TV news anchorman **Jack Latham**, who as a gay young blade worked as a stand-in on James Whale's 1935 horror epic *The Bride of Frankenstein* and also played small roles in the director's 1936 version of *Show Boat* and *The Great Garrick*, owned the home at 312 West Via Sol where he lived for eighteen years. In 1975, Latham was president and general manager of KPLM-TV (the original call letters for today's ABC affiliate in Palm Springs, KESQ). He died in 1987.

★   ★   ★

RCA recording artist **Jascha Heifetz**, dubbed "the Violinist of the Century," had sellout tours that took him around the world to such countries as Australia, Israel, and Japan, where his masterful interpretations of violin concertos by Bach, Beethoven, and Brahms delighted packed audiences.

He retired from performing in 1972 to spend the winters in this home with the red-tile roof at 373 West Via Sol. Industrialist W. J. Reynolds resided there in 1954. This house, where Heifetz's youngest son Jay also lived, was one of three that the master musician, one-time film star (*They Shall Have Music*, *Carnegie Hall*), and teacher at the University of Southern California School of Music, owned.

"No matter where the party, Beverly Hills, Malibu, Palm Springs," recalled acclaimed violinist Sherry Kloss, a former Heifetz student, "there was always the anticipation of joining together in the creation of music."

★   ★   ★

MGM dancer, choreographer, and director **Charles Walters**, who handled such coveted musical assignments for producers Arthur Freed, Joe Pasternak, and Lawrence Weingarten as *Easter Parade, Lili, Dangerous When Wet,* and *The Tender Trap*, built the house with the "Casa Contenta" sign in the front garden at 483 West Via Sol in 1956. This ultraelegant home was decorated by versatile set designer Paul Fox, whose twenty-year career included choosing the art and furnishings for *Laura, Three Coins in the Fountain, An Affair to Remember*, and *Cleopatra*.

Walters's sharp eye for talent matched his impeccable taste and vitality. Among his many screen accomplishments were reuniting Fred Astaire and Ginger Rogers after ten years in *The Barkleys of Broadway*, bringing Judy Garland and Gene Kelly together again in *Summer Stock*, and handling Joan Crawford's last musical assignment, *Torch Song*.

As well as directing, Walters owned and managed Chuck Walters Presents, a local clothing store that sold resort wear, gifts, and accessories for gentlemen. While living in this house with longtime companion John Darrow, Walters also directed his desert neighbors Frank Sinatra and Bing Crosby in *High Society*, as well as eliciting the best acting performance ever given by Debbie Reynolds in *The Unsinkable Molly Brown*. Walters's final film was *Walk Don't Run*, starring Cary Grant, yet another villager, in his last screen appearance.

★   ★   ★

At one time or another, **Liberace**, the recipient of six gold records and two Emmys for *The Liberace Show* for his unmatched ability to transform the classical music of Tchaikovsky and Chopin into popular hits, owned four different homes in Palm Springs.

"Some people collect stamps, I like to collect real estate," Lee, the name he went by offstage, kidded, grinning: "I am a firm believer in the good earth."

One of these residences, his third, was at 1441 North Kaweah Road and was decorated à la French Provincial with a Louis XIV room and a bubbling fountain. Today, Greek statues, Cupids, and lions courtesy of the home's next owner, Kevin Rizzotto, decorate the driveway and front entrance, where a bevy of effeminate young men in various stages of undress once preened and pranced at the behest of their joyous host. (Note: the piano-shaped black mailbox.)

★   ★   ★

Top: Liberace and his candelabra (Wayne Knight Collection). *Bottom:* Liberace's third residence at 1441 North Kaweah Road (Photo by Howard Johns).

In 1954, **H. Bruce Humberstone**, a fourteen-year veteran of 20th Century-Fox, where he directed four of the best *Charlie Chan* films, cracking murder mysteries at the racetrack, opera, Olympics, and Honolulu, as well as a quartet of snappy musicals starring John Payne, Alice Faye, Betty Grable, and Sonja Henie, rented the three-bedroom house at 1597 North Kaweah Road. There the easygoing director, known to his friends as "Lucky," basked in the success of his final big-budget film, *The Desert Song*, which paired Kathryn Grayson and Gordon MacRae in the best of three versions of this musical chestnut.

One of the founding members of the Screen Directors Guild (later Directors Guild of America), Humberstone so enjoyed his respite from Hollywood after more than a quarter of a century behind the camera that he didn't direct another film for nearly two years. He died in 1984.

Carolyn Jones without makeup (Steve Kiefer Collection).

★   ★   ★

Wide-eyed, reed-thin actress **Carolyn Jones**—best remembered as Morticia Addams, the sweetly sinister matriarch of TV's *The Addams Family*, dressed head-to-toe in black funereal attire and matching wits with her randy, tango-dancing husband, Gomez—lived with second real-life husband, *Strait-Jacket* assistant director Herbert Greene, at 368 West Stevens Road during her semiretirement in 1974.

Jones, who was nominated for a Best Supporting Actress Oscar in *The Bachelor Party*, had been married to producer Aaron Spelling for twelve years, during which time "Sissy," as he called her, played important screen roles with Elvis Presley, Alan Ladd, and Frank Sinatra. She died from colon cancer, age fifty-four, in 1983.

★   ★   ★

The life of trailblazing filmmaker **Howard Hawks** was nearly as exciting as the forty-five films he directed from speeding cars, trucks, planes, and helicopters to capture unforgettable moments of danger in *Scarface*, *The Dawn Patrol*, *Only Angels Have Wings*, and *Air Force*. He encouraged ad-libbing in the screwball comedies *Twentieth Century*, *Bringing Up Baby*, and *His Girl Friday* and talking dirty to get the right sexual tension in the crime melodramas *To Have and Have Not* and *The Big Sleep*.

He caused a ferocious cattle stampede in *Red River*, then hit all the right musical notes in *Gentlemen Prefer Blondes*. Hawks' talent for allegorical storytelling, mixing humor and pathos, has influenced such modern-day directors as Peter Bogdanovich, John Carpenter, Martin Scorsese, and Quentin Tarantino.

Offscreen, the introspective Hawks, who loved the desert, lived in this quiet neighborhood at 501 Stevens Road, with a separate entrance at 1455 Vine Avenue, for almost thirty years. Before that, he had rented different houses.

"If Howard took a house in Palm Springs for the winter, I went with him," recollected his second wife, Nancy Gross, a golden-haired *Harper's Bazaar* fashion model, nicknamed "Slim," whom the director married in 1941. In the same year, Hawks engaged celebrated architect Myron Hunt to design a horse ranch in the foothills of the Santa Monica Mountains. Hunt certainly had the requisite skill for the task having already executed grand commissions for railroad tycoon Henry Huntington in San Marino, the 100,000-seat Rose Bowl in Pasadena, the Ambassador Hotel in Los Angeles, I. Magnin in Beverly Hills, and the Mission Inn in Riverside—designated a National Historic Landmark in 1978.

Hawks's private three-bedroom, walled Stevens Road home, with the wrought-iron sign "Casa De Plata" above the gate, was built one year prior to his divorce from Gross in 1949. The storklike director spent more time here with his third wife, actress Dee Hartford, after making the lavish Egyptian spectacle, *Land of the Pharaohs*. He also made script changes during preproduction of two of his grittiest films, *Rio Bravo* and *El Dorado*, written by steadfast collaborator Leigh (*The Empire Strikes Back*) Brackett, while living here.

Hawks and his producing ally, friend, and agent Charles Feldman popped champagne corks here on New Year's Eve 1959. Three years later, Hawks unwound here after overseas filming was completed on *Hatari!* Another frequent houseguest was Hawks' friend and neighbor, Texas oilman Ted Weiner, who financed *El Dorado*, starring John Wayne and Robert Mitchum.

When he settled here permanently in 1967, Hawks' output slowed down, but he did produce the cult racing-car drama, *Red Line 7000*, with scenes filmed in Riverside, and his penultimate film, *Rio Lobo*, made in Mexico. Although he was seventy, Hawks, who helped launch the screen careers of Lauren Bacall, Joan Collins, and Angie Dickinson, still had an eye for pretty women. Visitors to his house often saw "one or more young beauties lying around his pool topless or completely nude," stated his biographer Todd McCarthy "although they never saw Hawks being physical with any of them."

Occasionally, neighbors complained about the noise of motorcycles, a mode of transportation that Hawks, a devoted racing enthusiast, and his twenty-three-year-old son,

Top: Howard Hawks goes for a spin in the desert (Courtesy of Barbara Hawks McCampbell). *Bottom:* Howard Hawks on location in Africa (Courtesy of Barbara Hawks McCampbell).

Gregg (named after the director's favorite cinematographer, Gregg Toland) preferred in the desert.

In 1975, Wayne, who had worked with Hawks five times, presented him with an honorary Oscar, underscoring the fact that Hawks was nominated only once as Best Director for *Sergeant York* in 1941. Their mutual friend, Palm Desert director John Ford, who'd won the award four times, always enjoyed ribbing Hawks about having beaten him.

Then tragedy struck. On December 26, 1977, Hawks, eighty-one, died in his home from complications resulting from a concussion he suffered in a fall several weeks earlier when he tripped over his one-hundred-pound black Belgian shepherd named Raven during the night. An embarrassed Hawks, who admitted to a friend of having "a whisky or two" the night of the accident, cut his head and broke a bone in his back, which never healed. Gregg Hawks sold his father's house and moved his personal belongings to Santa Monica. In 2003, Hawks' former home sold for $1,050,000.

Hawks' neighbor and good friend, **Harry Warner**, the oldest of the four Warner brothers who pioneered the use of sound, three-dimension (3-D), and television, otherwise known as the Idiot Box, lived in the large house with the long white wall at 591 Stevens Road (corner Via Monte Vista) where he walked with a cane in 1957.

Warner was the president of their worldwide company from 1923 when they made *Rin-Tin-Tin* movies for three unforgettable decades of moviemaking until he died from a stroke in 1958, two years after his younger brother, Jack Warner, sold the studio's film library for $22 million and was named the company's new president.

Four days after Harry Warner's funeral, Jack won two million francs in a six-hour game of baccarat in Monte Carlo. Harry's oldest and dearest daughter, Doris Warner, who married producer Mervyn LeRoy, director Charles Vidor, and composer Billy Rose, inherited her father's house, where she lived until her death in 1978.

Debbie Reynolds and her high-stakes gambler husband, **Harry Karl**—the dissolute owner of Karl's Shoe Stores, who had previously tied the knot with movieland bombshell Marie McDonald and Harry Cohn's widow Joan (she gave *him* $100,000 when their marriage was annulled after just twenty-one days)—took up residence in a five-bedroom home designed by city architect Howard Lapham at 670 West Stevens Road (Palm Vista Estates), in 1960.

"It had a pool and a panoramic view of the mountains," said Reynolds, who wed Karl while on the rebound from her breakup with Eddie Fisher. Fisher, as anyone breathing at the time remembers, married Elizabeth Taylor, who then divorced him and married Richard Burton.

While residing here, Reynolds, made some of her most-enjoyable movies, among them: the blockbuster action adventure *How the West Was Won* and *The Unsinkable Molly Brown*, for which she was nominated for a well-deserved Academy Award. Inevitably, as the trend for musicals waned, so did the musical comedy star's popularity, due in no small part to box-office flops like *Goodbye Charlie* and *The Singing Nun*, though she partly redeemed herself with the sprightly marital comedy *Divorce American Style*.

Unfortunately, the Reynolds-Karl marriage, like so many other well-publicized unions, was doomed. After Karl had gambled away virtually all of Debbie's money, as well as his own, the couple separated and divorced in 1973, leaving the embarrassed entertainer almost $2 million in debt.

★ ★ ★

In 1995, **John Phillips**, the bearded leader of the sixties folk-rock group, the Mamas and the Papas, and founder of the Monterey Pop Festival, paid $575,000 for the conservatively opulent home at 695 West Stevens Road where he resided for the last six years of his life.

The Mamas and the Papas (l to r): Denny Doherty, "Mama" Cass Elliott, Michelle Phillips, and John Phillips (Wayne Knight Collection).

The walled and gated house, which was guarded by three crouching cement lions, has a proud history. It was once the residence of Frankie James, the widow of Leo Spitz. Spitz was president of Universal-International Pictures, the Hollywood movie studio that turned out a long line of Gothic horror films and collegiate musical comedies, slowly embarking on more prestigious fare such as *The Glenn Miller Story*, *Imitation of Life*, and *Pillow Talk*. Its record label, MCA, later recorded Phillips's gypsy-style quartet. Former First Lady Eleanor Roosevelt was Mrs. Spitz's houseguest in 1960.

Phillips, who wrote the hits "California Dreamin'" and "Monday, Monday," waged a long, unsuccessful fight with substance abuse and underwent a liver transplant in 1992 shortly before moving to Palm Springs. He was often visited there by actress-daughter Mackenzie Phillips and her sister, Chynna Phillips, wife of actor William Baldwin.

In February 2001, Phillips was admitted to Desert Regional Medical Center after reportedly falling off a bar stool at his home and hurting his shoulder. His condition worsened, and the next month, he was transferred to UCLA Medical Center in Los Angeles where doctors found a stomach virus had severely damaged his weakened kidneys. He died of heart failure three days later, age sixty-five, but looking much older. Three months later, his home sold for $730,000.

★ ★ ★

When Oklahoma oilman **Louis Taubman** listed his palatial split-level, four-bedroom home at 925 Coronado Avenue (at the top of Stevens Road and Rose Avenue) for sale in 1987, its price tag was a modest $845,000—down from the inflated $1 million at which it had been originally listed. Taubman entertained President Lyndon B. Johnson at "the Desert White House," as it was called, during LBJ's historic February 1964 visit. Other guests have included Prince Philip, Duke of Edinburgh, who quipped "You can't do this in England," while swimming in the home's pool in the winter of 1966.

Yet another visitor was Jack Valenti, president of the Motion Picture Association of America, which gives those green-tinted censorship ratings you see on all movie previews. On one memorable occasion while renting the house, Caesar's Palace owner Cliff Pearlman hosted a small dinner party there for Frank and Barbara Sinatra, Kirk and Anne Douglas, and Suzanne Somers and her husband, Alan Hamel. The place settings were arranged so the couples were intermingled. Suzanne sat transfixed by Kirk Douglas in tight linen pants with no underwear. Sinatra told Somers he loved her Vegas show and thought she was a "doll."

Then Alan Hamel asked Cliff Pearlman if he had read the new unauthorized Meyer Lansky biography. The room fell deathly silent.

"Why would I want to do that?" he growled.

They all laughed. Taubman's home is one of the big mysteries of Las Palmas—everyone's seen it, but few have been inside. For the record, it has a wood-paneled billiard room and a view that overlooks the entire Coachella Valley. It is unlikely Taubman missed these and other amenities after he sold it since he also owned homes at The Springs in Rancho Mirage and in Beverly Hills.

Jackie Cooper, whom Roddy McDowall described as the most-gifted child star in movie history, endured a difficult adolescence, then grew up and became a successful producer-director. He moved to 1055 Rose Avenue with his second wife, Barbara, and three children Russell, Julie, and Christina, during network reruns of *The People's Choice* and *Hennessey* in 1962.

Interior designer Ford Munn decorated the home's interiors in lettuce-green and tangerine wallpaper with gold accents. Cooper, whose first house was in Racquet Club Estates, said he bought an old Model-T Ford to navigate the bumpy roads, taught his kids swimming, and took them horseback riding—all the stuff that families back then did in the desert. He even found time between jobs to learn to fly a Cessna 150 at Palm Springs Airport and eventually opened his own air taxi business, Desert Commuter Airlines—logging three thousand hours in the air.

When he tired of acting, this accomplished all-rounder, who could sing, dance, and play the drums, turned his experienced hand to directing TV shows, including fifteen memorable episodes of *M*A*S*H*—winning his first Emmy.

In 1968, actor-director **Hy Averback** moved to 1102 Rose Avenue from his satanically numbered previous home on 666 Alexander Way, the same year he directed the Peter Sellers cult classic *I Love You, Alice B. Toklas*. Formerly Bob Hope's radio announcer, the affable Averback, a friend of neighbor Jackie Cooper for thirty-five years, also helmed such cable favorites as *The Real McCoys* and *The Dukes of Hazzard*, along with various *M*A*S*H* episodes. He died, age seventy-six, following open-heart surgery in 1997.

According to watershed comedy writer, Larry Gelbart, who developed *M*A*S*H* for television, the decision to hire old pros like Cooper and Averback to direct many of the formative episodes, Gelbart said, "had a lot to do with establishing the quality and standard of the series."

Veteran MGM cameraman **Robert Surtees**, who was nominated for sixteen Oscars and won three of the gold statues for his lush cinematography on *King Solomon's Mines*, *The Bad and the Beautiful*, and *Ben-Hur*, lived at 1276 Rose Avenue in 1967—the year he was nominated twice, once for *Doctor Dolittle* and the second time for *The Graduate*.

Bruce Surtees, his cinematographer son, who was Oscar nominated for *Lenny*, has lensed twelve Clint Eastwood films, among them *Play Misty For Me*, *Dirty Harry*, and *Pale Rider*.

Maurice McDonald, who founded McDonald's restaurants, retired to 1293 Rose Avenue after selling his hamburger franchise to Ray Kroc in 1961. The plainly spoken McDonald, known as "Big Mac," was a friendly man with an abundance of energy and goodwill that extended to his support of local ball teams and children's charities.

His claim to fame as creator of the nation's leading fast-food company has been largely ignored. McDonald, who ran the day-to-day operations, and his younger brother, Richard, a marketing whiz who devised the famous Golden Arches logo, opened their first restaurant on the corner of 14th Street and E Street in San Bernardino in 1943. In 1954, they formed a business partnership with milkshake salesman Ray Kroc, opening franchise outlets state to state.

In five years, there were 228 stores, and in 1961 Kroc bought out the McDonald brothers for $2.7 million. Today, there are approximately 30,000 stores in 120 countries serving 45 million people a day. Mac died in his sleep here in 1971; Dick died in 1998.

Author **Sidney Sheldon**'s first desert house was at 1294 North Rose Avenue (near Via Vadera). The best-selling author lived there following publication of his second novel, *The Other Side of Midnight*, which spent an unprecedented fifty-two weeks on the *New York Times* best-seller list in 1974.

Cindy Williams looking chipper (Larry Edmunds Bookshop).

In 1983, **Cindy Williams**, the cute, smaller half of TV's lowbrow buddy comedy *Laverne & Shirley* about two loud-mouthed Milwaukee brewery workers, bought the gated home at 1155 Los Robles Drive. She lived there part time with actor-husband Bill Hudson until they filed for divorce. Williams put the home up for sale in 2002. One year later it sold for $500,000.

Williams first caught people's attention as Ron Howard's girlfriend in *American Graffiti*, which inspired the family sitcom *Happy Days* and led to Williams being cast as Shirley Feeney in her own series. Despite a reported long-running feud with costar Penny Marshall, which both actresses have denied, Williams remained on the show until its eighth season when she became pregnant with her first daughter, Emily, and asked to be written out of the script. These days, Williams works mostly behind the scenes as a producer.

Hollywood agent and helpful career booster **Lew Sherrell**, who turned straight-laced TV actor Adam West into an overnight sensation as the blue-caped crusader *Batman*, lived at 1354 Los Robles Drive until his death in 1996.

Actress **Ruta Lee**, whom her late neighbor Lew Sherrell once repped, currently lives with her Texas restaurateur-husband, Webster Lowe, at 1111 West Dolores Court. Lee is a tireless supporter and chairperson of the charitable Thalians, which was cofounded by her good friend, Debbie Reynolds. The volunteer showbiz organization, of which Reynolds is president, has so far raised more than $30 million for mental health research.

The first desert home of **George Hamilton** is located at 827 West Via Vadera (off Abrigo Road), where the perennially suntanned actor-producer lived while filming the life story of motorcycle daredevil *Evel Knievel* in 1971. Hamilton, a native of Memphis, Tennessee, became fast friends with finger-lickin' neighbors Elvis Presley and "Colonel" Tom Parker, who admired Hamilton's Southern hospitality, hearty appetite, and, best of all, his touching performance as country-and-western legend Hank Williams in *Your Cheatin' Heart*—one of a dozen films the underrated actor made after being signed to an MGM contract.

Mexican-American singer **Trini Lopez**, who went from the *barrios* to Beverly Hills, winning a gold record for his Latin-pop version of Peter, Paul and Mary's folk song "If I Had a Hammer," still plays the guitar around the corner at 1139 Abrigo Road where he has lived, surrounded by walls of record album covers and celebrity photographs, since 1981.

A native of Dallas, Trini's big break came when record producer Don Costa introduced the nightclub singer to Frank Sinatra. Sinatra signed him to an eight-year recording contract on his Reprise label. He even found a spot for Lopez in his woebegone 1965 sex comedy, *Marriage on the Rocks*. Lopez then traveled to England to play one of twelve death-row prisoners chosen for a suicide mission in the action-packed war movie, *The Dirty Dozen*.

Thirty years later, Lopez became a real-life criminal suspect when he was charged with assaulting his girlfriend, Rose Mihata, at his Las Palmas home on September 22, 1995. The incident occurred after Mihata said she found the earrings of another woman on Trini's dining room table, and when she demanded an explanation, he hit her. Mihata said it was the fifth time Lopez had assaulted her in ten years.

A humble Lopez testified in court that he had acted in self-defense against Mihata, who, he said, hit him with her fists, threw a porcelain elephant statue at his head, and tried to kick him between the legs. According to Lopez's testimony, he wrestled her to the floor where they struggled amid the Gary Jon designer furnishings. When she tried to bite him, he said, he pinned her arms back and placed his knee on her neck.

Trini Lopez when he was young and looking innocent (Wayne Knight Collection).

Mihata's chatterbox attorney Gloria Allred, who represented the family of murder victim Nicole Brown Simpson, was reportedly outraged that Lopez received only one misdemeanor charge instead of two felony charges as police recommended. At the end of the three-day trial, an eight-woman, four-man jury found him—surprise, surprise—not guilty.

★　★　★

The year was 1962, the year of *The Jetsons*, the Cuban missile crisis, and the House of Tomorrow at 1350 Ladera Circle (off Via Las Palmas). Charles DuBois, designed the octagonal-shaped structure, and owner **Robert Alexander,** whose construction firm helped popularize the midcentury modern architectural style, built it. Helene Alexander was overjoyed when she saw the finished product.

"Darling," she told her husband, "it's beautiful."

Look magazine gushed over the home's circular living room, faux lava rock walls, sixty-four-foot couch, thick shag carpeting, and gold-plated bathroom fixtures. There was something disquieting, however, about such blatant extravagance, especially when the Alexander family's two thousand other homes, which they sold for enormous profit, had none of it.

The Alexanders, it seemed, were impervious to criticism. They had become preachers of a new social order, people who believed in their own infallibility. At dusk on November 14, 1965, a green-and-white Lear jet took off from Palm Springs Airport with six passengers aboard: Bob and Helene Alexander; his parents, George and Mildred Alexander; New York handbag designer Richard Koret; and Peter Prescott, the eleven-year-old son of Flying Tigers Airlines president Robert Prescott, the plane's owner. They were destined for Burbank where a limousine was waiting to take them to a black-tie party in Hollywood.

Eight minutes after takeoff, the speeding plane entered the orbit of the Little Chocolate Mountains northwest of Indio and vanished. Motorists traveling east saw a ball of orange flame in the darkness. They were spared the sight of the plane's horrifying impact as red-hot metal and dismembered body parts spewed across the blackened rocks. There were no survivors.

In 1967, **Elvis Presley** and his twenty-one-year-old bride, Priscilla Beaulieu, who were secretly married in Las Vegas, flew back to Palm Springs on Frank Sinatra's Lear jet. They honeymooned at Robert Alexander's $300,000 showplace, which the couple rented for the reported sum of $21,000. Their daughter, Lisa Marie Presley, was born exactly nine months later.

William "Bill" Miller ran the Riviera nightclub in New Jersey where he booked Tony Martin, Frank Sinatra, Dean Martin, Jerry Lewis, Sammy Davis Jr., and Joey Bishop. Miller brokered a second career as entertainment director of the Sahara, Dunes, and International hotels in Las Vegas. In 1976, Miller retired to 1320 North Granito Circle, where the man known far and wide as "Mr. Entertainment" lived until his death, age ninety-eight, in 2002.

"Colonel" Tom Parker, the portly cigar-puffing Florida concert promoter, was Elvis Presley's personal manager for twenty-two years. He steered the Memphis rock 'n' roll singer from county fairs to national TV appearances, negotiated a long-term RCA recording contract and Paramount and MGM movie deals. Parker piled up millions of dollars off his biggest client while living at 1166 North Vista Vespero.

The Colonel, in his gaudy Hawaiian shirt and ubiquitous baseball cap, was an instantly recognizable figure, wielding a busy phone and fountain pen while gorging himself on a steady diet of rib eye steaks, and ham and eggs.

"The Colonel was fat—about five feet nine and 225 pounds—bald, semiliterate, shrewd, and vulgar," remembered Sammy Shore, who used to see his neighbor shopping for Cornish hens at Smith's Food King. Parker's former residence (since repainted) has several French Regency touches, including a concrete portico above the flagstone-faced main

Elvis and Priscilla Presley's wedding day (Larry Edmunds Bookshop).

entrance, where in past days, a constant stream of messengers, booking agents, and hotel owners bearing six- and seven-figure checks rang his doorbell.

Never one to look a gift horse in the mouth or refuse a bribe, the money-grubbing Parker loved publicity stunts—the bigger, the better. Presley wanted his wedding kept secret, but the Colonel couldn't resist and turned it into a photo opportunity for hundreds of photographers. To make sure no one entering Vegas might overlook Presley's appearances there, Parker rented huge billboards, and he hawked cheap souvenirs to thousands of mourners waiting outside Graceland after Presley's death in the summer of '77.

Five years later, after Parker and RCA were found guilty of collusion, conspiracy, and fraud in their mishandling of Presley's business affairs, the late entertainer's manager was paid $2 million for his rights to the estate and was subsequently evicted from his fourth-floor Hilton International hotel suite.

Parker moved his vast collection of Presley paraphernalia, including the singer's famous gold lamé suit, to the Vista Vespero house, where he spent his days lounging by the pool while his ailing wife, former carnival girl Marie Mott, received around-the-clock nursing care until her death in 1986. The Colonel then returned to Las Vegas, dropping as much as $25,000 a day at the casinos. He died in 1997 at age eighty-seven. Parker's former home sold for $185,000 in 1996. Three years later it was resold for $450,000.

★　★　★

Betty Grable (left) as Jenny Dolly and June Haver as Rosie Dolly in *The Dolly Sisters* (Wayne Knight Collection).

Rosie Dolly, of the famous vaudeville act *The Dolly Sisters*, lived the last three years of her life at 1200 Vista Vespero. Known as the Gabor Sisters of the flapper era, identical twins Roszika and Yansci Dolly danced and sang their way across the world's most-famous stages, from London to New York. They mixed music and millionaires, becoming wealthy along the way.

In 1932, Rosie Dolly married Chicago department store tycoon Irving Netcher, co-owner of the Boston Store. Her unhappy sister, known publicly as Jenny, was less fortunate. In 1941, she was found hanging from a curtain bar in her Hollywood home. Rosie went on to enjoy a brief revival in popularity, due in large part to *The Dolly Sisters*, the musical film loosely based on the sisters' lives starring Betty Grable and June Haver.

Rosie entertained many showbiz friends in this house. She would greet guests in a Mamie Eisenhower-style peau de soie gown, adorned with a necklace of sparkling diamonds. "If you drink Scotch," recommended the *oo-la-la* entertainer, "make it Black and White. It will never hang you over." Good advice. Rosie, age seventy-seven, died in 1970.

★　★　★

Resort builder **Milton Prell**, founder of the Sahara Hotel in Las Vegas and owner of the Aladdin Hotel where Elvis Presley and Priscilla Beaulieu were married, owned the house at 1254 Vista Vespero.

★　★　★

S.Z. "Cuddles" Sakall, the roly-poly character actor with the floppy jowls, enlivened scores of movies with his trademark nervous "*She-ee!*" notably in *Ball of Fire*, *Yankee Doodle Dandy*, and, best of all, as the flustered maitre d' of Rick's Café American in *Casablanca*. Sakall weekended at 1133 Camino del Mirasol in 1953—two years before his death from a heart attack.

★　★　★

Although best remembered as Jimmy Stewart's loving spouse in the Christmas perennial *It's a Wonderful Life*, it was her about-face role as a blowsy prostitute in 1953's *From Here to Eternity* that won peaches-and-cream beauty **Donna Reed** an Oscar for Best Supporting Actress. Reed and her second husband, Tony Owen (producer of *The Donna Reed Show*), lived at 1184 Camino del Mirasol until their 1971 divorce. Reed then began dating third husband Grover Asmus, who established the Donna Reed Foundation for the Performing Arts following his wife's death from pancreatic cancer in 1986.

In 1969, producer Robert Evans and his third wife, actress Ali MacGraw, honeymooned in this house after they were married at the Palm Springs courthouse where bottles of Dom Perignon were uncorked on the front lawn.

★　★　★

Buddy Adler, 20th Century-Fox's head of production and a founding member of the Screen Producers Guild, won an Oscar for bringing James Jones' profane army novel, *From Here to Eternity*, to the screen. Adler lived at 1255 Camino del Mirasol prior to his death from lung cancer in 1960. During his short tenure at Fox where he succeeded Darryl F. Zanuck, the gray-templed Adler (son of the creator of Adler Elevator Shoes), produced the Oscar-nominated *Love Is a Many-Splendored Thing*, *Bus Stop*, *Anastasia*, and *South Pacific*. Adler and his wife, screen star **Anita Louise** (*Madame DuBarry*, *A Midsummer Night's Dream*, *The Story of Louis Pasteur*, and *Anthony Adverse*) were very active in desert philanthropies. Louise died from a stroke in 1970.

★　★　★

Top: Donna Reed (Larry Edmunds Bookshop). *Left:* S.Z. "Cuddles" Sakall (Backlot Books & Movie Posters). *Right:* (Clockwise from left:) Buddy Adler, Robert Stack, Mervyn LeRoy, Anita Louise Adler and Kitty LeRoy (Courtesy of Palm Springs Historical Society).

Before the Adlers moved in, heart-shape-faced actress **Claudette Colbert**, who hitched up her skirt and stopped traffic with Clark Gable, winning both of them Oscars for *It Happened One Night*, lived at 1255 Camino del Mirasol with her husband, noted physician Joel Pressman. Dr. Pressman was on the staff of UCLA Medical Center and was a head and neck specialist who performed surgery on many movie folk.

A little-known fact is that Colbert, who resided here in 1958, ran an exclusive jewelry store on Palm Canyon Drive where well-to-do customers and friends shopped for expensive gifts. When Colbert found herself inundated with stage and film work in 1960, she sold the store.

★ ★ ★

Chi-Chi founder and Riviera Resort builder **Irwin Schuman**, who showcased hundreds of top variety acts such as Sophie Tucker, Milton Berle, Lena Horne, Sammy Davis Jr., and Eartha Kitt at his world-famous nightclub, lived at 201 Camino Norte. Reportedly honey-voiced ballad singer **Nat "King" Cole** stayed there between local nightclub appearances during the '58 season.

Cole became a controversial figure when six men attacked him after an Alabama concert. His TV show was cancelled following complaints from sponsors, and unfriendly neighbors picketed his home in the exclusive Hancock Park section of Los Angeles. But there was no denying the richness of his voice, which daughter Natalie Cole made popular all over again when she released a duet (using her dad's original vocal tracks) of "Unforgettable."

One of Cole's biggest hits had the distinction of being written by an unnoticed desert resident, Eben Ahbez (real name: Robert Bootzin). A practicing yogi and health food nut who lived out of a sleeping bag in the Hollywood Hills, Ahbez composed "Nature Boy" on a scrap of paper. He always complained he was never paid any royalties for the song, which earned its bow-tied singer a gold record. In 1995, Ahbez, age eighty-six, died in Desert Hospital from injuries he sustained when his 1974 Chevrolet van collided with a Plymouth Satellite in the high desert. Cole, a heavy smoker, had died thirty years earlier.

★ ★ ★

Harold Mirisch, the gregarious older brother of Marvin and Walter Mirisch, the exhibitor-producer trio whose independent company, formed in 1957, made *The Apartment*, *West Side Story*, and *In the Heat of the Night*—all of which won multiple

Top: Claudette Colbert in profile (Wayne Knight Collection). *Bottom:* Nat "King" Cole and concerned wife Maria Ellington (Wayne Knight Collection).

Oscars, including Best Picture, respectively, in 1960, 1961, and 1967—lived at 317 Camino Norte. It had a screening room where the brothers watched the latest movies until Harold's death in 1968. In 1983, Walter Mirisch received the Jean Hersholt Humanitarian Award. Marvin Mirisch died in 2002.

★   ★   ★

Bandleader **Paul Whiteman** resided at 320 Camino Norte while appearing at Romanoff's-On-the-Rocks, a local nightspot, in 1964. It was Whiteman and his thirty-five-piece orchestra who introduced George Gershwin's syncopated jazz arrangement of "Rhapsody in Blue," orchestrated by Ferde Grofe, in 1924. He played the marvelous tune, which became his trademark, in long and short versions for the next forty years. Whiteman appeared onscreen as himself in *The King of Jazz*, featuring his newest discovery Bing Crosby (who was arrested for drunk driving during the making of the film and jailed for forty days), *Thanks a Million*, *Strike Up the Band*, and, of course, *Rhapsody in Blue*. Whiteman died in 1967.

Actor Alan Ladd Dies in Palm Springs Home

Exclusive to The Times from a Staff Writer

PALM SPRINGS — Alan Ladd, the velvet-voiced, iron-jawed hero of 150 Hollywood films, died quietly Wednesday in his plush winter home here, the apparent victim of a heart attack.

Top: Alan Ladd (Steve Kiefer Collection). *Left:* Newspaper headline of Alan Ladd's death (Howard Johns Collection). *Bottom:* Alan Ladd's home at 323 Camino Norte (Courtesy of Palm Springs Historical Society).

★   ★   ★

On January 29, 1964, somber-looking, flaxen-haired movie tough guy and desert hardware store owner **Alan Ladd** died from a lethal combination of alcohol and barbiturates at 323 Camino Norte while spending a week alone drinking and talking on the phone to friends. Ladd, star of George Stevens' Western classic *Shane*, reportedly paid $49,000 in 1955 for this five-bedroom beige-colored home, designed by Donald Wexler and Richard Harrison (not the actor), and built by contractor Robert Higgins, a friend of Ladd's since they attended North Hollywood High School.

Ladd purchased the house from Robert Howard as part of a highly publicized reconciliation with second wife Sue Carol, formerly his agent, with whom he had been estranged since falling in love with costar June Allyson on the set of *The McConnell Story*. Although the Ladds publicly denied the separation, Sue stayed at the family compound in Holmby Hills, while Alan remained in seclusion at their second home in Rancho Sante Fe.

Palm Springs offered both husband and wife the time they needed to rekindle their relationship. Ladd, an expert swimmer, took great pride in the thirty-six-foot pool, situated beyond the covered patio and sliding glass doors. Sue Carol, a skilled decorator, painted the home's interior orange and brown, enlivened by touches of salad green to complement the Chinese modern furnishings.

For a while, it looked as if the attempt to reunite the family, which included Ladd's son from his first marriage, Alan Jr.; Sue's daughter, Carol Lee; their children, Alana and David, was working. In 1959, Carol Lee gave birth to a boy, making Ladd a first-time grandfather. "Dad would be lying on the couch, and when I went to fix the baby's bottle, I'd put the baby cradled up in his arms. It was adorable," Carol recalled of her emotionally distant stepfather.

Barely one year prior to his death, Ladd accidentally shot himself in the chest, he told reporters from his hospital bed, while investigating a nighttime prowler at his Camarillo ranch. The story was red-hot gossip for weeks in Hollywood where people who knew Ladd speculated on the real reasons for the shooting. Was he drunk or depressed?

When the news blazed across radio and TV stations that Alan Ladd, a top Hollywood star for three decades, had died, it was greeted with sadness rather than surprise. An autopsy performed by coroner Robert Drake showed that Ladd had a blood alcohol level nearly four times the legal limit and had ingested Seconal, Librium, and Sparine—the last drug prescribed by a concerned physician to counteract the effects of alcohol withdrawal. The official cause of death was cerebral edema due to chemical depressants on the central nervous system, but many believed he had committed suicide. After he was buried at Forest Lawn Memorial Park, Ladd's anguished widow, who was determined to keep the memory of her late husband alive, continued running the family's hardware store at the same time managing a thriving decorating business and a hotel.

Perky musical star **Mary Martin**, who displayed her winsome charms in the Broadway productions of *South Pacific*, *The Sound of Music*, and *Peter Pan*, once lived at 365 Camino Norte with her second husband and producer, Richard Halliday. The Hallidays, who were good friends of actress Janet Gaynor and her costume-designer husband, Gilbert Adrian, owned adjoining ranches in Brazil, where both couples took annual vacations.

Producer **Harry Joe Brown**, who gave Errol Flynn his first starring role in 1935's *Captain Blood*, teamed Tyrone Power and Alice Faye in *Alexander's Ragtime Band*, and later joined forces with Randolph Scott for a series of tense psychological Westerns, including *Ride Lonesome*, died of a heart attack in his home at 454 Camino Norte in 1972—ten years after Brown made film history when he signed Sean Flynn, whom he met at his father's funeral, to play *The Son of Captain Blood*. Brown produced 124 films and directed another 45 since 1922. His first wife, Sally Eilers, was previously married to actor Hoot Gibson.

Joseph Barbera, the younger half of Hanna-Barbera Productions, the mad creators of *Tom & Jerry*, *The Flintstones*, and *Yogi Bear*, is a thirty-year resident of 533 Camino Norte. Hanna-Barbera made more than two hundred of the playful cat-and-mouse cartoons, winning seven Oscars, then branched out into TV production. They pioneered the half-hour cartoon show format, which combined stylized animation and pop music, culminating in their canine investigative hero, *Scooby-Doo*. William Hanna, who was Barbera's business partner for more than half a century, died at age ninety in 2001.

★   ★   ★

Thirties matinee idol **William Powell**, an Oscar nominee for *The Thin Man*, *My Man Godfrey*, and *Life With Father*, shared the homey abode at 383 West Vereda Norte with his third wife, actress Diana Lewis, whom he nicknamed "Mousie," for forty-three years until his death from natural causes at age ninety-one on March 5, 1984.

One of the city's earliest and longest residents, Powell first set foot on the sandy peninsula, he recollected, while filming a 1926 Zane Grey Western called *Desert Gold*—a title he considered to be his lucky charm. The tall, droopy-eyed actor, who became the epitome of social etiquette, spent his early screen days playing mustache-twirling villains before winning the respect of critics in nearly sixty-five leading roles that cast him as worldly sophisticates and gentlemanly charmers, most frequently with courtly Myrna Loy in thirteen films, including *Manhattan Melodrama*, *The Great Ziegfeld*, and *The Senator Was Indiscreet*.

Top: Tom and Jerry co-creator Joseph Barbera's home at 533 Camino Norte (Photo by Howard Johns). *Bottom:* William Powell turns the water sprinkler on his wife Diana Lewis (Courtesy of Palm Springs Historical Society).

In 1938, after undergoing two painful operations for rectal cancer, Powell considered his acting career and his life, for that matter, to be finished. He was wrong. Audiences loved his intoxicated charm, part of which was the real thing. He drank, friends claimed, to ease his physical discomfort as well as the emotional distress at having to wear a colostomy bag. That all changed, however, when Powell met Diana Lewis, a dimple-cheeked actress, who was twenty-seven years his junior. They were married in 1940 and moved to the desert where he mixed martinis in his terry-cloth bathrobe, played poker, and when he regained his health, drove his ten-year-old Pontiac to the MGM studios to reprise the role of Nick Charles in five *Thin Man* sequels and play Florence Ziegfeld for a second time in *Ziegfeld Follies*.

"Powell was debonair and glamorous—very much like his movie characters," remembered Slim Keith, the ex-wife of Howard Hawks. "He had a fast wit, was well educated, and remarkably well read. His home was every bit what I'd imagined a movie star's house to be."

Unlike the actor's Georgian-style Beverly Hills mansion, which was painted white and had fur carpeting, this much-plainer home with rear additions by Albert Frey was furnished mostly in heavy wood.

"Later, I would come to see that Bill Powell had ghastly taste," said Keith, winner of the Neiman Marcus Award for fashion excellence in 1946.

Sensing that it was time to hang up his hat, Powell, whose wife affectionately called him "Poo the Cat," retired from the screen in 1955 after two final films, *How to Marry a Millionaire* and *Mister Roberts*. Powell did not have to work because the money he made during the era of low taxes was well invested.

With no more early morning studio calls, the Powells' playtime increasingly revolved around their two small poodles, Little Darling and Horatio (his middle name), as well as Diana's weekly Mouseburger tennis tournaments, where she grilled bite-sized hamburgers for their large circle of friends at the Racquet Club. Everyone marveled on the couple's idyllic life.

When William Powell's only son, Bill, an unfulfilled scriptwriter with kidney problems, committed suicide by slitting his throat in 1968, however, the normally resolute actor, who had endured the tragic loss of his girlfriend, Jean Harlow, from uremic poisoning and the death of his former wife, Carole Lombard, in a plane crash, was so brokenhearted that he withdrew from public view.

In 1982, Powell, now white-haired and suffering from diabetes, quietly celebrated his ninetieth birthday. Myrna Loy traveled all the way from her New York apartment to see him.

"How are you?" she asked.

"Not bad for a one-hundred-year-old man," he quipped.

Mousie continued to live in this house after her husband's death in 1984 and play golf until she died from cancer in 1997. Today, their former home, which sold for $540,000 in 1998, is registered with the Palm Springs Historic Site Preservation Board with a brass plaque near the front entrance that reads:

WILLIAM & "MOUSIE" POWELL RESIDENCE
BUILT c.1935-36
MEDITERRANEAN/SPANISH REVIVAL
HISTORIC SITE PRESERVATION BOARD #28

★   ★   ★

In 1967, Hollywood superagent **Irving "Swifty" Lazar**, who represented some of the world's foremost literary and musical geniuses, including Cole Porter, Noel Coward, Alan Jay Lerner, William Saroyan, Truman Capote, and Neil Simon, lived at 296 North Via Las Palmas, where the baldpated, nearsighted Lazar, whose glitzy Oscar parties at Spago were the hottest ticket in town, basked in the glory of having sold the movie rights to *The Sound of Music* for $1.25 million, *How to Succeed in Business Without Really Trying* ($1 million), and *Camelot* ($1.4 million).

When the finicky dealmaker negotiated the sale of Richard Nixon's memoirs for $2 million in 1974, it opened the floodgates for celebrity "tell-alls" by other Lazar clients such as John Huston, Lauren Bacall, Kirk Douglas, and Joan Collins.

Los Angeles criminal defense attorney **Harry Weiss**, whose celebrity clients included the campy sex siren Mae West, with whom he appeared on-screen as a Mafia don in the diabolically bad 1978 parody *Sextette*, owned the house at 230 North Via Las Palmas. There he kept shelves of framed photographs, many of them personally autographed by famous actors. The munchkinlike Weiss, who dressed flamboyantly in wide-brimmed hats and carried a silver-tipped cane, was a longstanding fixture of L.A. courtrooms. It was said he was on a first-name basis with all the judges and knew where the bodies, if any, were buried.

Weiss began his law career in the wild and woolly 1930s, when the lines between Hollywood and the mob were blurred. He saw and heard everything, he said, but was smart enough to keep his mouth shut. In 1994, Weiss suffered a heart attack and underwent surgery the following year. But it didn't stop him from throwing all-male pool parties at this house during the time he lived there.

In 1998 after Weiss sold the house for $325,000, the indefatigable attorney, then age eighty-two, was suspended by the California Bar Association and placed on probation for a period of two years for misconduct (i.e. illegally splitting fees with another attorney on a civil case). He has since retired.

Presidential inaugural ball dress designed by James Galanos (Courtesy of Los Angeles County Museum of Art).

Innovative Greek-American couturier **James Galanos** created the one-shoulder, silver-and-crystal-beaded white evening gown worn by former first lady Nancy Reagan at the inaugural celebrations for President Ronald Reagan. Galanos paid $492,500 for the home at 289 South Via Las Palmas, which was previously occupied by interior designer Arthur Elrod, in 1972.

Known to his deferential gay friends, who crowd around him at Hunter's Video Bar to buy drinks, as "Jimmy," Galanos began his career in Paris before moving to New York and Los Angeles. Assisting Hollywood costumer Jean Louis, Galanos developed his trademark sculptured, form-fitting style. He also designed coats, suits, and dresses for Betsy Bloomingdale, the wife of New York department store tycoon and Diners Club founder Alfred Bloomingdale.

Why not their husbands? "I don't do men," quipped Galanos, whose wit is as sharp as his scissors. Galanos's name is frequently included in the same fashion lists as Coco Chanel, Christian Dior, Hubert de Givenchy, and Yves Saint Laurent because he is the only American designer, it is said, whose stringent dressmaking and hand-finishing techniques meet the highest standards of French haute couture.

Always immaculately attired, Galanos eschews such strict formality at home, preferring simple classical décor, which would probably not endear him to some of today's interior design queens. "Embellishment is something so many overdo," he told *Architectural Digest*. "I'm not afraid to be simple. In design it's vitally important to know when to stop."

Fearless Hollywood gossip columnist **Rona Barrett**, who broke the David Begelman check-forging scandal that sent shock waves through Hollywood, among numerous other celebrity scoops, compiled many of her juicy stories while living at 357 South Via Las Palmas in 1978.

It was Barrett, described as "a platinum-frosted artichoke," who first told the world that Elizabeth Taylor and Richard Burton were breaking up; that Cary Grant was divorcing Dyan Cannon; and Elvis Presley was about to marry Priscilla Beaulieu. TV viewers loved her. Movie stars *hated* her. Mia Farrow poured champagne on her head. Ryan O'Neal mailed her a live tarantula in a box. Barrett lapped up the attention like a spoiled dog. A "bow wow" Frank Sinatra called her. Whatever the scoop—or the poop—she had her nose in it.

In 1959, cosmetics manufacturer **Davis Factor**, whose father Max was awarded an Oscar for his invention of modern movie makeup, owned the estate at 425 South Via Las Palmas, now the home of Jay and Anastasia Benoist. David's brother, Max Factor Jr., took over the family business after his father, who created the revolutionary Pan-Cake formula with his son, died in 1938.

Great grandson Davis Factor III and his younger brother, Dean, who was briefly engaged to actress Shannen Doherty, are the founders of SmashBox Photography and Cosmetics.

Broadway composer **Jerry Herman**, who struck box-office gold with *Hello, Dolly!*, *Mame*, and *La Cage aux Folles*, is happily ensconced on this street at 444 South Via Las Palmas, for which he paid $675,000 in 1999. It's the second desert home the clever songwriter has refurbished in between writing songs for stage, movies, and television. Herman's skillful talent for remodeling and decorating houses is well-known from coast-to-coast to buyers and sellers. "In a way," he said, "doing houses is like doing a Broadway musical, only without the chorus girls."

★　★　★

Perennial song-and-dance man **Donald O'Connor**, who partnered Gene Kelly and Debbie Reynolds in *Singin' in the Rain*, played the human sidekick to *Francis* the talking mule, and brought considerable pathos to his unsung portrayal of "The Great Stone Face" in *The Buster Keaton Story* (written and directed by Sidney Sheldon), reportedly kicked up his heels at two addresses on the same street— 700 and 840 South Via Las Palmas, although there is no official record of him having lived there. O'Connor died in 2003.

The actual homeowner of 840 South Via Las Palmas is Frank Carroll, an Olympic coach of the year, U.S. Figure Skating Association Hall of Famer, and three-time Professional Skating Association coach of the year. Carroll's students have won eleven world championships. They include seven-time U.S. national skating champion Michelle Kwan, who won silver and bronze medals in two Winter Olympics, as well as Linda Fratianne, Christopher Bowman, Tiffany Chan, and 2002 Olympic bronze medalist Timothy Goebel.

Top: Jerry Herman tasting success (Courtesy of Jerry Herman). *Left:* Rudy Vallee (Wayne Knight Collection). *Bottom:* Francis the talking mule and Donald O'Connor (Wayne Knight Collection).

★　★　★

Twenties "Heigh-ho!" megaphone crooner and early talkie musical star of *The Vagabond Lover* **Rudy Vallee** played offbeat comedy roles in writer-director Preston Sturges's *The Palm Beach Story*, *Unfaithfully Yours*, and *The Beautiful Blonde From Bashful Bend*, and later took Broadway and Hollywood by storm as J. B. Biggley, the lecherous company president in *How to Succeed in Business Without Really Trying*. Vallee resided at 484 West Vereda del Sur from 1946 until 1957. (Note: The house has since been razed to make way for a new home that was constructed at 475 South Via Las Palmas in 1992.)

★　★　★

Spencer Kellogg Jr., whose refining company (not the cereal manufacturer) was one of the world's largest distributors of vegetable oils and Soya bean extracts, lived at 321 West Vereda Sur, yet another Albert Frey design, in 1939. Kellogg took ill on Christmas Day 1944 and died the following day.

Top: Patrick Macnee and wife "Baba" Sekely (Courtesy of Bob Pollock). *Bottom:* Adolphe Menjou in tuxedo mode (Steve Kiefer Collection).

Bandleader and part-time actor, **Eddie LeBaron**, a native of Venezuela, who made cameo appearances in the film musicals *Trocadero* and *Casa Manana*, and his wife, Burnice Smith, the heir to typewriter manufacturer Smith-Corona, later resided at this home for seven years. He then moved to 328 West Mountain View Place.

★ ★ ★

Hungarian film director **Steve Sekely** fled the Nazis and settled in Hollywood where he directed the cult films *Revenge of the Zombies*, *The Scar*, and *The Day of the Triffids*, based on John Wyndham's creepy novel about man-eating plants. Sekely lived at 248 West Vereda Sur until his death in 1979. Nine years later, his widow, Karla (Baba) Majos de Nagyzsenye, married Patrick Macnee, the smooth-talking star of TV's *The Avengers*. Macnee has owned several desert homes since he arrived in 1968.

★ ★ ★

Tarzan producer **Sol Lesser** owned the film rights to the viable jungle franchise and leased them to MGM. He reclaimed them when aging star Johnny Weissmuller handed over his tree vine to newcomer Lex Barker. Lesser may or may not have worn a loincloth around his home at 357 Camino Sur where, in 1947, Edgar Rice Burroughs, creator of the ape man series, turned down an invitation to visit Lesser's tree house citing health reasons.

In addition to managing monkeys and elephants, Lesser also produced the schmaltzy *Our Town*, donated $1 million in profits from *Stage Door Canteen* to the American Theatre Wing, and collected a Best Documentary Oscar for *Kon-Tiki*.

In 1952, Lesser's home hit the news when a jewel thief made off with one of his precious sapphire rings valued at $10,000. A deserving recipient of the Jean Hersholt Humanitarian Award, Lesser died, age ninety, in 1980.

★ ★ ★

Donald W. Douglas Sr., the founder of Douglas Aircraft, the company that built the first DC-class transcontinental commercial airliners, lived at 377 Camino Sur until his death, age eighty-eight, in 1981. Douglas was one of America's youngest aeronautical engineers when he began manufacturing airplanes in 1920. His most successful invention, the DC-3, was launched in 1936. During World War II, his factory built thousands of military planes; he also developed wide-bodied passenger jets. Because of the high cost of production, Douglas's company merged with McDonnell Aircraft in 1967. Boeing acquired McDonnell Douglas Corporation in 1997, making it the largest aerospace firm in the world.

★ ★ ★

French-American leading man **Adolphe Menjou**, who was Oscar nominated for his showy role as crafty newspaper editor Walter Burns in 1931's *The Front Page* and gave a standout performance as flashy lawyer Billy Flynn in *Roxie Hart*, which inspired the play and film *Chicago*, often went shirtless at 523 Camino Sur. It was there that the actor, once voted "the best dressed man in Hollywood," wrote his autobiography titled *It Took Nine Tailors*, assisted by actress-wife Veree Teasdale, in 1946. Seventeen years and twenty-six movies later, Menjou, a vocal supporter of the House Un-American Activities Committee's investigation into communist infiltration in Hollywood, died from chronic hepatitis at age seventy-three.

When William Randolph Hearst's sad-eyed son **George Randolph Hearst**, who was publisher of the *San Francisco Chronicle* and the uncle of Patricia Hearst, died in 1972, his widow, Rosalie, dried her eyes and said, "No, more tears!" That was when she decided to devote her time to many philanthropic activities, holding numerous fundraising dinners at 550 Camino Sur for her late husband's Memorial Foundation for Diabetes Education, as well as Pathfinders and the Palm Springs Youth Center and Assistance League. Mrs. Hearst died in 1999 at age eighty-four. Her house sold for $850,000 in 2002.

Raunchy novelist **Harold Robbins**, whose trashy bestsellers, including *The Carpetbaggers* and *The Adventurers*, were based on the sex lives of the rich and famous, wrote his last three books at 601 Camino Sur (on the southwest corner of Via Monte Vista).

Robbins, who suffered a stroke in 1982 and was confined to a wheelchair since 1993, lived here with a sixty-inch TV set, a tropical fish tank, a Picasso, Leger, and four Chagalls, four dogs, three cats, and his third wife, Jann Stapp—a middle-aged nurse with a stripper's body—to keep him company. He died, age eighty-one, in 1997.

A two-fingered typist who started writing books on a $100 bet, Robbins won literary kudos for his first two novels, *Never Love a Stranger* and *A Stone For Danny Fisher*, before he realized the power of smut and became a one-man publishing cunnilinguist. Robbins' salacious tastes were formed early in his childhood. A New York orphan, he delivered cocaine, he said, to songwriter Cole Porter and gave horny men hand jobs in Harlem burlesque theaters. Variant forms of homosexuality and debauchery followed. His books sold an incredible 750 million copies and were translated into forty-two languages. Robbins' former home fetched $520,000 in 2001.

In 1958, big-voiced film and nightclub entertainer **Tony Martin** and his slinky ballet dancer-wife **Cyd Charisse** moved to 697 Camino Sur, where their two sons, Nicky and Tony Jr., rode bicycles and played handball. Four years later, Martin, who bought and sold three other Alexander-built homes as an investment, was a victim in an elaborate gam-

bling scam in which he was cheated out of $10,000 during a crooked gin rummy game with Harry Karl, Phil Silvers, Zeppo Marx, and others at the Friars Club in Beverly Hills—although Martin would never admit to having been taken. The group's total losses, it was later reported, amounted to $320,000.

Although Martin's records sold millions, he often signed on to weird acting roles such as singing "O Punchinello" to a monkey in one film and playing straight man to the Marx Brothers in another.

But a much bigger indignity befell Martin when he and Cyd Charisse, who strutted her long legs in *The Band Wagon*, *Brigadoon*, and *Silk Stockings*, were the only couple in town not invited to one of Frank Sinatra's swank New Year's Eve parties—"a dastardly deed," accused Martin, "and I doubt I'll ever forgive him."

Three decades later, Martin, whom Mel Torme called "the greatest singer of them all," proved he still had what it takes when he headlined at the Fabulous Palm Springs Follies, belting out his trademark song "Begin the Beguine"—at age eighty-seven.

★　★　★

With her magnesium-colored thick blonde hair, broad shoulders, and hefty bustline, Columbia Pictures discovery **Kim Novak** quickly took over as America's reigning love goddess, becoming the object of millions of men's sexual fantasies after they and their envious wives saw her slow-dance with William Holden in *Picnic*, tease Frank Sinatra in *Pal Joey*, and taunt James Stewart in *Vertigo*—these films were made ten years before Novak, wearing a scarf and dark glasses, rented Kay Banowit's four-bedroom

Top: Cyd Charisse and Tony Martin perform their double act (Wayne Knight Collection). *Bottom:* Kim Novak admires her portrait (Larry Edmunds Bookshop).

home at 740 Camino Sur (on the northwest corner of Vista Vespero).

Novak stayed here in the final days of her superstardom, which reached its zenith with her lusty portrayal of the schizophrenic bitch/heroine whose life is twice doomed in Robert Aldrich's cult movie *The Legend of Lylah Clare*, released in 1968.

Novak walked away from her career after being almost killed when her station wagon rolled over multiple times on an isolated stretch of coastline near Big Sur.

★　★　★

Studly, bronzed male pinup **George Nader**, whose 1953 sci-fi flick *Robot Monster* enjoys an inexplicable cult following and whose gay "coming out" novel, *Chrome*, was written during his convalescence from glaucoma, resided at 893 Camino Sur until his death in 2002. A minor-level star elevated to major camp status because of his close friendship with fellow gay icon Rock Hudson, the mellifluous-speaking Nader was the last of Universal's brilliantine-haired beefcake boys. His apparent lack of drive and ambition left him floundering after the studio failed to renew his seven-year contract amid mounting gossip about the actor's homosexuality.

Nader, to his credit, never looked back—and who could blame him after making such stinkers as *Sins of Jezebel* and *Lady Godiva*, though he did manage to appear in a few decent films, notably *Six Bridges to Cross* and *Away All Boats*.

His one consolation was Mark Miller, an aspiring opera singer, whom he met in the men's room at the Hollywood Bowl in 1943.

"He had on a white shirt with Camel cigarettes sticking out of the sleeve," remembered Miller, "and I said 'God, look at that beauty.'"

Four years later, their paths crossed again at the Pasadena Playhouse. It was instant love. The two men remained together for the next fifty-five years.

But it didn't mean total happiness. Being gay cost Nader some good roles, and when Rock Hudson was forced against his will to deal with adoring female fans, their friendship temporarily cooled. Nader found himself on the outs with producers and casting agents, and he grew increasingly resentful at the film industry's blatant hypocrisy, especially as exhibited by actors such as Anthony Perkins and Tab Hunter, who were gay and pretended they weren't. Nader considered this a betrayal.

Top: George Nader lifting weights (Steve Kiefer Collection). *Bottom:* George Nader's home on Camino Sur at the time of the Friendly triple murders (Courtesy of Palm Springs Historical Society).

His reluctance to play the Hollywood star game, "like William Haines a generation before," said William J. Mann, "made him suspect in a highly suspicious time," and he was forced to relocate to Europe where he became a top star of German detective films, playing FBI agent Jerry Cotton.

Nader's white-shuttered Vista Las Palmas home—his permanent address for the decade following Hudson's death from AIDS in 1985—was chosen for what Nader and Miller believed to be its absolute privacy. The house is located at the far end of a long street, but its whereabouts is known by more than Fed Ex and UPS drivers. It is the object of attention of the morbidly inclined, for it was at this address on the evening of October 3, 1978, that Palm Springs's first triple homicide occurred. This is where retired real estate developer Edward Friendly, his socially prominent wife, and their black maid were killed "execution-style" by a hired assassin.

The bloody crime ranks as one of the most violent in the city's history. The three victims were shot with a .45 caliber automatic weapon. The first to die was the maid, Frances Williams, who was hit at point-blank range when she went to answer a knock at the kitchen door. Next, the killer blew off Sophia Friendly's head when she attempted to flee the room. Then, he (or she) calmly ambushed Ed Friendly as he sat watching TV in the den, shooting him in the chest.

A possible motive for the killings: a $1-million trust fund that Sophia Friendly had set up for Ed "E. F." Hutton—her troubled son from a previous marriage to Curtis Hutton, the cousin of Woolworth heiress Barbara Hutton. Poor Ed, it was theorized, couldn't wait for his mother to die of natural causes so he hired a hit man to hurry things along.

What made this case even more newsworthy? Friendly was the brother of veteran CBS news producer Fred W. Friendly, who pioneered "live" coast-to-coast broadcasts and whose Peabody Award-winning documentaries and exposés on government corruption, civil rights issues, and white-collar crime, which he began on Edward R. Murrow's interview program "See It Now," was the forerunner of *60 Minutes.*

The killer was never brought to justice, partly due to a lack of real evidence. The murder weapon was never found, and there were no witnesses. Although police, the FBI, and Interpol tracked a prime suspect to Europe, efforts to extradite him to the U.S. failed, and he was last seen in Brazil. "We were never told about the murders," said Mark Miller, who purchased the home with Nader in 1991. "We found out two years later." The case remains unsolved.

Prior to this frightful episode, actress **Gregg Sherwood**, who played decorative roles in 1952's *The Merry Widow* and *The Girl Next Door* and was the ex-wife of Dodge Motors president Horace Dodge, also lived at 893 Camino Sur. In 1979, two years after Sherwood had moved out of this house, she pleaded no contest to defrauding a bank of $75,000 and looting $357,000 from the trust fund of her son, John Francis Dodge.

Born in 1924, Sherwood was a former Miss Wisconsin and Broadway show girl, who became the fifth wife of Horace Dodge Jr., the son of Dodge Motor Company's founder and heir to $57 million. Dodge divorced her after nine years of marriage because, he testified, he couldn't afford her wild spending. Sherwood settled for $11 million and married her bodyguard, Daniel Moran.

According to published reports, they embarked on a thirteen-year spending spree of $25,000-a-night parties and round-the-world flights in a private jet until all the money Dodge gave her was gone. Some speculated that the Friendlys were killed by mistake, and Sherwood was the intended victim. (A third celebrity homeowner, *Rhythm on Ice* producer George Arnold, lived there in 1961.)

Tin Pan Alley lyricist **Sammy Cahn**, who composed more than eighty finger-snapping tunes, including "Love and Marriage," "The Tender Trap," and "Come Fly With Me," lived at 1303 Via Monte Vista. The impish-looking Cahn—a cross between Groucho Marx and the Great Gazoo—scored his first Oscar for the title song *Three Coins in the Fountain* with Jule Styne.

Cahn purchased the Monte Vista house in 1952, he said, as a vacation getaway for his young bride, Gloria Delson, and their two children, Steven and Laurie—"just like all the 'in' people were doing." But marital pressures and a painful attack of ulcers for the overworked musical genius soon forced a trial separation from his wife, a former child actress who appeared in *Modern Times* and *Wonder Man*. A reconciliation attempt failed, and their twenty-year marriage ended in 1964. Cahn died, age seventy-nine, in 1993.

★ ★ ★

Actor, playboy, and presidential brother-in-law **Peter Lawford**, who melted female moviegoers' hearts as a bashful male pinup in MGM's *Son of Lassie*, *Little Women*, and *Royal Wedding*, surprised his fans when he forsook bachelorhood to marry JFK's younger sister, Patricia Kennedy, and became a member of Frank Sinatra's club-hopping Rat Pack. Lawford was said to have lived at 1295 North Via Monte Vista in the heady days of the Camelot presidency.

The upper-crust Lawford came from a prominent English family with a muddied reputation. His uncle, Herbert Lawford, was a Wimbledon tennis champion, but Peter's unexpected birth was a "mistake," according to his mother, May Sommerville. (Her husband, Major Ernest Aylen, shot himself when he learned of her adulterous affair and pregnancy with his commanding army officer, Sir Sidney Lawford.)

After May and Sir Sidney married, they moved to France, then settled in West Palm Beach, Florida, where their teenage son parked cars to help support him and his parents. Lawford's childhood read like an R-rated movie script. At age seven, he was smoking and

Top: Sammy Cahn playing a tune (Wayne Knight Collection). *Left:* Peter Lawford and Patricia Kennedy (Backlot Books and Movie Posters). *Bottom:* The Lawford-Kennedy home at 1295 North Via Monte Vista (Photo by John Waggaman).

drinking. His nanny and another man molested him when he was nine. At thirteen, he fell through a French glass door and severed the tendons of his upper right arm, leaving him with a permanent disability. Disenfranchised, sexually confused, and mostly broke, Lawford sought refuge in acting.

He quickly rose from extra to featured player and star, "the Popular Romantic Lead in the Movies" proclaimed *Collier's* magazine of the poised actor, whose impeccable manners and clipped speech made him the Hugh Grant of 1948. A passionate surfer, Lawford purchased his former studio boss Louis B. Mayer's twelve-room Santa Monica beach house in 1956, two years after his marriage to Pat Kennedy. But no records exist of this Vista Las Palmas home, which was built by George Alexander, ever being owned or lived in by the famous couple, together or separately.

The actor's career soon took a backseat to his subservient activities as the First Family's factotum; he was behind the production of *Ocean's 11* while appearing twice nightly with Sinatra, Dean Martin, and Sammy Davis Jr. at the Sands, planning the president's inaugural gala and his forty-fifth birthday bash, and being a pallbearer at Marilyn Monroe's funeral circus.

Lawford's drinking problem was exacerbated after his irrevocable split with Sinatra. The singer was insulted when the newly elected JFK canceled a trip to his Rancho Mirage house. Lawford's excessive drinking was compounded by the lifelong estrangement from his mother, Lady Lawford, who thought her son had turned into "an awful brat." She particularly disliked Sinatra, calling him "a dried-up piece of spaghetti" and denounced the boorish Kennedys as "barefoot Irish peasants."

After the events of November 22, 1963, things were never the same for Lawford who, frequently unemployed, became addicted to alcohol and drugs, eventually landing himself and bygone sweetheart Elizabeth Taylor in the Betty Ford Center for treatment. Pat Kennedy divorced Lawford, the father of her four children, Christopher, Sydney, Victoria, and Robin, in 1966. He died at sixty-one from liver and kidney disease on Christmas Eve 1984. Although it is conceivable that the Lawfords might have stayed at the Via Monte Vista home, it's anybody's guess if they actually did. However, it didn't stop the four-bedroom house from selling for $510,000 in 2001—largely on the strength of his tarnished name.

★ ★ ★

Dean Martin enjoying himself (Larry Edmunds Bookshop).

Dean Martin, the sleepy-eyed crooner of Italian *amore* songs, who loved to drink as much as he sang, proved he was much more than just a pretty voice, however. Martin, like many other business-minded stars, including Bob Hope, Bing Crosby, and Frank Sinatra, wisely invested his income in real estate. By 1968, the wealthy entertainer's assets included commercial land and residential property in San Francisco, Los Angeles, and Palm Springs where he spent increasing amounts of time hitting golf balls, drinking Scotch, and watching Westerns at 1123 Via Monte Vista.

Jeanne Biegger, Martin's second wife and the mother of three of his seven children, rented the family's first desert home during a trial separation from her husband in 1956, according to biographer William Schoell. At the time, Martin had split with goofy screen partner Jerry Lewis and was in hock to the IRS—their last film together was appropriately titled *Hollywood or Bust*. Ignoring fans' pleas for a reunion, Dean went solo and joined the carousing Rat Pack.

The Martins liked the desert so much that after the couple reconciled, they came back and bought a permanent home. In the wake of his record-breaking *Airport* success, Martin gave it to Jeanne as part of their 1973 divorce settlement. It was then that Gail, his second eldest daughter from his first marriage, and her lawyer-husband, Paul Polena, moved to town.

There was one thing missing from the twilight of the singer's life. His actor-son, Dean-Paul Martin, a captain in the Air National Guard, was killed when the F-4 Phantom jet he was piloting lost altitude and crashed into Mount San Gorgonio, exploding on impact. After Dino's death in 1987, his heartbroken father was unable to look at those mountains anymore. Frank Sinatra offered his despairing chum a concert tour in an attempt to console him. (Ten years earlier, Sinatra's mother perished with three others when a twin-engine Lear jet taking them to see her son's opening night at Caesar's Palace in Las Vegas hit the same snow-covered peaks at 375 mph and disintegrated.)

All of Martin's kids tried showbiz. Craig, his oldest son, worked in TV production. First and third daughters Claudia and Deana were singer-actresses. Youngest son Ricci cut an album. And his fourth daughter, Gina, married the Beach Boys' Carl Wilson. But the original is still the best.

Three blocks south of here, Liberace's violin-playing older brother, **George Liberace**, and his wife, Jayne, owned the house at 665 North Via Monte Vista in 1956, the year Lee broke through as a headliner. Because their ever-present mother was concerned about Liberace's lack of moral restraint, it was decided that George should live close by so he could keep an eye on him.

It obviously didn't work out, judging by the wealth of off-color stories and blue jokes that have made the rounds about the limp-wristed pianist. "My brother, George," as Lee always sarcastically introduced him, soon tired of his brother's professional and personal excesses, went into the food franchise business, and later became a successful music publisher. He died from leukemia in 1983.

★   ★   ★

George Liberace (left) and Lee showing brotherly love (Wayne Knight Collection).

Phil Regan, the New York policeman who turned in his badge for a microphone and went Hollywood, where his pot o' gold charm lit up the blarney-filled musicals *Sweet Adeline*, *Laughing Irish Eyes*, and *Sweet Rosie O'Grady*, lived at 610 North Via Monte Vista in 1939. A staunch political supporter, Regan performed his cheerful theme song "Happy Days Are Here Again" at numerous Democratic conventions. He also sang the national anthem at President Harry Truman's inauguration.

★   ★   ★

Quick-thinking theatrical agent **George "Bullets" Durgom**, praised for his friendship and loyalty to such high-energy clients as Jackie Gleason, Sammy Davis Jr., and Mickey Rooney, lived at 969 North Tuxedo Circle (off Via Monte Vista and Regal Drive) in 1972, twenty years before he died. It was Durgom who gave Merv Griffin a leg up the Hollywood ladder when he arranged an audition for the overweight band singer at Warner Brothers, leading to a variety of acting roles, which in turn opened the door for Griffin's successful stint as a game show inventor and talk show host.

★   ★   ★

Susan Bernard, the busty *Playboy* model, actress, and daughter of world-renowned photographer-to-the-stars Bruno Bernard, inherited the house at 997 North Tuxedo Circle from her father, who died in 1987. "Bernard of Hollywood" captured some of the most-iconoclastic images of movieland celebrities at work and play.

★   ★   ★

With his white tuxedo and golden trombone, **Tommy Dorsey** cut quite a figure as "the Sheik of Swing." Tommy, once the husband of MGM actress Patricia Dane, was the talented, but temperamental younger brother of trumpet-playing bandleader Jimmy Dorsey, whose jazz bands were at the forefront of the big band swing era. Their tumultuous personal lives were depicted onscreen in *The Fabulous Dorseys*, along with the music that made them famous, such as "Green Eyes" and "I'm Getting Sentimental Over You."

A heavy eater, Tommy choked to death in his sleep after consuming a hearty Thanksgiving dinner in 1956. Jimmy died from cancer one year later. In 1967, Tommy's widow, Janie, bought the house at 823 North Topaz Circle (off Leisure Way). She died in 2003.

★   ★   ★

Sandra Dee snuggling with husband Bobby Darin (Cinema Collectors).

Brash, pompadoured singer **Bobby Darin**'s renditions of "Splish Splash," "Dream Lover," and the finger-snapping "Mack the Knife" made him the hero of millions of teenage punks and prom girls. He reconciled his failing marriage to doll-like actress **Sandra Dee**, the screen's first *Gidget* and Debbie Reynolds's replacement in two *Tammy* films, while living at 845 North Fair Circle in 1964.

Darin's connection to the desert was strong if short lived. Darin was twenty-four and Dee sixteen when they were married. After miscarrying their first child, Dee developed signs of anorexia and alcoholism. While vacationing here in '61, Darin gave her much-needed good news: "You're gonna be a momma."

The next year, they returned with their son, Dodd, to spend time together as a family. A third pregnancy did not ease the couple's marital problems, although Darin's touching performance as a shell-shocked soldier in *Captain Newman, M.D.* received an Oscar nomination for Best Supporting Actor. Dee, who first hit it big as Troy Donahue's girlfriend in *A Summer Place*, joined her husband for *That Funny Feeling*, their third and last film together. Two years later, they separated and were divorced in 1967.

★   ★   ★

And, until 1995, the late *Los Angeles Times* travel editor **Jerry Hulse**, whose informative articles about Europe and Hawaii helped promote overseas tourism to the masses, wrote his weekly newspaper columns at 803 North High Road. Considered to be "the best travel writer in the country," Hulse was awarded the French Legion of Honor by President François Mitterrand in 1987. He also authored the acclaimed book *Jody* about his wife's search for her true identity, which was made into a TV movie starring Melissa Gilbert.

★   ★   ★

Chatty celebrity raconteur **George Hamilton** wrote his name in cement on the driveway of this two-story home at 591 North Patencio Road, where he and then-wife **Alana Collins** (parents of actor-musician Ashley Hamilton) lived in 1973. After Hamilton and Collins divorced, she married rock star Rod Stewart and he starred in the movie spoofs *Love at First Bite* and *Zorro, The Gay Blade* in between escorting a succession of famous and beautiful women, including Joan Collins, Elizabeth Taylor, and Philippines First Lady Imelda Marcos. (In 1995, the two ex-spouses reunited on TV's *The George and Alana Show*.)

Herbert F. Johnson, grandson of the founder of S. C. Johnson & Son, the parquet-flooring company and makers of the household cleaning products: Windex, Pledge, Mr. Muscle, and Raid, was the pleased owner of the same Patencio Road house from 1948 to 1954.

Top: George Hamilton (Howard Johns Collection). *Left:* George Hamilton's signature in cement (Photo by Howard Johns). *Bottom:* Hamilton's home at 591 North Patencio Road (Photo by Howard Johns).

Mario Lanza after his crash diet (Larry Edmunds Bookshop).

It was Johnson, the husband of MGM actress Irene Purcell, who hired Frank Lloyd Wright to design the brick-and-glass Johnson Wax administration building with its giant lily-pad interior columns, located in Racine, Wisconsin. Wright also designed "Wingspread," the Johnson family's thirty-six-acre prairie-style summer home, which was designated a National Historic Landmark in 1989. Johnson's former Las Palmas house on North Patencio Road sold for $575,000 in 1992.

★   ★   ★

When **Mario Lanza**, the bass-voiced, ham-sized operatic tenor—whom the press compared to Enrico Caruso, the Italian opera star he played in MGM's top-grosser *The Great Caruso*—slipped unseen into Palm Springs in January 1951, it was not to play tennis and golf or partake in the city's many fine restaurants and nightclubs. Lanza's mission was to lose weight, fifty pounds to be exact, before he began a national concert tour.

Each day for three weeks, Lanza ate a strict diet of boiled eggs, tomatoes, grapefruit, skimmed milk, and tangelos. He walked every morning in a heavy rubber sweat suit and boxed with a personal trainer in order to reduce his gargantuan size to a manageable two hundred pounds.

On February 11, Lanza left the desert with his arranger-conductor, Constantine Callinicos, and embarked on a grueling twenty-two-city, cross-country personal appearance tour. The effects of Lanza's treatment were restorative, giving him renewed vigor, but they did not last. The following year, in preparation for his forthcoming film, *The Student Prince*, Lanza rented a three-bedroom ranch house in Las Palmas and once again embarked on a crash diet to bring his rapidly ballooning weight under control.

MGM held up the film's production while Lanza even took daily singing lessons to improve his voice. However, it was apparent that he was fighting a losing battle against his insatiable appetite for food and drink. After returning to Hollywood, Lanza argued with the film's producer, Joe Pasternak, then walked out, and had to be replaced. His career in tatters, Lanza sunk into a severe depression and worsening alcoholism—the only saving grace was that his records were still popular.

In 1955, Lanza leased the house at 784 North Patencio Road from owner Frank Ryan for $3,000 a month, while dieting and training for a major Las Vegas comeback at the New Frontier Hotel. Once more he tried to reduce his weight, this time from an embarrassing 300 pounds to a more respectable 260, though he was still far from his slimmest. This put enormous emotional pressure on him.

As opening night approached, Lanza grew nervous and resumed drinking. Soon he was so intoxicated that he was incapable of singing, and the show had to be canceled. It was virtually the end of Lanza's professional career in America, and shortly thereafter, he relocated to Europe. His health destroyed by overeating, his heart weakened by strenuous dieting, it came as no surprise when Lanza died from a coronary thrombosis in Rome on October 7, 1959. The real surprise was his age: Lanza was just thirty-eight.

★   ★   ★

The bitchy dialogue and clever plot twists of husband-and-wife *Dynasty* writers **Bob** and **Eileen "Mike" Pollock** kept TV viewers glued to the weekly exploits of the oil-rich Carrington family for nine seasons. They are still writing stories and stage plays at their home at 975 North Patencio Road.

Dynasty story writers Bob and "Mike" Pollock with Jann Stapp and Harold Robbins (Courtesy of Bob Pollock).

★   ★   ★

Prior to moving into his second Las Palmas home at 990 North Patencio Road, millionaire author **Harold Robbins** paid $4 million for a mansion in Beverly Hills, bought homes in Acapulco, La Cannet in the south of France, and an eighty-five-foot yacht which he kept moored in the Mediterranean. A ten-year desert resident, Robbins' private life was every bit as glamorous as the characters in his stories of sex, power, and greed.

"We had an open marriage," boasted Grace Palermo, his second wife whom he divorced in 1992, "so our lives were orgies of sex and drugs."

A champion of free speech, he brought "amyl nitrate" and "anal intercourse" to the attention of the American literary mainstream, offended religious leaders with his constant blasphemy, and courted celebrity status as his books sold at the rate of thirty thousand copies a day.

Although he earned $40 million in his lifetime, Robbins reportedly died penniless, the bulk of his money spent on his favorite indulgence, women, which led to two costly divorces, three tax liens, and astronomical medical bills following a stroke.

★   ★   ★

Seattle hotel heiress **Jeannette Edris**, a divorced mother with two children, who married industrious Arkansas cattle breeder and future state governor Winthrop Rockefeller in 1956, was a major desert fundraising presence. She served on many medical boards including Desert Hospital and the AIDS Assistance Program while residing at 993 North Patencio Road until her death at age seventy-nine in 1997.

In a written statement, longtime family friend President Bill Clinton called her "a pioneering First Lady of Arkansas" and acknowledged Jeannette Rockefeller's humanitarian contributions, in particular, organizing a memorial service for slain civil rights activist Martin Luther King on the steps of the state capitol.

★   ★   ★

Contrary to what you may have heard, Madonna does not live here! Minnesota antique dealers George Shea and Gordon Locksley own 999 North Patencio Road. The star of *Little Caesar* and art collector **Edward G. Robinson** and his second wife, Jane Bodenheimer, were rumored to have rented the six-thousand-square-foot house, designed in modernistic tones by A. Quincy Jones and decorated in customary pastel shades by Arthur Elrod, when it was first built in 1959.

The fruit-laden, one-acre property is something of a star itself, having doubled for a Las Vegas mansion in the 2001 remake of *Ocean's 11*, where on three cool nights, the film's spiffy headliners, George Clooney, Brad Pitt, Matt Damon, Carl Reiner, Don Cheadle, Bernie Mac, Elliott Gould, Scott Caan, and Casey Affleck snacked between takes of the film's key scene where they plot a $150-million casino heist.

★   ★   ★

For avenue of the stars, however, you can't beat Via Lola. This lush development, part of the Merito Vista subdivision, has a profusion of historic star names whose various goings-on were, for the most part, shrouded in secrecy.

Powerful Los Angeles labor lawyer **Sidney Korshak**, the reputed mob "fixer" who defended Al Capone's gang and had close ties to the Chicago underworld, bought the six-bedroom home at 535 Via Lola in 1976. Korshak's list of clients included the Teamsters Union, Santa Anita racetrack, Hollywood Park, and the Los Angeles Dodgers.

"My husband and I were staying with Frank Sinatra when Kirk and Anne Douglas showed us a house that was for sale on their street," said Bernice Korshak, a beautiful blonde skater from the Ice Capades. "Sidney wasn't looking to buy a house, but they convinced us."

Celebrities and politicians fawned over Korshak—"possibly the highest-paid lawyer in the world," according to an FBI report.

"He's real big with the movie colony, lives in a mansion in Bel Air," said gangster Johnny Roselli. "His wife plays tennis with Dinah Shore, and he's been shacking up with Stella Stevens for years."

Korshak was MCA honcho Lew Wasserman's best friend and aide-de-camp with a national reputation as a problem solver. He brokered multimillion-dollar Hollywood deals and mediated labor disputes.

"A union cooks up a strike, and Sid arbitrates it," Roselli said. "Instead of a payoff under the table, he gets a big legal fee, pays taxes on it, and cuts it up."

Robert Evans claimed that a nod from Korshak "and the Teamsters change management . . . Santa Anita closes . . . Madison Square Garden stays open . . . Vegas shuts down . . . the Dodgers can play all-night baseball."

One time, Korshak, who represented several Las Vegas casinos, wanted to sell his neighbors, Kirk and Anne Douglas, a piece of the Riviera Hotel. They graciously declined.

"After a barbecue at Sidney Korshak's home one day," related Kirk, "I walked into the kitchen and was astounded to see George Raft doing the dishes. I backed out and mentioned this to Sidney. He said, 'Oh, George likes to do that!'"

Korshak, in his black shantung suit, starched white shirt, and tie, loved the limelight it seems despite his secretive business dealings. He supplied technical assistance on the James Bond caper, *Diamonds Are Forever*, and secured Al Pacino's unruly services for *The Godfather*. Korshak died in 1996, age eighty-eight, one day after his brother, Marshall, a Chicago politician and bootlegger, passed away. Four years later, Bernice Korshak sold the house for $800,000.

★　　★　　★

In 1957, **Kirk Douglas**, a three-time Oscar nominee as Best Actor for *Champion*, *The Bad and the Beautiful*, and *Lust for Life*, was at the peak of his career. A rugged Hollywood individualist, he and second wife Anne Buydens—voted one of the ten best-dressed women in the world—purchased their second desert home, located at 515 Via Lola.

This fine example of California-style desert modernism originally belonged to their neighbor, Robert Howard, the Los Angeles sportsman and investor, who owned land in Palm Springs. Howard had selected young architects Donald Wexler and Richard Harrison to design a home with low ceilings, lots of glass, and flagstone walls.

Top: Kirk and Anne Douglas with their young sons (Courtesy of Palm Springs Historical Society). *Bottom:* Kirk Douglas's home at 515 Via Lola (Courtesy of Kaminsky Productions).

"It was basically a modern post-and-beam structure with an asphalt and gravel roof," recounted Wexler, a Minnesota native who headed west to study architecture and was soon hired as a draftsman by Richard Neutra in his Silver Lake office. In 1952, Wexler went to work for William Cody, the chief architect of Tamarisk Country Club. There he met another young draftsman named Richard Harrison, and they started designing houses together.

One of their first commissions, Wexler said, was Bob Howard's residence, which was built by contractor Robert Higgins in 1954. Two years later, Howard listed the four-bedroom home for sale and shifted his family a few doors down the street. A buyer was quickly found in the person of Kirk Douglas, who immediately saw the home's potential and began making plans to enlarge it.

"It was a little house, and we intended to make it bigger," the actor remembered, purchasing adjoining land at the rear of the property so he could add a tennis court, gymnasium, and spa.

Kirk and Anne's enduring marriage, which has so far spanned almost as many decades as his acting career, reads like a movie script. They met at the Cannes Film Festival and became husband and wife in 1954. They have two sons, Peter, a producer, writer, and director; and Eric, an actor. Kirk's other two sons are Michael and Joel from his first marriage to actress Diana Dill, a member of a distinguished family in Bermuda.

Anne was pleasantly surprised when her husband took her to Palm Springs. "He told us we were going to the desert," she said, thinking they were headed for somewhere like the Sahara. When they flew over the mountains and Anne saw palm trees and swimming pools, she was impressed.

After moving into their dream house, they covered the walls with sculptures and art by Dubuffet, Braque, Vuillard, Mondrian, Chagall, Picasso, and Miro, enclosed the garage to make a guest suite, created a new facade with interior atriums, and added a three-car motor court.

The Douglas home became one of the street's most-noted residences as the couple welcomed friends and business associates Burt Lancaster, Gregory Peck, Billy Wilder, Yul Brynner, Warren Beatty, and Natalie Wood in a relaxed atmosphere that lasted for the next forty years.

Senator Robert Kennedy, Secretary of State Henry Kissinger, Lady Bird Johnson, and Lynda Bird Johnson stayed there. Spencer Tracy and Katharine Hepburn rented the house for two summers. MGM director Vincente Minnelli held his wedding reception to fourth wife Lee Anderson there. It was also in this house that Douglas, who formed his own production company Bryna (named after his Russian-born mother) met with fledgling director Stanley Kubrick and agent Ray Stark to discuss the making of *Spartacus* and where he wrote his probing autobiography, *The Ragman's Son*, and its cathartic follow-up, *Climbing the Mountain*.

In 1991 a small plane collided with Douglas's helicopter during take-off at Santa Paula Airport, fifty miles northwest of Los Angeles. Two people were killed and Douglas severely injured.

Four years later, Douglas began experiencing excruciating back pain and had to be flown to Los Angeles in his neighbor Lord Hanson's private plane for emergency surgery at Cedars-Sinai Medical Center. When Douglas suffered a stroke, fans feared the worst, but he waged a brave fight and was awarded a special Oscar presented by Steven Spielberg in 1996. Three years later, the plucky eighty-three-year-old performer, at the urging of his eldest son, Michael, who wanted his father and stepmother to be closer to their grandchildren, sold their Via Lola house for $1.3 million and moved to Montecito.

In 1960, wickedly humorous American playwright **Moss Hart**, who cowrote *You Can't Take It With You* and *The Man Who Came to Dinner* with George S. Kaufman and directed the Broadway stage triumphs, *My Fair Lady* and *Camelot*, sold his New York apartment. He and wife **Kitty Carlisle**, the actress, singer, and game show panelist on TV's *To Tell The Truth*, moved to a new house at 467 Via Lola. (Friend Edna Ferber, author of *Giant*, teasingly asked, "Lola who? Montez? Brigida?")

On the last night of Moss Hart's life, December 19, 1961, he had gone window-shopping with his family and actor Laurence Harvey along Palm Canyon Drive, enjoying the Christmas lights and carolers. The next morning, Hart complained to his wife that he had a bad toothache. They got dressed, and as she reversed their Cadillac out of the garage to take her husband to the dentist, he collapsed on the front lawn and died of a heart attack. He was fifty-seven.

Former Arkansas Governor **Winthrop Rockefeller** purchased Moss Hart's house in 1963—the same year George Hamilton valiantly failed to re-create the playwright's witty persona in the film version of his best-selling autobiography, *Act One*.

The chairman of Colonial Williamsburg Incorporated and longtime trustee of the National Urban League, Winthrop was the fourth of John D. Rockefeller Jr.'s five sons (the others were John III, Nelson, Laurance, and David). All Winthrop's money did not ease his marital woes with second wife Jeannette Edris, who soon tired of his moodiness and bouts of drinking.

"By 1969 she and Winthrop were living apart," said biographers Peter Collier and David Horowitz, "and had agreed on a divorce."

In 1973, the sixty-year-old Rockefeller died from cancer caused by years of smoking unfiltered Picayune cigarettes. Millions of dollars from his vast share of the family's empire were put into trust for future generations.

Thirties auburn-haired ingénue **Andrea Leeds**, a Howard Hawks discovery who received a Best Supporting Actress Oscar nomination for her suicidal histrionics in *Stage Door*, answered fan mail and posed for photographs with Jo-Jo, her blonde cocker spaniel, at 375 Via Lola.

Leeds "had a freshness that Hawks liked, wholesome but sassy," according to biographer A. Scott Berg, but she retired from the screen reportedly heartbroken after losing the sympathetic role of Melanie to Olivia de Havilland in *Gone With the Wind*.

As consolation, she married her dreamboat, Robert Howard, a big man with an eye for beautiful women. Howard's family owned the champion racehorse Seabiscuit, winner of the 1940 Santa Anita Handicap. His father, Charles Howard Sr., (played by Jeff Bridges in the 2003 movie version of Laura Hillenbrand's best-selling book, *Seabiscuit*) had amassed a fortune selling Buick automobiles and breeding cattle and horses. After his father died, Bob Howard squandered his million-dollar inheritance on gambling and hard liquor.

Sidney and Alexandra
Sheldon (Backlot
Books & Movie
Posters).

Leeds, who owned a downtown jewelry store, displayed a cheerful disposition despite her husband's struggle with alcoholism. In 1960, their nineteen-year-old son Robert Jr., who later became a noted herpetologist, made headlines when he was bitten by a rattlesnake that was one of several poisonous reptiles he kept in cages in the backyard. (He had already been bitten three times and was therefore immune to the antivenom.) Their twenty-six-year-old daughter, Leeann, died from cancer in 1971.

Bob Howard, whose health had declined after undergoing a kidney operation, died in a Las Vegas hospital in 1962. He was forty-five. Leeds survived him by two decades. She died, age seventy, in 1984.

★　★　★

Producer, director, screenwriter, and best-selling author **Sidney Sheldon**, a 1947 Oscar winner for his comical script of *The Bachelor and the Bobby-Soxer*, subsequently purchased the Leeds and Rockefeller homes and combined them into one gigantic estate, where he spends several months a year with second wife Alexandra Kostoff at 425 Via Lola. Their home, which was decorated in fancy yellow lollipop swirls by Arthur Elrod, previously served as the winter residence of Henry Ittleson Jr., the chairman and director of CIT Financial Corporation. Ittleson's New York family gave multimillion-dollar endowments for pioneering mental health research and continue through yearly grants to promote various medical programs as well as the fine arts.

Sheldon's seventeen sexually charged novels have sold more than 300 million copies in more than 100 countries, and he is proudly listed in *The Guinness Book of Records* as "the Most Translated Author in the World." A frequently traveled guest speaker, he donates generously of his time and money to literacy programs, schools, and libraries.

★　★　★

Independent producer **Edward Small**, one of the richest yet least-known men in Hollywood, who had lived on Racquet Club Road, took up residence at 367 Via Lola in 1951. It was unfairly said that he was the only producer who lived *up* to his name. Nevertheless, he was not afraid of shocking or taboo subjects including *The Christine Jorgensen Story*, which Small filmed. Jorgensen underwent the world's first sex change operation.

★　★　★

Producer **Bryan Foy**, the oldest member of the Seven Little Foys, directed the first "one

hundred-percent-talking" movie, *The Lights of New York*, and was known jokingly as Keeper of the Bs because of his long association with cheap moneymakers, many of them written by Crane Wilbur and starring Foy's friend Ronald Reagan. Foy lived at 350 Via Lola in 1946. His younger brother, Eddie Foy Jr., who played his own father in several movies, resided there later.

"Brynie," as he was called, earned some unwanted notoriety when he joined Eagle-Lion Studios in 1948 and put his friend, Chicago gangster Johnny Roselli, on the payroll. (Roselli was later implicated in a CIA plot to kill Cuban dictator Fidel Castro.) In 1955, Bob Hope portrayed Foy's dad in *The Seven Little Foys*, where he did a memorable tap dance on a banquet table with James Cagney.

He was Bugs Bunny, Daffy Duck, and Wile E. Coyote combined in one volatile human package. His name was **Jack L. Warner**, the cofounder of Warner Brothers Pictures, which ground out thousands of Merrie Melodies and Looney Tunes cartoons that preceded the company's main attractions, either a glossy Bette Davis picture, gritty Humphrey Bogart crime thriller, or a rousing Errol Flynn adventure.

At Warners, in real life as in cartoonland, anything could happen and often did: multiple hirings and firings, uproarious birthday pranks, noisy union strikes, even illicit liaisons. "JL," as his employees called him, was a man loved, feared, and hated—the unchallenged clown prince of Hollywood. That uncomplimentary assessment aside, Jack Warner's name as executive in charge of production emblazoned on the company's glowing shield at the start of more than two hundred films always guaranteed a high-class product.

Paradoxically, Warner Brothers was awarded fewer Oscars than any other studio during this time, although it had several impressive wins: Bette Davis twice for *Dangerous* and *Jezebel*, Paul Muni for *The Story of Louis Pasteur*, and James Cagney for *Yankee Doodle Dandy*. In 1942, *Casablanca* was a triple winner for Best Picture, Director, and Screenplay. The delighted Warner sprinted to the podium and claimed his prize. Unfortunately, the film's producer, Hal Wallis, felt he had been ignored and resigned in protest.

Twenty-two years later, *My Fair Lady*, Warner's greatest personal triumph, at a cost of $17 million to the studio, collected eight Oscars including Best Picture, Actor, and Director. It was sweet victory for the man who once sang for pennies in his family's nickelodeon.

Top: The Jack Warner estate at 285 Via Lola (Photo by John Waggaman). *Bottom:* Jack Warner cries foul (Courtesy of Palm Springs Historical Society).

But away from the moviemaking factory that he ruled with an iron fist, threatening actors with suspension if they refused a certain role or blackballing writers for inserting political subterfuge in their scripts, Warner was a discerning man of cultivated tastes, and he had the money and accolades to prove it when he moved to "Villa Aujourd'hui," his winter home at 285 Via Lola, named after the summer home he owned at Cap d'Antibes on the French Riviera.

Built in 1958, this four-thousand-square-foot property, ringed by giant palm and olive trees and enclosed by a high security wall, was almost as impregnable as his Burbank movie lot. Decorated by William Haines, the six-bedroom estate consisted of a neoclassical building where Warner and his second wife, Ann Boyar, lived in regal splendor with hand-painted Chinese wallpaper in the foyer, solid bronze pharaoh-head doorknobs, and Louis XVI furniture. Adorning the parklike grounds is a Bacchus fountain and Olympic-size swimming pool, plus two separate guest cottages and servants' quarters where Warner's uniformed chauffeur would polish his owner's Bentley after the three-hour drive from Los Angeles—a trip that his boss took frequently until the company was sold in 1969.

Warner was so smitten by desert living that he even bought his younger mistress a home nearby, according to biographer Cass Warner Sperling. However, after the retired mogul tripped and fell playing tennis in 1973, his health was never the same. He suffered a stroke and went blind four years later.

Ann Warner cared for her invalid husband until his death at eighty-six in 1978. Their beautiful daughter, **Barbara Warner**, who was married to *My Friend Irma* comedy writer Cy Howard, still resides next door at 1050 North Cahuilla Road. (Peek over the fence, and you'll see the name of one of the family's favorite films, *Casablanca*, painted on the awning.)

In 1990, gritty crime novelist and screenwriter **Steven Shagan**, a double Oscar nominee for Best Original Screenplay for *Save the Tiger* and Best Adapted Screenplay for *Voyage of the Damned*, purchased Jack Warner's former home for $1,315,000. There Shagan wrote the well-received HBO telefilm, *Gotti*, and the Richard Gere thriller, *Primal Fear*, which launched the screen-acting career of Edward Norton.

MCA chairman emeritus **Lew Wasserman**, the head of the powerful entertainment conglomerate that represented such important clients as Jimmy Stewart, Jane Wyman, Rock Hudson, Doris Day, and Cary Grant, packaged many successful TV series, and later instituted the NBC movie of the week, bought the ultracontemporary home at 295 Hermosa Place in 1960—two years before MCA's takeover of Universal Studios and its parent company, Decca Records.

Builder Joseph Pawling pulled out all the stops: a push-button sliding glass ceiling, African marble floors, and interior waterfalls that dominated the living room and dining area. Designed by Harold Levitt, this splendid five-bedroom residence "with its understated landscaping and secluded pool area," observed Wasserman's biographer Dennis McDougal, "was a perfect location for entertaining prospective clients, presidential aides, and priapic business associates." There, Wasserman and his wife, Edie, served cocktails and hosted generous luncheons and dinners, attended by agency founder and noted ophthalmologist Jules Stein, as well as agency partner Ronald Reagan and company stockholder Alfred Hitchcock.

"Sundays were reserved for their inner core of friends," said weekend guest and agency client Janet Leigh.

The absolute rule, however, was *no business!* All present observed a strict loyalty oath: "We never met. We never talked." At work, however, Wasserman was a fearsome adversary, inspiring fear and loathing in those who crossed his path. But he had a tender side that could charm and flatter those around him.

During a visit to Wasserman's plush estate, Universal's president Milton Rackmil fell for Gladys Stryker, a gift shop manager at the Racquet Club. Wasserman gave Rackmil the keys to his new home and told them to relax and enjoy themselves. The couple did, and they subsequently married. (Gladys Rackmil has since become a successful TV producer.)

In 1973, the year he was presented a special Oscar for his humanitarianism, Wasserman, who had worked his way up from a movie usher to account executive, was named chairman and CEO of MCA-Universal, which made the blockbusters *American Graffiti, Jaws, E. T., Back to the Future,* and *Jurassic Park.* Following a huge $5.7 billion company buyout by Edgar Bronfman Jr., owner of the Canadian distillery Seagram's, Wasserman, a 1995 Presidential Medal of Freedom winner, hung up his dark suit and tie. Two years later, he donated his Palm Springs home with the ghosts of countless parties past, to the UCLA Foundation. He died at eighty-nine in 2002.

★　★　★

Samuel Goldwyn, the tall, idiosyncratic movie mogul with an amusing knack for mangling the English language, but whose impeccable taste put him, literally, head and shoulders above the rest of Hollywood's "in" crowd, was a Palm Springs social fixture for several decades. A founding member of Famous Players-Lasky (renamed Paramount), Metro-Goldwyn-Mayer, and United Artists, he became a wealthy independent producer, winning numerous Academy Awards and other honors for his high-quality screen adaptations of *Dodsworth, Wuthering Heights, The Little Foxes, The Pride of the Yankees,* and *The Best Years of Our Lives*—the recipient of seven Oscars including Best Picture of 1946—the same year he was awarded the Irving Thalberg Memorial Award.

Goldwyn's "discoveries" included Ronald Colman, Miriam Hopkins, Eddie Cantor, Merle Oberon, David Niven, Teresa Wright, Joel McCrea, Dana Andrews, Virginia Mayo, Danny Kaye, Vera-Ellen, and Farley Granger, whom he showcased, along with Gary Cooper, Barbara Stanwyck, Bob Hope, Loretta Young, and Cary Grant.

Top: Judy Garland near the end of the rainbow (Wayne Knight Collection). *Bottom:* Samuel Goldwyn taking charge (Larry Edmunds Bookshop).

Actors weren't the only commodities that Goldwyn valued. He also had under contract at different times the stylish directors Sam Wood, John Ford, and William Wyler, as well as distinguished playwright Lillian Hellman and noted screenwriter George Oppenheimer. His most-cherished discovery, though, was his handpicked chorus line of shapely Goldwyn Girls, among them Virginia Bruce, Claire Dodd, Jean Howard, and a fledgling Betty Grable.

Goldwyn possessed a spontaneous wit and became famous for his twisted malapropisms, typified by these off-hand comments: "A verbal contract isn't worth the paper it's written on," and "I had a great idea this morning, but I didn't like it," or this pointed remark: "Anyone who goes to a psychiatrist should have his head examined." Goldwyn's seemingly mixed-up logic masked a strong business acumen and high intelligence that kept his career going longer than many of his counterparts in the fickle film industry. However, he would not endorse disparaging or subversive films, which makes you wonder how he would have managed in today's climate of moral ambiguity. Perhaps sensing upcoming changes in the industry, Goldwyn—after bringing the hit Broadway musical *Guys and Dolls* and George Gershwin's folk opera *Porgy and Bess* to the screen—quietly bowed out of the business he helped create and retired to this whitewashed, blue-tiled Spanish estate with the arched entranceway at 334 Hermosa Place, where he lived in 1960.

The home's previous owner, James Hammond, first rented the property to Goldwyn in 1955—the same year he gladly accommodated **Judy Garland** and her third husband, **Sid Luft**, in his adjoining house at 1045 North Cahuilla Road. Garland turned down a constant stream of party invitations while recovering from the difficult birth of her third child, Joey Luft. The baby was born two weeks prematurely and arrived just two days before the Academy Awards, which robbed her of an Oscar as Best Actress for *A Star is Born* (the award went to Grace Kelly for *The Country Girl*). It was Garland's last child, and she asked the doctor to tie her fallopian tubes after the delivery, according to biographer David Shipman.

Two years earlier, **Desi Arnaz** and **Lucille Ball** rented 334 Hermosa Place after they wrapped filming on the gag-laden comedy *The Long, Long Trailer*, which they made on summer hiatus from the third season of *I Love Lucy* in 1953. It was the same year her son, Desi Arnaz Jr., was born and two-year-old daughter Lucy Arnaz appeared with her mom on the cover of *TV Guide*. The home's design, like the best of Goldwyn's films, leaned toward the traditional: large rooms with heavy wooden beams, where the contented mogul spent his days reading books or playing tennis and croquet on the lawn. At night, he ate a simple dinner with his wife, Frances, and son Sam Jr. Afterward they'd sit in the den, drinking brandy and playing cards.

In contrast, the home's prior occupant, who rented it in 1950, was extroverted British director **Edmund Goulding** of *Grand Hotel* fame. He directed Gloria Swanson's first talking picture, *The Trespasser*, and was married for four years to professional ballroom dancer Marjorie Moss. It is here that Goulding, attired in his trademark blue blazer and white trousers, allegedly held Bacchanalian costume parties and bisexual orgies attended by the likes of Greta Garbo, Joan Crawford, and Cecil Beaton—the effete photographer to Britain's royal family.

The famous woman's director was particularly titillated, it's been said, at the notion of two of his favorite male actors, Errol Flynn and Tyrone Power, having sex with one another under his roof. Goldwyn, a firm believer in family values, would have had none of that. In 1962, more than one thousand people attended the devout producer's eightieth birthday party at the Beverly Hilton, including many Palm Springs celebrities and friends, among them William Wyler, Jack Benny, Danny Kaye, and Leonard Firestone. Frank Sinatra and Eddie Fisher sang a medley. Harpo Marx and Jimmy Durante performed "Inka Dinka Doo." Then amid rapt applause, Loretta Young kissed him on the cheek.

Goldwyn left a $16-million estate when he died at age ninety-four in 1974. Veteran entertainment lawyer **Seymour Lazar**, who represented Woody Allen, Lenny Bruce, and the Beatles, has owned this history-laden home for the past thirty years.

★   ★   ★

Film executive **Leo Spitz**, whose distributing company International Pictures merged with Universal, lived at 417 West Hermosa Place from 1950 until his death in 1956. This seven bedroom, nine-bathroom home, built in 1937, features an antique Italian-tiled swimming pool—valued at more than $300,000. While Universal-International's president, Spitz and production chief William Goetz, who was married to Louis B. Mayer's oldest daughter, Edith, oversaw the making of such profitable films as *The Egg and I*, *The Killers*, and *The Naked City*—helping turn the small studio into a major Hollywood player with diversified interests.

In 1957, barnstorming promoter **Mike Todd**, the inventor of Todd-AO, the high-definition, wide-screen process that provided unsurpassed visual clarity of cornfields in *Oklahoma!*, air travel in *Around the World in 80 Days*, and volcanic islands in *South Pacific*, leased the home from Spitz's widow.

Todd was looking forward to a carefree vacation with his third wife, Elizabeth Taylor, and her two children, Christopher and Michael Jr., from her previous marriage to actor

Mike Todd and Elizabeth Taylor doting on her sons Christopher and Michael Wilding, Jr. (Courtesy of Palm Springs Historical Society).

Michael Wilding. They ate, swam, and shopped together. The group was not to return to its Palm Springs idyll.

On March 22, 1958, a few hundred miles from White Sands Missile Range, the same desolate spot where Todd had filmed the high-speed rocket launch that ended the historic prologue to *Around the World in 80 Days*, his private plane, "The Lucky Liz," carrying Todd and biographer Art Cohn from Burbank to New York City where he was to be named Showman of the Year at the Friars Club, streaked from out of the sky and back to earth like a blazing comet, exploding in a blinding shower of fireworks near Grants, New Mexico.

Taylor was ill with bronchitis and had stayed at her Beverly Hills home that unlucky day. She allegedly awoke from her feverish sleep at the precise moment her husband died and had to be heavily sedated when informed he had, in fact, perished. Two years later, the five-time Oscar nominee recuperated from meningitis on Spitz's two-acre property with her fourth husband, singer Eddie Fisher, at her side. The interior of this richly furnished home, which was purchased by Seattle attorney Kenneth Shellan in 1994 for $1.5 million, is reportedly decorated with priceless works of art by Dali, Picasso, Renoir, Rembrandt, Chagall, Modigliani, Erte, and Remington.

★　　★　　★

A more recent convert to Palm Springs is Tony and Grammy award-winning songwriter **Jerry Herman**, who has been compared to Irving Berlin for his emotionally charged, toe-tapping songs. He is the only lyricist-composer, it's claimed, to have had three shows each run for more than fifteen hundred performances on Broadway: *Hello, Dolly!, La Cage aux Folles*, and *Mame*.

Herman has bought and sold twenty-six homes, including a New York penthouse and a mansion in Bel Air.

"This wasn't some hobby, you understand. It became my profession," he said. "I worked full time at this second career, and I made lots and lots of money at it."

Herman remodeled the former honeymoon cottage of Elizabeth Taylor and Michael Wilding in Beverly Hills, as well as Howard Hughes' bachelor pad on Londonderry Place in Los Angeles. He found the experience both rewarding and challenging, and it provided him with a much-needed outlet for his abundant creativity.

Inevitably, this passion for design work led him to the desert where Herman purchased and refurbished in toto the reputed former house of **Dinah Shore** at 432 West Hermosa Place. This seven-thousand-square-foot, five-bedroom home sits on nearly two manicured acres with mature citrus trees, a rose garden, a fifty-foot black-bottom swimming pool, and a tennis court. Built in 1965, the glass-and-stone compound was reportedly designed for the singer, variety show hostess, and talk show pioneer by modernist architects Donald Wexler and Richard Harrison.

The only problem with this piece of trivia is that it's not true. Shore never lived at this address, which will come as a shock to the hundreds of fans that take snapshots daily from passing tour buses. Here's the actual scoop: When Shore and actor George Montgomery divorced in 1962, she fell in love with Maurice Smith, a local building contractor and tennis player. They were married in 1963 and moved to a new home at 432 North Hermosa Drive—a totally different address in an entirely different neighborhood, which has since been redeveloped (now the Greenhouse condominiums). How this confusion started is a matter of debate, but the best guess is somebody didn't know his (or her) north from west. The home's real owner at that time was Palm Springs jeweler William Burke, who died in 1970. Five years later, the property was split into two parcels of land, and neighbor Kirk Douglas purchased a quarter of an acre to build an adjoining tennis court.

In 1976, James Greenbaum, a philanthropic Louisiana businessman whose charity fundraisers have attracted many big-name entertainers, including "Mr. Television" himself, Milton Berle, acquired the existing house from Burke's estate. Jerry Herman, who bought the property from Greenbaum in 1995, sold the remodeled home for $1,725,000 in 1999. It quickly sold again for $2,599,000.

The family of **Harry Grabiner**, secretary and vice president from 1939 to 1945 of the Chicago White Sox baseball team, were longtime villagers. They rented Raymond Cree's former home, at 442 Hermosa Place, where his brother, Joseph Grabiner, and wife Mary lived for ten years. On February 2, 1936, Grabiner's sedan overturned in the rain near Cabazon. The rain had washed away part of the treacherous road causing Harry to lose control of his car, which skidded in the mud and flipped over four times. It was reported that Al Jolson administered first aid until help arrived. Grabiner's daughter was brunette actress June Travis, another village resident. Travis was signed by Warner Brothers to a seven-year contract, where she played opposite James Cagney in *Ceiling Zero* and Ronald Reagan in *Love Is On the Air*.

Los Angeles KTLA-TV *Talk of the Town* personality **Toni Holt** and her husband, Santa Monica automobile dealer Robert Kramer, are the owners of this historic estate, built in 1928, at 457 Hermosa Place, where **Donald Duncan**, president of Duncan Meter Corporation, inventor of Good Humor ice cream, and originator of the spinning "yo-yo," lived in 1951.

Among Duncan's dinner guests at the rollicking home, erected by T. A. Hood, who is credited with building the Miami to Key West causeway, were famed *American Weekly* illus-

Tap-dancing queen Ann Miller (Cinema Collectors).

trator Henry Clive and his Sioux Indian wife, Acquanetta. They visited here when Clive was commissioned to paint an oil portrait of the meter man's wife. It was also here at a cocktail party in 1949 that an enraged Frank Sinatra slugged Duncan's bartender, Jack Wintermeyer, for not giving him an *extra dry* martini!

Ann Miller, who danced up a storm with Sinatra and Gene Kelly in *On the Town*, was too darn hot in *Kiss Me Kate*, but kept her cool in *Hit The Deck*, and her third husband, oil magnate Arthur Cameron, later acquired the home from Duncan. Duncan died in 1971 after being allegedly "muscled" out of the parking meter business by the Chicago mob. By then Miller, whose love of dancing is exceeded only by her taste for moneyed men, had already been twice more married and divorced from ironworks king Reese Milner and millionaire William Moss.

With her plaid shirt, hand-stitched jeans, and full-length boots, **Zaddie Bunker** could have been mistaken for a country farmer or a lesbian. In fact, this widowed, doughty pioneer, who built Palm Springs' first movie theater and handled the city's first motorized mail and passenger service, was an honorary colonel in the U.S. Air Force when she lived at 474 Hermosa Place in 1965. Known as the Flying Great-grandmother, Bunker became the first woman pilot to break the sound barrier in 1961. She died, age eighty-one, in 1969.

Multibillionaire Las Vegas casino owner **Kirk Kerkorian** played a lot of tennis with National Rifle Association hero Charlton Heston at 735 Prescott Drive, which Kerkorian purchased in 1970. Described as "a poor man's Howard Hughes," the eighty-five-year-old Kerkorian—who was recently the subject of a failed paternity suit by thirty-something tennis pro Lisa Bonder—was an eighth-grade dropout and one-time used car salesman when he founded a small airline. He eventually traded it for Transamerica stock worth millions.

The wily entrepreneur later borrowed more money and bought the Flamingo Hotel, merged it with his fifteen-hundred-room International Hotel, then took over failing Hollywood giant MGM—for whom Heston starred in *Skyjacked* and *Soylent Green*—all in 1969. Kerkorian cut back the studio's film production, sold its valuable back lots, and auctioned off props and costumes to help finance the MGM Grand Hotel in Las Vegas. In 1981, MGM bought out United Artists, a successful corporate merger that lasted ten years and continued the money-spinning *Rocky* and *James Bond* franchise.

★ ★ ★

In 1966, **Robert L. Lippert Sr.**, a one-time Alameda theater owner and drive-in promoter, whose company Lippert Pictures made more than two hundred low-budget films, most of them in the Western and science fiction genres, lived at 875 Prescott Drive. Called "The Quickie King" by *Time* magazine, Lippert's brilliant moves included casting a bespectacled George Reeves as Superman and selling hot buttered popcorn to hungry movie audiences. While in charge of 20th Century-Fox's second unit division, Lippert produced such films as *Murder, Inc.*, *Cabinet of Dr. Caligari*, and *Curse of the Fly*.

★   ★   ★

One name from the desert's past that made a big impact on its future is **Carl Lykken**, the first postmaster of Palm Springs, who lived at 242 West Mountain View Place in 1946. Lykken served under Presidents Woodrow Wilson, Warren Harding, and Calvin Coolidge, in addition to operating the city's first mercantile store, which he established in 1914 and where customers purchased dry goods and availed themselves of the only mail service and telephone line in the village. Lykken died in 1972 age eighty-seven.

★   ★   ★

San Francisco theater owner **Homer Curran**, who created Broadway's musical extravaganza *Song of Norway*, moved into the six-bedroom home at 325 West Mountain View Place shortly before Curran, in failing health, played his last encore at the age of sixty-seven in 1952.

Thirty years earlier, the Curran Theatre, which stands at 445 Geary Street, opened to the San Francisco public. Its rose, tan, and blue interiors, twenty rows of brown leather seats, four hundred crystal chandeliers, embroidered blue and purple curtain, and pastoral wall murals receiving high praise as "the handsomest theatre on the coast."

Broadway theater impresarios Sam and Lee Shubert helped Curran raise the initial investment of $800,000 to build the 1,667-seat theater, which was the regular venue of the San Francisco Civic Light Opera. In 1993, the theater was extensively renovated to accommodate the five-year run of Andrew Lloyd Webber's hi-tech stage musical *The Phantom of the Opera*. Curran's former Palm Springs home sold for $1.65 million in 2000.

★   ★   ★

In the summer of 1983, gung-ho TV producer **Glen A. Larson**, who created the prime-time hits *Battlestar Galactica*, *Knight Rider*, *Magnum P.I.*, and the Palm Springs detective series *P.S. I Luv U*, bought the Moroccan-style home that looms large on 328 West Mountain View Place. A former member of the Four Preps, whose hit songs include "26 Miles" and "Down By the Station," Larson struck ratings gold with the detective buddy series *It Takes a Thief* and *Alias Smith and Jones*, launching the one-time singer on a successful producing career.

Actors are not the only people who suffer delusions of grandeur. In the mid-1970s, Larson found himself in *mucho agua caliente* when James Garner, the cantankerous star of *The Rockford Files*, ambled up to the cocky hit maker and punched him for allegedly stealing scripts and reworking them for a rival TV series *Switch*, starring Robert Wagner and Eddie Albert. Larson's desert showplace, where he entertained clients and friends with the latest films and disco music, was built in 1940. The palatial home, which boasts seven bedroom suites, sits on two acres and includes a private screening room with two-tier seating and mandatory projection booth where Larson watched rough cuts of his weekly TV shows.

An earlier resident was pioneering meteorologist **Irving P. Krick**, who predicted the best time for the burning of Atlanta in *Gone With the Wind*, when hundreds of gallons of gasoline ignited old movie sets on the MGM back lot.

On December 10, 1938, the wind-free night that mastermind David Selznick lit the match sending flames roaring into the Los Angeles sky, three captains and thirty firemen stood ready with water hoses in case the blazing inferno jumped the studio walls and ignited surrounding homes in Culver City.

Exuding confidence, Selznick told the hundreds of onlookers not to worry—even though the film's producer had to take several steps back to avoid getting singed by the roasting heat. Krick's correct weather prediction saved the day, however, and the only things that went up in flames were fake storefronts and wood sidings as planned. Seven Technicolor cameras recorded two sets of stunt players dressed as Rhett Butler and Scarlett O'Hara dashing through thick jets of fire and dense smoke, which remains the highpoint of the most-popular film of all time.

Krick also selected the ideal weather conditions for the D-Day invasion of Normandy on June 6, 1944, when nine army divisions, including three airborne and six infantry, from the United States, Great Britain, and Canada crossed the English Channel on five thousand ships under heavy clouds, landing on the coast of France. Like a scene from a Hollywood war movie, which would be reenacted for the screen many times, one thousand airplanes dropped camouflaged paratroopers and amphibious craft deposited 130,000-armed troops into waist-deep water on five beaches.

In part because of the accuracy of Krick's long-range weather forecast, which afforded invading troops the element of surprise, allied forces were able to secure the beachhead within a few hours. It was the turning point of the war in Europe.

Krick was unable to prevent one calamity, however: the burglary of his own home, previously owned by bandleader Eddie LeBaron. In the early hours of January 18, 1974, four men wearing stockings over their heads and brandishing a .44 magnum handgun entered the house through an unlocked door, sexually assaulted his sleeping wife, Marie, and pistol-whipped their twenty-three-year-old son, Irving Jr. They escaped with $200,000 of jewelry and other personal items, including a 38-carat diamond ring valued at $50,000, and $1,600 cash. Now that's a story Larson should have filmed.

★ ★ ★

The Mountain View Place home, which Larson sold for $2 million in 1997, has another distinction beside Irving Krick's prognostications. It was the final residence of **Gene Autry**, Hollywood's first singing cowboy, who died from lymphoma in 1998, age ninety-one. A longstanding Saturday matinee attraction, the lariat-waving, guitar-plucking Autry, accompanied by his dimwitted sidekick Smiley Burnette and faithful horse Champion, starred in nearly one hundred musical Westerns, whose titles often doubled as songs—*Tumblin' Tumbleweeds*, *Mexicali Rose*, and *On Top of Old Smoky*, to name but a few. These "oaters" included several catchy tunes that Autry wrote himself and gladly sang at the drop of his white Stetson: "That Silver-Haired Daddy of Mine," "Back in the Saddle Again" (his theme song), and the Yuletide ditty, "Here Comes Santa Claus."

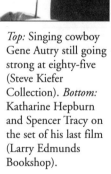

Autry's extensive business interests, financed with the money he made from movies, numbered assorted hotels, oil wells, ranches, and media companies, such as Los Angeles TV station KTLA, which he purchased in 1964, and the Autry Museum of Western Heritage, established by him in 1988. In Palm Springs, where the much-loved entertainer spent his winters, Autry owned Melody Ranch (formerly Holiday Inn), where he billeted his California Angels baseball team during local practice.

At the time of his death, Autry had accumulated a vast fortune, estimated at more than $200 million, much of which he personally deposited at Security Pacific Bank, where the actor's second wife, Jacqueline Ellam, whom he married in 1981, was vice president.

★   ★   ★

Robert Hanson, the wealthy playboy-son of British industrialist Lord Hanson, owner of Quantum Chemicals and Eastern Group, purchased 460 West Canyon Place (off Mission Road) in 1991. A cutthroat businessman and horse-racing enthusiast, Hanson Sr.'s past loves included Joan Collins and Audrey Hepburn, to whom he was engaged for one year. (Peter Giles played Hanson to Jennifer Love Hewitt's Hepburn in the TV movie *The Audrey Hepburn Story*). Son Robert was featured prominently in British tabloids throughout the 1990s trying vainly to match his father's amorous conquests.

Top: Singing cowboy Gene Autry still going strong at eighty-five (Steve Kiefer Collection). *Bottom:* Katharine Hepburn and Spencer Tracy on the set of his last film (Larry Edmunds Bookshop).

★   ★   ★

It's unlikely that **Katharine Hepburn** tended to an ailing **Spencer Tracy** at 776 North Mission Road, as claimed, during desert filming of *It's a Mad, Mad, Mad, Mad World* in 1963. That's because Tracy stayed with Hepburn at Kirk Douglas's house on Via Lola instead.

"They had lived together for several years while pretending publicly that they were just good friends," producer-director Stanley Kramer commented about Hepburn's love for Tracy, who died in 1967. Yet despite her great affection for him, Hepburn boycotted his funeral, stating he had refused to marry her.

Buddy Rich, hailed as the world's greatest drummer for his astonishing precision, energy, and speed, practiced the drums on the same street at 775 North Mission Road. Rich's exuberant personality and versatile big band style made him a favorite with jazz and swing buffs alike, and he recorded many top-selling albums.

"The beats never stopped," said Suzanne Somers, who toured with Rich while on hiatus from *Three's Company* in 1980. "It translated to his hands until it built to an incredible orgasmic frenzy night after night."

Although he was sidelined by a serious heart attack in 1983, Buddy was back on the road two months later, bringing audiences to their feet with his fast-paced drum solos. He died from brain cancer in 1987. Rich's one-time home sold for $770,000 in 1990.

Twenties cowboy hero and former rodeo champion **Hoot Gibson** demonstrated his expert horsemanship in two hundred silent and sound films, ranging from the John Ford two-reeler *Action* to the exciting one-hour feature *Spurs*. Married to actress Sally Eilers, Gibson reputedly built the home at 481 Merito Place. A top box-office star for more than a decade, Edmund Gibson earned his unusual nickname, he explained, when children hooted at him during his early days as a Los Angeles deliveryman for the Owl Drug Company. He died in 1962.

New York Irish actor **William Gargan**, an Oscar nominee for the adulterous comedy, *They Knew What They Wanted*, lived at 478 Merito Place with his real-life wife, Mary Kenny, in 1940. Twenty years later, Gargan lost his gruff voice when his larynx was removed during an operation to cure him of throat cancer, prompting the mute actor, who died in 1979, to ask the soul-searching question "Why Me?"—the title of his autobiography.

Sultry nightclub entertainer and civil rights activist **Lena Horne**, whose electrifying appearances lit up the screen in *Cabin in the Sky* and *Stormy Weather*, swam every day down the street at 465 West Merito Place where composer Roger Edens, who won Oscars for *Easter Parade*, *On the Town*, and *Annie Get Your Gun*, played piano whenever he visited her. Because of widespread racial discrimination, Horne, whose interracial marriage was kept a secret for three years, had purchased the home in the late 1950s "under an assumed name," according to biographers James Haskins and Kathleen Benson.

Horne's white husband, musical arranger and conductor **Lennie Hayton**, a two-time Oscar winner for *On the Town* and *Hello, Dolly!*, with whom she enjoyed playing Scrabble, died here from a heart ailment in 1971. Horne sold the house after a jewelry robbery at Christmas 1974. Another Oscar-nominated visitor, Sidney Lumet, who was married to Horne's daughter, Gail Jones, later directed his mother-in-law as Glinda the Good Witch in the all-black Emerald City remake, *The Wiz*.

★   ★   ★

Emmy-winning TV comedienne and nightclub monologist **Lily Tomlin**, who originated the pinch-faced character of Ernestine, the nosy telephone operator on *Laugh-In* and gained a bigger audience via the big screen where she was nominated for a Best Supporting Actress Oscar in Robert Altman's *Nashville*, fantasized about murdering her boss with Jane Fonda and Dolly Parton in *9 to 5*, and played Steve Martin's female alter ego in *All of Me*, among other memorable comic roles, owned the house at 443 West Merito Place, which she bought in 1997.

A lesbian in every way except by name (she astutely avoids any mention of the word), Tomlin used the well-hidden house as a personal retreat, where she spent several months each year with her lifetime partner, Jane Wagner. They have collaborated together on six comedy television specials and two feature films: *Moment by Moment*, with buffed costar John Travolta; and *The Incredible Shrinking Woman*, a clever spoof on the dangers of product consumerism.

Tomlin's well-honed ability to prick society's collective conscience rather than marginalizing the sexes is what separates her from lesbian propagandists such as Sandra Bernhard, Melissa Etheridge, and Ellen DeGeneres, although she has appeared in the pro-gay films *And the Band Played On* and *The Celluloid Closet*. Tomlin's home sold for $995,000 in 2003.

★   ★   ★

In 1939, Hollywood scriptwriter **Claude Binyon**, a former newspaper journalist who ten years earlier penned the attention-getting *Variety* stock market crash headline, "Wall Street

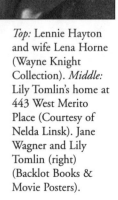

Top: Lennie Hayton and wife Lena Horne (Wayne Knight Collection). *Middle:* Lily Tomlin's home at 443 West Merito Place (Courtesy of Nelda Linsk). Jane Wagner and Lily Tomlin (right) (Backlot Books & Movie Posters).

Lays an Egg," put his feet up on the couch at 348 Merito Place and rewrote his screenplay for *Arizona*, starring William Holden, then embarked on the song-filled Bing Crosby vehicles *Dixie* and *Holiday Inn*. Thirteen years later, Binyon directed Dinah Shore in *Aaron Slick from Punkin Crick* and Bob Hope in *Here Come the Girls*. He died in 1976 at seventy-two.

★ ★ ★

Lithuanian-born actor **Laurence Harvey**, whose best roles were as a ruthless social climber in *Room at the Top* and a brainwashed political assassin in *The Manchurian Candidate*, commissioned the large compound at 300 West Merito Place in 1969. Harvey, who costarred with John Wayne in *The Alamo* and romanced his neighbor Elizabeth Taylor in *Butterfield 8*, although they were hardly on the best of speaking terms (he called her "the Bitch" and "Fat Ass" behind her back), lived here while married to his second wife, Joan Cohn. He died from stomach cancer in 1973. The flagstone-walled house, called "Villa Serena," is now worth a reported $1.85 million.

★ ★ ★

Gallant expatriate Australian actor **Rod Taylor**, who showed great sensitivity as Irish playwright Sean O'Casey in *Young Cassidy* and revealed a surprising gift for comedy as Jane Fonda's suitor in *Sunday in New York*, drank his fill of margaritas at 271 Merito Place, but still managed to go jogging most mornings. Taylor—father of New York's WNBC Channel 4 coanchor Felicia Taylor—lived there for five years with his third wife, Carol Kikumura, whom he met on the set of the TV series *Hong Kong* and married in 1980. George Rosenthal, the owner of Raleigh Studios, where such classic movies as *Whatever Happened to Baby Jane?* was filmed, bought Taylor's home in 1989.

Top: Laurence Harvey (Steve Kiefer Collection). *Bottom:* Rod Taylor sunbathing (Courtesy of Rod Taylor).

★ ★ ★

Snap! Crackle! Pop! **William Keith Kellogg**, whose Battle Creek, Michigan, factory produced millions of boxes of Corn Flakes invented by his older brother, John Harvey Kellogg, occupied 141 West Chino Drive (since demolished) in 1939. Five years later, Kellogg moved to new premises at 427 Tamarisk Road. He died in 1951. (Kellogg's much-talked-about celebrity neighbor, Clark Gable, was rumored to have lived at 222 West Chino Drive, but did not actually buy a house in the desert until he moved to Bermuda Dunes Country Club with fifth wife Kay Spreckles shortly before his death from a heart attack in 1960.)

★ ★ ★

Syndicated newspaper gossip columnist **Dorothy Manners**, who interviewed practically every movie star that ever twinkled for *Photoplay* and other top-selling fanzines, lived at 456 North Belardo Road in 1955 with her long-suffering husband, John Haskell. Manners, like her bitchy predecessor, Louella Parsons, whose column she took over from 1965 to 1977, was well schooled in the art of Hollywood scuttlebutt, knowing exactly how much sugar and vinegar to mix for a juicy tidbit or other tasty morsel about so-and-so's secret love affair, aborted pregnancy, or attempted suicide. Of Parsons' long-running feud with archrival Hedda Hopper, Manners, age ninety-five when she died at Hallmark Retirement Assisted Living in 1998, chortled, "Louella hated her guts."

If age is a state of mind, then ageless is the term that best describes The Cloisters, a rambling Spanish-Mexican colonial at 226 West Alejo Road (renumbered 501 North Belardo Road). Lush gardens, bubbling fountains, and paved courtyards lend an air of peace and serenity. The tiled roofs, observation tower, and white stucco walls create the impression that this stately building might well have been a monastery.

But there was nothing monastic about the life of its former owner, **Wladziu Valentino Liberace**, the flamboyant concert pianist who spent half of every year here for nearly two decades and where he died from AIDS, amid a frenzy of media controversy, in 1987. This was Liberace's fourth and last Palm Springs home, not counting two others he purchased nearby for his brother, George, and their elderly mother: a total of six consecutive houses—which may be a local real estate record.

The Cloisters is steeped in history. In 1930, Alvah Hicks, who built approximately twenty homes in the Vista Acres subdivision, according to his grandson Jim Hicks, including Our Lady of Solitude Church, which conveniently sits across the street, finished construction of a three-bedroom house on this corner site named "Villa Teresa" in honor of his wife. Hicks also owned Palm Springs Water Company, which supplied the valley's liquid life force (founded by Scottish settler John McCallum, a former Indian agent and land developer).

The growing Hicks family lived in the house until 1936 when they sold it to Ludovica Graham, a wealthy Reno, Nevada, socialite who turned the modest home into an elegant showplace. In quick succession, she built two more bedrooms and expanded the living area, adding more annexes to the property. Graham's house became renowned for its Saturday soirees, attracting carriages filled with guests. By this time, the house contained five bedrooms, a huge family room, formal dining room, full kitchen with butler's pantry, and two large trunk-storage rooms, not to mention the huge Olympic-size swimming pool where people gathered from all over town for cocktails and dinner.

In 1945, Graham sold the home to retired commercial furrier Walter Glatter, who added a barroom. Fifteen years later, Muriel Fulton, a local realtor, purchased the house from Glatter with the intention of turning it into an exclusive hotel. Fulton's business partner in the venture was the prominent Pasadena architect Wallace Neff, who had designed more than two hundred homes for superrich clients, including Los Angeles oil millionaire Edward Doheny, Culver City real estate developer Harry Culver, and *Los Angeles Times* publisher Norman Chandler.

Described by his son, Wallace Neff Jr., as "a master of the California Mediterranean idiom," Neff's specialty was Spanish-revival architecture, typified by his use of graceful archways, enclosed courtyards, sheltered patios and verandahs, high wood-beamed ceilings, and lofty entrance halls with grand staircases.

Neff had remodeled the plush Pickfair estate in Beverly Hills and created the private domains for such Hollywood luminaries as Louis B. Mayer, Darryl F. Zanuck, King Vidor, Douglas Fairbanks Jr., Charlie Chaplin, and Joan Bennett. In addition, he created four different homes for Metropolitan opera star Amelita Galli-Curci, a San Diego resident. Brad Pitt and Jennifer Aniston recently paid $13.5 million for a Beverly Hills mansion that Neff designed for actors Fredric March and Florence Eldridge in 1934.

Fulton and Neff changed the five bedrooms into self-contained guest suites. They converted the family room into a lobby and made the dining room a banquet room. A small, separate building, originally built as a vault, was converted into a tearoom. Separate hallways connected all the rooms, which opened onto four patios leading to the swimming pool. Fulton, overjoyed, christened the house The Cloisters—a place, she said, "where you can get away from it all." Six years later, owing to poor business, the hotel closed.

When Liberace bought The Cloisters for a reported $185,000 in 1967, it was rundown and badly in need of repair. He lavished a lot of time and spent $136,000 restoring the hotel to its former glory. The ceilings, floors, gallery, and tower remained, but everything else was changed. The original roof was removed and each handmade tile repaired and replaced. The guest suites were redecorated as theme rooms, and a small chapel was installed with a stained-glass window—previously it had been the snack bar. Crystal chandeliers were hung from the ceilings and gold-leafed mirrors fastened to the walls.

Liberace spared no expense on The Cloisters, and he delighted in taking visitors on guided tours of his dazzling home. He even gave it a new name: "Casa de Liberace."

"The art in the Gloria Vanderbilt Suite includes the Liberace memorabilia collage that Miss Vanderbilt created especially for me and presented to me on *The Mike Douglas Show*," he gushed in 1985. "The Valentino Room [named after Rudolph Valentino] features the sleigh bed from Falcon's Lair, the legendary star's Hollywood home," he raved. "There is also the Zebra room and, off the pool, the Persian Tent Room."

Christmas was the most-cherished time in Liberace's home. Before sixteen people sat down for dinner, a church choir would sing carols in the garden, and a priest said Mass in a shrine dedicated to Saint Anthony, filled with burning incense, where Liberace prayed each day.

"For extra guests," he winked, "I reserve nearby private villas, which are decorated with Christmas poinsettias in advance of their arrival."

Each departing guest was presented with terry-cloth robes and slippers, plus Liberace sandalwood soaps made in the shape of small pianos. But there was a darker side to Liberace. After moving in, he filled the house with his vast collection of priceless antiques, assorted bric-a-brac, and male pornography. There were nonstop parties and countless orgies where Liberace danced naked and had Greek-style sex with sixteen-year-old French boys.

That's not all. Aside from owning several valuable pianos and a fleet of vintage cars, it was said Liberace also operated illegal slot machines that he kept in the basement. Police later allegedly confiscated the one-armed bandits, and somebody, presumably an angry "trick," gave Lee a black eye. In 1982, Liberace's former "live-in" male companion, Scott Thorson, sued him for $100 million after he was thrown out of the house and replaced by a new boyfriend. Thorson, who had undergone expensive and painful cosmetic surgery to look like his pianist-lover, received only a fraction of that amount—$95,000.

Although Liberace's prudish mother, Frances Zuchowski, strongly disapproved of her son's gay lifestyle, she seemed strangely oblivious of these and other sordid goings-on while living next door at 274 West Alejo Road. After she died, the home was bought by

Casa de Liberace's dining room (Howard Johns Collection).

gift shop owners Vince Fronza and Ken Fosler. Liberace prevailed upon them to cut a hole in the wall so they could visit each other, and the three men became fast friends.

Despite his foibles, Liberace brought considerable glamour back to Palm Springs at a time when glamour and the city were in decline. His memorable holiday dinners, major shopping excursions to Bullock's and Saks Fifth Avenue, and frequent restaurant visits to Delmonico's, helped boost the local economy. Liberace's final days were reportedly spent in bed watching his favorite TV show, *The Golden Girls*, surrounded by his beloved family: two Chinese Shar-Peis, Wrinkles and Prunella; a West Highland terrier, Lady Di; a chow, Suzie Wong; and Gretel, a Dutch keeshond.

When the end grew near, a priest was summoned to administer the last rites. Two days later, Liberace drew his last breath as fans stood crying outside, some of them holding candles, others clutching rosary beads and flowers. A black hearse slowly arrived as news helicopters swooped low overhead and tabloid photographers scaled the walls. It was complete pandemonium. Police arrested a handful of trespassers, and several women fainted. Hundreds of mourners, many of them celebrities, packed Our Lady of Solitude Church for a memorial service where Father William Erstad read telegrams from President Ronald Reagan and First Lady Nancy Reagan, praising Liberace as a gifted musician, a caring individual, and a kind man who brought much joy to the world and left a rich legacy of memories.

Shortly after Liberace's death, it was announced that developers planned to turn the entertainer's home into a private museum. Then-mayor Sonny Bono toured the estate, but the city was unable to reach a logistical or financial agreement. In 1990, most of the household contents were sold to raise money for the Liberace Foundation for the Performing and Creative Arts. More than three thousand items ranging from small knick-knacks to large luxury automobiles, with an estimated value of half a million dollars, went under the auctioneer's gavel at the Plaza Theatre. Among the items sold: a red boat-tailed Auburn speedster, a white-and-gold Steinway piano, and a black mink bedspread embroidered with Liberace's candelabra logo. The home itself, however, remained unsold, tainted by the specter of AIDS.

Later that year, however, Stefan Hemming, a real estate investor from San Francisco, purchased "Casa de Liberace" for $725,000. He spent another $100,000 on improvements and furnishings. Hemming even managed to track down many items previously owned by Liberace and returned them to their rightful place. Los Angeles designer Bret Barber assisted with the renovations. Old plumbing and electrical wiring were replaced, rooms freshly painted, and broken statues reattached. It was long, hard work, but the results were well worth it. The home attracts hundreds of curious visitors to the city each year.

Looking out over the outlying homes and shops, is "Ojo del Desierto" or Eye of the Desert, the Mediterranean Revival-style home with red-tile gable roof and second-story verandah, which was designed and built in 1925 by Charles Tanner for **Thomas O'Donnell**, the president of California Petroleum Company, who resided at 447 West Alejo Road. It was O'Donnell who founded the city's first golf club, where Bob Hope, Jack Benny, Hoagy Carmichael, Bing Crosby, and Ben Hogan played on the "members only" nine-hole course, called Desert Golf Club, now O'Donnell Golf Club (entrance: 301 North Belardo Road).

Chapter 4
The Strip

Palm Canyon Drive, the teeming hub of local tourism and commerce known as "the Strip," connects the main sections of the city like an enormous heart pumping blood into the myriad of arteries that make up its surrounding streets. The two-mile long thoroughfare was originally called Main Avenue. It was renamed Palm Canyon Boulevard in 1930, and it's where circus parades and rodeo festivals thrilled crowds of onlookers for nearly five decades.

Indian Canyon Drive is of equal significance. It was here (now the Spa Hotel, 100 North Indian Canyon Drive) that Indians gathered food and lived in palm-thatched *ramadas* many hundreds of years ago. Today, the names of pioneers and Hollywood luminaries who have made important civic contributions are engraved in approximately 200 granite stars that are embedded along both sidewalks.

A casual stroll, stopping at the many pavilions selling antiques and souvenirs, rekindles memories of long-lost movie palaces, fashion boutiques, and malt shops where residents and tourists gathered each season. Chromium-plated storefronts, striped canvas awnings, and neon-lit signs have come and gone, but much of the day-to-day visage remains the same.

Billy Reed's, which is named after the impish vaudeville performer who danced "Tip-Toe Through the Tulips With Me" in *Gold Diggers of Broadway* and who later operated the New York niteries El Morocco, Copacabana, and the Little Club, opened for business at 1800 North Palm Canyon Drive in 1974—the same year that Reed, age sixty, died from a heart attack in New York City.

At the nadir of her media infamy, the constant subject of probing investigations on NBC's *Dateline* and Court TV, she was pegged America's Most Wanted Woman for scamming insurance companies, blowing up houses, and killing trusted friends and employees. Her face and name were printed on New York Police Department handouts distributed all over the city. She is **Sante Kimes**, now serving 130 years in federal prison for the cold-blooded murder of New York socialite Irene Silverman, ending a thirty-year spree of professional grifting, credit card fraud, and slavery that took the blowzy housewife from Los Angeles to Washington, D.C., the Bahamas, and back again.

Kimes's trail of deadly deception began in 1968 when she lived with her con artist-lover Clyde Wainwright at the Fountain Hotel at 1777 North Palm Canyon Drive. Wearing her Elizabeth Taylor-like getup of flowing white lace gown, bustier, oversized sunglasses, black wig, and turban, she engaged in stealing cars, clothes, furniture, and food while preying on the rich and gullible.

It was in Palm Springs that this gardenia-scented sociopath, then known by her married name Sante (pronounced *Shan-tay*) Walker, courted William Holden and Trini Lopez, bilked millionaire airline owner Robert Prescott, and finally set her sights on Kenneth Kimes, the wealthy builder of ten luxury hotels, including the Arabian-themed Mecca Hotel opposite Disneyland and the 150-room Polynesian-style Tropics Hotel, located on East Palm Canyon Drive.

Here, the unscrupulous Walker, in between dodging subpoenas and hiding from police, seduced Kimes into a fake marriage, making him a submissive Clyde Barrow to her domineering Bonnie Parker, hitting the road together for twenty years of cons, thefts, burglaries, and arson fires that ended with his own death, which she covered up, and her eventual arrest in 1998.

★   ★   ★

In 1982, curly-haired "insult" comedian **Sammy Shore**, who was Elvis Presley's opening act at the Las Vegas Hilton International for four years and also warmed up concert audiences for Diana Ross, Ann-Margret, and Tony Orlando, ran La Siesta Villas, a nineteen-room hotel, designed by Albert Frey at 247 West Stevens Road (off North Palm Canyon Drive). Shore, who considered himself a summertime pioneer, practiced new jokes on unsuspecting guests while he manned the front desk.

Talk about showbiz career turnaround. Just ten years earlier, Shore's name had been ablaze in neon lights up and down L.A.'s Sunset Strip when he founded the Comedy Store—the same place that Freddie Prinze, Gabe Kaplan, Robin Williams, David Letterman, and Jim Carrey were discovered and jive-talking Richard Pryor staged his famous free-basing comeback.

But a nasty temper aggravated by binge drinking side-railed Shore's career, and he lost the club to his soon-to-be ex-wife Mitzi Saidel, who still reigns supreme on the comedy circuit as Mitzi Shore. Their son, if you haven't already guessed, is MTV comedian Pauly Shore, star of *In the Army Now* and *Jury Duty*. His kid sister is comedy event producer Sandi C. Shore, who spots new talent and books club acts.

★   ★   ★

Go two blocks east, and you'll find the former site of **Bono's Restaurant** at 1700 North Indian Canyon Drive where George Hamilton, Joan Collins, and Sylvester Stallone ordered steaming veal and chicken entrees from Gucci-clad host Sonny Bono. Bono opened his third trattoria, costing $100,000, here in 1986—three years after founding his first restaurant, which he described as "the hottest hangout in LA," on the site of a boarded-up taco stand near the corner of Melrose Avenue and La Cienega Boulevard. At the L.A. restaurant, the fifty-year-old entertainer met and fell in love with Mary Whitaker, a twenty-two-year-old USC graduate working two waitressing jobs.

★   ★   ★

Riviera Resort
(Howard Johns
Collection).

Irwin Schuman's **Riviera Resort** at 1600 North Indian Canyon Drive is where Frank Sinatra organized several of his big charity shows with Rat Pack members Dean Martin and Sammy Davis Jr., who sang and clowned about on the stage of the thirteen-hundred-seat Mediterranean Room. Patterned after its more-famous Las Vegas cousin, the Palm Springs Riviera, designed by Pacific Palisades architect Homer Rissman at a cost of $3 million in 1959, was the city's first resort hotel boasting 250 rooms, four tennis courts, an eighteen-hole golf course (now the Riviera Gardens), and the largest Olympic-size heated swimming pool in Southern California. It's still going strong forty-five years later.

★   ★   ★

Musical Knights bandleader **Horace Heidt** owned and ran the star-filled **Lone Palm Hotel**, which stood at 1276 North Indian Canyon Drive, on the corner of Paseo El Mirador, well into the 1960s. Bert Wheeler, the smiling, baby-faced half of the slaphappy comedy team Wheeler and Woolsey that starred in 1929's Technicolor musical romp *Rio Rita*, was a hotel guest in 1938, the same year his partner, Robert Woolsey, died of kidney failure.

Frank Sinatra, his first wife, Nancy Barbato, and their family stayed here on the singer's first trip to the desert in 1944. Liberace spent the summer of 1953 as a guest of

Bandleader Horace Heidt between musical numbers (Wayne Knight Collection).

Heidt's TV director Louis "Duke" Goldstone, who also supervised the pianist's weekly half-hour variety show. Rock Hudson, who shot to stardom in *Magnificent Obsession* and *All That Heaven Allows*, slept in separate beds with fiancée Phyllis Gates in 1955. In the mid-fifties, Heidt grudgingly decided to curtail his swing and rumba dances and devote more time to his real estate holdings, which included a 180-unit senior living apartment complex in Sherman Oaks. He died there in 1986.

★   ★   ★

In 1957, **Hoagy Carmichael** was president of **Barbara Wills Interiors**, where they designed living spaces for preferred customers at 1078 North Palm Canyon Drive whenever the composer grew tired of writing songs and wanted to play decorator.

★   ★   ★

Dorothy Gray Women's Clothing in the Brown-Gray Building at 1074 North Palm Canyon Drive was headquarters of Dorothy Gray, the fashion consultant-wife of producer Harry Joe Brown, who as a young child gave angelic performances in the films *Princess O'Hara* and *Three Russian Girls*.

★   ★   ★

Attorneys, agents, and accountants were encouraged to lease office space at the **Sol Lesser Building** at 1050 North Palm Canyon Drive, where the bespectacled *Tarzan* producer would routinely show up on the first of every month to collect the rent.

★   ★   ★

If you hung out with the stars, chances are that you and they would ask hosts George and Ethel Strebe for your regular table at the **Doll House** (later Sorrentino's Seafood House) at 1032 North Palm Canyon Drive, where dining celebrities were serenaded by Guadalajara Chuy and his Muchachos.

If the Doll House was full, and it was on many nights, you'd dash across the busy street and order a Hawaiian steak and several Mai Tai's in one of the candle-lit amber wicker booths of **Don the Beachcomber** at 1101 North Palm Canyon Drive on the corner of Via Lola. It was here that gossip columnist Rona Barrett saw Joan Collins's fiancé, Warren Beatty, make a drunken pass at Robert Wagner's wife, Natalie Wood, on a triple date with the Kirk Douglases and Tony Curtises in 1961. (Note: Although it's been closed for two decades, six gas tiki torches still observe passing traffic from the restaurant's wood shingle roof.)

★   ★   ★

Sunset Tower Apartment Hotel, directly next door at 140 Via Lola, was a bachelor's paradise for many celebrity headline grabbers who owned or leased penthouses there in 1956. Among them were Sacramento political lobbyist Arthur Samish, who received millions of dollars in bribes from the liquor and trucking industries. He moved here after being paroled from federal prison where he served two years for tax evasion. El Mirador hotel owner and high-stakes gambler Ray Ryan, who rubbed Chicago mob bosses the wrong way when he reportedly cheated on a card game, played five-stud poker in his executive suite with oil producer George Cameron Jr., Zeppo Marx, the fourth Marx Brother, who starred with his exuberant siblings in five films, moved into an upstairs apartment after divorcing Marion Benda. Two years later, Zeppo, who ran a theatrical agency with fifth brother Gummo, won the heart of Las Vegas show girl Barbara Blakeley, and they became husband and wife.

Alan Ladd's widow, **Sue Carol**, the Charleston-dancing star of *Girls Gone Wild* and *The Exalted Flapper*, purchased the **Spanish Inn** (now boarded up) at 640 North Indian Canyon Drive in 1972. After being closed for a decade, it is poised to reopen, the same year that the family hardware store that Ladd founded closed its doors.

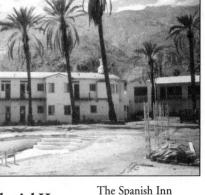

The Spanish Inn undergoing extensive renovation in 2003 (Photo by Howard Johns).

In 1951, Los Angeles millionaires **Bob** and **Andrea Howard** bought the **Colonial House**, a luxury two-story hotel with white colonnades and a red tile roof at 572 North Indian Canyon Drive, on the corner of Via Colusa, where long verandahs provided dramatic vistas of the surrounding city and mountains.

Built in 1936 by Al Wertheimer, a member of Detroit's iniquitous Purple Gang, the forty-four-room hotel featured a high-class restaurant and bar, as well as a "members only" Key Club—an illegal gambling casino that could only be reached through a secret passageway in the basement.

Prominent local architect Stewart Williams and artist/designer O. E. L. Graves were hired to remodel the plush hotel, which reopened for the 1952 season as Howard Manor. It featured live entertainment by such renowned singers as Diahann Carroll. Three-time world heavyweight champion Jack Dempsey and his fourth wife, Deanna Paitelli, whom he married in 1958, maintained a permanent suite. It's now the Palms—a private health resort.

Two blocks west, bouncy teenage performer **Peggy Ryan**, who sang and jitterbugged with Donald O'Connor in a dozen Universal minimusicals decades before moving to Hawaii and playing Steve McGarrett's secretary on *Hawaii Five-O*, welcomed students to her dance academy at 400 North Belardo Road (now American Legion Post headquarters) in 1965.

Sy DeVore not only lived in Palm Springs, but he sold high-quality sportswear and haberdashery at 249 North Palm Canyon Drive in 1959, where the likes of Sammy Davis Jr., Elvis Presley, and Ricky Nelson, stocked up on coats, pants, and other accouterments. One time, in need of a new wardrobe, Liberace, on the suggestion of William Holden, consulted DeVore who threw out the pianist's oversized "zoot suits" and fitted him in elegant white tails for his Hollywood Bowl concert. The makeover created such a lasting impression that Liberace asked DeVore to design him a gold lamé smoking jacket, gray silk suit, and black tuxedo with gold polka dots for the film *Sincerely Yours*.

Ruby's Dunes (now Hair of the Dog) at 238 North Palm Canyon Drive was the popular watering hole for glassy-eyed movie stars and shady characters that had been a part of the bar's scenery since it first opened for business in 1941. Everyone from frog-voiced crooner Phil Harris and his wife, Alice Faye, to Frank Sinatra and chain-smoking Harry Guardino went there. Owner Irwin Rubenstein's wife, Connie Barleau, sang and played the piano.

True story. One night, Kirk Douglas and Burt Lancaster were enjoying several rounds of cocktails in a booth when a drunk walked in, sat down next to the cleft-chinned one, and started melting him with his bad breath. "Mr. Mitchum," the drunk blabbed to Douglas, "I want to tell you how great you were in *Trapeze*!" Lancaster, who was the film's ignored star, laughed so much he nearly choked on a pretzel.

But for sheer showmanship, you couldn't (and still can't) surpass Irwin Schuman's souped-up version of the Stork Club, 21, Mocambo, and Ciro's rolled into one big, fat, smoke-filled supper club called **Chi-Chi** that stood at 217 North Palm Canyon Drive for thirty years and where, if you were wearing the appropriate attire and had a well-stacked dame on your arm, five bucks and fifty cents got you ringside seats to see Sophie Tucker, Milton Berle, Peggy Lee, Nat "King" Cole, Lena Horne, Sammy Davis Jr., Rosemary Clooney, Tony Martin, Ella Fitzgerald, or Louis Armstrong and his All Stars any night of the week.

This eye-boggling sight wasn't that different from the ancient Indian custom of tribal ceremonies or *fiestas* that took place hundreds of years earlier on the same ground. Men and women adorned in turquoise jewelry and beaded moccasins smoked tobacco and fraternized with one another—except that cars have since replaced ponies as the preferred mode of transportation. It's hardly surprising that the dark-skinned natives addressed their white neighbors as *Mel-ki-chem*—the noisy people.

Chi-Chi nightclub headliners (Courtesy of Bill Alexander).

Desert folklore says that Frank Sinatra met his second wife, Ava Gardner, at Chi-Chi in 1950. It was late in the evening. Ol' Red Eyes was dancing with Lana Turner, and Howard Hughes was trying to keep up with Southern belle Gardner. When the bandleader said, "Change partners," Frank and Ava danced off together and ended up waltzing back at Sinatra's house.

Mae West presented her campy nightclub act at the club's celestial Starlite Room. The "act" consisted of six bulging musclemen parading around the spot-lit stage in leopard skin loincloths while black comedienne Louise Beavers, dressed in a maid's uniform, served tea to a corseted West, who reclined provocatively on a chaise longue covered in eiderdown—fluttering her eyes and cooing like a pigeon. One of the men in the group, Paul Novak, soon became the aging star's live-in companion, chauffeur, bodyguard, and personal trainer. Cary Grant raved about the show for weeks. Ann Sheridan was also a big fan.

Mob boss Sam Giancana, a veteran of more than seventy police arrests with links to organized crime stretching across three states, took a special interest in the singing careers of the McGuire Sisters, whose three-part harmony of "Sincerely," "Moonglow," and "Sugartime" made them the darlings of the dinner-show circuit. Giancana was so smitten by Phyllis McGuire, the youngest and sexiest member of the satin-gowned trio, that he ordered a fresh bouquet of flowers sent to her dressing room at every performance.

The club's high times, like consuming too much hard liquor, were contrasted by a few terrible lows. In 1960, Dorothy Dandridge, the coffee-colored singing sensation of *Carmen Jones* and *Porgy and Bess*, accepted a last-minute booking to replace MGM's coloratura soprano Kathryn Grayson, who had taken ill. Miss Dandridge's voice was not at its best, however, due to emotional problems, and the show was poorly reviewed. Two years later, Dandridge bravely returned to Chi-Chi's stage for a limited eight-day engagement—one of her last public appearances. Looking stunning in a body-hugging white gown designed by William Travilla, Dandridge mesmerized the audience with her seductive rendering of "What Is This Thing Called Love?" and "Blow Out the Candle."

After the show closed, Dandridge threw a party for the orchestra and slowly got drunk on champagne. On September 8, 1965, the deeply troubled performer was found dead on the bathroom floor of her Hollywood apartment. She was forty-one. The official cause of death was an overdose of drugs used to treat mental depression.

Another Chi-Chi headliner, Marie McDonald, suffered an even more pathetic fate. In 1957, the shapely star, once touted by Hollywood press flacks as "the Body," was discovered wandering in a daze, clad only in her pajamas, along a road near Indio, California. McDonald told reporters she had been kidnapped, but had managed to escape her captors. Later she admitted it was a publicity stunt. Shortly afterward, the washed-up actress was arrested on drug charges, then booked for drunk driving. In 1963, she had a nervous breakdown while touring Australia and was arrested a third time for forging a drug prescription. Finally, two years later, McDonald swallowed a fatal overdose of Percodan.

The end of the great nightclub era when Ciro's filed for bankruptcy and Romanoff's finally went out of business signaled the imminent closure of Chi-Chi, which underwent several changes of ownership until, finally on a hot summer's day in 1977, the building was torn down, its massive center stage, wings, and tiered seating leveled to make room for a shopping center.

★   ★   ★

In 1955, **Marion Davies**, the giggling, ice-cream blonde star of *Show People*, *Hollywood Revue of 1929*, and *Going Hollywood* costarring whisky-sour crooner Bing Crosby, remarked to a friend that it might be nice to own a small bed-and-breakfast. "Wouldn't that be fun?" she lisped. And so, on a whim, Davies purchased the Mission-style **Desert Inn** at 153 North Palm Canyon Drive (now Desert Fashion Plaza and the adjoining Hyatt Regency Suites).

Attorneys Greg Bautzer and Arnold Grant reportedly negotiated the sale of the thirty-three-acre property, numbering one hundred hotel rooms, an à la carte restaurant, beauty shop, barber salon, and parking garage for the giveaway price of $1,750,000, which Davies paid owners Earl Coffman and his brother, George Roberson. The brothers cried when they signed the legal papers giving up the old homestead that had been in their family for three generations.

What Nellie Coffman, a divorced grandmother, started half a century earlier as a healing place for "broken bodies and broken spirits" evolved into an elite hotel for the healthy and wealthy: silent screen greats Billie Dove, Colleen Moore, Anita Stewart, Dolores del Rio and William S. Hart, professional racing car driver Ralph de Palma, U.S. Steel chairman Benjamin Fairless, and Charles Wilson, the vice president of General Motors.

For the convenience of guests, Wall Street stockbroker E. F. Hutton maintained offices next door with a ticker tape for investors to monitor the day's changing share prices. In 1926, Louella Parsons, the motion picture editor for William Randolph Hearst's *New York American*, interviewed English novelist John Galsworthy, author of *The Forsyte Saga*, while both were staying at the inn, where she was recovering from tuberculosis. Upon her return to Los Angeles, Hearst promoted his star reporter to motion picture editor of the *Los Angeles Examiner* and syndicated Parsons's column in five more broadsheets—a post she held for almost forty years.

In 1937, nine-year old Shirley Temple, Hollywood's number one star for five consecutive years, stayed at the inn while her chaperon-mother Gertrude Temple recovered from bronchitis. The curly-haired moppet and recipient of a miniature Oscar passed the time rehearsing "The Toy Trumpet" musical finale from her forthcoming film, *Rebecca of Sunnybrook Farm* with costar Bill "Bojangles" Robinson. Because he was black, Robinson had to make do with a tiny room in the servants' quarters.

When MGM songbird Jeanette MacDonald was felled with the flu midway through production of *San Francisco*, the studio's expensive re-creation of the 1906 earthquake, she was flown in Amelia Earhart's private plane to Palm Springs for several days recuperation at the inn.

Marion Davies and gay leading man William Haines (Courtesy of the Academy of Motion Picture Arts and Sciences).

"Jeanette returned, tanned and rested but still underweight," claimed biographer Edward Baron Turk, "to film her scenes from the frilly operas *Faust* and *La Traviata*."

Hot on her heels were Oscar-winning pantomimist Charlie Chaplin and his third wife, Paulette Goddard, *Andy Hardy* actress Ann Rutherford with May Company department store co-owner David May, *Duel in the Sun* author Niven Busch, actor John Payne and singer-wife Gloria de Haven, who met at the inn for cocktails each afternoon at Jimmy Van Heusen's Piano Lounge.

In 1953, veteran CBS news commentator Lowell Thomas made his sixth annual radio broadcast from the Fiesta House at the Desert Inn, where he was nursing a broken leg suffered in a skiing accident. Fans of the wide-screen travelogue, *This is Cinerama*, which Thomas narrated and produced, banged on windows and doors hoping to see him. "What does he look like?" someone asked. "I don't know," replied a young man standing on an apple box. "I just know his voice!"

Marion Davies, who had been spoiled her entire adult life, was the perfect choice to run a hotel: She knew how to pamper stars. A once-promising comedienne whose desultory screen career had been bankrolled by newspaper publisher William Randolph Hearst at a loss of $7 million, Davies, despite critics' barbs about her adulterous relationship with the grandfatherly Hearst, was well liked by virtually everyone.

"Marion, an utterly genuine person, had no illusions about her talents," said David Niven.

Although people sometimes made fun of the high-spirited actress because of her nervous stutter, Davies must have learned a thing or two from her megabucks sponsor because she eventually became wealthy in her own right, acquiring office buildings in New York and Los Angeles, a seven-acre estate in Beverly Hills, a 110-room Santa Monica beach house, and property in Palm Springs, as well as thousands of acres of land in Vera Cruz, Mexico.

However, the acquisition of the Desert Inn was a "toy" in comparison with the lumbering 127-acre Mediterranean-style Hearst Castle at San Simeon, complete with its own art museum and private petting zoo, where Davies, dressed in pink, ruled like a Chinese courtesan over busloads of excited guests who were wined and dined then stuffed like human olives into each of the 165 ornamental bedroom suites. Davies' absurdly monied lifestyle—depicted none too flatteringly by Orson Welles who renamed her Susan Alexander in *Citizen Kane*—hid an underlying history of family alcoholism that contributed to the early deaths of her invalid mother; a teenage brother who died in a boating accident; the suicide of her young niece; one sister who drowned in the family's swimming pool; another who choked to death on a piece of steak; and lastly, Davies herself, who, ravaged by years of consuming too many gin fizzes and pink ladies, was diagnosed with cancer of the jaw.

In 1960, Davies sold the Desert Inn for $2,500,000, "making a considerable profit on the deal, as she usually did in real estate ventures," claimed her biographer, Fred Lawrence Guiles. When she died eighteen months later, conservative estimates put the sixty-four-year-old's personal wealth at $20 million.

★   ★   ★

Director Charles Walters (left) welcomes Bing Crosby to his menswear store (Courtesy of Palm Springs Historical Society).

Resort wear for gentlemen was the specialty of **Chuck Walters Presents** at 137 North Palm Canyon Drive. The openly gay film director, who displayed signed photographs of star-friends Bing Crosby, Lucille Ball, Fred Astaire, Judy Garland, Peter Lawford, and Esther Williams, managed the boutique with tailor Manuel Alvarez in between supervising left-footed actors, limp-wristed choreographers, and over-the-hill chorus girls in more than two dozen musical films.

★   ★   ★

Built in 1924 by Pearl McManus, whose orderly Sunday attire was accented by a pearl necklace, bracelet, and earrings befitting her cultured name, the **Oasis Hotel Building** at 121 South Palm Canyon Drive (hotel entrance: 177 West Tahquitz Canyon Way) was designed by second-generation architect Lloyd Wright. His foppish father, Frank Lloyd Wright, was a leading proponent of "organic architecture," which he considered superior to all other man-made designs.

Lloyd Wright had closer ties to Hollywood than many working architects. He contributed set designs for a number of films, as well as designing private homes for actors Ramon Novarro, Claudette Colbert, and Raymond Griffith. He also crafted an early version of the Hollywood Bowl's elliptical acoustic shell (now the center of a preservation battle) where music lovers have gathered for outdoor symphony concerts for more than seventy years.

Wright's blueprint for the Oasis, set amid orange groves and cottonwood trees, included a large fountain, patio court, and ninety-foot dining room heated by charcoal braziers on chilly winter nights. When it first opened, the stylized concrete pueblo attracted desert newcomers John Wayne, Spencer Tracy, and Loretta Young, who customarily stayed on the top floor in the forty-foot Mayan Tower with its fusion of moderne interiors and American Colonial copper and leather furnishings. In 1943, the hotel's new owner, Dewey Metzdorf, expanded the 42-unit hostelry to 125 rooms.

Metzdorf was one of four frostbitten survivors of a 1943 Alaskan air disaster that killed two other passengers when their Lockheed aircraft crash-landed near Annette

Island. The men were stranded in subzero temperatures for thirty-three days. Metzdorf, the vice president of Western International Hotels (now Westin Hotels & Resorts), died from a heart attack one day before his sixty-eighth birthday on February 9, 1966.

★　★　★

The historic **Plaza Theatre** at 128 South Palm Canyon Drive is shrouded in history like an Egyptian mummy. If this was a hidden tomb and an archaeologist broke it open, the cheering ghosts of hundreds of singers, dancers, jugglers, and acrobats would escape into the air.

Dayton, Ohio, architect Harry Williams designed this three-story terraced Spanish Colonial as the centerpiece of the Plaza, a two-story shopping center and apartment complex reportedly commissioned by Julia Carnell, wife of National Cash Register cofounder Frank Patterson. The project employed a small army of stonemasons who labored on its construction for two years.

The Fabulous Palm Springs Follies (Photo by Brian Davis).

On December 12, 1936, the curtain went up on a sneak preview of MGM's much-trumpeted Parisian love story, *Camille*, starring Greta Garbo and Robert Taylor. Ralph Bellamy, the evening's smiling emcee, got a big laugh when he asked the largely ambivalent Hollywood audience, which included the film's two stars, "You really don't want to watch a movie tonight, do you?"

Since that history-making day, thousands of ticket buyers have trooped up and down the wooden aisles to applaud such big marquee names as Jack Benny, Bob Hope, Bing Crosby, Dinah Shore, and Eddie Cantor. For the past decade, the theater has hosted the Fabulous Palm Springs Follies, a high-kicking parade of geriatric crooners, chorines, and chorus boys. Who said vaudeville was dead?

★　★　★

Bernard of Hollywood photographed some of Tinseltown's brightest stars behind the glass doors of his walk-in studio at 138 South Canyon Drive (now Birkenstock Shoes) in 1945. One can only imagine the household names that had their faces photographed here for posterity: Clark Gable, John Wayne, Rita Hayworth, Kirk Douglas, Robert Mitchum, Marilyn Monroe, Gregory Peck, and others.

★　★　★

In the swank jewelry store of **Andrea of Palm Springs** at 193 South Palm Canyon Drive, proprietor Andrea Leeds, who looked like she had just stepped out of a beauty parlor, never faltered in her belief that the customer is always right, showing off her exclusive collection of gold bracelets and diamond rings.

★   ★   ★

The hip, San Francisco-style **Muriel's Supper Club** (now Atlas Restaurant & Dance Bar) at 210 South Palm Canyon Drive was packed to its metal rafters in 1999 for the opening-night appearance of Eartha Kitt, who had tables of long-time admirers of both sexes caterwauling at the slinky singer's double-entendre songs. Following Miss Kitt's show-stopping, one-night act was Nancy Sinatra and k.d. lang, who serenaded two hundred fans there in November 2000. This is the congested gateway to Arenas Road, the city's "red-light district," where gays and lesbians eat, drink, and make merry in one of several restaurants and honky-tonk saloons, which include Badlands, Rainbow Cactus Café, Tomboyz, Streetbar, and Hunter's Video Bar.

★   ★   ★

Thirty-five years ago, the biggest concern of Palm Springs law enforcement was controlling water fights during spring break when college kids drank too much beer and some teenage girls found themselves pregnant. Hot rods were all the rage; so was the Twist. Loving couples frequently peered in the curtain-fringed windows of **Jolie Gabor Pearl Salon** at 219 South Palm Canyon Drive, which the canary-frocked Gabor purchased from previous storeowner Claudette Colbert.

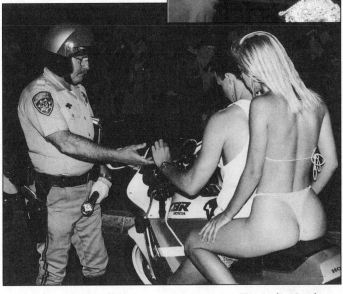

Top: Andrea Leeds weighs her jewelry (Courtesy of Palm Springs Historical Society). *Bottom:* A police officer stops a teenage motorcycle rider during spring break on Palm Canyon Drive (Photo by Steve Kiefer).

The moment Colbert upped and left, Gabor replaced her high-priced collection of imported objets d'art with cultured pearls and costume jewelry priced from $5 to $5,000.

The gems are long gone. The space is now occupied by the Agua Caliente Cultural Museum and is in the Village Green at 221 South Palm Canyon Drive, the home of McCallum Adobe—the city's oldest remaining building. Built in 1885, McCallum Adobe sits between Ruddy's General Store and Miss Cornelia White's Little House, a few of the remaining relics from the desert's outmoded past.

★   ★   ★

Modernism in all its architectural forms is common in everyday desert life—from gas stations and banks to schools and department stores. What separated the marble and quartz diametrical design of **Robinson's Specialty Shop** (now the Alley) at 333 South Palm

Canyon Drive from Bullock's, W & J Sloane, Saks Fifth Avenue, and other contemporary buildings that are now a distant memory on the Palm Springs Strip, however, is this store's gold anodized aluminum fascia created by Hollywood production designer William L. Pereira and his partner, Charles Luckman.

Pereira-Luckman were jointly responsible for designing some of Southern California's most-impressive commercial structures: the Marineland aquarium, Los Angeles International Airport, Malibu campus of Pepperdine University, and the pyramid-shaped Transamerica building in San Francisco. The preppy, urbane Pereira, who shared an Oscar for Best Special Effects on 1942's *Reap the Wild Wind*, was the younger brother of Hal Pereira, the supervising art director of Paramount's Melrose Avenue studios for twenty-five years and himself a twenty-three-time Oscar nominee and winner for *The Rose Tattoo*.

Bill Pereira, however, felt unfulfilled constructing movie sets, so he decided to build real buildings instead. The first of these was Robinson's Department Store in Pasadena, followed by CBS Television City, Disneyland Hotel, and Los Angeles County Museum of Art.

"Big Chief" Frank Sinatra with bar owner Jilly Rizzo (right) (Courtesy of Palm Springs Historical Society).

Jilly's at 424 South Indian Avenue (later Flower Drum Restaurant), run by Sinatra's shadow, Jilly Rizzo, was modeled after the popular Manhattan West Side establishment of the same name—featured in many Sinatra films from *The Manchurian Candidate* to *The Detective*—that attracted the likes of lounge singers Gordon MacRae and Jack Jones to its oak-paneled bar, where they ordered freshly cooked delicacies such as king crab and prime rib and ran up huge bar tabs with manager Eddie King. In 1974, Jilly's moved to a new location at 262 South Palm Canyon Drive (now the Chop House).

Afterward dining at Jilly's, everyone jumped in their sedans and sports cars and drove around the corner to **Pal Joey's** at 233 East Saturnino Road for a nightcap. This swinging discotheque, run by Sam Bianco and Joe Hanna, was named in honor of Sinatra's 1957 film of the same name, in which "Mr. S" crooned the sardonic love song "The Lady Is a Tramp" to a peeved Rita Hayworth. It was here that waistcoated, bell-bottomed nightclubbers Lucille Ball, Harold Robbins, Victoria Principal, and her boyfriend, Andy Gibb, whiled away the late-night hours drinking at the bar and dancing the Hustle.

★　★　★

Tony Roma's at 450 South Palm Canyon Drive was hardly on a par, say, with Morton's or La Dome, but for greasy barbecued ribs, it was considered to be among the best. What separated this family restaurant from the other 260 outlets in 27 different countries, however, was that its ingenious founder wasn't just a world-famous name—he dined at the restaurant and lived here, too. A five-year South Palm Springs resident until his death, age seventy-eight, in 2003, it was Roma (real name: Anthony Lopresti) who invented the tasty red sauce that chef David Smith ladled over the charbroiled beef and cobs of corn they sold at Roma's first rib joint in North Miami, Florida. Three months after Roma's passing, the Palm Springs location closed.

★   ★   ★

Another local landmark is **Alan Ladd's**, at 500 South Palm Canyon Drive, on the east corner of Ramon Road. The Ladd family-owned retail store, selling hardware items, painting supplies, home appliances, and sporting goods, opened in late 1955 in partnership with contractor Bob Higgins, who had attended North Hollywood High School with Ladd.

"During construction, Alan was on the scene every day," trumpeted *The Palm Springs Villager*, "watering the seeded lawn and practically stopping traffic on South Palm Canyon Drive. The tourists couldn't believe their eyes!"

Neither could some of the city's residents, who were slack-jawed at the sight of Ladd himself making the rounds each day behind the wheel of a delivery truck. This was no mere publicity stunt, however. Ladd personally welcomed customers to the store where his son, David, was paid twenty-five cents an hour to dust shelves while his staff filled orders. The bold retail venture, continued *The Villager*, seemed to be in "keeping with the trend of other film and stage personalities who not only have established homes here, but have acquired businesses (primarily hotels) as testimony to their belief in the unlimited future of this resort area."

After nearly forty-six years in business, however, when it diversified into selling exclusive gifts and other merchandise, the store abruptly closed in mid-2002. The new owners, who have negotiated a license with the Ladd family to keep the building's gold-plated name, plan to lease the downstairs floor space and upstairs loggia to a group of select tenants.

★   ★   ★

Bob Lippert's Steak House (now Pizza Hut) at 1180 South Palm Canyon Drive was managed by the same barnstorming father-and-son movie producers who owned Desert Ho Hotel (now La Posada) in Palm Springs and later built the Thunderbird Hotel in Indio. Lippert's modestly made Westerns and science fiction flicks turned a hefty profit for distributor 20th Century-Fox when other much costlier undertakings such as *Cleopatra* and *Doctor Dolittle* nearly bankrupted the studio. The studio was forced to sell off its famous back lot, which was redeveloped as Century City.

In 1972, Paul Di Amico took over Lippert's restaurant, renaming it Di Amico's

Steakhouse and turning it into a popular meeting place for Frank Sinatra, Harry Guardino, Governor Jerry Brown, and several former legislators representing Riverside County. It was here that Republican Congressman Jerry Lewis, then a 67th District assemblyman, was introduced to Frank "Big Frank" Matranga, a reputed Los Angeles organized crime figure. It's been theorized Di Amico's unsavory clientele, like Big Frank, may have led to his problems, though Paul himself was unable or unwilling to provide any clues.

What is known is that on April 13, 1989, Di Amico's Steakhouse suspiciously caught fire and burned to the ground. Fire marshals said the blaze had all the characteristics of a hot, fast-paced fire that was accelerated with the use of a petroleum product. No arrests were made. Three years later, Di Amico's bookkeeper, Roger Smith, was kidnapped from a bank parking lot, robbed, and shot to death. Finally, on June 27, 1994, a second arson fire destroyed Di Amico's new restaurant that he had opened a few blocks away. The inferno, which broke out in the mezzanine level where a framed oil painting of Frank Sinatra hung on the wall, took twenty-seven firefighters two hours to bring under control. By that time, the building was a burned-out shell. The three crimes are still unsolved.

Casa Blanca Motor Hotel (now Musicland Hotel) at 1342 South Palm Canyon Drive (southeast corner of Morongo Road) was once owned by low-budget filmmaker Al Adamson and his wife, actress Regina Carrol. There they billeted their casts and crew, most of whom were washed-up actors, go-go dancers, and Hell's Angel bikers. Thirty years on, it's still a place for drifters and people with no fixed address. Adamson's own addresses in Los Angeles, Palm Springs, and Las Vegas were much spiffier. He later moved to Indio where he was found murdered in 1995.

Continuing southeast, blond, well-coiffed decorator extraordinaire Bill Hamilton, George's younger brother, welcomed clients to **Eva Gabor Interiors** at 190 East Palm Canyon Drive, where the cultivated Hungarian actress, who later launched her own collection of shag-style and bobbed wigs, could be found several days a week at her office desk supervising design layouts.

Chapter 5

Tennis Club Chatter

The Tennis Club district, which takes its name from the modernistic sport's establishment of the same name at the far end of Baristo Road, spans several blocks west of Palm Canyon Drive—from Tahquitz Canyon Way, where such widely known local personages as Cornelia White, Pearl McManus, and J. Smeaton Chase's widow lived in stone cottages at the base of the mountain—east to Belardo Road and south to Ramon Road.

This low-lying area, once covered by fruit orchards, is now mostly a patchwork of baroque hotels and inns quaintly named Apache Lodge, Arenas Gardens, El Poco, Holiday House, Korakia, La Serena, Orchid Tree, San Marino, and Skye Jordan. Desert Hills, for example, was built in 1956 on part of the old Pearl McManus property. Estrella Inn underwent a $4-million renovation in 1997. Among the other hotels that have been refitted and given new names are Andalusian Court, Chase, Coyote, and Orbit.

Desert Museum at 101 Museum Drive has been publicly supported by private contributions ever since its conception as a stuffed wildlife exhibit in 1938. Former presidents, ambassadors, movie stars, and business leaders are some of its major benefactors.

The present-day museum building and 450-seat Annenberg Theater, which was constructed from multicolored brown, sienna, and charcoal-colored volcanic rock in 1976, offers a wide-ranging display of art—from Native American and European masters, to abstract and pop. In 1995, architect Stewart Williams came out of retirement twenty years after designing the original premises to oversee construction of the Steve Chase Art Wing and Education Center—a $10-million, second-story addition that houses, among other valuable items, permanent collections of Asian, African, and Western art that were bequeathed to the museum by William Holden and George Montgomery.

George Roberson, whose mother Nellie Coffman owned the Desert Inn, built the Mediterranean/Spanish Revival stone-walled house located at 385 West Tahquitz Canyon Way in 1924. It is reputed that General George S. Patton, among other visiting dignitaries, once sat in Roberson's sitting room and smoked cigars. The design is credited to Alfred Heineman, the younger brother of Glendale bungalow-court architect Arthur S. Heineman, who coined the term "motel." (Some sources give credit to Charles Tanner.) The home was part of Tahquitz Desert Estates. Roberson died in 1968.

Today, the stately, well-preserved home complete with brick-tiled verandah and Colonial fireplace is Le Vallauris, the much-lauded French restaurant owned and operated by Paul Bruggemans, who previously ran Le St. Germain in Hollywood. Diners ordering meals on the sun-dappled terrace of the old Roberson home have included *TV Guide* publisher and foreign diplomat Walter Annenberg, Firestone Tire & Rubber Company president Leonard Firestone, as well as Chrysler Motors chairman Lee Iacocca, fashion designers Hubert de Givenchy and James Galanos, and Isadore Sharp, founder of the Four Seasons Hotels. Bruggemans and his partner, Michel Despras, reopened St. Germain in Indian Wells in 1995.

★　　★　　★

Former U.S. Secretary of the Treasury and famed New York attorney **Samuel Untermyer** lived in the Mediterranean villa at 412 West Tahquitz Canyon Way, which is now the Willows Historic Inn. Untermyer, a staunch advocate of various legal reforms, practiced corporate, civil, criminal, labor, family, and international law and administered business affairs for the Rockefellers and Hearsts.

Top: Albert Einstein chatting with Samuel Untermyer (Courtesy of Palm Springs Historical Society). *Bottom:* The Willows Historic Inn (Courtesy of Tracy Conrad).

Built in 1927, Untermyer's eight-room terraced home, where he continued practicing law into his eighties, was a gathering place for many nationally prominent figures of the day, from New York mayor and constant partygoer James "Jimmy" Walker to Swiss aeronautical pioneering twin brothers Auguste and Jean Piccard, who admired the mahogany-beamed frescoed ceilings and solid stone floors. A real curiosity was the visit by German physicist Albert Einstein and his wife, Mileva Maric, who vacationed with Untermyer in 1933 and marveled at the bountiful selection of desert flora and fauna that can still be viewed from the glass portals of this mountainside home.

After Untermyer's death in 1940, his eldest son, Alvin, who was also an attorney, resided here until 1952. Marion Davies later reportedly occupied the home when she owned the Desert Inn. (The assertion that Davies's sister, Rose Douras, who died in 1963, was found dead in the house next door is pure fiction.)

This historic home was restored to its original art deco ambience over a two-year period commencing in 1994 by new owners Paul Marut and Tracy Conrad.

★ ★ ★

In 1963, **Albert Frey**, whose work lives on in the unique designs of so many desert homes and commercial buildings, began construction on a second residence known as "Frey House II," at 686 Palisades Drive, on a private road overlooking the Desert Museum.

"After looking up at the mountains for almost twenty years, I thought it might be nice to live there," Frey professed. The only problem was that nobody could figure out how to build a house on the vertical mountainside. Unlike the relatively simple design of Frey's first house, this project almost defied gravity. Concrete had to be poured in a perfect slab on a steep hill with jagged rock outcroppings. Instead of fighting the elements, Frey decided to incorporate them into the building's contemporary design, hence a large boulder protruding into the living-room and a swimming pool that sticks out two hundred feet above the city skyline.

Frey was justifiably proud of the finished product, which has been featured in numerous magazine photo shoots, and after construction of this unique aluminum, glass, and cinder-block house was completed, he rarely left it. In his nineties, he could still be seen perched like a scarecrow on the rocks, flinging birdseed into the air to be gobbled up by hungry doves and quail.

★ ★ ★

British-born director **James Whale**, whose talent for Grand Guignol sent chills up and down people's spines with his frightening versions of *Frankenstein*, *The Old Dark House*, and *The Invisible Man*, was a worthy Palm Springs candidate. But horror wasn't Whale's only forte. He displayed a genuine love of American musical theater in 1936's *Show Boat* and exhibited a thirst for rousing adventure in 1939's *The Man In the Iron Mask*, starring fellow village resident Louis Hayward.

Campy film director James Whale was a hotel owner (Courtesy of Academy of Motion Picture Arts and Sciences).

Unfortunately, Whale's defiant homosexuality alienated many people around him. When his movie career slowly petered out, he replaced it with traveling and painting. By 1954, having invested his life savings in Los Angeles commercial real estate, Whale owned and operated Town & Desert, an eight-unit hotel designed and built by modernist architect Herbert Burns with a forty-foot, heated pool and complimentary bicycles for guests at 370 West Arenas Road.

Here, shielded by mesquite and tamarisk trees, Whale spent his mornings sketching and afternoons entertaining handsome young men in a poolside cabana—a habit he had picked up after installing a swimming pool in his Pacific Palisades home to ward off the boredom of his early retirement.

"Whale made rather a fool of himself during this period," stated biographer James Curtis, "ignoring his old friends and ogling the bronzed beauties that frequented his home. He sunbathed, waded cautiously in the shallow end of the pool, and kept a pornographic diary from which he occasionally read aloud."

Three years later, in rapidly failing health, Whale threw himself headfirst into his home's beloved swimming pool and drowned, leaving behind a cryptic suicide note. The director's colorful gay life, played by openly gay actor Ian McKellen, was dramatized in the 1999 film *Gods and Monsters*.

San Marino Hotel, which opened for business as Del Marcos at 225 West Baristo Road in 1948, was the first commercial venture of William F. Cody. The architect combined elements of Frank Lloyd Wright's prairie style with European modernism to create a two-story, redwood and stone configuration of sixteen guest rooms arranged in a classic "U"-shape around a twenty-by-forty-foot swimming pool, supplemented by an inner courtyard and overhead walkway. Cody's blueprint received a favorable mention from the American Institute of Architects for its clean and efficient design. (Fifty-five years on, the hotel reverted to its original name.)

Nancy Kulp (center) in *The Beverly Hillbillies* (Steve Kiefer Collection).

When hatchet-faced character actress **Nancy Kulp**, who played Miss Jane Hathaway, the sex-starved bank secretary on TV's *The Beverly Hillbillies*, was diagnosed with cancer of the larynx in 1989, she went to stay at her friend Joseph Baier's house at 377 West Baristo Road. Kulp's condition gradually worsened, and the mannish comedy actress and unsuccessful 1984 Congressional Democratic candidate died here on February 3, 1991, setting off a firestorm of tabloid stories about her lesbianism.

Contrary to what tour bus operators may say, twice-married sixties pop singer **Nancy Sinatra**, who is definitely not a lesbian, although she chanted the suggestively worded disco hit "These Boots Are Made for Walking," never lived at "Villa Nane II," a gated, cypress-lined corner estate at 300 South Patencio Road. For the record, independent oil broker Albert Stevenson of Long Beach is the home's one and only owner.

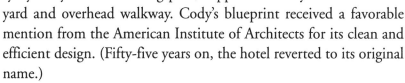

The Tennis Club, where baby-faced sexpot Terry Moore, an Oscar nominee for *Come Back Little Sheba*, posed fetchingly in a two-piece bathing suit while looking skyward, began operation at 701 West Baristo Road in 1937. A former teenage model, Moore's ample bosom attracted the roving eye of Howard Hughes, whom she secretly married aboard his yacht, she said, and later bore him a stillborn baby girl. The couple's desert comings and goings were typical celebrity fodder of the day, when photographers followed them from one hotel restaurant to another, aimed their flashbulbs—and *snap!*

When the Tennis Club was first built by Tahquitz Park landowner Pearl McManus, who had lived on the property as a child, there were bountiful gardens and a trout farm, on which were later constructed two championship tennis courts considered by a number of players to be the best in the world. The V-shaped palm trees set at the back of the oval-shaped swimming pool were widely imitated by landscape designers.

The inspiration for the club's wide terrace was the Capuchin Monastery in Amalfi, Italy. An International-style rooftop restaurant and bar, designed with typical modernistic flair by architects A. Quincy Jones and Paul R. Williams, who also redesigned the Beverly Hills Hotel's Polo Lounge and coffee shop, and created the black-and-white check design of Perino's Restaurant on Wilshire Boulevard, was added in 1946. So impressed were visitors at Williams's unerring ability to create gilded pomp out of mere wood and plaster that he was commissioned to revamp, in rapid succession, the Knickerbocker and Beverly-Wilshire hotels, Chasen's Restaurant, and the Flamingo Hotel in Las Vegas.

The late TV director Alan Rafkin, who handled hundreds of sitcom episodes stretching from *The Dick Van Dyke Show* to *Suddenly Susan*, was an active Tennis Club member until his death in 2001. Founder Pearl McManus's Mediterranean-style villa called "the Pink Mansion," where she died in 1966, was located at 281 South Tahquitz Drive. It has since been replaced by time-share condominiums.

★   ★   ★

Top: Character actor J. Carrol Naish dressed up (Larry Edmunds Bookshop). *Bottom:* J. Carrol Naish's home at 139 South Tahquitz Drive (Photo by Howard Johns).

Swarthy Irish character actor **J. Carrol Naish** was a master of dialects who was the voice of Luigi Basco on radio and later played the proverb-spouting detective Charlie Chan on television. He was a double Oscar nominee for *Sahara* and *A Medal For Benny* when he lived in the two-story home, labeled "Villa Amalfi," at 139 South Tahquitz Drive in 1945. (Note: This is one of five vintage homes in the area known as the Art Colony that are being fully restored by hotel owners David and Trudy Johnston.)

★   ★   ★

The blissful spot where **Rudolph Valentino**, the florid, womanizing star of *The Sheik* and *The Four Horsemen of the Apocalypse*, disrobed and made passionate love to Natacha Rambova on a four-poster bed swathed in soft Egyptian cotton sheets and where after that, rumor has it, British Prime Minister Winston Churchill set up his easel, canvas, and painting brushes is not a desert mirage or a movie back lot—it is Korakia Pensione at 257 South Patencio Road.

Scottish artist Gordon Coutts, a member of the Royal Academy of London, built this historic French-Moroccan style villa with solid pine floors and turret windows, in 1924. An incurable romantic and itinerant traveler, Coutts erected this exquisite desert palace, which he named "Dar Marroc," as a reminder of his days in Tangier. He died from heart failure in 1937. Twenty years later, the hotel, repainted pink, became known as Gracia Grande.

Current owner Douglas Smith, who delights in telling this touching story, purchased Coutt's garden estate in 1988 and refurbished the flaking building. Hollywood personages Ted Danson, Alicia Silverstone, Chris O'Donnell, and Elisabeth Shue are said to have dipped their toes and other extremities, as Valentino once did, in the mosaic-tiled pool.

★   ★   ★

San Marino playboy **Arthur K. Bourne**, whose late father was the director of Singer Sewing Machine Company, commissioned Wallace Neff to design a Mediterranean Revival-style party home for him with a blue-tiled swimming pool at 466 South Patencio Road. Bourne entertained lots of lovelies in the pool's cooling waters and air-conditioned cabana. "Neff grasped the possibilities of Palm Springs readily," his son, Wallace Jr., explained of this home, built in 1933, "as demonstrated by the inclusion of a small second-story room and loggia."

★   ★   ★

Herman Ridder, grandson of the founder of Knight-Ridder, the country's second-largest newspaper group, publishing thirty-two dailies, including the *Philadelphia Inquirer*, *Miami Herald*, and *San Jose Mercury News*, resided at 421 West Santa Rosa Drive for more than twelve years.

★   ★   ★

Top: Korakia Pensione when it was Gracia Grande (Courtesy of Palm Springs Historical Society). *Bottom:* Rudolph Valentino in *The Four Horsemen of the Apocalypse* (Courtesy of Palm Springs Historical Society).

Broken-nosed, oafish-looking **William Bendix**, a 1942 Best Supporting Actor Oscar nominee for *Wake Island*, was unkindly described by one critic as "Neanderthal Man reincarnated in Brooklyn," but he could always be counted on to give effective performances both in comedies like *Woman of the Year* and dramas such as *Lifeboat* and *The Hairy Ape*. He cooled off with a beer in the summertime with his wife, Theresa, at 372 South Monte Vista Drive.

★　★　★

William Gargan, who played dry-humored heroes in nearly one hundred murder mysteries, including three turns as Ellery Queen and the lead on TV's *Martin Kane, Private Eye*, memorized his lines on Nellie Coffman's former estate, where he lived at 115 South Cahuilla Road in 1958.

★　★　★

Polly Bergen, who played the female love interest in a trio of Dean Martin-Jerry Lewis sophomoric comedies, including *That's My Boy*, took a four-year sabbatical from acting and managed Apache Lodge at 161 South Cahuilla Road, where she lived after divorcing her first of three husbands, actor Jerome Courtland, in 1955. Bergen's career received a welcome boost the following year when she married high-powered MCA talent agent Freddie Fields, later the successful producer of *Crimes Of the Heart, Glory*, etc.

The chipper actress and Pepsi spokesperson won an Emmy for TV's *The Helen Morgan Story* and later played Gregory Peck's terrified wife in 1962's *Cape Fear*. Fields, meanwhile, became a familiar sight driving around town making deals for clients Barbra Streisand, Paul Newman, Kirk Douglas, and Peter Sellers on the car phone of his white Bentley. He also chose locations for Richard Gere's breakthrough film, *American Gigolo*, which was partly set and photographed in the desert. But their luxuriant lifestyle came crashing down around them.

"I went from being an extremely wealthy woman living in a four-thousand-square-foot apartment on Park Avenue, and suddenly found myself at one point with $35 in the bank," said Bergen, whose last important role was Robert Mitchum's hobnobbing wife in the TV miniseries *The Winds of War*.

★　★　★

Top: Sue Carol and Alan Ladd with friends Tess and William Bendix (Courtesy of Palm Springs Historical Society). *Bottom:* Apache Lodge owner Polly Bergen (Steve Kiefer Collection).

Harriet Cody, the widow of Harold Cody (the first cousin to Wild West showman Buffalo Bill) and proprietor of the city's first livery stable where Western actors Tom Mix and Jack Holt boarded horses, built the Southwestern-style Casa Cody Bed and Breakfast Inn at 175 South Cahuilla Road. Erected in 1936, the tile-and-stucco hotel was reputedly designed by Myron Hunt, the architect of Caltech, Pomona, and Occidental College campuses, as well as the Pasadena Public Library—listed in the National Register of Historic Places. The main adobe building was extensively damaged in a 1948 earthquake and rebuilt shortly before Harriet Cody's death in 1954 when her daughter Patricia Rogers inherited it. After she died, the seventeen-room property underwent several changes of ownership until Frank Tysen and Therese Hayes acquired the hotel in 1986 and merged it with Apache Lodge.

Artist **Earl Cordrey**, whose watercolor and pastel illustrations of modern-day Americana were featured on everything from soft drink advertisements to *Cosmopolitan* and *Good Housekeeping* magazine covers, sketched and painted in his studio on the grounds of the Colony Bungalows at 430 South Cahuilla Road in 1944. Cordrey, who also designed the city of Palm Springs official seal, did some of his best paintings in Puerto Vallarta, Mexico.

Garbo slept here! Travolta danced! And Minnelli sang! These are just some of the silver screen luminaries who have dined or stayed at the **Ingleside Inn** at 200 West Ramon Road. Originally called Twin Palms, this parklike estate of Spanish eclectic annexed buildings was commissioned in 1922 by Carrie Birge, the widow of George Birge, president of Pierce Arrow Motor Car Company. She resided there from the time the home was built until her death in 1932.

Eight years later, Jackson Hardy, the husband of Ruth Hardy, the city's first councilwoman and former owner of Casitas Del Monte, purchased Birge's home. They reversed the main entrance at 482 South Cahuilla Road to its current address and converted the building into a twenty-nine-room hotel, where operatic soprano Lily Pons, who married musical conductor Andre Kostelanetz in 1938, lived for thirteen years.

On October 12, 1946, star-crossed lovers Howard Hughes and Ava Gardner registered at the front desk under the assumed names of Hughes's mechanic, Earl Martyn, and his secretary, Mrs. Clark. Other famous guests have included Norman Vincent Peale, Salvador Dali, and the family of San Francisco banker A. P. Giannini, the founder of Bank of Italy (precursor to Bank of America).

In 1975, the Ingleside Inn was bought and fully restored by New York businessman Melvyn Haber, who added a fine-dining restaurant and piano lounge, the venue for Frank and Barbara Sinatra's prewedding dinner for eighty guests in 1976. Actress June Allyson and third husband David Ashrow were married there that same year. Debbie Reynolds celebrated her fiftieth birthday at the inn in 1982. A few years later, Kurt Russell and Goldie Hawn flew down in his plane for lunch.

★　★　★

Age-defying actor **Robert Stack**, who gave Deanna Durbin her first screen kiss in *First Love* and was Carole Lombard's young admirer in *To Be Or Not To Be*, lived with his actress-wife, Rosemarie Bowe, at 460 South Belardo Road in 1957. That was the same year he was nominated for an Oscar as Lauren Bacall's impotent, alcoholic husband in *Written on the Wind.*

★　★　★

A short trek southwest is the superstition-filled Indian canyon called Tahquitz (pronounced *Ta-co-wits*), identifiable by the weathered impression resembling a witch's hat that can be seen from miles away. Legend has it the malevolent spirit that dwells in the caves above the swimming hole where Ronald Colman and Jane Wyatt dabbled in Frank Capra's mystical fable *Lost Horizon* steals human souls and lures unsuspecting people to their doom.

This may explain why so many hikers have been injured trying to climb the slippery rocks. When floodwaters roared down the mountain in winter, it was said the gods were punishing those people below. Today any overflow from Tahquitz Falls is diverted along concrete spillways and under a road bridge into Tahquitz Creek, which runs eastward to Cathedral City.

★　★　★

National Geographic photographer **Fred Payne Clatworthy**, who popularized the use of autochrome color photography whereby lifelike images are registered on a glass plate using a layer of microscopic filters made from millions of grains of dyed potato starch, lived at 698 West Ramon Road in 1938. Clatworthy, whose territory covered the western United States, Mexico, and Hawaii, was among the first camera-ready artists, along with Ansel Adams, to have his work widely published. Yet this particular home, now long gone, where Clatworthy kept a makeshift darkroom, was surprisingly modest, consisting of mud walls, a thatched roof, and an irrigation ditch. He died in 1952.

Chapter 6

Movie Colony Mayhem

The Movie Colony, which contains the second largest grouping of celebrity homes, is located east of Indian Canyon Drive and extends from Tamarisk Road south to Alejo Road, and east all the way to Sunrise Way. It includes the area just north of Tachevah Road, known as El Mirador, named after the former hotel, and Ruth Hardy Park (formerly Tamarisk Park) between Via Miraleste and Avenida Caballeros.

Most of the homes found in its interlocking subdivisions are white-stucco, terra-cotta-tiled Spanish estates built in the 1930s with an intermittent sprinkling of mid-century modern and California ranch-style designs. After years of neglect, it is in the middle of resurgence as new residents busily restore the neighborhood.

Few of the original hotels, evocatively named Avalon, Bahama, Capri, Golden Gate, Mira Loma, Silver Sands, and Sunset Palms, where guests once sat around the pool in their Bermuda shorts sipping ice-cold drinks, have survived the area's extensive rebuilding. Modern-day incarnations, such as Chaps Inn, Colibri, Desert Bear, East Canyon Hotel, Indianola Tiki House, and Villa Escondida Resort, now target gay visitors only, although some "retro" establishments, such as Ballantine's, cater to club-hopping swingers.

Desert Shadows Inn, a full-service naturalist resort for men and women at 1533 Chaparral Road, would bring a smile to the face of Australian-born rebel **Errol Flynn**, the screen's favored incarnation of Robin Hood and Don Juan, who reportedly built his own clothing-optional hotel, called Casa del Sol, on this site (renamed Normandy Village Inn, 1550 North Indian Canyon Drive) after he was acquitted of charges of statutory rape in 1943.

It all began innocently enough on a weekend cruise aboard Flynn's yacht, *Sirocco*, which sailed from San Pedro to Santa Catalina Island with its skipper, Flynn, and two willing young girls, Elaine Patterson and Peggy Satterlee, in tow. Nothing untoward occurred—or so Flynn testified in court. The shit hit the fan, so to speak, when Satterlee's father later demanded $5,000 hush money, and another girl Betty Hansen, who had met

Errol Flynn on his best behavior (Larry Edmunds Bookshop).

Flynn at a party, complained she had been molested. It was, as things turned out, a trumped-up case of extortion, the fictitious sordid details of which took the wind out of Flynn's sails (he contemplated suicide and flight from jurisdiction) before a jury found him not guilty, and he was saved from a mental breakdown.

But the damage had been done; tennis and swimming now took a backseat in the actor's life of boozing and depravity. No longer a hero in green tights, Flynn had good reason to flee to the desert. His stormy seven-year marriage to French actress Lili Damita, whom he called "Tiger Lil," was over, and he had become increasingly unhappy with the pedestrian roles foisted on him by his employer, Jack Warner, who insisted on casting the virile performer in unsuitable parts that Flynn thought bordered on castration.

The rebellious actor did not want the cumbersome burden of added tax debt and alimony payments to Damita (the mother of their son, Sean Flynn), so Errol wisely kept his famous name off any legal papers. The hotel's official owner was Leon Gordon, the British writer-producer of two of Flynn's most-incongruous films, *That Forsyte Woman* opposite Greer Garson, and *Kim*, which costarred Dean Stockwell, Paul Lukas, and Reginald Owen. Flynn's hotel ownership coincided with his move into real estate, spending a king's ransom on a palatial two-story home, which he built on eleven acres atop Mulholland Drive in Los Angeles, and a cattle ranch on the island of Hawaii that he purchased for $250,000—two valuable properties the impulsive actor owned in the course of his periodic visits to Palm Springs.

Back then, Flynn's lodge was packed with the sybaritic star's hard-drinking cronies, who partied until dawn in a choice of luxury suites. But following the fun-loving performer's death, age fifty in 1959, the building was sold and lay abandoned until gutted by fire in 1990.

Nearby **Desert Arches**, a small complex of thirty-nine, two-bedroom condominiums, is an unexpected celebrity address, but that's exactly what it was some forty years ago when actors and other showbiz folk on a budget rented by the month in one of a dozen garden-style apartments, all of them since replaced by the current structure, which was built in 1973.

This is where the mother of late cult B-movie actor **John Agar** lived in the Trinidad Apartments at 448 East Cottonwood Road in 1960, when she managed a women's fashion boutique at El Mirador Hotel. Agar visited his mother each winter, but avoided the summer, he said, because of the intense desert heat.

Lillian Agar's youthful-looking son, who was married to Shirley Temple for four years, got his start in two classic John Wayne Westerns, *Fort Apache* and *She Wore a Yellow Ribbon*, which helped to make him the dependable star of such popular science fiction movies as *Revenge of the Creature* and *Tarantula*. A losing fight with alcoholism changed all that, and Agar sunk into supporting roles that paid well, but did his reputation little good.

★ ★ ★

White-haired, bushy-browed **Henry Travers** was nominated for an Oscar as Best Supporting Actor in *Mrs. Miniver* and played Clarence Oddbody, the benevolent angel who saves Jimmy Stewart from drowning in Frank Capra's Yuletide classic *It's a Wonderful Life*. In 1964, he spent his next-to-last winter in the Seabrooke Apartments at 720 East Cottonwood Road. The following year, at age ninety-one, he finally earned his wings and was heaven sent. Travers's understanding look and kind words in *Dark Victory*, *The Bells of St. Mary's*, and *The Yearling* had audiences reaching for their handkerchiefs. However, this quintessential Englishman, who always looked like he just awoke from a nap, preferred to reach for something much tastier—a glass of sherry.

The first home of hotel orchestra leader and Dixieland drummer **Ben Pollack**, who worked as Chico Marx's musical director and played himself in *The Glenn Miller Story* and *The Benny Goodman Story*, was in the Fountain D'Or Apartments at 807 East Cottonwood Road. He lived there in 1966 while running the downtown nightclub, Easy Street North, which he soon learned was anything but easy. Pollack's dance band arrangements of "Sweet Sue" (dedicated to actress Sue Carol), "Wait Til You See 'Ma Cherie,'" and "Louise" were all the rage of twenties jazz age America.

Unfortunately, by the time he moved to the desert, Pollack's music was a relic of the past, and the money he had hoped to make from this expensive nightclub venture never materialized, sending him into a spiral of debt. He spent a great deal of time in costly litigation against Benny Goodman and Bing Crosby, as well as Paramount Pictures and Camel cigarettes, claiming they cheated him out of more than $5 million in earnings.

Internationally syndicated cartoonist **Milton Caniff** was dubbed "Rembrandt of the Comics" for his action-packed weekly comic strip *Terry and the Pirates*, in which his young airborne hero battled an assortment of Eastern potentates and deadly spies, including the evil Dragon Lady. He later drew weekly installments for another long-running comic strip, *Steve Canyon*, about the adventures of a heroic fighter pilot, while staying at 443 East Chuckwalla Road in 1975. Caniff's twenty million fans included Orson Welles and Italian filmmaker Federico Fellini, who were heavily influenced, they said, by his high contrast, black-and-white style. The Milton Caniff Spirit of Flight Award, given each year by the National Aviation Hall of Fame, is named in memory of Caniff, who died in 1988.

In 1928, Prescott Stevens, a grizzled cattleman from Colorado who codeveloped Vista Acres subdivision with Alvah Hicks, built **El Mirador Hotel**, a three-hundred-room configuration of suites and cottages at 1150 North Indian Avenue, for the vast sum of

$750,000. The triple-story Spanish Colonial Revival style enclosed forecourt and *ramada* with its distinctive green, yellow, and blue chevron-striped bell tower was conceived by Los Angeles architects Albert Walker and Percy Eisen, designers of the Hollywood Plaza and Beverly-Wilshire hotels in Los Angeles.

Walker and Eisen's comfortable design stayed within the confines of beaux-arts tradition by giving the main building and adjoining rooms a red-tile roof, wrought-iron balustrades with Mexican tiled walkways, giant chandeliers, hand-tufted rugs, and potted palms that appealed to discriminating visitors of the period. Many of these visitors were initially taken aback then embraced the daring fashion concept of ladies' bare midriffs and cabana shorts that supposedly originated there.

Four years after it opened, El Mirador, despite doing brisk business, went bankrupt due to the lingering effects of the Wall Street stock market crash and was sold to a consortium headed by Los Angeles attorney Warren Pinney. In an effort to increase patronage, said Frank Bogert, who functioned as the hotel's public relations director, "Pinney created a glamorous resort with bellboys in fancy uniforms," mandating that his staff wear brass-buttoned tunics with epaulets and braided caps.

Clockwise from top left: Bonita Granville and Jackie Cooper kiss underwater. Jeanne Martin, El Mirador owner Ray Ryan and Dean Martin. Randolph Scott, Marion DuPont and Claudette Colbert on a bicycle in front of El Mirador's tower. Marlene Dietrich with actor Leslie Howard. (All photos courtesy of Palm Springs Historical Society.)

When exhausted playwright Moss Hart was recovering at El Mirador from a nervous collapse in 1932, he noted in his diary the sheer opulence of the hotel—"horribly expensive but a fairyland"—and made wisecracks about the white-suited male nurses that attended him around the clock.

As America pulled itself out of the Depression, business picked up at El Mirador, and before long, it was fully booked with lines of noteworthy silver screeners. Al Jolson, Ruby Keeler, Gary Cooper, Marlene Dietrich, John Wayne, Loretta Young, Jimmy Durante, Constance Bennett, Joan Bennett, Cary Grant, Ginger Rogers, James Cagney, and the Marx Brothers sunned themselves in one of fifteen glass-walled cabanas, just feet from the huge four-lane swimming pool with its submerged porthole used for underwater photography. Freestyle swimmer Johnny Weissmuller, winner of five Olympic gold medals, practiced his laps. U.S. diving champion Harold "Dutch" Smith, who won silver and gold at the 1932 Olympics, made El Mirador his permanent home in 1937.

From 1935 onward, actors Freeman Gosden and Charles Correll broadcast their weekly *Amos 'n' Andy* radio show from the hotel tower's second floor on a special telephone line to NBC Studios, which was relayed to an estimated forty million listeners. Another frequent visitor, composer George Gershwin, played "Someone To Watch Over Me" and other tunes on the dining room's grand piano after supper each evening. Walter Chrysler, founder of Chrysler Corporation, *Saturday Evening Post* editor George Lorimer, and Grover Magnin, the son of retail store founder Isaac Magnin, were among the nation's leading corporate names that registered at El Mirador during the 1936 winter.

"The hotel garage, usually filled with Rolls-Royces and Cadillacs, was equipped with eight chauffeur's rooms," Bogert stated.

In 1942, the federal government purchased El Mirador and converted it into Torney General Hospital, where hundreds of American and British soldiers recuperated from illnesses and other injuries. Large numbers of Italian prisoners of war captured during the Libyan campaign were placed in internment camps two blocks away on the present-day site of Ruth Hardy Park and worked as hospital orderlies until the war ended.

El Mirador finally reopened for business in 1952 "more glamorous than it had been before the war," with a $2-million facelift courtesy of the hotel's new owner, Roy Fitzgerald of Chicago. African-American architect Paul R. Williams, who designed Palm Springs Tennis Club and Town & Country Restaurant (now Zelda's Nightclub) with A. Quincy Jones, as well as Saks Fifth Avenue and Milton Kreis Drug Store (Starbucks) on Palm Canyon Drive, handled the hotel renovations.

El Mirador's subsequent owners included Indiana oilman Ray Ryan, whose beaming countenance was its main attraction along with weekly Polynesian buffets in the South Pacific Room when he ran the hotel in 1959. After Ryan came *Matinee Theater* actor-host John Conte's Palm Springs KMIR-TV station, an NBC affiliate, started broadcasting there in 1968. Hoping to attract extra patronage, Conte added a motorized fountain called Dancing Waters prior to relocating to larger studios in Palm Desert.

But the hotel, which went the way of so many great establishments, never recaptured its past glory and permanently closed its doors to the public in 1973. Razed to make way for Desert Hospital (renamed Desert Regional Medical Center), the only reminder of El Mirador is a replica of its pink-stucco tower, now painted white, constructed in 1991 two years after the original was destroyed by fire.

Today, a different kind of monument, the five-story Sinatra Patient Tower, along with the Frederick Loewe Intensive Care Center, Dinah Shore Family Waiting Area, and an atrium dedicated to Andrea Leeds Howard, occupies pride of place on the hospital's manicured lawns where cancer-stricken "My Blue Heaven" singer Gene Austin, Hopalong Cassidy's sidekick Russell Hayden, and Guy Madison, star of TV's *The Adventures of Wild Bill Hickok*, ended their days.

Because of its closeness to such a hallowed piece of ground as that of El Mirador, many people think this neighborhood of creosote and brittle-bush retains a nostalgic charm not found elsewhere in the city. They might be right. The ghosts of once-famous vacationers and distinguished homeowners surely dwell in the trees among the cobblestone pathways, flagstone facades, and picket fences of surrounding streets. When the wind blows, insists one resident, you can almost hear their voices calling in the breeze.

Judy Canova talking her mouth off (Larry Edmunds Bookshop).

★　　★　　★

In 1994, skinny, bespectacled actor **Herbert Anderson**, who played Jay North's hapless father in the popular 1960s TV sitcom *Dennis the Menace*, died at the Rancho El Mirador condominiums at 291 Mel Avenue, next door to Desert Hospital, after a long illness. He was seventy-seven.

★　　★　　★

Two blocks east, hillbilly singer-comedienne **Judy Canova**, the mother of *Soap* actress Diana Canova, lived in the Spanish revival estate at 1194 North Via Miraleste from 1956 to 1959. Judy Canova's big grin and corn-fed humor was the highpoint of scores of Republic second features such as *Sis Hopkins, Sleepytime Gal,* and *Louisiana Hayride.*

Canova's tasteful clothes and beautifully furnished home, formerly owned by automobile dealer Albert Stuebing, often surprised visitors who expected to see her surrounded by barnyard animals. (This address is sometimes mistaken for that of another loud-mouthed comedienne, Lucille Ball, who was supposed to have stayed there, but never owned it.)

★　　★　　★

One of the more prestigious residents of the Movie Colony, however, was someone that few people outside today's fast-track motion picture industry have ever heard of: handsome, "lavender" leading man **William Haines**, whose wise-cracking personality and reckless behavior was perfectly suited to the gin-soaked Roaring Twenties.

Haines shot to stardom as MGM's smart-alecky sports hero in *Brown of Harvard, Slide Kelly Slide,* and *Spring Fever.* He quickly became the cinema's favorite bad boy in such cheeky outings as *Tell It to the Marines, Alias Jimmy Valentine,* and *Speedway*—films that are now forgotten, but were tremendous moneymakers in their day. However, when talk of Haines's open homosexuality began making the rounds, studio boss Louis B. Mayer dumped him, after some fifty films, in favor of conservative newcomer Robert Montgomery, who mimicked Haines's mugging style, but had none of his panache.

Undeterred, Haines reinvented himself as Hollywood's ebullient decorator-to-the-stars. He went on to win fame and fortune as the Beverly Hills interior designer who created the living spaces for Marion Davies, Carole Lombard, and his lifelong friend, Joan Crawford, whom he called "Cranberry" because she detested the name Crawford. "It sounds like crawfish," she said.

Among Haines's most-noteworthy paying clients were *Dinner at Eight* director George Cukor, whose Sunset Strip house he totally remodeled in 1935, Warner Brothers studio chief Jack Warner, and William Goetz, the head of production at 20th Century-Fox—at a starting price of $50,000 per bedroom!

Haines imbued his designs with his signature Chippendale furniture, hand-painted Chinese wallpaper, Ming chests, and lotus-patterned Lowestoft china. According to film historian Richard Lamparski, Haines did a lot of entertaining in his Brentwood home, which he greatly expanded from its humble Federal Housing Authority beginnings. However, the actor-decorator soon began spending an increasing amount of his time in the desert where many of his friends, past and present, were residing. Naturally, they needed his services, and he happily obliged.

By the end of the 1950s, Haines and his longtime companion, James Shields, were semiretired and living in quiet splendor in an elegant five-bedroom manor house that Haines had purchased in 1957 at 651 East Paseo El Mirador, the walls encased with "wormwood" paneling. In 1966, Haines, assisted by his business partner, Ted Graber, designed the modish interiors for *Philadelphia Inquirer*, *Seventeen*, and *TV Guide* publisher Walter Annenberg's three-million-dollar Sunnylands estate in Rancho Mirage. Declared *The Hollywood Reporter*, "No matter what the colors, the desert will definitely be greener."

When President Richard Nixon appointed Annenberg, his close friend and political ally, as U.S. ambassador to Great Britain in 1969, Haines was dispatched to London where he completely overhauled the ambassador's faded, three-story, thirty-five-room Georgian mansion in Regent's Park. What began as a painstaking challenge turned into an artistic triumph, and Haines, at age seventy, was lauded as few interior designers before or since. The $1-million restoration, which took nine hectic months, was profiled in *Architectural Digest*.

Regrettably, it was Haines's last important commission. On December 26, 1973, the ever-cheerful actor and artisan succumbed to cancer at seventy-three. Jimmy Shields, his lover of forty-seven years, took a fatal drug overdose three months later, after telling a friend, "It's no good without Billy."

Popular stage and film entertainer **Eddie Cantor**, nicknamed "Banjo Eyes," and the woman he always talked about on his weekly radio show—wife Ida—lived at 720 Paseo El Mirador for more than twenty years. Cantor was one of the few Broadway performers (he starred in four Ziegfeld Follies) to attract a large movie following via his appearances in the early Hollywood musical spectaculars *Whoopee, The Kid From Spain*, and *Kid Millions*.

Cantor's freewheeling style and high-pitched voice were ideally suited to radio where he entertained millions of listeners, clapping his hands and singing "If You Knew Suzie." While residing here, Cantor—an enthusiastic supporter of the Palm Springs Boys Club who also donated his time and talent each year to the annual Palm Springs Police Benefit Show—wrote several autobiographies chronicling his lengthy career. Despite being a poor film, he enjoyed a resurgence in popularity after release of *The Eddie Cantor Story* in 1953.

Throughout his lifetime, Cantor, who also did double duty as a songwriter ("Merrily We Roll Along") and author (*Ziegfeld, the Great Glorifier*), was eagerly sought after as a private teacher. He gave singing lessons to Dinah Shore and showed sixteen-year-old Joel Grey, the future star of Bob Fosse's *Cabaret*, how to dance.

Cantor received a special Academy Award in 1956 and was awarded a U.S. Service Medal for his humanitarianism and generosity of spirit, in particular for creating the March of Dimes campaign to help fight infantile paralysis.

Cantor was never in the best of health after suffering a heart attack in 1952. He succumbed to a second one in 1964—four months after he and Ida, who predeceased him by two years, would have celebrated their fiftieth wedding anniversary. (Note: Cantor's home, which sold for $115,000 in 1998, is one of few on the street without a swimming pool. He insisted it be filled in after the birth of his youngest daughter, Janet, so she would not be in any danger.)

Clockwise from top: Eddie Cantor's house in 2002 (Photo by Howard Johns). Lawrence Welk (right) with wife Fern (Backlot Books & Movie Posters). Eddie Cantor plugs a Palm Springs Police Benefit Show (Courtesy of Palm Springs Historical Society).

★   ★   ★

Champagne music maestro **Lawrence Welk**, whose TV variety show ran on ABC for twenty-five years, practiced the accordion and danced the polka at 730 Paseo El Mirador, where he resided until 1978. Welk's fireside sing-alongs and ballroom waltzes were the mainstay of several generations of immigrant American families, so much so that when

Truman Capote before his facelift (Larry Edmunds Bookshop).

the German-speaking bandleader went into the real estate business, his fans followed him to live in Cathedral City, San Diego, and Branson, Missouri, where he built a string of senior living resorts.

Welk's corny catch phrases "wunnerful, wunnerful" and "ah-one and ah-two" became household expressions; his license plate reportedly read: A1NA2. Although Welk died, age eighty-nine, in 1992, his company is still going strong.

★   ★   ★

Southern gothic writer and social pixie **Truman Capote**, who went from being a heralded literary genius with the publication of his first novel, *Other Voices, Other Rooms*, to being an impotent failure with his last unfinished work, *Answered Prayers*, took the generous advance he had received for this highly anticipated magnum opus and rented the house that he later bought and remodeled at 853 Paseo El Mirador in 1968.

Capote's winter home was carefully chosen for its privacy, explained biographer Gerald Clarke. "A high wall enclosed the garden and pool, and all that could be seen of the world outside was the tops of nodding palm trees and purple desert mountains." But the falsetto-voiced storyteller, who became the darling of TV talk shows with two number-one bestsellers, *Breakfast at Tiffany's* and *In Cold Blood*, did not anticipate the desert's captivating allure, and he spent most of the daytime being pampered at the Spa Hotel and dancing at night in the city's discos.

Instead of writing, Capote gossiped incessantly on the phone or gulped cocktails at the parties of Frank Sinatra, Bob Hope, and Walter Annenberg, where he paraded a succession of hunky male lovers, including an air-conditioning repairman from Illinois and a Times Square barman, in front of shocked dinner guests. In 1974, Capote was admitted to Eisenhower Medical Center suffering from "exhaustion." (He was hospitalized four times in 1981, seven times in 1982, and sixteen times in 1983 for alcohol-related illnesses.) Not long after, bored and depressed, he packed his bags and left the desert for Key West, Florida. The incomplete book that was to have been his masterpiece went unpublished until his premature death, age fifty-nine, from a drug overdose in 1984. Capote's home sold for $140,000 in 1996.

★   ★   ★

If you visited Sin City in the 1950s, their names were everywhere. Grammy-winning jazz and blues vocalist **Keely Smith**, voted the First Lady of Las Vegas, and her face-contorting, trumpet-blowing, singer-husband **Louis Prima**, literally had hundreds of tuxedoed fans, including the Rat Pack, storming the Sahara Hotel's Casbar (sic) Room to see their crazy act. For the price of two drinks, you'd be treated to the spectacle of a loud-mouthed Italian man in a bad toupee standing on stage making goo-goo eyes at his poker-faced, young wife, flailing his arms about, and singing up a storm.

It didn't matter what blasé critics said about them; audiences went wild over this manic musical duo as they tugged and teased each other for ten years until Keely finally shouted, "No, more!"

Prima, who fathered her two daughters, Toni and Luanne, later attempted a solo comeback. He died of complications from a brain tumor in 1978 at age sixty-seven. But Smith, who divorced him in 1961 citing "extreme mental cruelty" and went on to become a star on her own, still swings, swings, swings with third husband Bobby Milano at 1055 Paseo El Mirador. Now seventy-one and still sounding great (she even sports the same short-bobbed hair), Smith is enjoying a resurgence in popularity thanks to new recordings of her timeless songs, including "It's Magic" and "I Wish You Love," as well as renewed interest in Prima's Dixieland-style music by *Stray Cats'* Brian Setzer, who recorded "Jump, Jive An' Wail," and David Lee Roth, who used Prima's original arrangement of "Just a Gigolo."

Top: Keely Smith's home at 1055 Paseo El Mirador (Photo by Howard Johns). *Bottom:* Keely Smith, voted the First Lady of Las Vegas (Wayne Knight Collection).

But a singer's life isn't all music and applause. On July 11, 1986, Smith was arrested for allegedly failing to pay state disability insurance and taxes in connection with a restaurant she managed with her brother, Norman, and two others in Palm Desert. Smith was released on $1,500 bail. (She was previously cited with violating the state labor code in connection with another nightclub venture, but was acquitted of those charges.)

That same night, she awoke to find two masked gunmen in her bedroom. They had pistol-whipped Norman and were busily ransacking the Paseo El Mirador house looking for jewelry. The robbers fled with $300,000 worth of emerald rings, gold necklaces, and bracelets including a flawless eighteen-carat diamond ring. The items were later recovered. Two men were found guilty of the crime and sent to prison.

In 1998, Smith's singer-husband Bobby Milano, also known as Charles Caci, and his older brother, Vincent, reputedly a captain of La Cosa Nostra in Los Angeles, were named in a federal racketeering indictment that accused them of selling counterfeit traveler's checks for fraudulent use, according to an article in the *Las Vegas Sun*. Four years later, the brothers pleaded guilty to the charges. Prosecutors agreed to seek minimum sentences for both men because of their advanced age and health. It's one of many showbiz anomalies that organized crime is attracted to the entertainment spotlight and vice versa.

Recently, Smith released three brand-new CDs: *Swing, Swing, Swing*, followed by *Keely Sings Sinatra*, which she recorded with the seventeen-piece Frankie Capp Orchestra, and *Keely Swings Basie Style*.

Another Paseo El Mirador landmark is "Frey House I," the first desert home of Swiss-born architect **Albert Frey** at 1150 Paseo El Mirador (renumbered 1210 North Via Donna)—on the site of the defunct El Mirador golf course. A disciple of the French architectural scholar, Le Corbusier, who preached geometric simplicity, Frey said he originally conceived the Flash Gordon-style home as an experiment. He used prefabricated building materials such as plywood and corrugated metal sheeting when he designed and built a small cottage here in 1940, then extended it, adding a separate living room and floating dining table in 1947 and a suspended staircase leading to a second-floor circular bedroom in 1953 (later removed).

The harsh practicalities of desert living caused problems with the higher living space's exterior, which was sheathed in aluminum panels and insulated with vinyl padding. These were not the best components for non-air-conditioned summer heat. Frey painted the house in rich primary colors to combat the high temperatures. He also planted groves of date palms, citrus trees, and cacti around the swimming pool. Although this unusual house has undergone many structural changes and modifications, most recently with the architect's assistance over a two-year period ending with his death in 1998, the floor plan remains faithful to Frey's original concept of integrated living, and several key features, including the floor-to-ceiling sliding-glass doors, pool, and courtyard have been preserved.

But the most attention-grabbing house on the street, aesthetically speaking, surely is the one that was designed by fellow architect **E. Stewart Williams** for his family at 1250 Paseo El Mirador in 1954. A second-generation architect (his father, Harry, designed the Plaza, the city's first shopping center), Williams not only designed this unique home, he built it, too, combining natural and man-made materials such as wood and glass to create a free-flowing plan for relaxed living.

In 1997, Seattle-based contemporary glass artist **Dale Chihuly**, whose giant ornamental red, blue, and yellow clamshells are popular living-room centerpieces, paid $350,000 for Williams's house, which is nestled at the end of a private drive off the main street. Chihuly painted it different colors in an attempt to modernize the home's interior, but did not make any major structural changes. In 2001, real estate investor Marc Sanders bought the home from Chihuly for $575,000 and reversed what he considered had been incorrectly done. He repainted the chartreuse exterior in softer café au lait tones and decorated the home with authentic midcentury modern furnishings.

★ ★ ★

In 1981, Groucho Marx's third and last wife, **Eden Hartford**, moved to 1265 Serena Circle—four years after the comedian's death at eighty-six. The two were married in 1954 during the run of the CBS quiz show *You Bet Your Life* when he was sixty-four and she was twenty-three. Groucho divorced Eden in 1969. The younger sister of *Vogue* model Dee Hartford, Eden, who died in 1983, "was as nice a person as you would ever want to meet," recalled Sammy Cahn.

★ ★ ★

Actor **Charles Irwin**, who emceed Universal's first color film musical, *King of Jazz*, and announced the "Little Johnny Jones" musical number in *Yankee Doodle Dandy*, retired to 511 Linda Vista Road in 1958.

★ ★ ★

The first of several homes occupied by Lorenz Hart's younger brother, **Teddy Hart**, can be found at 1120 Linda Vista Road. Teddy, who played the Indian "Crowbar" in three Ma and Pa Kettle comedies and received a lifetime royalty from his late brother's music, moved there in 1955.

★ ★ ★

Top: Howard Hughes's house at 1185 Pasatiempo Road (Photo by Howard Johns). *Bottom:* Howard Hughes testifies at a grand jury hearing (Backlot Books & Movie Posters).

Howard Hughes had a highly developed understanding of both economics and aerodynamics, which helped to make him America's first billionaire, as well as one of the most talked-about celebrities of his era. A brilliant industrialist, aviator, and movie producer, he knew the desert as few others did—from the air, having flown over its stony terrain many times.

Hughes, who financed the making of *Hell's Angels*, *Scarface*, and *The Outlaw*, rented his first Palm Springs home in 1940 as a place to "stash" his then-fifteen-year-old acting protégée, Faith Domergue. In succeeding years, he piloted various aircraft, among them an experimental D-2 bomber, on test flights across the desert. These flights were conducted in total secrecy with only Hughes's trusted mechanic, Earl Martyn, in attendance.

In 1947, Hughes entertained Pan American Airways president Juan Trippe in another desert home he had rented for the season. The following year, Hughes returned by air under cover of darkness to negotiate the purchase of RKO Radio Pictures from its owner, Floyd Odlum, who lived in Indio.

Less than a decade later, Hughes sold RKO's seven-hundred-film library and studio back lot. He then moved to 1451 North Paseo de Anza. Hughes and his second wife, **Jean Peters** (Tyrone Power's sulking leading lady in *Captain from Castile*), secretly honeymooned here in early 1957, "where they were surrounded by guards as they walked the desert gardens," according to biographer Richard Hack, "and watched the grapefruit grow."

Their rented home was located directly behind the Ranch Club, both of which have since been replaced by condominiums (now the Ranch: 1600 North Chia Road). When Hughes and Peters lived there, however, the Ranch Club at 1445 North Sunrise Way (not to be confused with the Racquet Club) was the premier holiday spot for city slickers that liked horse rides and hoedowns. Oscar winners Broderick Crawford, Jane Wyman, and lanky lawman Hugh O'Brian of TV's *Wyatt Earp* were a few of the actors that showed up there in Western attire.

Then, in 1963, Hughes shifted his operations to a modest tract home with a painted wooden fence at 1185 Pasatiempo Road, where he hid from the press during his highly publicized Trans World Airlines antitrust lawsuit. If you think the digs are modest—and they are—remember that Hughes tried to keep things low key in his private life. Still, from this inauspicious address, million-dollar business deals were made on extra phone lines he had installed during negotiations to purchase six Las Vegas casinos, including the Desert Inn, Frontier, Sands, and Silver Slipper.

★ ★ ★

Nick Castle, the dance director for Shirley Temple, George Murphy, Betty Grable, and Gene Kelly, lived at 1220 Pasatiempo Road. He choreographed the famous dancing-on-the-walls sequence for Fred Astaire in *Royal Wedding*. Castle's son, Nick Jr., wrote and directed *Tap*, a 1989 homage to his father's musical career, starring Gregory Hines.

★ ★ ★

Walt Disney movie director **Norman Tokar**, whose fondness for animal stories got the better of him judging by their titles—*Sammy the Way Out Seal, The Ugly Dachshund, The Horse in the Gray Flannel Suit, The Cat From Outer Space*—read these and other scripts, surrounded by the animals he loved, at 1225 Pasatiempo Road.

★ ★ ★

The boyhood home of new wave Hollywood auteur **Cameron Crowe**, who grew up to write and direct the Oscar-winning *Jerry Maguire, Almost Famous* (based on his exploits as a young *Rolling Stone* contributor), and *Vanilla Sky*, is located at 1240 Pasatiempo Road. Crowe, also the author of the revealing book *Conversations with Wilder*, lived there with his Realtor-father, James Crowe, until the family moved to Indio in 1973.

Hyperactive musical comedy star **Betty Hutton**, who matched rifles with Howard Keel as Wild West show performers in *Annie Get Your Gun* and swung on a circus trapeze in *The Greatest Show on Earth*, was more than just a funny face. Hutton, whom costar Bob Hope called "a vitamin pill with legs," was also an accomplished rhythm singer, belting out novelty songs such as "Doctor, Lawyer, Indian Chief," which peaked at number one on the music charts. (Marion Hutton, her older sister, was a vocalist with the Glenn Miller Orchestra.)

Betty Hutton prior to her nervous breakdown (Wayne Knight Collection).

The highly competitive tomboy was crowned Queen of the Desert Circus in 1954 when she rode down Palm Canyon Drive with grand marshal Walt Disney, show master Phil Harris, and high sheriff Ray Ryan. Ten years on, this high-spirited performer became a casualty of her own fame, suffering a nervous breakdown and attempting suicide before she was finally saved, Hutton said, by religion. She staged a brief comeback before disappearing from view again.

Many years passed without any mention of her name. Then in 1999, an alert fan spotted the blonde-wigged star alighting from a taxicab outside her Ranch Club condominium at 1415 Chia Road—the same location where, intriguingly, Hutton and her third husband, Capitol Records president Alan Livingston, had stayed with her two daughters, Candy and Lindsay, when it was a private club forty-five years earlier. The resulting publicity sent her packing to Desert Dorado Villas where she suffered a ministroke and was hospitalized in 2001. She has since moved.

Fifties composer/conductor/arranger **Les Baxter**, who wrote the music for American-International Pictures's *Beach Party* series and its creepy Edgar Allan Poe anthologies, lived at 1540 East Mel Avenue (off North Sunrise Way). Baxter's exotic rhythms, featuring chiming xylophones and pulsating bongo drums, started the Hawaiian "tiki music" craze. For lovers of high camp, Baxter's go-go-dancing film score (sung by the Supremes) for the Vincent Price spy spoof, *Dr. Goldfoot and the Bikini Machine*, is a classic. Baxter was seventy-three when he died of a massive heart attack due to kidney failure in 1996.

Edmund Goulding, who locked horns with Oscar-winning spitfire Bette Davis when he directed three of her all-time best pictures, *Dark Victory*, *The Old Maid*, and *The Great Lie*, and guided sensitive Tyrone Power to dramatic greatness in *The Razor's Edge* and *Nightmare Alley*, played "Mam'selle" and other songs he had written on the piano for dinner guests at 1431 East Tachevah Road—one year before he died at Cedars Lebanon Hospital on Christmas Eve 1959 undergoing surgery for a ruptured aorta.

★　　★　　★

Cuban-born bandleader **Miguelito Valdes**, one of the original Mambo Kings, first recorded the song "Babalu" years ahead of his competitor, Desi Arnaz. Valdes's distinctive voice made him one of the great romantic male vocalists of his time. He lived at 1265 East Tachevah Road in 1968.

★　　★　　★

William McClatchy, great grandson of James McClatchy, founder of the *Sacramento Bee* newspaper, owns the $2.5 million home with nine bedrooms and eleven baths at 650 East Tachevah Drive. McClatchy's family-run company, whose mastheads include *Anchorage Daily News* and *Star-Tribune* in Minneapolis, is the eighth largest newspaper publisher in the country.

★　　★　　★

Charlie Farrell spent the last decade of his life, drinking malt Scotch and watching reruns of his old movies in the four-bedroom Spanish home at 630 East Tachevah Drive, on the northeast corner of Via Miraleste. It was said that Farrell deeply grieved the loss of his wife, actress Virginia Valli, who died in 1968 after suffering a stroke at age seventy. He subsequently withdrew from public life and became a recluse.

(Note: Farrell's initials "C.D.F." which stand for Charles David Farrell are welded in wrought iron above the front entrance of this home, where he died of cardiac arrest, age eighty-nine, on May 6, 1990, although his death went strangely unreported for almost one week.) Farrell's home, recently remodeled, sold for $285,000 in 1994.

Charlie Farrell and Virginia Valli take a stroll outside their Tachevah Drive home (Courtesy of Palm Springs Historical Society).

★　　★　　★

For six months in 1987, **Tammy Faye Bakker** and her televangelist husband, Jim Bakker, who admitted to having an extramarital affair with church secretary Jessica Hahn and embezzling more than $150 million from their Praise The Lord "and-give-us-your-money" ministry, tried to hide from the clamoring news media at 688 East Vereda Sur (one block from the Katherine Finchy Middle School).

The Bakkers reportedly paid $600,000 for this five-bedroom home where the contributions of their gullible flock, it was claimed, unknowingly paid for $500 shower curtains and plated the bathroom fixtures in solid gold—a charge that Tammy, as usual, denied. "All we had were gold-colored swans instead of silver-colored knobs," she whined.

In the midst of the PTL controversy, Moral Majority leader Jerry Falwell, Assemblies of God minister Richard Dortch, and Falwell's lawyer, Norman Roy Grutman, whose high-end clients included *Penthouse* publisher Bob Guccione (producer of the X-rated film *Caligula*), flew to Palm Springs in Falwell's private plane and persuaded Jim Bakker to sign a letter of resignation that gave them control of the ministry.

"With a single stroke of that pen," wept Tammy, "I knew it was all over." It's hard to believe the fuss that these two Minnesota opportunists engendered in the Washington political arena, but they did—and how they were turned into national celebrities.

Tammy Faye Bakker deep in prayer (Backlot Books & Movie Posters).

"Outside our house the road was three and four deep with reporters, TV trucks, and cameras," Tammy recounted with wide-eyed astonishment. "Lights like you'd see in a baseball stadium were erected for when it got dark. They had satellite dishes sticking up in the air. Rows of Porta-Johns were moved in to accommodate the hundreds of reporters."

As helicopters circled overhead like vultures, the Bakkers were forced to hide under blankets on the floor of other people's cars to outrun the media gauntlet. The congestion got so bad that six months later the besieged couple was forced to sell their house and move to a condominium in Palm Desert. The false-eyelashed celebrity and recurrent documentary film subject, who later divorced Bakker and married PTL building contractor Roe Messner, now preaches the good word about women's beauty products. Third-generation Chicago shoemaker **Irving Florsheim**, whose family surely would have balked at such distasteful controversy, owned the Bakker's home in 1957. Forty years later, it sold for $525,000.

MGM screenwriter **Irving Brecher**, a Best Screenplay Oscar nominee for his nineteenth-century charmer, *Meet Me In St. Louis*, who also created TV's *The Life of Riley* and *The People's Choice* featuring Cleo the basset hound and wrote the screenplay for *Bye Bye Birdie*, resided at 723 East Vereda Sur from 1959 through 1975. Talk about talent, undisputed talent! The last remaining writer from that studio's cherished Golden Age, Brecher, who turned eighty-eight in 2002, was hired by Mervyn LeRoy to write zingers for the cowardly lion, scarecrow, and tin man in *The Wizard of Oz* because, Brecher said, "they weren't funny enough." The result: more jokes, bigger laughs, and at least a half-dozen pratfalls that were the hallmark of Brecher's comedy style.

★   ★   ★

Noah Dietrich, Howard Hughes's financial adviser and trusted aide for more than thirty years, purchased Brecher's Vereda Sur home in 1976. It was Dietrich, a race car driver-turned-accountant, who transformed Hughes from a wealthy twenty-year-old tool company owner to a billionaire investor and corporate raider netting upwards of $50 million a year.

In 1957, Hughes fired Dietrich, sympathetically portrayed by actors Lew Ayres in *The Carpetbaggers* and Ed Flanders in *The Amazing Howard Hughes*, the latter based on Dietrich's unflattering biography of Hughes. The "bashful billionaire" retaliated by calling Dietrich "a no-good dishonest son of a bitch." Dietrich sued him for breach of contract and defamation—and won.

Varied accounts have related Hughes's descent into madness, storing his bodily waste in Mason jars he kept in a closet, injecting himself with dirty hypodermic needles, and rarely bathing except when he cleaned himself with rubbing alcohol. Two months after Dietrich secretly moved into this house, a shockingly emaciated Hughes died from kidney failure on a mercy flight from Acapulco to Houston. In 1982, Dietrich, his own health undermined by heart problems that were accelerated by his distressing rift with Hughes, died in Desert Hospital. He was ninety-two.

Dietrich's love-hate relationship with Hughes was not his only Hollywood connection. Noah's stepdaughter, Susan Brewer (from his marriage to showgirl Mary Brewer), was formerly married to actor Peter Fonda; their daughter is actress Bridget Fonda. (Note: This home, which has since been renumbered 700 Vereda Sur, is now owned by educational and travel writer Richard Hostrop.)

And this quiet neighborhood of cul-de-sacs, known as Tachevah Vista, is also the site of the first desert home of *Ulysses* star **Kirk Douglas**, who lived for two years at 1069 East Marshall Way. (Thunderbird Country Club golf pro Claude Harmon later resided there.) Current owner John McCarron paid $74,000 for the house in 1977.

Desert legend **Bob Hope**, who won more awards than he could possibly count in his lifetime, including five special Oscars, two Emmys, fifty-four doctorates, and an honorary knighthood, owned the tile-and-stucco house and the overgrown vacant lot behind it at 1014 Buena Vista Drive (on the corner of Avenida Caballeros). He purchased it way back in 1941 when he was radio and filmdom's brightest comedy star.

"We enjoyed that little house," reminisced Hope's wife of sixty-nine years, Dolores Reade, "but by 1946 we were bursting at the seams with four children [Linda, Tony, Nora, Kelly], so we moved into a larger home on El Alameda." Today, Dolores's sister, Mildred Malatesta, uses the home as a convenient guesthouse. Hope died in 2003, shortly after celebrating his one-hundredth birthday.

The second home of actor **Tom Neal**, where the unemployed actor who worked as a landscape gardener lived with his third wife, Gail Evatt, in 1964, is located at 1057 Buena Vista Drive. Neal's promising film career evaporated after his violent altercation with actor Franchot Tone over the affections of actress Barbara Payton, who had earlier engaged in a torrid affair with neighboring comedian Bob Hope. According to biographer Arthur Marx, Hope was introduced to Payton on a personal appearance tour of Dallas in the spring of 1949.

"Barbara was Hope's type: blond, with a curvaceous figure," Marx stated, "and willing, oh, so willing." Their afternoon trysts lasted for six months until Dolores put her foot down and Hope grudgingly ordered the brazen actress to hit the road. Neal and Payton were costarred in *The Great Jesse James Raid*, which Palm Springs producer Robert Lippert Jr. hoped would be a box-office smash because of their sexual chemistry. Nevertheless, the film failed to attract much interest. In 1965 the Neals moved to Little Tuscany, where Neal killed his wife.

"*Action!*" is the word most associated with lightning-paced director **Raoul Walsh**, and action is what moviegoers got when they paid fifty cents to see a film by the gruff, pipe-smoking director. Walsh began his film career as an actor in 1912, then lost his right eye in a freak accident when a jackrabbit smashed the windshield of his car. Thereafter Walsh, who reportedly lived in the walled and gated home at 1062 East Buena Vista Drive, retreated to behind the camera, his missing eye covered by a black patch. He directed many movies in many genres, among them, 1924's *The Thief of Bagdad*, *The Strawberry Blonde*, *High Sierra*, *Along the Great Divide*, and *The Naked and the Dead*.

Errol Flynn, whom Walsh directed in seven movies, often shared an invigorating swig between takes of *Objective, Burma!*—which was filmed during a 1944 summer heat wave in Palm Springs. Walsh was still going strong as a biographer and university lecturer at age eighty—though he was blind by the time of his death at ninety-three in 1981. Actor **Richard Harrison**, who partly remodeled the ranch-style home, which he purchased in 1994 and sold in 2003, says that Walsh, a heavy drinker and womanizer, even wrote his name in the cement. But, alas, there's no sign of the rascally Flynn!

Polish-born musical composer-conductor **Roman Ryterband**, whose classical compositions for harp, flute, and piano included Sonata Breve, Dialogue for Two Flutes, and Suite Polonaise, lived at 1073 Buena Vista Drive from 1967 until his death in 1979. Ryterband was the first American to study the culture and musical heritage of the Agua Caliente Band of Cahuilla Indians. He utilized some of their chants in his local composition Two Desert Scenes.

Actress Marjorie Rambeau in later years (Steve Kiefer Collection).

On July 7, 1970, former stage and screen beauty **Marjorie Rambeau**, nominated for Best Supporting Actress for *The Primrose Path* and *Torch Song*, died eight days shy of her eighty-first birthday at 1248 Buena Vista Drive. Police were alerted after longtime companion Frances Guerra found her body. Rambeau, whose worldly manner made her ideally suited to playing strong-willed women in *Tugboat Annie Sails Again* and *Tobacco Road*, suffered multiple injuries in an automobile accident in 1945 from which she never fully recovered. Many of her subsequent roles were played in a wheelchair or on crutches. Rambeau's third husband of thirty-seven years, Francis Gudger, a vice president of the Plastics Division of Du Pont Corporation and financier of Samuel Goldwyn, died in the same house three years earlier.

★ ★ ★

Gant Gaither, a veteran Broadway producer, director, and stage manager who had a long friendship with Grace Kelly and produced the Debbie Reynolds-Cliff Robertson film *My Six Loves*, moved to the ranch-style house at 1411 Buena Vista Drive in 1992. Gaither, who took up abstract painting at age forty-six and has authored several books, is a member of the board of trustees for the Princess Grace Foundation with Barbara (Cary) Grant, Karl Lagerfeld, Tony Randall, and Barbara Sinatra.

★ ★ ★

Loretta Young's oldest son, **Christopher Lewis**, who inexplicably directed the 1986 horror flick *Revenge* about a devil cult and moonlighted as a nighttime disc jockey on local "easy listening" radio station KWXY, lived at 1477 Buena Vista Drive until 1999. Twenty-six years earlier, Lewis pleaded no contest to child molestation charges after being accused of lewd conduct with two thirteen-year-old boys. He was sentenced to five years probation and a $500 fine.

★ ★ ★

20th-Century-Fox director of publicity **Harry Brand**, a sportswriter-turned-press agent for film financer Joseph Schenck, lived at 1575 East San Jacinto Way in 1956. Brand's early clients included Buster Keaton and Roscoe "Fatty" Arbuckle, whom he befriended after the notorious Coke-bottle rape trial of movie starlet Virginia Rappe in 1921. Brand also swapped stories with writer-pals Damon Runyon, Ring Lardner, and Walter Winchell and was on a first-name basis with most of the country's leaders—from Presidents Truman and Nixon, to California Governors Earl Warren and "Pat" Brown.

While at Fox, Brand, who died at ninety-two in 1989, helped make stars out of Shirley Temple, Alice Faye, Tyrone Power, Betty Grable, and Jeffrey Hunter. His hardest job: transforming stuffy young British actor Rex Harrison into a suave matinee idol nicknamed "Sexy Rexy." Harrison's actress-lover Carole Landis and his fourth wife, Rachel Roberts, killed themselves when he rejected them.

However, Brand's most-publicized *bon mot* came when his biggest client, Marilyn Monroe, whom he wagered $10,000 on a star-making bet, married Joe DiMaggio in 1954. "We're not losing a star," he gleefully announced at a packed press conference. "We're gaining an outfielder." Twenty years after Brand's famous pronouncement, TV director Richard Lang (son of 20th Century-Fox musical taskmaster Walter Lang) bought this home, and Brand moved to South Palm Springs.

★ ★ ★

What is said to be the home of America's favorite piece of cheesecake, **Betty Grable**, who sang and danced her way through such Technicolor trifles as *Moon Over Miami*, *Springtime In the Rockies*, and *Pin-Up Girl*, is located at 1145 East San Jacinto Way. A lack of hard evidence that Grable hid out here between films with her trumpet-playing second husband, **Harry James**, hasn't stopped the rumors.

★ ★ ★

Hungarian-born stage and film lothario **Francis Lederer**'s career spanned half a century from German-made silent films, notably *Pandora's Box*, and the Broadway triumph *Autumn Crocus*, to scores of chic Hollywood talkies and, finally, TV's Cold War espionage series *Mission: Impossible*. He reached an important milestone, his one-hundredth birthday, shortly before dying on May 25, 2000, at the home he shared for almost thirty years with his socialite-wife, Marion Irvine, at 1385 East El Alameda.

Lederer played smooth Continental charmers in many screwball comedies and propagandistic war films such as *Midnight* and *Confessions of a Nazi Spy*. In addition to acting, Lederer owned 250 acres of land in the Los Angeles suburb of Canoga Park. He was honorary mayor there for twenty-five years. He later founded the American National Academy of Performing Arts where he taught weekly acting classes. Many of his students went on to become stars, among them *Dynasty*'s Michael Nader (the nephew of actor George Nader) and *Mad About You*'s Helen Hunt, who made a successful leap to the big screen, notably in *As Good as It Gets*, for which she won an Oscar.

Top: Francis Lederer and Marion Irvine (Courtesy of Marion Lederer). *Bottom:* Hedy Lamarr tempting fate (Larry Edmunds Bookshop).

★ ★ ★

The big rumor on El Alameda is that exotic Austrian-born actress and outdoor naturalist **Hedy Lamarr**, whose full-frontal nudity in the German film *Ecstasy* caused a commotion when it was released in 1932, once owned the home at 1232 El Alameda (on the corner of Hermosa Drive). There's even a brass plaque on the front door, which was recently stolen by a fan, proclaiming it:

HOUSE OF
HEDY LAMARR
ESTABLISHED
1938

However, the rumor of Lamarr's home ownership isn't true—it's a myth. Married six times, Lamarr played temptresses in *Algiers*, *White Cargo*, and *Samson and Delilah* then dropped out of sight. In 1966 and 1991, she was arrested for shoplifting. Lamarr instigated several lawsuits for unauthorized use of her likeness, the last one against E & J Gallo Winery. The case was still pending when police found the eighty-six-year-old actress dead in her Altamonte Springs home near Orlando, Florida, on January 19, 2000.

Dolores Reade keeping a watchful eye on husband Bob Hope (Courtesy of Ward Grant).

In 1946, **Bob Hope**, an honorary mayor of Palm Springs**,** bought his second desert house, this one at 1188 El Alameda, on the corner of Hermosa Drive (part of La Rambla tract development). The house was just doors away from the home of his longtime secretary, Jan King, who answered the comedian's fan mail for more than two decades.

The high-walled, seven-room home was decorated by Loretta Young's mother, Gladys Belzer. It was redone ten years later by interior designers Joan Billings and Gary Jon.

"On El Alameda, we put the pool in and built a wall around the property and did some landscaping, all kinds of things," said Dolores Hope. "Our family grew up in that house, and we had some wonderful times there: weekends and Easter and 'Classic' parties and Memorial Day weekends, when it was too hot to play golf, but just the right temperature for Bob's famous frozen daiquiris."

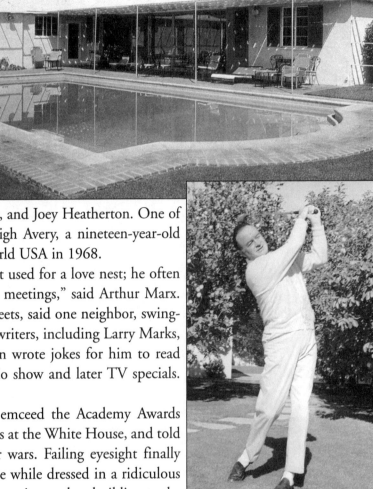

One of Hope's favorite pastimes when he wasn't snacking on hamburgers was "spotting" female talent. When his affair with Barbara Payton cooled off, Hope reportedly took up with a succession of buxom starlets, including Marilyn Maxwell, Rhonda Fleming, and Joey Heatherton. One of his most talked-about flings was Johnine Leigh Avery, a nineteen-year-old beauty contestant who was crowned Miss World USA in 1968.

"Hope's Palm Springs house was not just used for a love nest; he often worked on his scripts there, or held business meetings," said Arthur Marx. To help his timing, Hope would walk the streets, said one neighbor, swinging a golf club for exercise, while an army of writers, including Larry Marks, Norman Sullivan, and gag man Barney Dean wrote jokes for him to read when he went on the air for his weekly radio show and later TV specials. Hope didn't retire until 1996.

During the time he lived here, Hope emceed the Academy Awards twenty-six times, entertained eleven presidents at the White House, and told 100,000 jokes to ten million troops in four wars. Failing eyesight finally forced him to use cue cards, milking applause while dressed in a ridiculous costume or leering at a red-faced beauty contest winner, then building to the next punch line, calling out: *But-I-wanna-tell-ya!*

Top: Bob Hope's "love nest" at 1188 East El Alameda (Howard Johns Collection). *Bottom:* Bob Hope practicing his golf swing (Courtesy of *Palm Springs Life*).

And it was here, in the summer of 2000, that Hope suffered gastrointestinal bleeding three days after his ninety-seventh birthday. A male nurse found him lying unconscious on the bedroom floor and dialed 911. Within minutes, two fire trucks raced to the scene and lifted the stricken comedian onto a stretcher. Hope was taken by ambulance to Desert Regional Medical Center, placed on oxygen, and given two blood transfusions. He was then transferred to Eisenhower Medical Center where his condition improved. He was sent home one week later, quipping, "I'm not dead yet!"

★   ★   ★

In 1968, Pied Pipers band singer and Los Angeles KMPC-AM radio disc jockey **Dick Whittinghill**, who appeared as himself in the films *Will Success Spoil Rock Hunter?*, *It's Only Money*, and *The Lively Set*, lived at 1165 East El Alameda.

★   ★   ★

Hollywood Reporter columnist and bit-part actor **George Christy**, whose weekly column "The Great Life" was suspended when it was alleged that he took roles in some twenty films, including *Die Hard* and *The Thomas Crown Affair* as paid compensation for writing glowing endorsements, resided at 1075 East El Alameda in 1974.

Paramount's sloe-eyed singing star **Dorothy Lamour**, dubbed "Queen of the Sarong," is supposed to have bought the house at 1029 East El Alameda so she could be next to her chummy, pipe-smoking *Road* costar Bing Crosby. Sounds like a nice reason, but it wasn't the case.

The former New Orleans beauty queen, who played virginal island princesses in *The Hurricane* and *Aloma of the South Seas* when she wasn't being the butt of the team's jokes, was never particularly close to either of her costars. (Crosby was too "cold," said Lamour, although she did enjoy Hope's company.)

Indeed, their laughing camaraderie was strictly for the cameras, and offscreen she was never considered a part of the team. "My feelings were hurt," griped the actress after being omitted from a profit-sharing deal on their fifth film together, *Road To Rio*. When it was decided to make a seventh installment, *The Road to Hong Kong*, without her, she was justifiably outraged.

Bing Crosby, meanwhile, supposedly moved into 1011 East El Alameda with first wife Dixie Lee and their three young sons Gary, Philip, and Dennis (Lindsay wasn't yet born) in 1936. This house has had its share of famous occupants: Bill Hamilton lived there when he worked as a design associate for Eva Gabor Interiors in 1971, and Elyane Valdes, the widow of Cuban bandleader Miguelito Valdes, purchased the home in 1979 where she still lives more than twenty years after his death.

Award-winning architect **Donald A. Wexler**, who designed the glass-walled concourse at Palm Springs International Airport, as well as numerous schools and offices, built the house at 1272 Verbena Drive, which sold for $635,000 in 2001. In the same year, the Historic Site Preservation Board proclaimed Wexler's steel-framed houses (located in the northern end of the city) landmarks.

Hip-wiggling, Brazilian bombshell **Carmen Miranda**, who met and fell in love with future husband David Sebastian on the set of the 1948 comedy *Copacabana*, lived in this quaint cottage at 1285 East Verbena Drive prior to moving to Deep Well.

Left: Carmen Miranda wearing fruit (Wayne Knight Collection). *Right:* Carmen Miranda's cottage at 1285 East Verbena Drive (Photo by Howard Johns).

Joan Davis stepping out (Steve Kiefer Collection).

Rubber-faced comedienne **Joan Davis** was once radio's highest-paid actress. Her brazen slapstick humor enlivened many commonplace films, especially as the frightened radio screamer in Abbott and Costello's haunted-house comedy *Hold That Ghost* and the hit TV show *I Married Joan*. She died from a heart attack in 1961 while living in the house she had owned for ten years at 1400 Tamarisk Road.

★　★　★

Winston Hibler, who narrated Walt Disney's Oscar-winning feature-length documentary *The Living Desert* as well as its acclaimed sequel, *The Vanishing Prairie*, lived at 1280 East Tamarisk Road. Hibler's fascinating observations of wild animal behavior, which he cowrote with partner James Algar, helped pave the way for future nature conservation programs on Discovery Channel and Animal Planet. Hibler also directed Disney's *Charlie, the Lonesome Cougar* and *Napoleon and Samantha*, starring an African lion. His son, Chris, has directed episodes of TV's *Remington Steele*, *Matlock*, *Father Dowling Mysteries*, and *Diagnosis Murder*.

★　★　★

In 1953, Academy-winning director **Norman Taurog**, who guided hyperkinetic actor Mickey Rooney to an Oscar in *Boys Town* during a ten-year stint at MGM, lived at 1188 East Tamarisk Road. Taurog then switched to Paramount where he tried to control Dean Martin and Jerry Lewis in the military farce *Jumping Jacks*—the first of five films he made with the boisterous team. A glutton for punishment, he next took on nine middling Elvis Presley musical assignments and kept a tight rein on Robert Conrad, Troy Donahue, and Connie Stevens as party-crashing teenagers in *Palm Springs Weekend*.

★　★　★

Five-time world champion ice skater **Carol Heiss**, who starred in 1961's *Snow White and the Three Stooges* and married fellow Olympic gold medalist figure skater Hayes Jenkins, was reportedly a guest in this elegant home, owned in 1963 by the Ice Capades Corporation, at 1129 East Tamarisk Road. Norwegian ice-skating champion Sonja Henie's name was written in wrought-iron letters on one side of the main entrance and the words Ice Capades were displayed on the other.

Eight years earlier, Louis B. Mayer's son-in-law, **William Goetz**, who was head of production at 20th Century-Fox and Universal, leased the same home from prior owner

Louise Celestin, while producing the Joan Crawford-Cliff Robertson romance *Autumn Leaves*. A Best Picture Oscar nominee for *The House of Rothschild* and *Sayonara*, Goetz was among the first producers to encourage actors to take a percentage of a film's profits in lieu of salaries, thus helping defer expensive production costs.

★   ★   ★

It's long been assumed that the double "H" blue-tiled, monogrammed gateposts of this old-fashioned estate were the initials of a famous Hutton. Neither Barbara nor Betty, however, was the home's actual owner. Nor did the house belong to eccentric billionaire Howard Hughes or A & P grocery chain heir Huntington Hartford as surmised.

That special honor belongs to **Harry Hanbury**, a self-made millionaire and former Oklahoma "wildcatter" who built the home at 796 Via Miraleste, on the southeast corner of Tamarisk Road. In 1933, Hanbury contracted

Harry Hanbury's home at 796 Via Miraleste (Photo by John Waggaman).

tuberculosis, and doctors advised him to relocate to a warmer, dryer climate. He purchased three acres of land in central Palm Springs and erected an enormous two-story house for his wife, Margaret, son Harry Jr., and daughter Helene. The colossal eight-bedroom, seven-bathroom home, completed in 1934, is a wonderful example of early Spanish Colonial Revival architecture, characterized by decorative arches, staircases, and a courtyard entry that was designed by Los Angeles architect Ross Montgomery.

Montgomery conceived the pueblo-themed Our Lady of Mount Carmel Church in Santa Barbara and the ornate Spanish-style St. Andrew's Church in Pasadena. At the time of its completion in 1934, the home's turquoise swimming pool was the largest ever sunk in the city—a source of immense pride for the owner and the envy of all who saw it.

Because of its nostalgic Old World charm and luxurious accommodations, the Hanbury Estate became a home away from home for many visiting politicians and celebrities. **Cary Grant** and his second wife, Woolworth heiress **Barbara Hutton**, whom the press nicknamed "Cash and Cary," reportedly spent their honeymoon in the white stucco main house, which was, at the time, painted pink with a white terra-cotta-tiled roof. The newlyweds made front-page news when they were quietly married on July 8, 1942, at the Lake Arrowhead home of Grant's agent, Frank Vincent. Afterward, the happy couple slipped back unnoticed to Beverly Hills. There is no record of the Grant's Palm Springs honeymoon, but a decade later, the good-looking actor, recalling the fun times he had in the desert, bought his own home less than one block away.

In 1944, Hanbury, who had fallen badly into debt, sold his cherished estate for

$55,000 to Fresno winemaker Krikor Arakelian. Two years later, Hanbury, fifty-nine, died in a Los Angeles sanitarium. The home itself made headlines in 1947 when a bearded faith healer named Avak Hakopian showed up to offer a miracle cure for Arakelian's sickly son. Gawkers stopped traffic to catch a glimpse of the white-robed man making daily pronouncements outside the house, but no cure came out of it.

★　　★　　★

Jennifer Jones relaxes with husband David Selznick (Larry Edmunds Bookshop).

One famous name did spend time at 796 Via Miraleste.

Revered as a master showman, reviled as "the great dictator" for his overbearing pomposity, the achievements of **David O. Selznick**, who either preplanned or scripted many of his films in Palm Springs, is the stuff of legend. Among his long list of credits are *King Kong, Dinner at Eight, David Copperfield, A Tale of Two Cities, A Star Is Born, Rebecca,* and *The Third Man.* Selznick's all-time monument to himself, the Technicolor Civil War epic, *Gone With the Wind,* which won a record ten Academy Awards in 1939, including Best Picture, Director, and Actress, eventually grossed more than $800 million! But the film's masochistically inclined creator was forced to give up part ownership to his imperious father-in-law, Louis B. Mayer, receiving only a faint trickle of its gushing profits in return for worldwide distribution.

When MGM planned a wide-screen reissue of *Gone With the Wind* in 1954, Selznick leaped at the chance to earn additional income from his greatest work. That March, the chain-smoking producer and his actress-wife, Jennifer Jones, four months pregnant with their daughter, Mary, rented the former Hanbury Estate where a butler and maid administered to their personal needs while Selznick dictated a flood of memos and telegrams, advising the studio on how best to show his beloved film. Selznick's efforts paid off, and the picture again achieved enormous profits. There was talk of a sequel, a remake, and even a musical—none of which materialized in his lifetime.

Ten years later, Selznick, in the advanced stages of heart disease, stayed at the Racquet Club in January 1964 while looking for another house to rent.

"He was spending time at Palm Springs and La Quinta, doing his best to rest, playing a little golf, but hating the cold that set in around three in the afternoon," according to biographer David Thomson.

On June 22, 1965, Selznick suffered a fifth heart attack, which proved fatal. He was sixty-three. Two years later, Leonora Cole, his personal secretary and aide for thirty-eight years, who took daily dictation from her obsessive employer and kept bulging files on all his films, retired to a South Palm Springs condominium where she died in 1987 at eighty-one. On May 11, 1976, Jennifer Jones's emotionally troubled daughter, Mary Selznick, jumped to her death from the twenty-second floor of her psychiatrist's office in Westwood, alarming pedestrians whose shrill cries of "Oh, my God!" could be heard above the noise of traffic on Wilshire Boulevard. Mary was twenty-one.

★   ★   ★

In the meantime, Irish singer, Democratic fundraiser, and property developer **Phil Regan** and his wife, Josephine Dwyer, who had been Palm Springs socialites since his arrival in 1934, bought Harry Hanbury's former home. The mansion became a meeting place for such prominent political figures as President Harry Truman, Chicago Mayor Richard Daley, Los Angeles Mayor Sam Yorty, and Governor Edmund "Pat" Brown. In 1974, a Santa Barbara judge sentenced Regan to fourteen years in prison for attempting to bribe a county supervisor to gain rezoning of valuable coastal land above a popular nude beach where Regan planned to build a residential development. Regan's Palm Springs home, listed for sale at $250,000, had been stripped of its outstanding collection of Irish Beleek and stood eerily vacant. After Governor Jerry Brown pardoned him, Regan moved to Santa Barbara where he died in 1996 at the age of eighty-nine.

★   ★   ★

Top: The Zanuck family compound at 346 East Tamarisk Road (Courtesy of Palm Springs Historical Society). *Bottom:* Darryl Zanuck and wife Virginia Fox contemplate his many awards (Courtesy of Darrylin Zanuck Pineda).

Buck-toothed, cigar-chomping movie mogul, producer, and screenwriter **Darryl F. Zanuck**, who was in charge of production at 20th Century-Fox where he put his courageous stamp on nearly two hundred topical films, including *Young Mr. Lincoln*, *The Grapes of Wrath*, *Gentleman's Agreement*, *The Snake Pit*, and *Viva Zapata!*, entertained family and friends at 346 East Tamarisk Road. Zanuck reportedly won this fabulous ten-bedroom, eight-bathroom estate in a poker game with film executive and United Artists president Joseph Schenck, who built the house soon after he divorced his actress-wife Norma Talmadge in 1934.

A former New York pharmacist and amusement park owner, Schenck bankrolled all of Buster Keaton's silent comedies, as well as the films of his former wife and her two sisters, Natalie and Constance Talmadge. He founded Twentieth Century Pictures with Zanuck in 1933 and merged it with William Fox's Film Corporation two years later, renaming the company 20th Century-Fox with Zanuck at the helm.

The polo-playing maverick first left his mark at Warner Brothers where he produced forty films, among them *The Jazz Singer* and *Little Caesar*. But when Jack Warner made it clear to Zanuck that he was only a hired hand, he defected and found a willing ally in Schenck, who saw a great opportunity to consolidate his holdings. They drank a toast to success, and Zanuck saying "Let's beat the bastards!"

Schenck's checkered past caught up with him soon afterward. An IRS audit of his income taxes revealed that he had received thousands of dollars in unreported cash as president of the Motion Picture Producers Association, while making illegal payoffs to mob-controlled Hollywood unions to settle strikes and other labor disputes. Charged with tax fraud and facing a long prison stretch, Schenck testified that he was the innocent victim of two Chicago racketeers, Willie Bioff and George Browne, who, he claimed, had extorted millions of dollars from the studios. Schenck was sentenced to a year in jail and replaced as company president by Spyros Skouras, though he was later exonerated.

Zanuck purchased Schenck's house, helping to ease his friend's financial woes, during the time of Fox's biggest growth in 1943. The acquisition of this fine home, whether won in a card game as claimed or secured with a customary loan, represented Zanuck's strong faith in the desert, both as a place for business and pleasure.

"The walled-off compound, which took up most of a block near the town's center, contained two structures," according to Zanuck's biographer Marlys J. Harris, "— a two-story main house, where the family and servants stayed, and a pool house with four bedrooms and a living room, which guests came to call the 'casino.'"

Between the two white-stucco buildings was a seventy-foot swimming pool, surrounded by mature fruit groves and tamarisk trees. After settling in, Zanuck built a flood-lit tennis court behind the pool house. His wife, Virginia Fox, a former Mack Sennett bathing beauty who loved rhyming words, christened their new home Ric-Su-Dar after the couple's three children, Richard, Susan, and Darrylin. Visitors often referred to it as the desert's royal palace because it was always filled with European nobility, five-star generals, and heads of state.

While living here, Zanuck collected three Best Picture Oscars for *How Green Was My Valley*, *Gentleman's Agreement*, and *All About Eve*—which received a total of fourteen nominations. Zanuck proudly displayed these and other awards on the mantel of his Movie Colony home, which became the setting for high-stakes croquet games with Samuel Goldwyn, Harpo Marx, and George Sanders, as well as lawn parties attended by some of Hollywood's biggest names—Charlie Chaplin, Bette Davis, Clark Gable, Olivia de Havilland, Joseph Cotten, Marilyn Monroe, David Niven, Judy Garland, and Tyrone Power.

"Tyrone and I would wander off for walks or take long lazy drives," remembered Lana Turner. "Although we had separate rooms," she said, "sometimes at night he'd sneak into mine."

They weren't the only ones who enjoyed nighttime dalliances. Many husbands kissed their wives goodnight then prowled the halls looking for unlocked bedroom doors. Once inside, they'd slip beneath the covers of a solitary sleeping guest—or if rejected, beat a hasty retreat. Weekends were the busiest time at Ric-Su-Dar with dozens of luxury automobiles lining both sides of the street. Visitors to the house were never bored. There were amusing games of charades, lively conversations, and an ever-changing menu prepared by the family chef.

"Virginia Zanuck was a sweet and gentle hostess," recalled Kitty Carlisle. Carlisle and her husband, playwright Moss Hart, were houseguests in 1946. Hart discussed the script he would write for *Gentleman's Agreement*, the watershed film that attacked anti-Semitism. Other great literary names that stayed there included John Steinbeck, John Gunther, and William Faulkner. Henry Luce, the cofounder and editor-in-chief of *Time*, and his sharp-tongued wife, Claire Booth Luce, author of the catty stage play *The Women*, were also frequent guests.

Not all was croquet and fancy dinners at the Zanuck home, however. In 1953, three years before Zanuck became an independent producer and was replaced by Spyrous Skouras as head of production at 20th Century-Fox, his teenage heir apparent, Richard, who went on to produce two Best Picture Oscar nominees, *Jaws* and *The Verdict*, as well as 1989's Best Picture winner *Driving Miss Daisy*, was involved in a knife fight with local Indians and was arrested by police. Susan Zanuck, who dated Robert Wagner, later died of complications resulting from alcoholism, and Darrylin, formerly the wife of producer Robert Jacks, was charged with forging her father's will.

To add insult to injury, Zanuck's grandson Dino Hakim (son of Egyptian-born film producer Andre Hakim and Susan Zanuck) was arrested for drug dealing and later died of a heroin overdose. Zanuck himself wasn't immune to the temptations of his own success. His cravings for French food, wine, and women nearly ended his marriage. After he bolted from Hollywood in the midst of male menopause ("He'll be back," said Virginia Zanuck), he was linked to a succession of Parisians with visions of stardom: Bella Darvi, who costarred in *The Egyptian* (she gassed herself to death in 1971); cabaret singer Juliette Greco, who received second billing to Errol Flynn in *The Roots of Heaven*; Irina Demick, one of forty-two international stars in *The Longest Day*; and Genevieve Gilles, who appeared in his next-to-last film, *Hello-Goodbye*.

When Zanuck returned from his fifteen-year European exile, he found Hollywood had changed. His despotic rule was no longer tolerated, and in 1971 he was forced to resign from Fox. Zanuck's own health, like his crumbling empire, was failing him. He flew back to Palm Springs where he sat watching TV, stroking and petting his two Yorkshire terriers, Lisa and Tina, while plotting his nonexistent comeback. On December 22, 1979, his body ravaged by a variety of maladies, including senile dementia, Zanuck died in Desert Hospital following a heart attack. He was seventy-seven.

Unable to come to terms with the loss of her husband, Virginia rearranged family photographs and stared blankly at his empty chair at the head of the dining table. By the

Rory Calhoun's stardom was tempered by heavy drinking and smoking (Backlot Books & Movie Posters).

time of her own death three years later, the surviving family members were embroiled in a bitter feud to get as much money as possible out of their parents' estate.

In 1994, after more than a decade of legal wrangling over the property's ownership, Joseph Clayes, a San Francisco doctor, purchased the home with its sun-streaked canopies, bird-spotted statuaries, and weed-filled lawns for the rock bottom price of $350,000. The only reminder of Zanuck's time there was the empty tennis courts, their spotlights doused like a closed movie set.

★ ★ ★

Gimlet-eyed cowboy actor **Rory Calhoun**, was discovered riding a horse by Alan Ladd and put under contract at Fox. The athletic newcomer starred in a stampede of Westerns, *River of No Return*, *The Treasure of Pancho Villa*, and *Red Sundown*, among them, headlined on TV's *The Texan*, and later wrote several Western novels. He moved to this high-walled residence at 333 East Tamarisk Road in 1970, following his divorce from actress Lita Baron. Seven years later, someone paid the small bounty of $50,000 for Calhoun's house.

★ ★ ★

Producer **David E. Rose** (not the *Bonanza* theme composer who was briefly married to Judy Garland) lived at 330 West El Alameda (off Tamarisk Road and North Avenida Olivos) in 1960. While based in England, the somber-looking Rose—previously head of United Artists Productions and vice president of Samuel Goldwyn Incorporated—produced *Island of Desire*, *Port Afrique*, *The House of the Seven Hawks*, and other films that employed many Palm Springs "villagers" such as Rock Hudson, Linda Christian, and Van Johnson.

★ ★ ★

And, in 1974, **Dale Wasserman**, the inspired playwright of *One Flew Over the Cuckoo's Nest* and the record-breaking theatrical smash, *Man of La Mancha*, rested on his laurels at 770 North Avenida Palos Verdes in between fleeting appearances on the desert cocktail circuit. Local party gossip was that Wasserman, who had written the first draft of *The Vikings* and the initial script of *Cleopatra*, sued Kirk Douglas over the rights to his *Cuckoo's Nest* play, which the actor's son, Michael, eventually made into an Oscar-winning film—without his father who had first played the role on Broadway. Wasserman's unresolved gripe soon turned into a marathon Douglas father-and-son feud that took more than ten years to heal.

★   ★   ★

Tall, broad-shouldered leading man **George Montgomery** alternated between bare-knuckle town tamers in 20th Century-Fox's *The Last of the Duanes*, *Riders of the Purple Sage*, and *Ten Gentlemen From West Point* to well-dressed civilians in *Orchestra Wives*, *Roxie Hart*, and *Coney Island* then back again, finally inheriting the role of streetwise gumshoe Philip Marlowe in *The Brasher Doubloon*. He built the home at 877 North Avenida Palos Verdes in 1952 on land the actor said he purchased from adjoining neighbor and one-time boss Darryl Zanuck.

Montana born and bred, with a distrust of anything phony, Montgomery felt more comfortable in buckskin than gray flannel, though he looked equally good in both. By the time the husky six-footer moved to the desert, his days as Fox's reigning pretty boy were behind him, and the flinty roles he played as Davy Crockett, Bat Masterson, and Pat Garrett asserted his macho independence. Married since 1943 to honey-blonde singer **Dinah Shore**, who was a featured performer in such song-and-dance films as *Thank Your Lucky Stars*, *Up in Arms*, and *Till the Clouds Roll By*, the Montgomerys were the perfect stay-at-home couple. He was handy around the house, and she was an excellent cook.

Dinah Shore and wandering husband George Montgomery. (Courtesy of Palm Springs Historical Society).

More than anything else, George liked carpentry and architecture, and when not working at the studio, he could be found sawing and hammering wood in his garage workshop.

"I found that this hobby of mine became a profitable business, as well as a source of relaxation and pleasure that in no way interfered with my career in pictures," said Montgomery, who built a total of eleven homes for his family and actor-friends, including John Wayne, William Holden, and Ronald Reagan, and handcrafted Colonial-style furniture for many of them.

Because of the couple's joint popularity on TV—he in the Western series *Cimarron City*; she as host of *The Dinah Shore Show*—their Palm Springs house, which was photographed on souvenir postcards, received widespread publicity. One unusual feature: miniature bathroom sinks that were installed for the couple's two children, Melissa and John. By the end of the decade, however, their careers had diverged to such an extent that husband and wife were increasingly apart. It was obvious to other people, too. In June 1961, George and Dinah sat at the kitchen table and talked about a trial separation.

"We have to do what's best for the children," she pleaded. "It's no good," he said. "It's over." They clasped hands. Then George got up and left Dinah alone with the kids. When the Montgomerys divorced in 1962, a mutual friend, Dr. Daniel Kaplan, bought their home. The next year, in a headline-making case of near-fatal attraction,

Jack Benny at home reading a good book (Courtesy of *Palm Springs Life*).

Montgomery's infatuated housekeeper, Ruth Wenzel, with whom he had a brief affair, attempted to shoot the star then herself. She snatched a .38 revolver from under a pillow in the actor's bedroom and fired it at his head, but missed. Montgomery subdued her and called police.

Ladies Professional Golf Association member **Linda Christiansen**, who purchased the house from Kaplan for $320,000 in 1995, said Montgomery's former home, which sold again three years later for $410,000, was full of happy memories. That's probably why Miss Shore, who lost a brave fight with cancer in 1994, and her ex-husband, who survived her by six years, stayed good friends.

★   ★   ★

In 1951, **Jack Benny**, labeled the Meanest Man in the World for his apparent stinginess, but who was, in fact, one of the nicest guys around, putted golf balls in the backyard and picked fruit at his second home at 987 Avenida Palos Verdes (note the letter "B" on the front gates). Built in 1947 for William Perlberg, who produced two of Benny's funniest films, including the uproarious *Charley's Aunt*, and subsequently relocated one street away, this was the first desert house that Benny owned.

"My parents and I spent almost every holiday there, except in summer, and almost every weekend," said their daughter, Joan Benny. Her father relished inviting an eclectic mixture of guests to dinner: Elizabeth Taylor and Michael Wilding, for example, would be seated on one side of Jack Benny and Mary Livingstone with Stewart Granger and Jean Simmons on the other. His tightwad reputation notwithstanding, the Benny's were generous hosts, showering guests with gifts, but in later years after moving to Las Palmas, many of their social activities were curtailed because of his exhausting schedule and Mary's fluctuating health.

Not that they lacked anything. Benny owned two priceless violins—a Stradivarius and Presenda—as well as valuable artworks by Pissarro and Utrillo. In 1997, two decades after the comedian's death, his neglected house was sold for $252,000. It was then totally remodeled with new limestone floors, Berber carpeting, a modern kitchen, and family room. David Lurie, then-general manager of Merv Griffin's Resort Hotel & Givenchy Spa, purchased the house for $545,000 in 1998.

★   ★   ★

From 1952 onward, squat, slick-haired Paramount producer **William Perlberg**, who was associated with many critical and commercial box office hits, among them *The Song of Bernadette*, *Miracle on 34th Street*, *The Country Girl*, and *The Counterfeit Traitor*, relaxed on the weekends with his singer-wife, Josephine Brock, at their 888 North Avenida Palmas estate, which was designed by William F. Cody. Bing Crosby, Grace Kelly, and William Holden, who costarred in Perlberg productions, were among this home's favored dinner guests. They chatted at the boomerang-shaped pool, listened to hi-fi music, and played Parcheesi.

After her husband's death in 1968, "Bobbe," who had sang and danced with siblings Eunice and Kathleen Brock (known professionally as the Brox Sisters) in *Hollywood Revue of 1929* and *Hollywood on Parade*, married songwriter Jimmy Van Heusen, and they moved to Yucca Valley.

★   ★   ★

Twenties daredevil comedian **Harold Lloyd**, who clung so tenuously to an office tower's clock face in *Safety Last* and went on hair-raising car rides and other exciting adventures in *Girl Shy*, *The Freshman*, *For Heaven's Sake*, and *The Kid Brother*, built this rustic country home at 899 North Avenida Palmas (rear entrance: 878 Avenida Palos Verdes) in 1925. This house was far smaller than Lloyd's thirty-two-room Italian Renaissance-style Beverly Hills mansion, christened "Greenacres," which billionaire supermarket tycoon Ron Burkle purchased in 1993 from Marshall Field heir Ted Field for $17.5 million. This four-thousand-square-foot desert house (completed while Greenacres was still under construction) where Lloyd and his actress-wife, Mildred Davis, spent much of their leisure time, has its own hallmarks.

A giant bell hung over the main entrance, where a tiled fountain and gravel courtyard welcomed visitors to the carved wooden front doors. Inside was the large living room with a rough-hewn beamed high ceiling and stone fireplace. There Lloyd, who liked to play endless parlor games, rejoiced following his 1952 win of a special Oscar. A millionaire at thirty-one, who grew up "dirt poor," the bespectacled Lloyd was, like his neighbor, Cary Grant, reluctant to spend a dollar—or spare a dime. He was also deeply superstitious, insisting he enter and leave his home or office through the same door and drive to and from a place along the same route every time. These insecurities probably stemmed from a near-life-and-death experience early in Lloyd's career. A prop movie bomb filled with gunpowder exploded in his face, almost blinding the accident-prone comedian and blowing off the thumb and forefinger of his right hand.

Top: Harold Lloyd's home at 899 North Avenida Palmas (Courtesy of the Asher-White Team). *Bottom:* Harold Lloyd and Mildred Davis (Larry Edmunds Bookshop).

In subsequent films, Lloyd wore a glove and prosthetic device to hide his deformity. It was said that the injured hand gradually became eroticized, although this claim has never been completely proven or dispelled. There were no such concerns at Lloyd's "desert jungle," however, where he entertained writer-directors Leo McCarey and Elliott Nugent, along with actor-friends Lionel Stander and Sterling Holloway (the soft-spoken voice of Winnie the Pooh).

Although a lifelong teetotaler, Lloyd loved a good party and would motor his three children, Gloria, Harold Jr., and Peggy, down for the weekend in one of his exotic cars: a blue Chandler phaeton, Cunningham, red Buick roadster, and closed Pierce-Arrow, as

well as a customized Chevrolet station wagon (he was the first to own a six-cylinder model), Lincoln, Packard, and two Rolls-Royces. Lloyd's other passion was breeding Great Danes and at one time, according to biographer Tom Dardis, he had sixty-five of them. The estate's swimming pool, constructed on land where ripe citrus trees and pink and white oleanders once stood, postdates Lloyd—unlike most stars of the period who relished their privacy—he preferred taking a public dip at El Mirador.

In 1975, four years after Lloyd died from prostate cancer, drive-in exploitation filmmaker **Al Adamson**, who gave the world such vulgar entertainment as *Satan's Sadists* and *Dracula vs. Frankenstein*, occupied these premises during the making of one of his kinky sex films. Lloyd's former house sold for $1.4 million in 2000, reflecting continued interest in his movie career.

Lloyd's father, **James Darsie Lloyd**, lived at 261 West Hermosa Place until his death at eighty-three in 1947.

★   ★   ★

Twice Oscar-nominated romantic screen idol **Cary Grant** and his third wife, actress Betsy Drake, purchased "Las Palomas," the six-bedroom home at 928 Avenida Palmas from Grant's attorney, Stanley Fox, in 1954, shortly after the actor celebrated his fiftieth birthday. Built in 1927, this two-story replica of a nineteenth-century Andalusian farmhouse with Spanish-tile roof, French blue shutters, and cathedral ceilings, is located on one-and-a-half tree-lined acres, surrounded by rose bushes, citrus, date, and olive trees.

"The Grants would rise early in the morning and ride out across the desert to see the sunrise," biographer Nancy Nelson said. "At night, after a long ride, they would cook steaks under the desert moon."

A longtime student of psychiatry, Grant kept an extensive library of books, includ-

Top: Cary Grant's home at 928 Avenida Palmas (Courtesy of Palm Springs Historical Society). *Bottom:* Cary Grant, wife Dyan Cannon and their baby Jennifer (Cinema Collectors).

ing (most tellingly) a three-volume set on the life of Sigmund Freud. Playwright Clifford Odets, a frequent houseguest, enjoyed the writings of Lord Byron and Wordsworth. Katharine Hepburn liked to sit in Betsy's bathtub for hours, she said, reading Sophocles. The home provided a tranquil environment for Grant, a self-confessed neurotic, who hadn't stopped working since he ran away from home at fourteen and joined the circus, sailing from England to America with Bob Pender's acrobatic troupe in 1920.

By the time of his marriage to Drake, however, Grant declared, "I'm retired." But Alfred Hitchcock, who had directed Grant in *Suspicion* and *Notorious*, failed to listen. He drove to the actor's house in early '54, the script of his next film, *To Catch A Thief*, tucked under his arm.

"Don't you think I'm a little too old for that sort of thing?" Grant grimaced as the two men ate lunch by the pool. Hitch chewed his food and smiled. "My wife, Alma, thinks you'd be perfect. So do I," he said. Although they were the best of friends, the bisexual Grant, who suffered from recurring hepatitis, was concerned about his jaundiced appearance in the high-definition Vista Vision process, which made every enlarged pore of an actor's skin look like a moon crater. Hitchcock, squinting in the sun, reassured his favorite star that it was not a problem.

"Grace Kelly wants to do it," he slurped between sips of iced tea. "Let me think it over," Grant cautiously replied. Betsy Drake flipped out when he told her the news. "But you have to do it, Cary," she squeaked at him, her poodle, April, barking in agreement. So Grant packed a suitcase and flew to France for his sixty-first film.

After they divorced, Drake's ex-husband, who was listed in the 1963 Palm Springs phone directory under his real name of Archibald Leach, drove to the Sunair Drive-in to see the Oscar-winning French documentary *The Sky Above, the Mud Below*, shaking his head at the primitive lifestyle of the film's New Guinea headhunters. "It reminds me of Hollywood," he quipped in mock disgust.

After making some of his best films, including *An Affair to Remember*, *Indiscreet*, *North By Northwest*, and *Charade*, Grant wrapped up his thirty-four-year acting career, encompassing seventy-two starring roles, while residing here with his fourth wife, actress Dyan Cannon (the mother of *Beverly Hills 90210* actress Jennifer Grant), whom he married in 1965 and divorced in 1968. Grant, who was awarded an honorary Oscar in 1970, stayed on alone at the house until he sold it in 1972. He died from a stroke in 1986.

Frank Zane, a former Mr. Olympia, who bought the actor's home in 1988, says he found scrapbooks and other mementos in the attic where they'd been stored and forgotten. Ten years later, Zane sold the house for the low price of $720,000 (down from $900,000) to Dr. Jane Cowles Smith, who embarked on a careful restoration supervised by Marty Newman of Historic Southwest Interiors.

★ ★ ★

The first desert home of the late singer-songwriter **John Phillips**, which he rented with fellow singer Scott McKenzie and model-daughter Bijou Phillips, is located at 982

Avenida Palmas. They lived there in 1994 when Phillips was recovering from a liver transplant. What appears from the street to be a normal, two-story Spanish Colonial with a forecourt fountain and cobblestone patio hid a neatly concealed gambling den that was used by anonymous high rollers when the home was built in 1935, complete with a ten-foot-by-eight-foot fireplace to warm visitors on cold winter nights. The house sold in "as is" condition for $620,000 in 1999. Completely restored, it fetched $1.5 million in 2002.

★   ★   ★

Busby Berkeley in rapture over two young bathing beauties (Courtesy of Academy of Motion Picture Arts and Sciences).

Question: "I'm a highly talented dance director, who was one of Hollywood's greatest technical innovators of synchronized dancing, breakaway sets, and overhead crane shots until I suffered a nervous breakdown and was forced to take an early retirement. Because I handled more Palm Springs stars than any other director (they include Eddie Cantor, Ruby Keeler, Al Jolson, Ginger Rogers, Alice Faye, Loretta Young, George Murphy, Carmen Miranda, Frank Sinatra, and Esther Williams), it's appropriate, don't you think, that I chose to live here. Who am I?"

Answer: This unassuming, gray-haired gentleman who was nominated three times for an Oscar was named William Enos, but if he'd told people his real identity, it would have caused a backstage riot. If you haven't already guessed, the man was **Busby Berkeley**, who choreographed the frenetic, geometric dance numbers for *42nd Street, Gold Diggers of 1933, Footlight Parade*, and *Dames*, and who went on to direct three knockout Mickey Rooney-Judy Garland "putting-on-a-show" musicals *Babes in Arms, Strike Up the Band*, and *Babes on Broadway*.

But Berkeley's fame came at a high price. In 1935, at the peak of his moviemaking career, this cinematic wizard's livelihood almost went up in a puff of smoke. On a silvery moonlit night, leaving a film's wrap party in Santa Monica, Berkeley, having drunk one-too-many martinis, crashed his white roadster into oncoming traffic on the Pacific Coast Highway, hitting two cars and killing three people. Berkeley was narrowly acquitted of second-degree murder, but he was never the same.

Following the death of his overbearing mother in 1946, Berkeley, who owned a beaux-arts Italian villa in Los Angeles, attempted suicide by slashing his wrists and was committed to a mental hospital. His comeback was slow, but provided more movie magic: water ballets in *Million Dollar Mermaid* and *Easy to Love*, a tom-tom number in *Rose Marie*, and the trapeze sequence in *Jumbo*. In 1958, Berkeley, slightly slower in body, but no less imaginative of mind, moved into this ranch-style house with a clay pot on the front wall at 318 Via Alta Mira (Palm Springs Estates) where he lived for the next eighteen years. In

1971, he came out of retirement to direct his friend, Ruby Keeler, in the Broadway revival of *No, No, Nanette!* He died here, age eighty, in 1976. (Berkeley's brother, Maurice Enos, lived at 550 Miraleste Court in 1974.)

★　★　★

Among Berkeley's many neighbors during his sunset years was silent screen actor **William "Buster" Collier Jr.**, the devil-may-care star of Raoul Walsh's *The Wanderer* and Frank Capra's *So This is Love*. Collier lived at 358 East Via Alta Mira with his wife, Marie Stevens, a Ziegfeld Follies performer whom Collier married after his retirement from acting in 1934. He later worked as a producer and agent, packaging TV shows for the William Morris Agency.

The adopted son of noted stage actor and playwright William Collier Sr., who cowrote the musical, *The Hottentot*, Collier ran in the same vaudeville circles as his famous father, which included close friendships with Eddie Cantor, Lillian Russell, and George M. Cohan, as well as business tycoon William Randolph Hearst and Constance Talmadge, whom Buster once romanced. He died, age eighty-four, in 1987.

★　★　★

Motown composer **Michael Masser** achieved fame as a white man writing love songs for black superstar Diana Ross, including the blockbuster hits "Do You Know Where You're Going To?" and "Touch Me in the Morning." Masser owned the home at 444 East Valmonte Norte, for which he paid $315,000 in 1991 and served as his desert base for the next several years. A ten-year valley resident, Masser composed the film scores for *Mahogany*, *The Greatest*, and *Stir Crazy*. He also produced Whitney Houston's top-selling album "Didn't We Almost Have It All." He now lives in Rancho Mirage.

★　★　★

Writer-producer **Milton Sperling**, who supervised the frivolous musicals *Sun Valley Serenade* and *Hello, Frisco, Hello*, then joined the U.S. Marine Corps where he oversaw the wartime sagas *To the Shores of Tripoli*, *Crash Dive*, and *Retreat, Hell!*, lived at 487 East Valmonte Norte in 1956—the same year he was named an Oscar nominee for Best Original Screenplay for his riveting script of *The Court-Martial of Billy Mitchell*, starring longtime friend Gary Cooper. Sperling (the husband of Harry Warner's youngest daughter, Betty) died in 1988. David Lyons, the proprietor of Lyon's English Grille, now owns Sperling's home.

★　★　★

Jack Benny, who left a $4-million estate when he died, rented his first home, located at 355 East Valmonte del Sur, in 1947. The Benny's next-door neighbors, according to his daughter, Joan Benny, were actor Tyrone Power and his first wife, French *gamine* Annabella, whom Power costarred with in *Suez* and divorced ten years later in 1948. (The Powers were long-time friends of the Bennys since Tyrone's guest appearance on his radio show.)

"One frequent visitor was Barbara Stanwyck, who usually brought her son, Skip, with her," Joan Benny said. "He was my first boyfriend, and our romance began in Palm Springs," where the two children rode their bicycles and participated in typical childish pranks until Mary Benny discovered they had stolen a jeweler's ring and lectured them on the dangers of shoplifting. Joan learned a valuable lesson, but Stanwyck's stepson disregarded the advice. A troubled youth that had been adopted from a foster home by the four-time Oscar nominated actress, he was later arrested for selling pornography to teenagers.

Pianist-arranger **John Scott Trotter**, who was Bing Crosby's musical director for seventeen years, resided at 419 East Valmonte del Sur during the time he conducted the NBC radio orchestra for its weekly Kraft Music Hall, which ran from 1937 to 1946. A native of North Carolina, Trotter's relaxed bonhomie was perfectly suited to a movie sound stage or big band recording session. In addition to his work on three Crosby films, *Pennies From Heaven*, *Dr. Rhythm*, and *Rhythm on the River*, Trotter served as arranger-composer for several TV series, including *The George Gobel Show*, *Ben Casey*, and *The Bing Crosby Show*. In 1969, he was nominated for an Oscar and Grammy for Best Original Song Score for the animated movie *A Boy Named Charlie Brown*. Trotter died in 1975.

Actress **Joan Perry**, who had been married to Columbia Pictures boss Harry Cohn and smarmy shoe manufacturer Harry Karl, lived at 475 Valmonte del Sur, following the death of her third husband, courtly actor Laurence Harvey, in 1973. When Perry, who costarred in the psychological thriller *Blind Alley* and also appeared in several *Lone Wolf* and *Maisie* movies, wed her first husband Cohn, whom Stanley Kramer called "vulgar, domineering, semiliterate, ruthless, boorish, and some might say malevolent" (he forgot to add wealthy), she promptly retired.

Cohn's stranglehold over actors and writers was as long and dangerous as sections of Ramon Road. He discovered Rita Hayworth, owned 50 percent of William Holden's contract, and invented Kim Novak, who supposedly gave him his first heart attack when informed that his biggest star was shacking up with Sammy Davis Jr. Despite his loathsome reputation, he was a perceptive judge of raw talent and, surprisingly, a man of his word, who expressed bitter disappointment over people's frequent lack of gratitude.

The Cohns often visited the desert to drink and gamble until his 1954 cancer operation, which left the caustic mogul weakened, but still in control of his studio empire, whose recent multiple Oscar winners had included *All the King's Men*, *Born Yesterday*, and *On the Waterfront*. Cohn died right after his greatest production, *The Bridge On the River*

Kwai—winner of seven awards, including Best Picture, Director, and Actor, in 1958. "Where once sat rough, tough basic Harry Cohn, who could belch shamelessly at a formal dinner—to see, at his place, at his table, the elegance of a Larry Harvey," observed songwriter Sammy Cahn, was a marked contrast, indeed.

★　　★　　★

Olympic Games ice skater **Ronnie Robertson**, who won two silver medals and earned a special place in the Guinness Book of Records as the World's Fastest Ice Skater, owned the house at 437 East Via Colusa, where he lived between Ice Capades shows in 1972. Robertson could spin faster than an electric fan (he was timed doing spins at the phenomenal rate of seven to eight revolutions per second or 420 to 480 revolutions per minute). Amazingly dexterous, he could execute as many as forty-five "butterflies" in a row and was even filmed performing a quadruple loop.

A longtime Ice Capades attraction, Robertson was sixty-two when he succumbed to AIDS in 2000. Fellow Ice Capades comedy star Bob MacDonald, who was Johnny Labrecque's skating partner for six years and now lives not far from Robertson's former home, explained the desert's appeal for him and many of his peers. "When we finished touring each year, all of us wanted to go somewhere exciting that wasn't cold," he said. "So we chose places like Hawaii or Palm Springs."

★　　★　　★

If it weren't for the runaway critical and commercial success of *The Jazz Singer* and *The Singing Fool*—the first two Vitaphone musical "talking pictures"—the career of blackface vaudeville entertainer **Al Jolson** might have been a small footnote in cinema history and Palm Springs would probably have been denied one of its most-colorful inhabitants.

Jolson had lobbied hard for the Jewish cantor-turned-jazz singer role, ad-libbing his own dialogue and singing his heart out. The pioneering Warner Brothers, meanwhile, which had invested a lot of time and money in this uncertain enterprise, was rewarded with a special Oscar. By 1929, as a result of this revolutionary new sound process, movies got their permanent voice, and Al Jolson, who insisted on being billed as "the World's Greatest Entertainer" or he wouldn't perform (similar to Michael Jackson's insistence on being called "the King of Pop"), received a much-needed career boost at age forty-three.

Jolson's first recorded visit to the desert, where he was to spend much of his remaining life, occurred in December 1933. That's when the middle-aged performer and his third bride, twenty-four-year-old tap-dancer Ruby Keeler, checked into El Mirador Hotel following completion of their respective solo films *Wonder Bar* and *Footlight Parade*—and prior to their one-and-only film together, *Go Into Your Dance*.

Earlier that same year, Jolson's brother, Harry, opened a small café in San Bernardino. Thereafter, Jolson sought out the therapeutic desert sunshine and golf that soothed his jangled nerves. He bought a big Colonial-style house and five-acre orange grove in

Al Jolson on borrowed time (Larry Edmunds Bookshop).

Encino, and the couple adopted an infant son, who they renamed Al Jolson Jr. The visits to Palm Springs continued until Jolson's growing jealousy of his wife, whose career was fast eclipsing his own, caused the couple to split up. They eventually divorced in 1939, Keeler charging her husband with "extreme cruelty."

A chastened Jolson returned to Broadway, playing 158 performances of *Hold On To Your Hats* until he was sidelined with pneumonia. In the meantime, Keeler married John Lowe Jr., a wealthy California realtor, and she retired. In 1942, Jolson embarked on USO tours of army hospitals in England, South America, North Africa, and Italy, performing in constant heat and rain. The fifty-seven-year-old started complaining of fatigue and was diagnosed with malaria.

In January 1945, after resting up in Palm Springs, Jolson hit the road again, but chest pains forced him to return to Los Angeles where he was hospitalized with a serious lung infection. Jack and Harry Warner arranged for two specialists to be flown in by special plane, and they performed a life-saving operation on the critically ill entertainer at Cedars of Lebanon Hospital, removing part of his rib cage and most of his diseased left lung.

Top: Al Jolson's home at 570 Via Corta (Photo by Howard Johns). *Bottom:* CBS President William Paley (left) and house-guest Freeman Gosden (Courtesy of Palm Springs Historical Society).

Two months later, Jolson proposed to his fourth wife, Erle Galbraith, a shy brunette from Arkansas. They took the train from Los Angeles to Palm Springs where they set off by car for Blythe, only to be told they weren't allowed to marry there. They went to Arizona instead. After he had recovered from surgery, Jolson drove to Columbia Pictures and recorded his catalog of best-selling songs, including "April Showers," "You Made Me Love You," and his biggest hit, "Swanee," for an upcoming Technicolor film biography about his life, starring Larry Parks. Titled *The Jolson Story*, it became the box office sensation of 1946, and Parks, giving the performance of a lifetime (his singing voice was dubbed by Jolson), was nominated for an Oscar as Best Actor.

To celebrate his long-awaited comeback, Jolson purchased the Palm Springs mansion of **Jay Paley**, the tall, debonair uncle and financial backer of CBS president and owner William Paley, at 570 Via Corta. Architect Paul R. Williams, who designed Jay Paley's Bel Air residence, accepted his social status as a "Negro," he said, without complaint, was nevertheless determined to prove himself the equal of his white employers, and what better way than working for some of Hollywood's top stars, designing city and country residences for Lon Chaney, ZaSu Pitts, Frank Sinatra, Lucille Ball, Danny Thomas, Barbara Stanwyck, and two homes for Tyrone Power.

Bill Paley, whose family-owned Congress Cigar Company had been bought by

American Tobacco for $13.75 million, was a neophyte Chicago cigar merchant when he acquired Columbia Broadcasting Systems with the help of his uncle in 1929. The younger Paley spent the next twenty-five years of his life turning the fledgling radio station into a vast media empire—making it, in that time, the most profitable of the three entertainment networks, beating out NBC and ABC. Jay Paley, who taught his nephew the basics of finance, "moved to California where he consorted with starlets and played the horses," according to biographer Sally Bedell Smith, and where, inevitably, Paley's pecuniary indulgences led him to buy this desert compound.

Built in 1934, the low slung, three-bedroom Bermuda-type home was set on one-and-a-half acres with an Olympic-size swimming pool, gazebo, fruit orchard, and tennis courts. Here, the Paleys gathered for their winter vacation, keeping score of their growing fortune in the *Wall Street Journal*, which was delivered to them each week by special messenger.

At the time Jolson purchased this home, Bill Paley was trying to lure some of radio's biggest names away from rival NBC. Therefore, it could be argued that the "sale" of Jay Paley's house was an inducement, if not a bribe, for Jolson's services. "After winning Jack Benny," admitted Bill Paley, "I went after Bing Crosby, whom I had wanted to get back on CBS for fourteen years." Paley's efforts paid off, and in rapid succession he signed, in addition to Crosby, Red Skelton, Edgar Bergen, Burns and Allen, Ed Wynn, Groucho Marx, Fred Waring, and, of course, Jolson. Even Frank Sinatra "who had left us," Paley scoffed, "came back." They weren't the only ones.

Charles Correll, the bass-voiced creator of Andy in the *Amos 'n' Andy* radio series with Freeman Gosden, had owned Jolson's house in 1942. Correll purchased the home for the then-hefty sum of $35,000 from William T. Walker, a Detroit neon sign businessman, who previously lived there. (Two years later, Paul Williams designed a thousand-square-foot Beverly Hills mansion for Charles Correll.) Stephen Goosson, the head of Columbia's art department, who crafted the sets for Frank Capra's *Lost Horizon*, is said to have redecorated Jolson's new home as a gift from studio boss Harry Cohn.

After moving in, the Jolsons adopted a baby boy and brought him to the desert where he was kept in a spare bedroom. Jolson used to lie nude on an upstairs sun deck for a perfect all-over tan while preparing for television and film appearances during the 1948-49 season, among them reprising more hit songs in *Jolson Sings Again*.

Following a strenuous two-week overseas tour of U.S. army bases in Hawaii, Japan, and Korea, Jolson, feeling ill, returned to Palm Springs where "he rested, soaked himself in sunlight, and felt better within days," Herbert Goldman said. On October 23, 1950, Jolson set off for San Francisco where he was slated to appear on Bing Crosby's radio show. That night, after checking in to the St. Francis Hotel, Jolson collapsed and died from a heart attack. He was sixty-four.

Once again, the participation of architect Paul Williams was sought to design a lasting tribute. His Al Jolson Memorial Shrine stands at Hillside Memorial Park. The next year, Jolson's widow married the successful Broadway playwright, **Norman Krasna**—the home's next owner through 1955. A three-time Oscar nominee, who won a fourth time for his screenplay of *Princess O'Rourke*, Krasna also wrote the romantic comedy *Indiscreet*, starring Cary Grant and Ingrid Bergman.

In addition to which, Frank Sinatra, driving straight from the set of *Pal Joey*, stayed at 570 Via Corta while awaiting completion of his Tamarisk Country Club home in 1957. Parking meter king Donald Duncan then owned the house in 1960. A seventh celebrity resident, singer Allan Jones, lived there with his third wife, Mary Florsheim, between nightclub gigs in 1965. Thirty hot summers later, *Hollywood Babylon* writer and avant-garde filmmaker Kenneth Anger occupied the guesthouse for five years while bus tour operators made daily stops outside the home, pointing out its peeling roof, weathered marble statues, and messy garden. Anger, kept awake at night by unseen noises, swore the property was haunted with Jolson's ghost—or was it a howling coyote? The current owner, James Stirbl from Costa Mesa, paid $775,000 for the house in 1985.

★   ★   ★

In 1960, Hollywood's then-hottest celebrity couple, **Tony Curtis** and **Janet Leigh**, paid $46,000 for this modern post-and-beam home built by Roy Fey at 641 North Camino Real (Caballeros Estates). They entertained close friends Frank Sinatra and Kirk Douglas, with whom the Curtises had recently costarred in *The Vikings*.

"One birthday we had a party, and Tony hired a plane to fly overhead with a banner, 'Happy Birthday Janet,'" remembered Leigh, who even had T-shirts printed with the house's nickname: Camp Curtis.

That year, Curtis, a Best Actor Oscar nominee for *The Defiant Ones*, had three of his biggest box-office hits: *Some Like It Hot*, *Operation Petticoat*, and *Spartacus*. To add to their joy, his wife had also been nominated for an Oscar as the bank-robbing heroine in *Psycho*.

Janet Leigh and Tony Curtis dry off their wet poodle after a swim (Courtesy of Palm Springs Historical Society).

"I waltzed around the living room and out onto the terrazzo floors of the patio, past the pool, and into the garden," said Leigh. But she didn't win.

The couple's fairy-tale marriage, which lasted ten years, ended in 1962. Janet kept the house for two more years then sold it to MCA talent agent Mort Viner, who represented such stars as Dean Martin, Shirley MacLaine, and Jimmy Stewart. Looking back, Curtis, who invested his money in property in California and Hawaii, where he parlayed smaller homes into bigger homes, reflected, "I never went broke," insisting "I've always had a flair for real estate."

He's not kidding. This home netted $265,000 for its lucky seller in 1994. The silver-haired star, who was feted at the 1995 Palm Springs International Film Festival, is now a highly sought-after artist of impressionist paintings. In 2002 the home sold for $840,000.

★   ★   ★

Donald Woods, the self-professed King of the Bs, who starred in two of Universal's Crime Club films with Nan Grey, *The Black Doll* and *Danger on the Air*, and played Lupe Velez's exasperated husband in RKO's first three *Mexican Spitfire* movies, had a dual career. He was also a successful desert realtor before retiring from both endeavors to this cul-de-sac home at 690 North Camino Real in 1988. Wood's home sold for $180,000 in 1997. He died in Hallmark Retirement Assisted Living the following year at age ninety-one.

★   ★   ★

Top: Donald Woods (right) playing second fiddle to Rin-Tin-Tin and child actor Bobby Blake (Steve Kiefer Collection). *Bottom Left:* Gloria Swanson at seventy-seven (Steve Kiefer Collection). *Bottom Right:* Singer Dick Haymes in fine voice (Wayne Knight Collection).

The Spanish Mediterranean-style home at 635 East Granvia Valmonte (on the corner of Via Miraleste) has a double mark of distinction. Argentine singing rave **Dick Haymes**, whose melodious tones turned "It Might As Well Be Spring" (a 1945 Oscar winner for Best Song from *State Fair*) and the St. Patrick Day standard "Irish Eyes Are Smiling" into number one hits, and his third of six wives, Nora Eddington, a stunning redhead who was previously married to Errol Flynn, resided on the grounds in 1952. The next year they divorced, and Haymes married voluptuous sexpot Rita Hayworth.

Two decades later, silent screen queen-turned-sculptor and health food advocate **Gloria Swanson** purchased the eight-room house and lived there part time from 1970 until her fourth comeback, in *Airport 1975*.

"When Universal Studios sent me the original script in the spring of 1974 and I realized they wanted me to play the aging alcoholic actress in it, I turned it down flat," she said.

William Frye, the film's producer, made a brilliant suggestion: Why not have her play herself? And Swanson did.

The next year, the erratic *Sunset Boulevard* diva returned to New York to marry her fifth husband, screenwriter William Dufty, and pen her long-awaited memoirs. In the book, she coyly revealed her numerous love affairs, notably her three-year relationship with banker and film producer Joseph Kennedy, a one-time bootlegger who financed several of her films, including the calamitous *Queen Kelly*. Despite repeated assertions that the couple stayed at various addresses in the desert, they did most of their snuggling at Kennedy's home in Palm Beach, Florida, which might account for the geographical mix-up.

However, Swanson did make periodic trips to the West Coast to see friends in nearby Palm Desert. Swanson's former Movie Colony home, which recently sold for $940,000, has had several other owners, none of them as fickle or fabulous as she. Swanson died in 1983 at age eighty-four.

The home of **Marion Huntington**, daughter of Pacific Electric Railway builder Henry Huntington, whose red streetcars provided the first rapid transit service throughout Los Angeles, is located at 735 Granvia Valmonte, on the corner of Los Nietos Road. The orange-walled estate has been featured in many TV series, most notably a lavish garden wedding in *The Bold and the Beautiful* and several exterior segments of *P.S. I Luv U*.

★ ★ ★

Smiling operatic tenor **Allan Jones** played dashing Gaylord Ravenal in the 1936 film version of *Show Boat*, costarring Irene Dunne, then courted Jeanette MacDonald in *The Firefly*, and was the cheerfully mixed-up hero of two frenzied Marx Brothers comedies, *A Night At the Opera* opposite Kitty Carlisle, and *A Day At the Races* with Maureen O'Sullivan. He hosted small gatherings with his second wife, actress Irene Hervey from 1939's *Destry Rides Again*, in the house with the wagon wheel in the front garden at 1036 Via Alta Mira (off Avenida Caballeros). Their Grammy-winning singer-son, Jack Jones grew up here prior to cutting his own records and joining neighbor Bob Hope on a USO tour of Vietnam. Jack remembers when the neighborhood was all dirt roads!

Top: Allan Jones (left) and son Jack Jones (Wayne Knight Collection). *Bottom:* Van Johnson and wife Eve Wynn (Larry Edmunds Bookshop).

Carrot-topped leading man **Van Johnson**, who hid his nervous stage fright in carefree musicals such as *In the Good Old Summertime* and *Brigadoon* and mustered additional courage in the hard-hitting dramas *Battleground* and *The Caine Mutiny*, first visited Palm Springs as a novice contract player in 1941. Two years later, Johnson was nearly killed when he crashed his DeSoto convertible driving to a private screening at MGM, but he survived with a metal plate implanted in his forehead to become the studio's reigning Boy Next Door, appearing opposite June Allyson, Esther Williams, Janet Leigh, and Elizabeth Taylor in quirky romantic comedies.

The smiling, freckle-faced actor vacationed at the Racquet Club prior to filming *The Last Time I Saw Paris* in 1954. He returned in 1955 after completing *Miracle in the Rain*, costarring Jane Wyman, with wife Eve Abbott, who had been married to his best friend, Keenan Wynn, and bought the ranch-style house at 1049 Via Alta Mira.

Johnson's unconventional marriage was a constant source of speculation. Eve and Van had custody of Wynn's two sons, Ned and Tracy. Wynn was a regular visitor to the Johnson home. Ned Wynn, who described his parents' unusual relationship as "an inseparable threesome," later observed of his middle-aged stepfather, "he seemed powdered up, rouged, florid, and soft"—alluding to Johnson's long-rumored homosexuality.

In 1962, while appearing in the London stage production of *The Music Man*, Johnson reportedly fell in love with the show's lead male dancer, according to biographer Ronald Davis, and Eve filed for divorce, which was granted after six years. Their home was sold by court order, and Johnson was forced to go on the road singing in dinner theaters to pay his bills. Two decades later, he replaced Gene Barry in the Broadway musical *La Cage aux Folles*.

European character actor **Gregory Gaye**, who cornered the market for playing sharp-tongued German generals and thick-accented Russian counts in more than one hundred films, including *Dodsworth*, *Ninotchka*, *Casablanca* (Bogart: "Your cash is good at the bar." Gaye: "What? Do you know who I am?" Bogart: "I do. You're lucky the bar's open to you."), and *Auntie Mame*, resided at 1066 Via Alta Mira in 1975. His nephew is George Gaynes, the daffy Commandant Eric Lassard in seven *Police Academy* movies.

At the spotless domicile of **Frank Sinatra**, there are no restless ghosts, only the lilting sounds of lullabies on acetate discs he made long ago: "I Fall In Love Too Easily," "Fools Rush In," and "Take My Love." When the skinny Columbia recording artist, MGM movie star, and teenage bobby-soxer idol first hit Palm Springs, the place was already jumping. After he arrived, things really started to hop. In fact, "the Voice" liked the night life so much, he built his first home, named Twin Palms, at 1148 East Alejo Road (renumbered 1145 East Via Colusa) so he could be close to all the downtown action.

Cruise by, and you'll see why it was such a popular party house. Built in sixty days for a reported cost of $110,000 in 1947, this redwood-clad, four-bedroom home was designed by longtime desert architect E. Stewart Williams, who went on to create some of the city's most-recognizable landmarks: Palm Springs High School, Desert Hospital, Temple Isaiah, Coachella Valley Savings (now Washington Mutual), and, last but not

Ava Gardner and Frank Sinatra in high spirits (Cinema Collectors).

Frank Sinatra's "Twin Palms" home at 1148 East Alejo Road (Courtesy of Palm Springs Historical Society).

least, Desert Museum.

Contrary to what has been alleged about the singer's behavior over the years, Sinatra was not a difficult client. "We got along just fine," shrugged Williams, an advocate of modernism, who decided to be creative and use natural building materials to complement the desert terrain.

Among the special features incorporated into the design of Sinatra's house were a movie projection room, studio-quality sound equipment for cutting his own records, a home-security intercom system, and electric automatic-opening front gates—a novel idea back in '47. A floor-to-ceiling, retractable sliding wall opened onto a wraparound patio, cabana, and swimming pool where a breezeway with architectural cutouts creates a black-and-white piano-key effect when the sun is at high noon—though Williams insisted that was not his intention. "It was an accident," he said.

At Christmastime, Sinatra filled the home with friends and guests. Phil Silvers, Jack and Mary Benny, George Burns, Gracie Allen, Sammy Cahn, and actor Don McGuire would take turns entertaining the assembled group. Cahn even wrote R-rated parodies of various songs that he performed after Frank's wife, Nancy, had tucked their three children Nancy Jr., Frank Jr., and Tina, into their bunk beds.

When Frank and Nancy divorced in 1951, Sinatra continued to live there with second wife **Ava Gardner**. When her career eclipsed his with her starring turns in *The Snows of Kilimanjaro* and *Mogambo*, jealousy was sparked, and the two separated in 1953. In 1954, Sinatra's career was revived when he won an Oscar for Best Supporting Actor as the murdered army private, Angelo Maggio, in *From Here to Eternity*.

The echoes of laughter, the rattle of ice cubes, and smell of freshly lit cigarettes still permeated the living room forty-five years later when *Fight Club*'s Brad Pitt was photographed reclining on the fireplace hearth wearing a sexy woman's dress and pursing his lips for the cover of *Rolling Stone*.

After Sinatra and Gardner's tumultuous parting—he threw her clothes onto the driveway in front of Lana Turner—the house was sold to Elsinore Machris, a strait-laced Los Angeles millionaire philanthropist and widow of George Machris, the founder and first president of Wilshire Oil Company. Mrs. Machris, who was unimpressed by Sinatra's extramarital shenanigans despite huge numbers of adoring fans that camped outside on the street, gave $1 million to the City of Hope Medical Center in Duarte and donated another $25,000 to the Desert Press Club, of which she was founder and honorary life president.

Prior to Sinatra's exit, Oscar-nominated playwright Moss Hart leased the house in preparation for writing an updated version of *A Star Is Born* as a comeback vehicle for Judy Garland. Garland had temporarily cured her blues by marrying Sid Luft, a professional gambler who owned the movie rights to the famous racehorse, Man O'War. Hart and Garland met at Sinatra's home where she excitedly spilled forth her ideas for playing the modernized role that had been fused into moviegoers' consciousness a generation earlier by Janet Gaynor. Hart was so bowled over by Garland's enthusiasm for the part, he turned in a finished script with musical interludes by Harold Arlen and Ira Gershwin in three months.

In 1954, Machris remarried and sold the home to Hugh Young, an avowed Sinatra fan, who owned the Rosemead-based chain of Boulevard Dry Cleaners. Because of a fall in real estate prices, Young paid approximately $55,000 for the home and its contents, according to his nephew, Howard Chester. Young eventually retired and moved into the house where he lived for the next forty years—refusing to change anything that Sinatra owned including the drapes and outmoded telephones. In failing health, still playing Sinatra's old records although he could barely hear them, Young died in 1997, age ninety-two. His wife, Maurine, whom he had married in Texas in 1928, preceded him in death two years earlier.

Their precious home, unchanged for forty-three years, was finally sold to Marc Sanders for $135,000. It was dilapidated and overgrown with thick vegetation. Ahead of Sanders lay ten months of extensive restoration, from tearing up worn floor coverings and replacing old doors and windows to remodeling the kitchen. Concrete living room floors were washed and acid-etched. Wood-framed windows were refitted with metal-framed, dual-tempered glass; and a wood-paneled dividing wall, where the movie projector had been located, was replaced with Arizona flagstone to match the stone in the rest of the house.

Because the original wood siding was badly deteriorated, it was removed and the exterior walls restuccoed. The wooden gates and fence posts where Sinatra and his paramours had noisily come and gone were dismantled, and a concrete-block wall and steel gates erected in their place to keep out unwanted trespassers. Sanders's painstaking restoration of Sinatra's home resulted in the preservation of a crucial piece of local history, which became by fortuitous timing (a revival in midcentury modern architecture, booming real estate prices, the death of Sinatra), a touchstone for Palm Springs's financial rejuvenation. This achievement was reflected in the home's jaw-dropping selling price of $1,345,000 in 2000.

Chapter 7

Palm Springs Central

This gentrified neighborhood of low-priced homes and condominiums, typified by Veterans Tract, were built in the immediate postwar boom and are indicative of the city's urban sprawl. It encompasses the heavily populated residential and commercial areas fanning out from Avenida Caballeros along Alejo Road east to Palm Springs International Airport and further south to Ramon Road. These subdivisions include Palm Springs Mall, Los Compadres, and Demuth Park.

Jerry Antes (right) dancing with June Allyson (Courtesy of Jerry Antes).

★　★　★

Actor-singer-dancer **Jerry Antes**, whose nimble feet graced many a Hollywood musical both as a performer and choreographer, including *Rear Window*, *The Opposite Sex*, *Under the Yum Yum Tree*, and the 1973 revival of *No, No, Nanette!*, now lives in a two-bedroom condominium at 865 East Arenas Road.

★　★　★

Could it be that **Menahem Golan**, who owns a Villa Caballeros condominium at 255 South Avenida Caballeros, is the same person who made those terrible Yiddish popcorn movies that cleared cinemas almost twenty years ago? It certainly appears that way. Golan's cultural legacy will be forever linked to cousin and former business partner Yoram Globus's boom-and-bust Cannon Films that dropped some of the biggest box office bombs in modern-day film history, including *Enter the Ninja*, *Death Wish 2, 3, 4,* and *5*, *Missing in Action*, *The Delta Force*, and *Masters of the Universe*. However, they did manage to score a critical hit or two: the Oscar-nominated *Runaway Train* and *Barfly*. Nice try, but no cigar.

★　★　★

185

Clara Bow in thoughtful repose (Larry Edmunds Bookshop).

A better bet artistically speaking is the home of the late actor **Roy Dean**, who retired to a Caballeros Estates one-bedroom condominium at 280 South Avenida Caballeros in 1998. Dean played minor roles as English menservants and officials in *Midnight Lace*, *The Music Man*, and *My Fair Lady*, but is more appreciated as a pioneer of male nude photography with publications of *A Time in Eden*, *In Search of Adam*, *Reflections of Men*, and his final book, *Adam Today*. He died in 2002.

★　　★　　★

Dimple-cheeked with bobbed red hair, cupid lips, and an insatiable appetite for living, **Clara Bow** was the personification of 1920's Flaming Youth—a star that was every bit as popular as Garbo and her box office rival, Louise Brooks. Dubbed the "It" girl because of her magnetic personality and pulsating sex appeal, Bow alternatively captivated, aroused, and enraged moviegoers with her realistic performances as man-crazy flappers in *Dancing Mothers*, *Mantrap*, and *It*, the film that brought her eternal fame and everlasting personal shame.

With the coming of sound, Bow continued to strut her stuff in *The Wild Party*, *Dangerous Curves*, and *The Saturday Night Kid*. Following a nervous breakdown and failed suicide attempt, Bow received electric shock treatment during a prolonged stay in a Los Angeles sanitarium. After separating from her actor-turned-politician husband, Rex Bell, a frumpy, middle-aged Bow made periodic trips to the desert where she visited *Wings* costar Charles "Buddy" Rogers, Janet Gaynor, and Bob Hope. Bow's mental illnesses, real and imagined, could fill up both sides of a psychiatrist's notebook: bulimia, claustrophobia, hysteria, insomnia, hypochondria, nymphomania, and schizophrenia.

Her father dead, husband away, and two sons, Tony and George, serving in the armed forces, "Clara spent Christmas of 1959 without her family," stated biographer David Stenn, the same year she or her namesake was listed in the phone book at 200 North Avenida Caballeros, which was the location of Cliff's Stables. (Other Bow sightings were reported as far south as the Mesa.) Bow died from a heart attack, age sixty, in 1965.

★　　★　　★

If Clara Bow had been around for two more decades, she would have been a welcome guest at **La Mancha Private Villas** at 444 North Avenida Caballeros, where Mickey Rooney, Elizabeth Taylor, Harry Belafonte, Barbra Streisand, and James Brolin have all stayed. The twenty-acre, gated compound is located on the site of the old Palm Springs airstrip where, before the advent of jet air travel, the likes of Howard Hughes, Edgar Bergen, and Jimmy Van Heusen landed their planes. Then in 1949, construction began on a new, bigger runway further east where Palm Springs International Airport, the final destination of golfing millionaires in their Lear jets, and U.S. presidents alighting from Air Force One, stands today.

★　　★　　★

What do the Broadway musicals *Bye Bye Birdie*, *How to Succeed in Business Without Really Trying*, and *Funny Girl* have in common? They featured resplendent lighting and scenery by veteran set designer **Robert Randolph**, an eight-year resident of the Palm Regency condominiums at 1360 East Andreas Road. Randolph's impressive list of credits includes *Funny Girl* starring Barbra Streisand, Gwen Verdon as *Sweet Charity*, and Lauren Bacall in *Applause!* During the 1964-65 season, he had eleven shows running on Broadway, receiving a total of eight Tony Award nominations, but never won.

If the loss bothered him, he didn't show it. On TV, Randolph designed *Liza with a Z*, which was Liza Minnelli's first musical special, as well as 1985's *Night of 100 Stars*. He also designed Broadway revivals of *Gypsy*, *Porgy and Bess*, and *Seven Brides for Seven Brothers*. He died, age seventy-seven, in 2003.

Emmy-winning screenwriter **Martin Ragaway**, who concocted the scripts for *Abbott & Costello In the Foreign Legion* and *Ma & Pa Kettle Go to Town,* and later wrote episodes of *The Brady Bunch*, *The Partridge Family*, and *Diff'rent Strokes*, maintained a weekend home for ten years in the Greenhouse at 1172 East Casa Verde Way, where he wrote humor books about golf and fishing until his death in 1989.

British writer-comedian **Michael Bentine**, a founding member of *The Goon Show* with Spike Milligan, Harry Secombe, and Peter Sellers, was a ten-year winter resident at 433 North Hermosa Drive until he died in 1996.

Top: Ben Pollack playing the drums (Wayne Knight Collection). *Bottom:* The home at 550 North Paseo De Anza where Ben Pollack hanged himself (Photo by Howard Johns).

★   ★   ★

Ben Pollack was known as the Father of Swing during the infancy of the big band craze when he had Benny Goodman, Harry James, and Glenn Miller, among other top "sidemen" such as Victor Young, Jack Teagarden, and Charlie Spivak, in his New York orchestra's lineup.

On June 7, 1971, Pollack was found dead in the bathroom of his home at 550 North Paseo De Anza (off East Alejo Road). He had hanged himself two weeks before his sixty-eighth birthday. Frank Marty, a friend, discovered the bandleader's body dangling from a shower rail. After moving to the desert in 1965, Pollack, who gambled and lost his money in a failed nightclub venture, left two suicide notes complaining of despondency. "Songs of the Islands," the musical theme that he played with verve at every performance, was in stark contrast to the rancor Pollack felt towards the cutthroat music business. His death touched off stories about failed litigation and unpaid royalties. The final insult was that his televised funeral drew hundreds of people the bandleader had most despised, including many individuals who, he claimed, owed him money.

Bearded character actor **Mickey Finn** (not the late British *T. Rex* rock band drummer), who played a variety of lummoxes, cowboys, and pirates in *Pardners*, *The Alamo*, *One-Eyed Jacks*, and *Sergeants 3*, lived at 505 North Calle Marcus in 1960.

Kazowee! Gangly, loose-limbed vaudevillian **Gil Lamb** whose contortions got big laughs in the World War II servicemen's comedies *The Fleet's In* and *Star Spangled Rhythm*, moved to a three-bedroom condominium owned by his de-facto wife, Irene Griffith, at 792 North Madrid Circle in 1986. Lamb was reportedly one of the first actors to portray Bozo the Clown on TV (followed by Larry Harmon and Willard Scott). In 1960, he inherited Jack Haley's role as the Tin Woodman in NBC's color special *The Land of Oz*. Gil appeared as himself in the memorable party scene of *Breakfast at Tiffany's*. He also played comical characters in *Bye Bye Birdie*, *Good Neighbor Sam*, and *The Love Bug*. A heavy drinker and smoker, who became reproachful of other comedians, Lamb was eighty-nine when he died in 1995.

Child actor **Bob Anderson**, who played Jimmy Stewart as a boy in *It's a Wonderful Life*, now lives at 540 North Lujo Circle (off Alejo Road and Sunrise Way). Anderson also portrayed childhood versions of Zachary Scott in *Ruthless* and John Payne in *Maryland*. Today, Anderson works as a sound mixer and production manager for various film studios, having racked up screen credits on *My Cousin Vinny*, *Sgt. Bilko*, *My Favorite Martian*, and most recently, *The Scorpion King*. He also worked as a line producer and production consultant on the Wesley Snipes thriller, *Passenger 57*, *Demolition Man*, and *Heat*.

Two-fisted movie bad guy and former Hollywood Palladium bouncer **Chris Alcaide** played sneering thugs in more than eighty TV Westerns and took a savage beating from Glenn Ford in *The Big Heat*. He lives at 502 North Cerritos Road with his Turkish-born photographer-wife Peri Hatman, who enjoyed her own fifteen minutes of fame when she played a travel guide in the Errol Flynn melodrama *Istanbul*.

In 1956, Argentine rave **Fernando Lamas**, who swept Lana Turner off her feet in *The Merry Widow*, kept pace with Esther Williams in *Dangerous When Wet*, and made passionate love to his third wife, Arlene Dahl, in the 3-D adventure *Sangaree*, was Ernest Dunlevie's houseguest, along with Dahl, the mother of their future son, Lorenzo Lamas, at 1897 East Alejo Road (Desert Palm Estates).

★　★　★

Stephen Boyd, the granite-jawed Irish leading man who rose to international prominence as Messala, the villainous opponent of Charlton Heston, whipping his horses and locking wheels with him in the rousing chariot race of *Ben-Hur*, was able to indulge his passion for solitary sports while living in the desert.

"I'm a loner, I always have been," revealed Boyd, who was thirty-seven years old and unmarried when he resided at 501 North Juanita Road (off Farrell Drive and Alejo Road) in 1965—the same year a ticket seller spotted him watching *Lord Jim* at the Palm Springs Drive-In. Despite efforts to broaden his dramatic range, however, Boyd became typecast in marathon sixties historical epics such as *The Fall of the Roman Empire*, *Genghis Khan*, and *The Bible*. His career fizzled out in cheaply made Spanish films, and he died from a heart attack while playing golf in 1977.

★　★　★

Huell Howser, the aw-shucks host of *California's Gold* on PBS, which has presented more than thirty programs about Palm Springs history and lifestyle, recently bought and renovated the house at 247 North Monterey Road, in the Alejo Palms subdivision, which was first developed by Jack Meiselman in 1960. When these non-Alexander homes first came on the market, they boasted such useful features as Youngstown kitchens with built-ins and American Standard fixtures. The model home that launched one hundred others just like it still stands at 506 North Monterey Road.

★　★　★

Top: Fernando Lamas makes love to Arlene Dahl (Larry Edmunds Bookshop). *Middle:* Stephen Boyd exuding virility (Cinema Collectors). *Bottom:* Huell Howser out and about (Courtesy of Huell Howser Productions).

Renegade architect **William F. Cody**, whose technical brilliance was compromised, it was said, by his contempt for authority and a serious drinking problem, resided at 1950 East Desert Palms Drive, where he suffered a stroke and was confined to a wheelchair for the last eight years of his life. Cody (no relation to Buffalo Bill) designed the Spa Hotel, Palm Springs Library Center, Sunrize Plaza, and Saint Theresa Catholic Church—the place of his memorial service in 1978. Most of Cody's peers agree that he, more than any other architect, pioneered desert architecture in its purest form. But his bellicose nature caused him to be denied that honor in his lifetime. In death, however, he has earned his rightful place as a true innovator.

Zsa Zsa Gabor's second husband, **Conrad Hilton**, the self-made founder of the world-wide hotel chain that bears his name (he also wrote the autobiographical tome *Be My Guest*, a copy of which was placed in every room by his diligent staff), gave the short-tempered Hollywood actress a daughter named Francesca before she dumped him for actor George Sanders. Hilton slept in the recessed, double tennis court estate that he owned at 1961 East Desert Palms Drive (off North Sunrise Way between Alejo and Amado Roads).

Hilton's son, Conrad Jr., was Elizabeth Taylor's first of eight husbands. His grandson, Rick, is the father of actress-models Paris and Nicky Hilton, who are heirs to their great-grandfather's fortune—a respectable $108 million at the time of his death in 1979!

In 1957, Hollywood composer **Ted Grouya**, who cowrote the love songs "Flamingo," "In My Arms," and "I Heard You Cried Last Night," which spent thirteen weeks on the hit parade, resided one block south at 2155 East McManus Drive. His son is independent filmmaker Ted Grouya Jr., who wrote, directed, and produced *Jerks*.

Andrew Morgan Maree III, the former president of A. Morgan Maree, Jr., & Associates, which assisted in the preparation of income tax returns and business investments for a select group of Hollywood clients, is now retired at 246 North Saturmino Drive (off Tahquitz Canyon Drive). Andy Maree's late father, A. Morgan Maree Jr., was David O. Selznick's business manager from 1944 until 1952. He also was the trusted adviser to Humphrey Bogart and Lauren Bacall, and arranged the purchase of the novel, *Beat the Devil*, which became a cult film under the supervision of another Maree client, director John Huston.

Over the years, Maree Jr. invested stars' salaries in oil wells, shopping centers, and office buildings, even a production company—Four Star Television, founded by Dick Powell, Charles Boyer, David Niven, and Ida Lupino. Maree III's artist-wife, Wendy Smith, who passed away from cancer in 2000, was previously married to singer Dick Haymes.

Harper Goff is a Hollywood art director who did not receive the credit he deserved. Among his many accomplishments is creating the vivid storyboards for Walt Disney's live-action classic *20,000 Leagues Under the Sea*, complete with a man-eating giant squid. His futuristic design of Captain Nemo's Victorian submarine "Nautilus" became a featured attraction for several decades at Disneyland, where Goff also drew the turn-of-the-century firehouse, city hall, and emporium for Main Street U.S.A. (based on his hometown of Fort Collins, Colorado) and the Jungle Cruise (modeled on John Huston's *The African Queen*), among other memorable rides.

Harper Goff's vision of microscopic man in *Fantastic Voyage* (Larry Edmunds Bookshop).

Goff lived at 266 North Sunset Way in 1963. Perhaps his most-remarkable achievement was his oversized movie set designs that re-created various organs in the human body into which a miniaturized group of scientists were injected by hypodermic needle. Their mission? Stop a lethal blood clot from reaching a man's brain in 20th Century-Fox's *Fantastic Voyage*.

As unfair as it was, Goff was deprived of *two* Oscars for Best Color Art Direction that were awarded to *20,000 Leagues Under the Sea* and *Fantastic Voyage* because he was not a union member. Goff had to accept commiserations from his peers on the first loss and a small acknowledgment for "creative production research" on the second, while others claimed the awards.

Twice-elected city mayor and jack-of-all-trades **Frank Bogert**, who eked out a profitable living as a horse wrangler, hotel manager, and magazine publisher, is older than the street he lives on at 2787 East Plaimor Avenue (Sunmor Estates). A valley resident since 1927, Bogert, who recently turned ninety, does not need to worry about his place in history. He is immortalized in bronze riding a galloping steed outside the steps of City Hall and the connecting council chambers, which were designed by Albert Frey.

In 1964, actor Peter Lawford attended the dedication ceremony of a bronze bust of President John F. Kennedy, located on the center island of Tahquitz Canyon Way and Civic Drive, across the street from a third bronze, unveiled on the fiftieth anniversary of Palm Springs Airport, of Bogert's mayoral predecessor, Charles Farrell.

Robert Lippert Jr, a college football star, stunt pilot, and second generation independent film producer who made the minor Western classic, *The Tall Texan*, lived at 212 North Jill Circle in 1960.

The second house of **Liberace**, complete with the letter "L" on the front gates, is located at 231 North Lyn Circle, part of the Enchanted Homes development near the present-day Palm Springs Mall. Erected in 1958, this curious home, one of two rental houses on this street that the TV and recording star kept for the exclusive use of male guests, was customized for Liberace by local contractor George Alexander. "After buying his own luxury house," wrote journalist Bob Thomas, "Lee purchased less ostentatious quarters for his visitors."

★　★　★

Mournful, long-faced, character actor **Sheppard Sanders**, who had featured roles in such big-screen blockbusters as *The Sand Pebbles* and *Kelly's Heroes*, and later taught acting classes at College of the Desert, lived at 2002 Paseo Roseta in 1975.

★　★　★

Variety columnist **Frank Scully**, an imperious George Washington-like figure whose entertaining potpourri "Scully's Scrapbook" was the longest-running column in the newspaper's history, died at 2100 Calle Felicia in 1964, where he had resided for seven years after having his right leg amputated and one lung removed. Believing no literary task to be too small or unimportant, Scully, the recipient of an honorary papal knighthood, found time to take on a varied range of subjects, ghostwriting Frank Harris's biography of George Bernard Shaw, for example, and authoring the first book published about UFOs, *Behind the Flying Saucers*.

When he was invested as a Knight of the Order of St. Gregory in 1957, hundreds of well-wishers besieged Scully's home, where they ate from a banquet of turkeys and hams supplied by Andrea Leeds Howard and "Sir Francis" held court for attending media on the front lawn.

★　★　★

A writer of a different temperament, **Thomas Ardies**, a former newspaperman, whose reputation derives chiefly from turning out cheap potboilers, resided at 2122 East Baristo Road (San Jacinto Estates) in 1978 while completing his bawdy novel about thieves and liars chasing rainbows in the desert's hot spots, suitably titled *Palm Springs*.

★　★　★

The original **Camelot Theatre** at 2300 East Baristo Road was hailed as "California's Most Modern Theater" when it was built in 1967. The cinema featured a Dimension 150 distortion-free "curvilinear" screen measuring sixty-eight-feet wide by thirty-feet high with six different magnetic soundtracks.

In 1974, actor William Holden made a rare personal appearance at the theater for the opening of *The Towering Inferno*. The theater closed in 1992 following the opening of a new multiplex, Courtyard 10, on Tahquitz Canyon Way. After being converted into a smaller three-screen complex, Camelot Theatres reopened in 1999 as the showplace for European and independently made films. In 2002, Olivia Newton-John and Beau Bridges were among the cast members who appeared on stage for the first anniversary screening of the cult gay film, *Sordid Lives*. In 2003, George Clooney attended the premiere of his directorial film debut, *Confessions of a Dangerous Mind*.

★　★　★

Laura La Plante, the elfin silent screen star who appeared in more than eighty seminal movies and serials, mostly at Universal where she battled an unseen killer in *The Cat and the Canary* and was Magnolia in the first screen version of *Show Boat*, moved to the Rose Garden at 1369 Tiffany Circle (off Baristo Road) in 1989, following the death of her second husband, Warner Brothers producer Irving Asher. La Plante died from Alzheimer's disease in 1996, age ninety-four.

★　★　★

Blue-collar stage and film actor **Harry Guardino**, who went from playing cocky soldiers and rogue cops in *Pork Chop Hill* and *Madigan* to romancing Lauren Bacall on Broadway in seven hundred performances of the musical, *Woman of the Year*, spent his final three years with ballerina-wife Elyssa Paternoster at 2949 East Via Vaquero Road. Guardino portrayed Clint Eastwood's worried boss in several *Dirty Harry* movies, but was upstaged by Clyde the Orangutan in Eastwood's one-two comedy punch-ups *Every Which Way But Loose* and *Any Which Way You Can*.

Before Guardino's tenure, **Travis Rogers**, a member of the Desert Riders and manager of Rogers Ranch (nicknamed the Mink-and-Manure Club by William Gargan, where such rowdy stars as Alice Faye, Phil Harris, Sonja Henie, and Gordon MacRae helped prop up the bar), was the previous owner of this home. Guardino, a twenty-year city resident, rebuilt it extensively. He died from lung cancer, age sixty-nine, in 1995.

★　★　★

MGM special effects pioneer **A. Arnold Gillespie**, a highly skilled painter and animator known to his colleagues as "Buddy," designed sets and built miniatures for more than two

Top: George Clooney at the Palm Springs premiere of *Confessions of a Dangerous Mind* (Photo by Steve Kiefer). *Bottom:* Harry Guardino frowning (Larry Edmunds Bookshop).

hundred films and received twelve Oscar nominations. He lived at 660 Compadre Road in 1964.

Gillespie won his first gold statuette for the matte, miniature, and back projection work that provided a bird's-eye view of aerial bombing raids in *Thirty Seconds Over Tokyo*, followed by two more awards for *Green Dolphin Street* and *Plymouth Adventure*. He also supervised the Roman galley scenes of the 1925 original and 1959 remake of *Ben-Hur*, which won him a fourth Oscar, and worked on both 1935 and 1962 versions of *Mutiny on the Bounty*.

Several blocks east, off Ramon Road, is the former home of actor **Robert Dix** and his wife, AIP beach bunny **Darlene Lucht**, at 717 Mountain View Drive. Dix, the twin son of 1931's *Cimarron* actor Richard Dix, had a less-successful stint in middling Western roles than his accomplished father, his biggest achievement being *Young Jesse James* (as Frank James). He then sunk into cheap horror films, e.g. *Blood of Dracula's Castle*, which were directed by his friend and Palm Springs neighbor, Al Adamson.

The mile-long stretch of housing known as **Veterans Tract** was constructed after World War II for returning servicemen, spurred by the availability of low-interest home loans. Much of the city's rapid postwar growth, when the total number of building permits reached $70-million worth of construction in 1956, was accelerated by developers Jack Meiselman, Sy Simon, and Dick Weiss and his father, Jack Weiss. They supplemented the building of tract homes with condominiums that surpassed an estimated twelve thousand in number by 1987.

And what better person to realize its real estate potential than big band singer **Eadie Adams**, who appeared in *Restless Knights* with the Three Stooges, *After the Thin Man* alongside William Powell and Myrna Loy, and *The Big City* with Spencer Tracy? Adams lived at 760 South Calle Santa Cruz, opposite Demuth Park. In 1962, the boisterous entertainer (no relation to Edie Adams, the actress-wife of TV comedian Ernie Kovacs) founded Eadie Adams Realty that grew into one of the largest unaffiliated companies selling homes in the Coachella Valley. In 1991, eight years after her death, Eadie Adams Realty merged with Coldwell Banker, increasing its size to two offices, thirty-seven full-time residential specialists, and five commercial agents.

Polish-born composer **Paul Sawtell**, who resided for two years at 975 South Paseo Dorotea, wrote background music for nearly six hundred movies and hundreds more TV shows—how else could he afford the alimony payments to his many ex-wives? But it's the creepy film scores that Sawtell composed for the science fiction classics *Kronos*, *The Fly*, and *It! The Terror From Beyond Space*, plus the swirling main themes for Irwin Allen's *The Lost World*, *Five Weeks in a Balloon*, and *Voyage to the Bottom of the Sea* with its beeping sonar, that won him greatest acclaim.

Six months after Darryl Zanuck, the highly competitive cofounder of 20th Century-Fox, was laid to rest in Westwood Memorial Park, Los Angeles, his second oldest daughter, **Susan Zanuck**, who had abandoned her dreams of becoming an actress to be a wife and mother to her first husband, Andre Hakim, and their three children, Andre Jr., Raymond, and Sharon, accomplished what she had been secretly trying to do for ten years. She killed herself.

On June 10, 1980, nineteen-year-old Sharon returned to check on her forty-six-year-old mother at their rented cul-de-sac home at 2320 East El Chorro Way (off South Farrell Drive and East Palm Canyon Drive). When the apprehensive teenager opened the bedroom door, she found Susan lying deathly still on her king-size bed. She had been living on a $1-million trust fund that provided $3,000 allowance each month. It was widely known around town that she was an alcoholic whose sons were hooked on drugs.

Actress Terry Moore, who had known Susan when they were both pretty young things zipping around Hollywood in matching Thunderbirds, later said, "Susan drank quite a bit even when she was very young." Rumors quickly circulated of theft and murder, but the coroner was unable to find any evidence of foul play. The official cause of death was cardiac arrhythmia that had been aggravated by an enlarged liver.

Writer-producer **Paul Henning**, the mastermind behind three of television's looniest sitcoms, *The Beverly Hillbillies*, *Petticoat Junction*, and *Green Acres*, lived at 1112 San Joaquin Drive (off South Farrell Drive)—one year after these popular network shows were axed by CBS in 1971, but lived on to amuse millions more viewers in countless syndication reruns.

Chapter 8
Deepwell Dish

This eclectic combination of private homes and hotels begins at the intersection of South Indian Canyon Drive and Ramon Road, where the Indians once raised livestock and grew manzanita (small apple) trees. It then crosses over Sunny Dunes Road to Mesquite Avenue and wraps around East Palm Canyon Drive, ending at the junction of South Sunrise Way. In between is Vista Santa Rosa, sometimes facetiously called "Little Mexico" because of the high number of Spanish-speaking inhabitants, connected by Warm Sands Park, Tahquitz River Estates, and, lastly, Deep Well itself.

Biblical actor Henry Wilcoxon (Backlot Books & Movie Posters).

★   ★   ★

Strapping, hawk-nosed actor **Henry Wilcoxon**, who wore a metal breast-plate as Marc Antony in Cecil B. DeMille's Roman spectacle *Cleopatra* with Claudette Colbert and played a grim-faced Richard the Lionhearted in *The Crusades* with Loretta Young, lived at 524 South Calle Abronia (now a triplex) in 1959. Wilcoxon, who drove a white Ford Thunderbird, bought the house for his second wife, actress Joan Woodbury, and their three small children shortly after the death of Wilcoxon's longtime colleague DeMille.

Wilcoxon was DeMille's associate producer on *Samson and Delilah*, *The Greatest Show on Earth*, and the 1956 remake of *The Ten Commandments*—a massive five-year production that took the film's cast and crew to Egypt for the gigantic exodus and the parting of the Red Sea, the single-most spectacular sequence ever filmed. However, Wilcoxon, whom DeMille pegged as "an avid shaper of ideas and craftsman of dramatic construction," fell out with the director over the ill-advised remake of *The Buccaneer*, directed by DeMille's son-in-law Anthony Quinn.

★   ★   ★

RKO contract player and future real estate developer **Russell Wade**, who enjoyed brief prominence as a wavy-haired juvenile in producer Val Lewton's eerie chillers *The Ghost Ship* and *The Body Snatcher* with those venerated masters of horror Boris Karloff and Bela Lugosi, lived at 594 South Calle Abronia (now a duplex), on the corner of Camino Parocela, in 1948. Fifty years later, the home's selling price was a mere $69,000.

Artist **Paul Grimm**, a forty-two-year desert resident, whose landscape paintings of Mount San Jacinto and the High Sierras in brilliant turquoise, gold, and magenta hues have been praised by critics as among the finest works of their kind ever produced, lived at 526 Calle Palo Fierro until his death in 1974.

★ ★ ★

Magnificent Obsession director John Stahl lines up a shot (Larry Edmunds Bookshop).

In 1939, English-Chinese author **Leslie Charteris**, creator of the Saint, the cunning amateur sleuth who solved mysteries in London, New York, and Miami, wrote his twenty-third novel, *The Saint Goes West* (filmed as *The Saint in Palm Springs*), while staying in the Mediterranean-style house with a miniature bell tower at 504 South Indian Trail.

Architect Wallace Neff designed the vintage tile-and-stucco home, which sits opposite a center island divided by a grove of fifty palm trees, for nationally syndicated radio personality Cal Pearce. Pearce rented his house for one season to Charteris after the writer had crisscrossed the country conducting research for his various stories, while living in a homemade trailer. The erudite author cut an impressive, if odd-looking figure whenever dressed in his red-checked Western attire, cowboy hat, and polished monocle, but he was no fool. According to biographer Richard Vanderbeets, "The series ended over a dispute between RKO and Charteris, who grew dissatisfied with the Saint's screen exploits in plots only remotely related to the author's storylines." Charteris, who published a total of fifty-two books in his lifetime, died, age eighty-five, in 1993.

★ ★ ★

Pre-eminent Hollywood filmmaker **John M. Stahl**, a man of infinite good taste, directed some of the most stylish and profitable women's pictures ever made, several of these so-called "four handkerchief weepies" that were adapted from the novels of Fannie Hurst and starred Irene Dunne, included the definitive screen versions of *Back Street*, *Imitation of Life*, and *Magnificent Obsession* (all of them slickly remade by Universal producer Ross

Hunter). In 1946 Stahl lived at 527 South Indian Trail. Stahl launched Gregory Peck in *Keys of the Kingdom*, sent Gene Tierney into a flurry in the classic tearjerker, *Leave Her to Heaven*, and unleashed Rex Harrison on Maureen O'Hara in *The Foxes of Harrow*—ensuring strong sales of Kleenex.

★　★　★

And in 1938, Pepsodent Toothpaste radio announcer **Bill Hay**, whose dulcet tones introduced more than five thousand *Amos 'n' Andy* "live-to-air" radio programs on the NBC network, lived at 539 Vista Oro.

★　★　★

Warm Sands Park, between Ramon Road and Sunny Dunes Road, is a neat configuration of duplexes, triplexes, and hotel apartments, where sleep-deprived vacationers and rowdy spring breakers once booked accommodations at Golden Palm, Sun & Sands, Vista Grande, and Warm Sands Villa—where actor Lloyd Pantages, whose father owned the Pantages Theatre in Hollywood, was a guest in 1954.

Most of the hotels, as they were originally built and named, still exist, though their clientele is no longer family oriented. These resorts are now "clothing optional" and almost all of them gay owned. At last count, there are fifteen all-male resorts with rates ranging from $69 to $250 a night. The new kids on the block are All Worlds, Atrium, Avalon, Bacchanal, Cobalt, Columns, Desert Paradise, El Mirasol, Inn Exile, Inndulge, and Mirage, where Hollywood still has a tenuous connection. It is the favorite locale for many of the adult porn industry's hottest young bucks, who frequently take it off and get it on with each other here for the X-rated cameras, although it's extremely doubtful you'll find the abundance of gay sex films, among them *Palm Springs 92264*, *Desert Maneuvers*, *Guest Services*, and *Men in Exile* for rent at Blockbuster or Hollywood Video. Aaron Austin, Todd Stevens, and Robert Harvey are a few of the city's gay porn stars-in-residence.

★　★　★

The operatic performances of Hungarian soprano **Gitta Alpar** in *The Magic Flute*, *Rigoletto*, and *La Traviata* made her a star of pre-Nazi Berlin—especially *Madame DuBarry*, which won her international acclaim. But political turmoil caused Alpar, who was married at one time to *Metropolis* film star Gustav Froelich, to leave Germany and seek safe haven abroad. In the sixties, Alpar settled in this contemporary California-style

Top: Warm Sands water sports (Courtesy of All Worlds Resort). *Bottom:* German opera star Gitta Alpar (Courtesy of Hans Franke).

Top: A young-looking Della Reese (Backlot Books & Movie Posters). *Bottom:* Don Durant as "Johnny Ringo" (Steve Kiefer Collection).

home, appropriately named "Villa DuBarry," at 671 Grenfall Road, where she became a sought-after singing teacher.

The blonde opera star's former home, which was bedecked with signed mementos from her career, located a few doors away from the old Kauai and Bahia hotels, is one of a few private residences on this street—now a popular men's cruising spot. But Alpar, who lived in the desert for three decades, wasn't the least bit concerned. When she died, age eighty-eight, in 1991, having moved several times, her remains were interred near the graves of fellow opera divas Miliza Korjus and Wagnerian soprano Helen Traubel at Westwood Memorial Park in Los Angeles.

★　★　★

Outspoken *Touched By an Angel* TV star **Della Reese**, an ordained Baptist minister and civil rights activist, was just starting her remarkable career when she lived in this tiny motor home at 217 Minnehaha Street in Ramon Park (entrance: 1441 East Ramon Road). Prior to acting, Reese was a gospel and blues singer, whose million-selling hits included "And That Reminds Me" and "Don't You Know," which she sang with gusto more than twenty times on *The Ed Sullivan Show*.

Reese was the first woman to guest host for Johnny Carson on *The Tonight Show* where, on October 3, 1980, she suffered a near-fatal aneurysm. But the resilient performer bounced back with notable appearances in *Designing Women*, *L.A. Law*, *Picket Fences*, and the short-lived sitcom, *The Royal Family*, with the late Redd Foxx.

★　★　★

Actor **Don Durant**, better known to TV viewers as square-jawed, clean-cut *Johnny Ringo*— "the fastest gun in all the West" battling pesky outlaws and marauding Indians —finally hung up his .45 holster at 1742 Camino Parocela (off Ramon Road and Sunrise Way) in the Sunflower condominiums before moving to Palm Desert.

★　★　★

Also at the Sunflower: Western crooner **Fred Scott**, "The Silvery Voiced Buckaroo," who rode the plains in thirteen low-budget shoot-'em-ups, among them *The Fighting Deputy* and *In Old Montana* that played the Depression-era prairie theater circuit. Scott, a 1988 Golden Boot Awards honoree, liked the simple life at 1716 Camino Parocela. He then moved to 1765 E. Ramon Road, where he died two days before his ninetieth birthday in 1992.

★　★　★

Beverly Hills developer Paul Trousdale and contractor Robert Higgins built approximately two hundred houses, many of them designed by Donald Wexler and Richard Harrison in adjoining **Tahquitz River Estates**, where small hotels such as Impala, Matador, and A Place in the Sun provided overnight lodgings for short-term visitors. Today, it is a shady haven for gay groups at Triangle Inn, Chestnutz, Santiago, and Tortuga Del Sol.

In 1994, short-haired, goateed Los Angeles interior designer **Brad Dunning**, who remodeled NBC West Coast president Don Ohlmeyer's Indian Wells retreat as well as the home of CAA agent Bryan Lourd, purchased the three-bedroom house at 844 North Riverside Drive for $150,000. Dunning moved to the desert, he said, when houses, including his own "were practically being given away." Not anymore. Like tumbleweeds in a sandstorm, these fleeting bargains have been swept away, replaced by row upon row of shiny remodels that are commanding a high selling price. And Dunning's residence, no doubt, will eventually be one of them. But would these homes have the same appeal if it weren't for the phantoms of their former owners?

French-born leading lady **Lili Damita** (real name: Liliane Carre), who was married to Errol Flynn from 1935 to 1942, supposedly lived at 952 North Riverside Drive in 1956—three years before her gallivanting ex-husband suffered a fatal heart attack in Vancouver, Canada. Lili was brought to Hollywood by Samuel Goldwyn to replace Vilma Banky in *The Rescue* opposite Ronald Colman. She costarred in eighteen movies, including *Fighting Caravans* with Gary Cooper and *This Is the Night*, which introduced Cary Grant.

Lili's marriage to Flynn was made in hell, however; they hated each other. To obtain a quick divorce, Flynn foolishly agreed to pay her $12,000 a year. "She'd remained single to keep the alimony flowing," said Jeffrey Meyers, "but in 1962 married Allen Loomis, a wealthy businessman who invented Eskimo Pies."

They moved to Palm Beach, Florida. Damita's actor-son Sean Flynn was moonlighting as a *Paris Match* photojournalist in war-torn Cambodia when he and a male friend were captured by the Vietcong and vanished without a trace in 1970. Lili spent the rest of her life searching in vain for her missing son. She died from Alzheimer's disease, age ninety-two, in 1994.

Russian-born character actor **Akim Tamiroff**—a two-time Best Supporting Actor Oscar nominee for his convincing portrayal of a Chinese warlord in *The General Died at Dawn* and a Russian loyalist in *For Whom the Bell Tolls*, owned the house at 1150 North Riverside Drive, where he relaxed between films in 1960.

Tamiroff enjoyed a long association with director Cecil B. DeMille, as well as working with Orson Welles on many of his pet projects (memorably as Mexican crime boss Joe Grandi in *Touch of Evil* and Sancho Panza in the unfinished *Don Quixote*). He also played a multitude of ethnic roles, mostly as sweating, flustered rascals. Tamiroff's widow, actress Tamara Shayne, continued living in the house after her husband died here from cancer in 1972. She died in 1983. Their home sold for $62,500 in 1992.

On the other side of Tahquitz Creek, in 1959, scriptwriter **Anthony Veiller**, who collaborated with director John Huston on the screen adaptations of *The Killers*, *Moulin Rouge*, and *The Night of the Iguana*, rented the house for his wife and two children at 1177 Riverside Drive South.

Werner Groebli, the knee-bending, lederhosen-clad half of famous Ice Follies comedy team Frick and Frack (with late partner Hans Mauch), who performed much-imitated trick maneuvers such as the "cantilever spread-eagle," resided in the San Lorenzo Apartments at 777 San Lorenzo Road until the death of his wife Yvonne Baumgartner in 2002. He has since moved.

★ ★ ★

It's a documented fact. **William Wyler** is the most-honored producer-director of all time. A relentless taskmaster, whose meticulous preparation and attention to detail made him one of the most-respected and feared directors in the film business, Wyler lived

Top: Akim Tamiroff mugs for the camera (Backlot Books & Movie Posters). *Bottom:* William Wyler and *Funny Girl* star Barbra Streisand (Courtesy of Academy of Motion Picture Arts and Sciences).

unnoticed a few doors away. An inconspicuous Palm Springs resident for fifteen years, Wyler's grandiose productions spanned almost half a century and nearly every conceivable subject from classic literature in *Wuthering Heights* to popular stage plays with *The Little Foxes*, glossy melodramas like *Jezebel* and the sophisticated comedy *Roman Holiday*.

Toward the end of his career, he delved into the mind of psychological drama with *The Collector* and tackled blatant racism in *The Liberation of L.B. Jones*. Wyler's feature films won forty Academy Awards and netted 128 nominations! Wyler himself received three well-deserved Oscars as Best Director for *Mrs. Miniver*, *The Best Years of Our Lives*, and the gargantuan Roman epic *Ben-Hur*. He was also presented with the Irving Thalberg Memorial Award.

Offscreen, Wyler rode motorcycles, played the violin, and was an expert bartender. When he wasn't working, "Willy," as his friends called him, spent the weekends at 976 San Lorenzo Road, where such favored guests as Lillian Hellman, John Huston, and neighbor Fay Bainter chatted over drinks in his backyard. Wyler owned this house from 1951 until 1967—the period of his greatest achievement and fame. He relaxed here at the completion of every film—and nearly undertook another assignment, while residing here, that would have been the crowning glory of his career. The film was *Patton*, but he did not direct it. Instead, Wyler announced his retirement. He died, age seventy-nine, in 1981. Wyler wasn't the only illustrious director to live on San Lorenzo Road (now full of gay-owned hotels), where a buyer paid $133,000 for his home in 1994. The street's countrified setting has attracted plenty of interesting personalities.

Comedy virtuoso **William A. Seiter**, who directed the screen teams of Laurel and Hardy in *Sons of the Desert*, Fred Astaire and Ginger Rogers in *Roberta*, and the Marx Brothers in *Room Service*, lived in the whitewashed, brick home at 1128 San Lorenzo Road in 1951. In addition to these distinctions, Seiter helmed two Shirley Temple vehicles, *Dimples* and *Stowaway*, and guided Rita Hayworth through the lively musical *You Were Never Lovelier* after which, Seiter and his actress-wife Marian Nixon, who enjoyed the good things in life, drifted away from films. He subsequently moved to Palm Desert and died in 1964.

Writer **Don Hartman**, who supplied the hilarious visual gags such as a talking camel for many of the Crosby-Hope-Lamour *Road* movies, lived at 1151 San Lorenzo Road, named "Casa Sonrisa," in 1955 during his tenure as head of production at Paramount Pictures. Three years later, weighed down by the pressure of running a movie studio, Hartman was stricken by a fatal heart attack while sleeping in his second home at 1356 San Lorenzo Road.

Beverly Hills real estate developer **Paul Trousdale**, owner of Trousdale Construction Company that built variations of the ranch, Colonial, Monterey, and Regency styles both here and elsewhere, must have believed in what he was selling or else he wouldn't have lived in the custom-built house with the tall fichus hedge at 1179 San Lorenzo Road, on the corner of Hermosa Drive, in 1956.

Landscape architect Edward Huntsman-Trout gave the home and others like it a look of increased affluence by his well-chosen placement of gates, lamps, fountains, and lawns.

Billie Dove in all her splendor (Larry Edmunds Bookshop).

In 1963, **Anthony Veiller**, whom John Huston declared "my favorite American screenwriter," wrote the script for *The List of Adrian Messenger*, a gimmicky murder mystery with cameos by Frank Sinatra, Tony Curtis, and Kirk Douglas, while residing at 1228 San Lorenzo Road.

★   ★   ★

One of the street's more-illustrious inhabitants was former Ziegfeld Follies discovery and silent screen leading lady **Billie Dove**, the demure costar of swashbuckler Douglas Fairbanks Sr. in 1926's *The Black Pirate*—the first two-strip Technicolor feature to be widely released. Dubbed "the American Beauty" because of her flawless complexion, luscious lips, and hazel eyes, Dove's romantic appeal briefly eclipsed that of Mary Pickford, Gloria Swanson, and Garbo. However, the strong-willed actress chose marriage to action-adventure director Irvin Willat over her promising career—to the disappointment of millions of fans. Six years later, Miss Dove divorced Willat and became the sweetheart of eccentric film producer Howard Hughes, living with him for two years, but canceling their proposed wedding, it was later claimed, when she learned he had contracted syphilis.

Following her retirement from acting in 1932, Dove wed her second husband, Robert Kenaston, a wealthy rancher and real estate investor, and they moved to this white-and-gray, brick-walled home lined with cypress trees at 1328 San Lorenzo Road, where they raised a son, Robert Jr., and adopted a daughter, Gail. Preferring painting to performing, Billie, a member of the Palm Springs Palette Club, turned down subsequent movie offers, including the role of Belle Watling in *Gone With the Wind*, but she did play a small part in the Hawaiian love story *Diamond Head*, as a lark in 1962.

★   ★   ★

Action-movie producer **Sam Zimbalist**, who oversaw the rigorous and often-dangerous location filming of *King Solomon's Mines* and *Mogambo* in Africa, reportedly occupied this charming Spanish estate at 245 Palo Verde Avenue. Sadly, Zimbalist was felled by a massive heart attack midway through production of *Ben-Hur* in 1958. His death was hardly surprising given the film's overwhelming logistics: three hundred constructed sets, eight thousand cheering extras, and forty thousand tons of imported sand for the chariot race at Circus Maximus, which took one thousand workers a year to build at Cinecittà Studios in Rome.

★   ★   ★

Illinois architect **William Gray Purcell**, who helped popularize the flat prairie-style house that originated in the Midwest, designed this simple-yet-functional, two-bedroom home at 252 East Ocotillo Avenue, where he lived in 1933. Purcell designed many important commercial structures (offices, banks, churches) in Minnesota until he contracted tuberculosis and moved to California where he died in 1965.

★　★　★

Podiatrist **Dr. William M. Scholl**, the original "Dr. Scholl" whose footwear company invented the corn pads, rubber insoles, and orthopedic sandals and whose contoured products later became an unlikely fashion statement for a generation of pot-smoking hippies, built the California Spanish-style house with tennis courts at 211 East Morongo Road, where Scholl modified his inventions from 1944 until his death, age eighty-six, in 1968.

The home's second owner, **Robert H. Cohn**, the founder and chairman of CFS Continental, a $2-billion Chicago food-services distributor, purchased Scholl's estate in 1969, which, despite increased local development, remains the largest single residence on a street with its own indelible history.

★　★　★

Sharon Tate, the ill-fated blonde starlet, first visited the desert when she was dating French actor Philippe Forquet in 1963, according to her biographer, Greg King. However, there exists a curious listing for a woman also named Sharon Tate at 156 East Morongo Road two years earlier. (Tate's family resided in Italy from late 1960 to early 1962 where her father, Paul Tate, was a captain in the U.S. Army.)

If it is indeed the same person, then Tate was no stranger to these parts. In 1961, the only year her name appears in the Palm Springs phone directory, Tate had not yet begun her film career. The eighteen-year-old was still single, taking acting classes, and modeling in L.A.-based TV commercials and magazine photo shoots.

Intriguingly, the Morongo Road home where Tate or her namesake roomed was that of statuesque woman-about-town Roma Marvin, who ran La Roma Originals ladies wear store, advertised as "The Elegance in Hand Knits and Sportswear." Tate's love of fashion and photography may well have led to her looking for work in local fashion shows, as it did other aspiring models. Her presence in the desert at this time certainly seems plausible, given that many performers also tried to break into show business here. It was reported, for example, that city resident Kathleen Lavigne had once coached Tate in modeling.

Sharon Tate at her glamorous best (Backlot Books & Movie Posters).

But where other star-struck hopefuls may have failed, Tate's patience and perseverance was generously rewarded. In 1963, Filmways president and producer Martin Ransohoff signed the novice actress to an exclusive seven-year contract. Her first major film was prophetically titled *Eye of the Devil*, followed by *The Fearless Vampire Killers*, a horror spoof. After the release of the pill-popping showbiz parable *Valley of the Dolls* in 1967, Tate and her husband, Czech director Roman Polanski, along with actress Mia Farrow and comedian Peter Sellers, went hiking at Joshua Tree National Monument, where they spent the weekend sitting around a campfire, getting stoned, King said, and watching the sky for UFOs.

One year later, Tate was back in the desert, this time to film scenes at the Palm Springs Aerial Tramway for the Matt Helm tongue-in-cheek spy adventure *The Wrecking Crew*, starring Dean Martin. It was her last film. On August 9, 1969, a pregnant Tate, men's hairdresser Jay Sebring, coffee heiress Abigail Folger, and Polish playboy Voytek Frykowski were among five people tortured to death in the Benedict Canyon home of absentee record producer Terry Melcher (the son of Doris Day and husband-agent Marty Melcher) by four crazed members of cult leader Charles Manson's "family."

Two years later, at the tail end of the headline-grabbing Tate murder trial, fifteen jurors and two sheriff's deputies took a restful Sunday bus trip to the desert, ate lunch at El Mirador Hotel, and enjoyed an exhilarating ride on the Aerial Tramway. Fourteen days later, the refreshed jury found all four Manson defendants guilty of first-degree murder.

If anyone can solve the puzzle of whether Tate was in the desert in 1961, it would be desert mystery writer and pulp fiction devotee **Arthur Lyons** who has resided at 646 East Morongo Road since the death of his father, Arthur Lyons Sr., in 1980. Lyons Sr. ran the natty Los Angeles eatery Saddle and Sirloin, as well as the Players, where Robert Benchley, John Barrymore, Lillian Hellman, and Dashiell Hammett ordered dinner each night when the bistro was owned by Preston Sturges. Lyons also managed the Radio Room, which featured the first moving neon sign in Southern California, according to his namesake son, who cowrote the crime thrillers *Unnatural Causes* and *Physical Evidence* with retired L.A. medical examiner Thomas Noguchi. (Coincidentally, Noguchi also toiled for many months on the Tate murder case.)

In addition, Lyons, a former city council member and current director of the Palm Springs Film Noir Festival, has researched two books on the cult of Satanism. His novel *Castles Burning* became the neo film noir *Slow Burn*, filmed partly in the desert.

Max Factor Jr., son of the world-famous cosmetics founder, once lived in the triple-sided home at 297 Avenida Olancha, which borders three streets: Avenida Olancha, Via Entrada, and Avenida Ortega. In 1973, Factor sold his father's company to Proctor & Gamble for $480 million—the equivalent of more than $2 billion today. (Note: Factor's address was changed to 238 Avenida Ortega in 1974.) Donald Factor, his son, now owns this house, since repainted terra-cotta red with black trim.

In July 2000, Max Factor Sr.'s errant thirty-six-year-old great-grandson, Andrew Luster, was arrested and charged with raping three women after giving them the date-rape drug, gamma hydroxybutyrate, and liquid Ecstasy. Two years later, midway through his criminal trial, Luster, dubbed "the Lipstick Rapist," jumped $1-million bail and became a wanted FBI fugitive. On January 21, 2003, his whereabouts still unknown, Luster was convicted on eighty-six counts, including, rape, sodomy, and drug possession. A judge sentenced him *in absentia* to 124 years in state prison and ordered the missing felon to pay $1 million in restitution to his victims. American authorities had no idea Luster was watching it all on TV—from a bar in the Mexican beach resort of Puerto Vallarta, where U.S. bounty hunters nabbed him at a taco stand five months later and turned him over to the police.

Mexican-American bandleader-composer **Don Tosti**, who had a major crossover hit with *Pachuco Boogie*, lives at 360 Avenida Olancha, off East Palm Canyon Drive. A forty-year city resident, Tosti now teaches piano, bass, and guitar.

Deep Well, the city's third-most-important celebrity neighborhood, begins at Mesquite Avenue, which runs east off South Palm Canyon Drive and continues south to Sunrise Way. It is named after the adjoining and privately owned Deep Well Ranch, which stood on the 1000 block of East Palm Canyon Drive. Built seventy-five years ago by Charles Doyle, the original horse ranch turned belly up and reopened soon after under the management of Frank and Melba Bennett. It was gradually supplemented over the next three decades by rows of tract homes, collectively called Deep Well Ranch Estates. These individual homes are a mixture of Spanish revival, classic ranch style, and California modern, now enjoying a resurgence in popularity.

Ruddy-faced stage, film, and TV actor **Patrick Macnee** spent fifteen years battling overindulgence in booze brought on by severe depression and two bad marriages, he said, while living at 748 East Mesquite Avenue, which he purchased during a career lull in 1973. Macnee's seriously ill asthmatic daughter, Jennifer, who was living with him at the time, transformed the dreary home into a cozy Spanish-style ranch house with mimosa, grapefruit, and lemon trees. It soon became Macnee's favorite place to ventilate when he wasn't rehearsing or traveling abroad.

Although it took another thirteen years for him to get completely sober, Macnee kept working. He returned to England for a second go-round as dandified secret agent John Steed in *The New Avengers*, journeyed to India for *The Sea Wolves*, then flew to France for the James Bond film, *A View to a Kill*. In between, he undertook the assignment of annunciating in his best pontifical tones the opening narration of TV's *Battlestar Galactica*: "There are those who believe that life here began out there far across the universe...." He has since garnered a strong cult following playing eccentric doctors and scientists in such scary video fare as *The Howling*, *This Is Spinal Tap*, *Waxwork*, and *Lobster Man From Mars*.

Los Angeles KTLA-TV sports commentator and glib actor **Richard Lane**, who played Inspector Farraday in sixteen *Boston Blackie* films, lived at 1022 East Mesquite Avenue during his semiretirement in 1974. Lane—the voice of wrestling, roller derby, and midget-car racing throughout Los Angeles in the fifties and sixties—was the regular announcer for the L.A. Thunderbirds roller derby team for more than twenty years, yelling *"Whoooooaaaaah Nellie!"* in his familiar Irish brogue whenever a player head-butted or tackled an opponent. He even made up impromptu names for numerous wrestling moves, most of which are still in common use today.

Ginny Simms, who performed the entrancing ballads "All The Things You Are" from *Broadway Rhythm* and the duet "You're the Top" with Cary Grant in *Night and Day*, lived for six years in her favorite abode with a Japanese bonsai garden at 1139 East Mesquite Avenue. The Texas-born singer first occupied the house in 1956 after divorcing her first and second husbands, Hyatt Von Dehn and Bob Calhoun. Formerly the lead vocalist and one-time lover of mortarboard-and-gowned orchestra leader Kay Kyser, Simms "had a natural voice, with two octaves, and a magical glissando," said biographer Charles Higham. When she rebuffed the advances of MGM's Louis B. Mayer, who offered her $1 million to marry him, Simms was banished from the studio forever, and her career faltered. In 1999, her beloved home sold for $315,000.

Top: Ginny Simms (Courtesy of Palm Springs Historical Society). *Bottom:* Charles Winninger as Cap'n Andy (Backlot Books & Movie Posters).

The second home of actor and businessman **Russell Wade**, where he lived in 1957 during construction of the twelve-acre William Cody-designed Cameron Center shopping complex, is at 1422 Mesquite Avenue. Wade's home sold for $175,000 in 1998.

Character actor **Charles Winninger**, who originated the pixilated expression *"Happ-y new year!"* as Cap'n Andy in the 1927 stage production of *Show Boat*, a role he reprised in the 1936 film version, retired to 1580 Mesquite Avenue where he died as the result of a broken hip at age eighty-four in 1969. Winninger's widow, Gertrude Walker, wrote crime stories, one of them filmed as a Joan Crawford vehicle, *The Damned Don't Cry*, which was partially shot nearby at Frank Sinatra's house. Walker died on her ninety-third birthday in 1995. Their home fetched $140,000 that same year.

★　★　★

Actor-producer **Richard Whorf**, who had varied success in dramatic roles on Broadway before switching to films, most notably as the incarnation of theatrical impresario Sam H. Harris, the business partner of vaudeville dynamo George M. Cohan (played by James Cagney) in *Yankee Doodle Dandy*, fared better on the other side of the camera directing many classic TV series that needed a light touch—*My Three Sons*, *The Beverly Hillbillies*, and *The Wild, Wild West*—while living at 1680 Mesquite Avenue until his death from a heart attack in 1966. Ten years later, the home sold for the price of a luxury car: $48,500.

★　★　★

"Tennessee" Ernie Ford, a genuine Southern native of Bristol, Tennessee, and former San Bernardino radio disk jockey, became the first country singer to star at the London Palladium where he performed "Mule Train," "Ballad of Davy Crockett," and his biggest hit, "Sixteen Tons." Ford lived in a two-bedroom Sunrise Villas condominium at 1012 St. George Circle (off Mesquite and Sunrise Way) in 1980. Ford's thundering voice, backed by lush string arrangements and heavenly choirs, catapulted the black-haired baritone to TV stardom, releasing a total of eighty-three albums for Capitol Records over twenty-seven years. When Ford, grand marshal of the 1982 Desert Circus Parade, died in 1991, his ode to Kentucky coal miners: "You load sixteen tons and what do you get? Another day older and deeper in debt...." jammed the airwaves all over again.

★　★　★

Oscar-nominated screenwriter **Oscar Brodney**, who wrote the audacious scripts for fifty film musicals, comedies, and dramas, including *If You Knew Susie*, *The Glenn Miller Story*, *The Black Shield of Falworth*, *Lady Godiva*, and *The Purple Mask*, resided at 1700 West Grand Bahama Drive in 1975.

★　★　★

Top: Richard Whorf performed Shakespeare's plays for weary GI's (Backlot Books & Movie Posters). *Bottom:* "Tennessee" Ernie Ford (Larry Edmunds Bookshop).

Oscar-winning Czech filmmaker **Frantisek Daniel**, who produced the 1965 Best Foreign Film, *Shop on Main Street* and was the first foreigner invited by the Soviet Union to attend the Moscow Film Institute, owned the Sunrise Villas condominium at 1971 Grand Bahama Drive East, where he died from a heart attack, age sixty-nine, in 1996.

One of the neighborhood's most-dependable residents until his death, age eighty-five, in 2002, was strong-jawed fifties leading man **Kenneth Tobey**, who saved the planet from aliens and monsters in *The Thing from Another World*, *The Beast from 20,000 Fathoms*, and *It Came from Beneath the Sea*. Another Tobey role was that of Admiral William Halsey in *MacArthur*—one of several films he made with lifelong friend Gregory Peck, who died six months after he did. Tobey lived with his daughter, Tina, at 1070 South Calle Marcus.

William H. Pine, one half of the Paramount producing team with William C. Thomas known as the "Two Dollar Bills" because none of their films ever lost money, owned the house at 1470 South Calle Marcus. After turning out humdrum aviation and crime sagas for nearly a decade, Pine-Thomas hit their stride with a rash of Technicolor Westerns, pirate tales, and jungle adventures, the quality of which, despite limited budgets, was consistently good, especially *Run for Cover* with James Cagney, John Payne in *Hell's Island*, and Jane Wyman as *Lucy Gallant*. Their greatest success, *The Far Horizons*, starring Fred MacMurray and Charlton Heston, was released the year of Pine's death in 1955.

Shortly before fruit-wearing, samba-dancing nightclub and film entertainer **Carmen Miranda** collapsed and died from a heart attack in 1955, induced, it was claimed, by her abundant use of cocaine, "the Lady in the Tutti-Frutti Hat" resided with manager-husband David Sebastian at 1044 South Calle Rolph. It was here, amid the scent of orange and lemon blossoms, that Miranda sought refuge for a "chronic sinus problem," according to publicity reports, but where, following her final film appearances in *Nancy Goes to Rio* and the Martin and Lewis comedy *Scared Stiff* (a musical remake of Bob Hope's *The Ghost Breakers*), she recovered from electric shock treatment in a futile effort to cure her of depression.

"In her latter years, chemical stimulants more often than not fueled the astonishing energy she displayed on stage," revealed biographer Martha Gil-Montero, adding that even a black bag containing pills and injections could not relieve Miranda's debilitating malaise. A three-hour funeral procession drew more than one million spectators who lined the streets of Rio de Janeiro for a glimpse of her bronze casket draped in the national flag—a bigger turnout than memorial services held for President Getulio Vargas the previous year.

Wild-haired, shrill-voiced actress **Marjorie Main**, who played Percy Kilbride's shotgun-wielding hillbilly wife in nine *Ma and Pa Kettle* comedies, dwelled in the pink-and-green, two-story house (since repainted yellow and brown) at 1280 South Calle Rolph, where, according to film historian Richard Lamparski, she did her own cooking and housecleaning.

Broadway-trained, Main first showed her dramatic flair as teary-eyed slum mothers in *Dead End* and *Stella Dallas*, but she was even better when she hemmed and hawed in the musicals *Meet Me in St. Louis* and *The Harvey Girls*. Main, an Oscar nominee for *The Egg and I*, was a breakfast regular at Louise's Pantry and spent her summers in the alpine village of Idyllwild. A lifelong nonsmoker and teetotaler, she attributed hard work to her prevailing good health. She died at eighty-five in 1975.

★ ★ ★

In 1952, bright-eyed cowboy star **Robert Livingston**, who played Stony Brooke, the cheerful leader of *The Three Mesquiteers* in twenty-nine Republic Westerns and later portrayed the masked avenger in the fifteen-episode serial, *The Lone Ranger Rides Again*, entered semiretirement at 1321 South Calle Rolph. Twenty years on, Al Adamson coaxed Livingston back in front of the cameras for a couple of films of a different nature than those he had made before, *Girls for Rent* and *Blazing Stewardesses*.

★ ★ ★

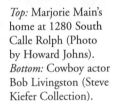

In 1955, **Oscar G. Mayer**, president and chairman of his late father's meat company that sold prepackaged wieners, bologna, and bacon, owned the house at 1353 South Calle Rolph. Among the company's delectable "firsts:" introducing sliced bacon and wrapping its sausages with a yellow paper band. They also pioneered the sponsorship of family TV shows which had kids everywhere singing its advertising jingle "The Wiener Song." The Oscar Mayer Company was bought by Kraft Foods in 1989.

Top: Marjorie Main's home at 1280 South Calle Rolph (Photo by Howard Johns). *Bottom:* Cowboy actor Bob Livingston (Steve Kiefer Collection).

★ ★ ★

Hey laaaaady! Klutzy comedian **Jerry Lewis**, the "do-it-all" star of *The Bellboy*, *The Nutty Professor* (remade with Eddie Murphy), and *The Disorderly Orderly*, laughed it up with his wife of thirty-six years, Patti Calonico, and their six children, Gary, Ron, Scott, Chris, Anthony, and baby Joseph, in the family's small ranch-style home with a wooden swing in the front yard at 1349 Sagebrush Road in 1963—the same year the nonstop motor-mouth did a whirlwind thirty-five city personal appearance tour and starred in *Who's Minding the Store?*

Two years later, Lewis, who played many desert golf and charity benefits, got hooked on Percodan after a slip and fall at the Sands Hotel in Las Vegas. The following year, he held the first of his insufferable yearly muscular dystrophy telethons, then hightailed it back here, where he swam and suntanned until 1975. If Lewis's popularity were measured by the price of real estate, he'd be considered *real* cheap judging by the rock-bottom selling price of his former home in 1994. Lewis' recent health woes have landed him in hospitals in Australia and England. He suffers back pain so severe that he needs a battery-powered pulse generator to send electric impulses to his spinal cord, while undergoing ongoing treatment for diabetes and pulmonary fibrosis. Despite his medical problems, Lewis will still perform anywhere, it seems, even Spain, at the drop of an airline ticket.

Producer **Bryan Foy**, who made a middle-aged star of Vincent Price in the first 3-D horror film *House of Wax* and threw political caution to the wind with his red-baiting propaganda piece *I Was a Communist for the FBI*, which inconceivably was nominated for an Academy Award, lived at 1377 Paseo de Marcia in 1963. That was the same year he made his final film, *PT 109*, a sanitized version of John F. Kennedy's naval exploits in the South Pacific. Foy died in 1977.

★ ★ ★

Hollywood composer **Frank Skinner**, who arranged, conducted, and wrote the music for five hundred films made at Universal Studios, including *Destry Rides Again*, *My Little Chickadee*, and *Tammy and the Bachelor*, lived with his lyricist-wife, Grace Shannon, at 1380 South Paseo de Marcia until his death from cancer in 1968.

Top: Funnyman Jerry Lewis and family (Courtesy of Palm Springs Historical Society). *Middle:* William Holden controlling his demons (Cinema Collectors). *Bottom:* William Holden's home at 1323 South Driftwood Drive (Courtesy of Palm Springs Historical Society).

★ ★ ★

Hollywood superstar **William Holden**'s youthful, sunny disposition gradually gave way to grim-faced weariness, the result of his ever-increasing dissatisfaction with the moviemaking business. A Best Actor Oscar winner for *Stalag 17*, he was a top box-office draw for two decades in such films as *Sunset Boulevard*, *Sabrina*, *Picnic*, and *The Bridge on the River Kwai*.

Holden took up permanent residence in this contemporary Japanese-style house at 1323 South Driftwood Drive in 1967. He decorated his home with many rare artifacts and primitive artworks that he collected during his frequent trips to Africa and Asia.

"I found myself too spread out," the craggy actor explained when he was fifty. "You gotta have one place where everything is there." By "there," the world traveler meant Palm Springs, which he first visited as the fresh-faced star of *Golden Boy*, based on Clifford Odets's boxing play, in 1939. "It was the place where you could get the cleanest air and an instant suntan for a healthy onscreen look," he said.

A big-game hunter and early protector of endangered species, Holden was co-owner with millionaire investor Ray Ryan of the Mount Kenya Safari Club, a full-service tourist resort in Nairobi where visiting film stars and members of royalty sipped gin and tonics and gazed out over the plains at galloping herds of antelopes and prides of yawning lions. In 1969, Holden held poolside meetings at his Deepwell home with publicist Jay Bernstein during promotion of his controversial anti-Western *The Wild Bunch*, which was produced by fellow desert resident Phil Feldman.

Away from the cameras, Holden rarely socialized, preferring to charbroil a steak with producer-friend Ray Stark and his longtime buddy, Richard Quine, who directed him in *The World of Suzie Wong*—and showing the group home movies of his recent trips to Hong Kong. The introspective actor also stayed up late reading books on the two subjects he liked best, art and history, as well as contemplating thick bundles of film scripts, among them *The Towering Inferno*, which he accepted and *The Omen*, which he declined.

He rehearsed his third Oscar-nominated role in *Network* and embarked on a ten-year love affair with actress Stefanie Powers while living here. Holden was a familiar sight driving his Mercedes 500 to the market or racing his Honda 1000 motorcycle across the desert. A keen botanist, he donated thousands of African tree plantings to nurseries and parks throughout the valley. Holden sold his treasured house when he moved to Southridge in 1977—the same year his friend, Ray Ryan, who testified against Chicago mobster Marshall Caifano, was killed by a car bomb. Holden died in 1981.

Los Angeles KABC-TV Eyewitness News reporter **David Jackson**, who was embedded with American troops in the recent war with Iraq, paid $750,000 for the actor's former home in 1999.

★　★　★

Classical pianist **Phil Moody**, a graduate of London's Royal Academy of Music, who performs a nightly cabaret show at Livreri's Italian Restaurant, lives at 1440 South Driftwood Drive. In addition to his career as a virtuoso performer, Moody and his late songwriting partner, Pony Sherrell, penned the songs for two movie musicals—*So This Is Paris*, starring Tony Curtis and Gloria DeHaven, and *The Second Greatest Sex* with Jeanne Crain and George Nader.

★　★　★

For eight years, glamorous film and TV legend **Loretta Young** left an everlasting impression as the smiling hostess of *Letter to Loretta*, appearing each week dressed in sumptuous gowns designed by her third husband, French-born costume designer **Jean Louis**. In 1993, she and Louis moved to 1075 Manzanita Avenue where the pious, swanlike actress,

who starred in 103 films from 1917 to 1989, still received fan mail from people that remembered her strong-willed performances in *The Bishop's Wife* alongside Cary Grant, *The Story of Alexander Graham Bell* with Henry Fonda, *Suez* with Tyrone Power, and *Call of the Wild* in the arms of Clark Gable, with whom it has been repeatedly alleged she bore an illegitimate daughter.

A devout Catholic, Young caused an Oscar upset in 1947 when she walked off with the Best Actress award for *The Farmer's Daughter*, beating out Joan Crawford, Dorothy McGuire, Susan Hayward, and Rosalind Russell. She was nominated a second time as a determined nun in *Come to the Stable*.

Jean Louis was nominated for an Oscar more than a dozen times, finally receiving his own statuette for *The Solid Gold Cadillac*. Memorable among his other credits is Rita Hayworth's strapless black gown in *Gilda*. He also designed the flesh-colored, beaded dress worn by Marilyn Monroe when she sang "Happy Birthday, Mr. President" to J.F.K. at Madison Square Garden. Louis was eighty-nine when he died sitting on the patio on a glorious spring day in 1997—the same year Young's two older sisters, Polly Ann Young and Sally Blane, died. Young survived them by three years, succumbing to ovarian cancer at age eighty-seven in 2000.

Their home with its distinctive circular white living room, fourteen-foot ceilings, indirect lighting, and suspended fireplace sold twelve months later for $630,000—nearly double what Young paid for it.

Top Left: Loretta Young modeling a gown by Jean-Louis (Larry Edmunds Bookshop). *Top Right:* The circular living room of Loretta Young's home at 1075 Manzanita Avenue (Courtesy of the Asher-White Team). *Middle:* Dragnet star Jack Webb (Backlot Books & Movie Posters). *Bottom:* Torch singer Julie London (Wayne Knight Collection).

★　★　★

Jack Webb, the gravel-voiced star and producer of *Dragnet* and *Pete Kelly's Blues*, lived at 1255 South Manzanita Avenue while preparing his sixth TV police series *Adam-12* in 1965. The four-times married Webb, however, consoled himself with a bottle of bourbon most nights waiting for the love of his life and next-door neighbor to come back to him. Confused? Don't be.

Webb's lost love was his first wife, singer **Julie London** of 1297 South Manzanita Avenue, whose mournful torch song "Cry Me a River" was a number one hit in 1956. A native of San Bernardino, London recorded more than thirty albums of haunting romantic ballads, appearing frequently on TV variety shows hosted by Dinah Shore, Bob Hope, and Perry Como. When London fell on hard times, Webb rode to her rescue, casting her as the head nurse on his hit series, *Emergency!* The couple remained close friends even though they were both remarried to other people (he to former Miss USA Jackie

Loughery; she to actor-drummer Bobby Troup). Webb's end came first in 1982. Then in 1996, their oldest daughter, Stacey Webb, who was the pride and joy of both parents, was killed in a drunk-driving accident with her boyfriend when their GMC truck collided with a California Highway Patrol car in Morongo Valley. Heartbroken, London suffered a stroke and died in 2000.

★　★　★

Las Vegas hotel pioneer **Thomas Hull** built one of the city's first casino-resorts, El Rancho, with its trademark red and yellow windmill signage that welcomed millions of gamblers to the state of Nevada and was the venue for Paul Newman's splashy wedding to Joanne Woodward. Hull enjoyed the last four years of his life at 1350 Manzanita Avenue with actress-wife Lynn Starr until he died, age seventy, in 1964.

★　★　★

Five-times married **Eva Gabor**, youngest and prettiest of the Hungarian sisters, reportedly lived at 1509 Manzanita Avenue in 1978. Although she had good roles in *The Last Time I Saw Paris* and *Gigi*, Eva is best remembered as the spoiled Park Avenue wife of Hooterville farm owner Eddie Albert in the hokey TV sitcom *Green Acres*, which also starred desert colleagues Pat Buttram and Alvy Moore.

★　★　★

Liberace's first desert home, where he greeted visitors in 1957, can be found at 1516 South Manzanita Avenue. It was here that the effervescent concert performer admitted gentlemen callers through a sky-blue front door with tropical plants in the entrance hall and past a baby grand piano where each day he relentlessly practiced twenty-five songs a week for his popular TV show. During Lee's stay, a large fireplace hood decorated with harlequin diamonds dominated the black-and-white living room. In the rose-pink kitchen, the fussy pianist, wearing a "Kiss-the-cook" apron, prepared and served homemade lasagna. Outside, under the light of candelabra-shaped garden torches, shimmered a rectangular swimming pool with black and white stone fingers arranged in a keyboard flowerbed pattern at one end, flanked by muscular bodybuilders. A stickler in every way, Liberace even decorated the house himself—adorning the walls with plastic flowers, cupids, and portraits of his two French poodles, Mambo and Minuet, who slept on their own plump-cushioned bed.

★　★　★

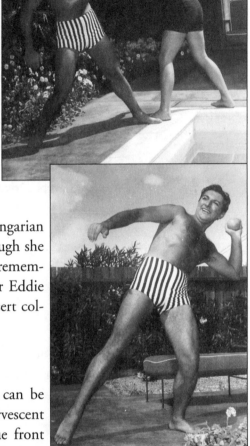

Top: Liberace doing some male bonding at his Deepwell home (Photo by Bill Anderson). *Bottom:* Liberace picking grapefruit in his backyard (Photo by Bill Anderson).

215

Harriet Parsons, the pioneering feminist producer of *The Enchanted Cottage, I Remember Mama,* and *Clash By Night*, bought the house at 1115 East Deepwell Drive after leaving RKO in 1955. The lesbian daughter of syndicated Hearst newspaper columnist Louella Parsons, Harriet was a self-acknowledged "tomboy" who began her career as a child actor, then segued into journalism and documentary filmmaking. It's been suggested that she retired from the business because of studio interference—a subtle form of sexual discrimination. Unlike her scatterbrained mother, "Harriet was a straightforward, no-nonsense girl," said biographer George Eells, "who might have found real happiness teaching English classics at college or university." In 1958, Parsons and her lifetime partner, Evelyn Farney, moved to a new home at 613 South Beverly Drive in Ramon Rise Estates. Parsons died in 1983.

Husky-voiced actress **Joanna Moore**—the ex-wife of Ryan O'Neal and mother of actor-siblings Griffin and Tatum O'Neal—played flirtatious roles in *Walk on the Wild Side, Son of Flubber*, and *Never a Dull Moment*. She lived in Deepwell Ranch condominiums at 1302 Primavera Drive in 1980.

The present home of midcentury modern architect **Donald Wexler**, who designed the Sinatra Medical Education Center at Desert Hospital and the Indio Juvenile Hall of Detention and Treatment Center, is located at 1320 North Primavera Drive.

Broadway producer, theater owner, and manager **Richard Horner**, who collaborated with partner Lester Osterman on dozens of plays, including the 1974 revival of Eugene O'Neill's *A Moon for the Misbegotten*, starring Colleen Dewhurst and Jason Robards, resided with actress-wife **Lynne Stuart** at 1339 Primavera Drive from 1994 until Horner's death, age eighty-two, in 2002. Horner-Stuart produced the Tony Award-winning stage play *The Crucifer of Blood*, which was filmed with Charlton Heston as Sherlock Holmes.

Talent agent **Victor Orsatti**, who was married to leggy showgirl Marie "the Body" McDonald and produced five films with actor Rory Calhoun, including *Apache Territory*, lived at 1356 Primavera Drive in 1975. Vic Orsatti was the youngest of three brothers: Frank founded the Orsatti Agency, whose clients included Betty Grable, Alice Faye, Judy Garland, Margaret O'Brien, and Edward G. Robinson; and Ernie Orsatti was a baseball player with the St. Louis Cardinals.

Violin virtuoso **Murray Korda**, a leading expert on Gypsy music, whose twenty-piece orchestra played for eight U.S. presidents and serenaded party guests at the wedding of Barbra Streisand and James Brolin, lived for twenty years at 852 East Biltmore Place with his wife, Joan Allen, and four children until his death at age seventy. While on his way to Yom Kippur services in Orwell, Vermont, on September 30, 1998, Korda was killed in a head-on collision when an oncoming car crossed the center line.

★　★　★

Actress **Nina Wayne**, a well-rounded graduate of Columbia Pictures's charm school, who had eye-catching roles in *Dead Heat on a Merry-Go-Round, Luv,* and *The Comic,* lives in a two-bedroom Biltmore condominium at 1370 South Camino Real. Her sister, Carol Wayne, who played Johnny Carson's much-ogled Tea Time Movie Matinee lady on *The Tonight Show,* mysteriously drowned in Manzanillo, Mexico, in 1985.

★　★　★

MGM director **Richard Thorpe** amassed an incredible 114 directorial credits during his thirty-three-year tenure with that studio, including several *Tarzan, The Thin Man,* and *Lassie* installments. He spent his sunset years roaming in apartment number 222 at 1550 South Camino Real. Thorpe's spicy tastes ran from traditional Americana in *Huckleberry Finn* to the decorative costume adventures *The Prisoner of Zenda* to classical music in *The Student Prince.* He guided some of MGM's finest talents, among them Ava Gardner, Robert Taylor, and Lana Turner. In addition, Thorpe, who died in 1991 at age ninety-four, directed the studio's first Cinemascope medieval epic, *Knights of the Round Table,* as well as Elvis Presley's best film, *Jailhouse Rock.* Jerry Thorpe, his son, directed the long-running TV series *Kung Fu.*

Director Richard Thorpe (Larry Edmunds Bookshop).

★　★　★

If Richard Thorpe and his cohorts wanted to order lunch or dinner, they simply walked across the street to Villa Royale at 1620 South Indian Trail where customers meet at the Europa Restaurant and Bar, which is part owned by Lebanese-American actor **Tony Shalhoub**, who plays the obsessive-compulsive detective in the Emmy-winning TV series *Monk,* and his actress-wife, **Brooke Adams**. A Los Angeles investment group paid $1,362,000 for the thirty-one-room hotel-restaurant in 1997.

★　★　★

Marjorie Main dons a life preserver at the Biltmore Hotel (Courtesy of Palm Springs Historical Society).

To the east is "motel row," a selection of medium-priced lodgings exotically named Aloha, Alpine Gardens, Blue Palms, Caliente Tropics, Caribbean, Ironside, Palm Tee, and Royal Sun, which cater to impromptu visitors and seasonal travelers. Several of these hotels are now decidedly gay—the Citadel, Casitas Laquita, Desert Knight, Queen of Hearts, Terrazzo, and Viola's Resort.

The most famous of these antiquated hotels is a long, grayish building that occupied almost an entire city block. Built in 1948 by San Francisco theater owner Samuel H. Levin and designed by Los Angeles architect Frederick Monhoff, the crescent-shaped **Biltmore Hotel** at 1000 East Palm Canyon Drive, where autograph hounds once chased the Rat Pack and poolside waiters were kept busy serving cocktails to sunbathers reclining on gaily colored beach chairs under striped parasols, has the unfortunate distinction of being, perhaps, the city's most-jinxed hotel. This is no flight of fancy, but rather fact.

"The World's Finest Desert Resort," as it was called, had been open for business less than six months when a mysterious early-morning fire gutted the hotel's warehouse, scaring cleaning staff and causing $10,000 in damage. Over the years, strange accidents have plagued the hotel's twenty-five buildings and fifty private guest suites—all of them since deserted, telephones still sitting on desks, chairs arranged around dusty tables in the glass-walled lobby as if waiting for the next guest.

These unexplained occurrences didn't stop the parade of movie stars and wealthy Midwesterners that made yearly reservations during the hotel's golden era. They crowded around the bar and hit golf balls on the nine-hole putting green (now an empty lot), but it did put a crimp in the day-to-day hotel operations, which finally caused the hotel to cease operating on its fortieth anniversary.

That's not to say the Biltmore had never been popular, but time had somehow passed her by until, by the end of her lifetime, she resembled a lonely old spinster—like Miss Habersham staring out the window in her unused wedding dress in Charles Dickens' *Great Expectations.*

One unpleasant incident took place in the Biltmore's fancy restaurant, the Garden Room, which advertised "superb food prepared by our famous chef." It was here at a private party on October 12, 1979, that four socially prominent diners became violently ill after they contracted type-A hepatitis from eating contaminated food. Palm Springs businessman Ray Blumenthal, journalist Allene Arthur, socialite June Linthicum, and beauty-salon owner Ron Smith sued the hotel for $4 million, claiming they nearly died. Three years later, Blumenthal was awarded $75,000 in damages, and the other plaintiffs settled out of court.

"Move and I'll blow your fuckin' head off!" Those were the terrifying words that echoed in the ears of Robert Shannon, the retired president of I. Magnin, when he and his wife were abducted at gunpoint from the Biltmore Hotel's parking lot after dining there on Christmas Day 1983. Shannon was about to unlock the driver's door of his tan Mercedes when he felt the cold steel of a sawed-off .12 gauge shotgun pressed against the back of his head.

"Please don't hurt us," begged Kathleen Shannon. "Shuddup!" yelled the gunman, grabbing Shannon's wallet and car keys, then unlocking the trunk. "Get in!" ordered the man, pointing the gun at them. The elderly couple clambered into the trunk. Then he slammed the lid shut and locked it. Several hours elapsed before the Shannons were freed outside their Rancho Sante Fe home and taken inside where they were bound and gagged while their home was ransacked by the gunman and another man who then fled the scene with $78,000 of cash, furs, and jewels in Shannon's stolen car. The kidnappers were arrested two months later and eventually sentenced to life in prison.

Then on May 1, 1986, a man claiming to be a terrorist for Libyan dictator Muammar Khadafy telephoned police and told them he had placed explosives in the Biltmore Hotel. Two fire trucks and eight firefighters rushed to the scene. Every room was searched and forty people evacuated. Fortunately, it was a hoax. Police traced the call to the home of a thirty-eight-year-old man named Stephen Honey and arrested him.

The accumulation of bad press involving fires, kidnapping, and food poisoning, proved to be a public relations disaster for the ailing hotel and in 1988 it closed—never to reopen. Samuel Levin's two sons, Richard and Robert, put the darkened lodging up for sale, but there were no takers. Rats soon infested the kitchen, vandals broke windows and doors, and transients squatted inside the rooms, leaving a trail of filth, debris, and human excrement on the floors.

In 1999, Los Angeles businesswoman Linda Grant paid an undisclosed sum for the abandoned property, which had been listed for sale for $3.9 million. Instead of knocking it down, she planned to resurrect the rotting hotel, which leaned more precariously each day. In October 2001, the city council ordered Grant to clean up the property or have it razed. Time ticked by; there were more structural problems and more odd fires. The comatose hotel was finally put out of its misery and reduced to rubble in September 2003.

Thirties child star **Bonita Granville**, who played juvenile screen detective Nancy Drew, and her rich oilman-husband **Jack Wrather Jr.**, who produced the TV series *Lassie* and *The Lone Ranger*, owned L'Horizon, where they lived on-site at 1050 East Palm Canyon Drive in 1954.

In addition to changing beds and brewing coffee, the Wrathers built and ran Disneyland Hotel, founded Los Angeles PBS station KCET-TV, and turned the Spruce Goose and Queen Mary into Long Beach's top tourist attractions. Because of the well-liked couple's strong political affiliations, they also were advisers to President Ronald Reagan when he took office in 1980. (In 1988, the Walt Disney Company bought Wrather Corporation for $152 million.)

Although the husband-and-wife business team has been deceased for more than a decade, L'Horizon is still open for business. Gucci fashion designer Tom Ford, who was voted VH1/Vogue Fashion Awards Designer of the Year in 2001, stays at the taupe-colored hotel, designed by William Cody, whenever he's in the desert. He's the latest in a long line of celebrities who have signed the guest register. *Beloved Infidel* screenwriter Sy Bartlett and brunette actress Patricia Owens exchanged wedding vows on the hotel grounds in 1956. The William Wylers, Don Hartmans, Gregory Pecks, Kirk Douglases, and Alan Ladds attended the ceremony. Six months later, Mrs. Bartlett underwent an emergency appendectomy while filming *Sayonara* in Japan, but sufficiently recovered to play the shrieking heroine of 1958's *The Fly*.

Baseball legend **Leo Durocher**, who played shortstop for seventeen years with the Brooklyn Dodgers, Cincinnati Reds, St. Louis Cardinals, and New York Yankees, winning an exhausting total of 2,009 games out of 3,740 played, as well as claiming victory at the 1954 World Series, retired to the Joshua Tree Apartments (now Tennis Court Apartments) at 1400 East Palm Canyon Drive, in 1976.

Married for thirteen years to MGM actress Laraine Day (Nurse Mary Lamont in the *Dr. Kildare* film series), the highly competitive and combative Durocher, who coined the expression "nice guys finish last" and later managed the Dodgers, New York Giants, Chicago Cubs, and Houston Astros, was seriously injured in a 1989 traffic accident when an oncoming motorist struck his Cadillac Seville outside Jensen's Finest Foods on South Sunrise Way. Three years after the eighty-six year-old sports hero and crony of Frank Sinatra died a virtual recluse in 1991, he was posthumously inducted into the Baseball Hall of Fame.

When Paramount director **A. Edward Sutherland**, the owner of a Calypso Palms apartment at 1643 Andee Drive (off East Palm Canyon Drive) died largely forgotten, age seventy-seven, in 1974, his passing barely rated a mention. "A lousy no-good bastard," Clara Bow had called him. But Sutherland, who had worked with Bow, Eddie Cantor, W.C. Fields, Mae West, and Laurel and Hardy, deserved better.

Decades earlier, he had directed each of them in *The Saturday Night Kid*, *Palmy Days*, *Mississippi*, *Every Day's A Holiday*, and *The Flying Deuces*, respectively. His achievements didn't end there, however. A former vaudevillian and member of the Keystone Kops, Sutherland brought his considerable talents to more than fifty feature films, including *International House* and *Follow the Boys*—two marvelous all-star revues that showcased the

Comedy director Eddie Sutherland (right) gets an earful from orchestra leader Charlie Spivak (Larry Edmunds Bookshop).

live performances of George Burns, Gracie Allen, Rudy Vallee, Cab Calloway, Jeanette MacDonald, George Raft, and Dinah Shore, plus the absurd spectacle of black-cloaked magician Orson Welles sawing a sequined Marlene Dietrich in half! In 1933, Sutherland proved just how clever he could be with *Murders in the Zoo*—a surprisingly gory pre-Code horror entry.

One wonders if the patrons that crowded into Club Trinidad, just steps away, knew that Sutherland had been living next door—or gave him a second thought.

Chapter 9

Mesa By Moonlight

The appeal of Mesa, a favored secluded spot, lies in the Spanish and Southwestern architectural styles that have adorned the lower mountainside since it was first sub-divided by Edmond Fulford, a successful Los Angeles businessman and Builders Supply founder, who moved here in 1921. The majority of these adobe-style homes, collectively Tahquitz Desert Estates and Palm Canyon Mesa, were built in the 1930s and 1940s. Rocky hillside terrain, mature palm trees, and natural desert landscaping have preserved the area's uniqueness.

Hollywood movers and shakers have always valued its quiet, low-key appeal. Fulford's dream of a planned community accessible through a common main entrance predated today's gated country clubs. However, his abrupt passing in 1936 precluded this visionary developer from witnessing the trend firsthand. One gate still partially stands at the corner of South Palm Canyon Drive and El Portal, where Pasadena architect Alfred Heineman owned several parcels of land on which he intended to propagate with their elite building designs.

For better or worse, these plans never came to fruition, and Heineman sold the land for future residential development. Builder Joseph Pawling was among the developers who constructed many of these latter-day homes. But it was the stars, their scribes, or handlers who set the tone for this rustic desert living.

Michael Levee is not a name that most people remember, but he was, in his time, one of filmland's foremost agents. Levee began his career as vice president of First National Studios, which merged with Warner Brothers in 1929. He was a founding member and president of the Academy of Motion Picture Arts and Sciences (AMPAS), and he originated the concept of paying "residuals," which was later adopted by the Screen Actors Guild.

Levee's honest, straightforward style won him many friends, and his services as an agent were soon in great demand. On his client list were actors Joe E. Brown, Joan Crawford, Bette Davis, Leslie Howard, Jeanette MacDonald, Paul Muni, Mary Pickford, Dick Powell, and Claude Rains. He also represented such directors as Cecil B. DeMille, William Dieterle, Mervyn LeRoy, writer Ben Hecht, and Chicago opera star Madame Ernestine Schumann-Heink.

After he retired in 1956, Levee got itchy feet, and ten years later, on the eve of his seventy-fifth birthday, he took out full-page trade advertisements announcing that he had become president of the Royal Hawaiian Estates, a Polynesian-style village (on the corner of South Palm Canyon Drive and Twin Palms Drive). Levee, whose address was listed as 243 Twin Palms Drive, advertised that he had two beautifully furnished condominiums for sale. So, "Howz About Cummin Out 'N See Em Sum Time," he teased readers.

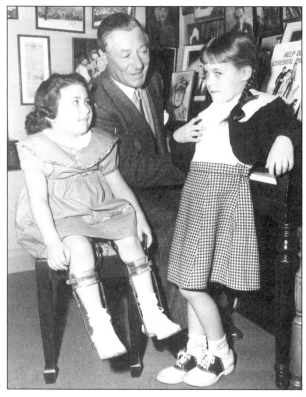

George Jessel and handicapped kids (Wayne Knight Collection).

Levee's ploy worked, and he quickly found two buyers. The first was **Milton Krasner**, the Oscar-winning Technicolor cinematographer of 1954's *Three Coins in the Fountain* and a seven-time nominee noted for his vibrant compositions on many of 20th Century-Fox's biggest Cinemascope crowd-pleasers from the previous decade, including *Demetrius and the Gladiators*, *The Seven Year Itch*, and *An Affair to Remember*. Krasner bought a unit at 117 Twin Palms Drive.

George Jessel, who starred in *The Jazz Singer* on Broadway and produced a handful of vaudeville-based film musicals such as *The Dolly Sisters* and *When My Baby Smiles At Me*, is better remembered as America's Toastmaster General, the monocle-wearing master of ceremonies and eulogist. Jessel grabbed the second unit at 1788 South Palm Canyon Drive. Levee, who ate breakfast every day across the road at Lindy Lou's Pancake House (now Tarbell Realtors), designed by Howard Lapham, lived at the Royal Hawaiian Estates until his death, age eighty-one, in 1972.

★　★　★

Chester Moorten, the desert's first horticulturalist, known to his green-thumbed friends as "Cactus Slim," founded **Moorten Botanical Garden** at 1701 South Palm Canyon Drive. A former Hollywood stuntman and character actor who was billed as the Human Pin Cushion in W.C. Fields's two-reeler *Two Flaming Youths* and played the Thin Man novelty attraction in *The Sideshow*, Moorten moved to the desert for his health in 1933 where he opened his first nursery five years later on the corner of Indian Avenue and Tahquitz Canyon Way.

In 1940, Moorten married Patricia Haliday-Pagan in Beverly Hills. The best man at their wedding was James Edwards, the founder, chairman, and CEO of Edwards Theatres Circuit. In 1955, Moorten relocated his garden center to the present two-acre site, where he maintained an extensive variety of cacti and other succulents that were eagerly purchased by village homeowners, including Frank Sinatra, Bing Crosby, Red Skelton, and Ginger Rogers. Moorten was especially pleased when Walt Disney asked him to landscape Frontierland at the newly opened Disneyland.

Although Chester Moorten died in 1980, visitors are still welcome at his nursery, which hosts weddings and private parties. His widow, Patricia, lives in an adjoining two-bedroom stone cottage dubbed "Castle Cactus" at 1735 South Palm Canyon Drive, which was previously the home of *Touring Topics* scenic photographer Stephen Willard.

★   ★   ★

Palm Springs mayor Sonny Bono (Backlot Books & Movie Posters).

British character actor **Reginald Owen** occupied the Spanish adobe home at 1757 South Palm Canyon Drive—the same year he played Scrooge in 1938's *A Christmas Carol*. Owen's specialty was impersonating emperors and silver-haired aristocrats, which he played in more than 125 films, among them *Queen Christina*, *Of Human Bondage*, and *Anna Karenina*. Two of his funniest roles were the cannon-firing Admiral Boom in *Mary Poppins* and General Teagler in *Bedknobs and Broomsticks*.

★   ★   ★

The former home of **Sonny Bono**, where he lived with fourth wife Mary Whitaker until his untimely death at age sixty-two in a Lake Tahoe skiing accident, is at 301 El Camino Way (rear entrance: 294 Crestview Drive).

"I loved the sun, the quiet, the solitude of a desert night, the picturesque landscape, and the tranquility," enthused Bono, whose passing drew unprecedented media attention in spring of 1998. Never in the history of Palm Springs or any other city for that matter had a politician/movie star/pop icon garnered so much airtime simultaneously on *all* three major television networks, as well as cable and satellite stations around the world. *Los Angeles Times* TV critic Howard Rosenberg likened the marathon news coverage to "a thundering drum roll," drawing comparisons of Bono's funeral to Princess Diana's fatal automobile crash the previous year.

And in a sad twist of fate, Bono and ex-wife Cher were finally back together after more than twenty years apart. "I landed at LAX and went straight to Palm Springs," said Cher, who found herself at Bono's home with its arched doorways, hardwood floors, and Edward Fields area rugs, breaking bread with his extended family—their daughter

Chastity, her son Elijah (from Cher's marriage to Gregg Allman), stepdaughter Christy and her son, Nico, and Mary's two children by Bono, Chesare and Chianna.

This monstrous nine-thousand-square-foot Mediterranean-style estate, actually two houses joined together, sits on one-and-a-half acres and boasts seven bedrooms, formal living rooms and dining rooms, gourmet kitchen, media room, outdoor barbecue pit, and tennis courts, plus a separate two-bedroom guesthouse. When Bono purchased the property, however, it was in poor condition. He decided to remodel the house—starting with a $10,000 concrete wall whose unauthorized construction earned the ire of city building inspectors. That costly dilemma, coupled with the added expenditure of running a restaurant, launched the singer-songwriter-turned-restaurateur on an unlikely political career.

Was Bono smart or stupid? According to his former press agent, Jay Bernstein, Sonny had no illusions about himself. "It was a PR stunt," said Bernstein, who was hoping to get some extra publicity for the restaurant. But instead of being welcomed with open arms, Bono was treated as a joke—and he didn't like it.

"As a businessman, taxpayer, and resident, that did not strike me as fair. Nor was it democratic," he complained.

Deciding to fight what he considered to be an adversarial bureaucracy at City Hall, Bono ran for mayor and, to everyone's surprise, won. (Coincidentally, he was elected to public office the day after his former spouse won a Best Actress Oscar for *Moonstruck*.) Among the notable achievements during his five-year term: erasing a $2.5-million deficit without raising city taxes and founding the Palm Springs Film Festival. Bono was elected to Congress in 1994 and was re-elected two years later.

Suzanne Somers and Alan Hamel standing in front of their Mesa home (Courtesy of Kaminsky Productions).

After he was buried with full honors, Sonny's widow assumed his congressional job. She sold their house for $1.4 million and moved the family to a new home in Bellamonte Estates. But in typical tabloid fashion, Bono was not allowed to rest in peace. It was revealed that he was addicted to painkillers, which he took for chronic neck and back trouble. Bono was one of several celebrity patients of Dr. Milton Reber, a Park Avenue physician who prescribed cocaine as a pain reliever for severe back problems. Bono began taking the drug in 1968 while he was still married to Cher and staying at the Waldorf-Astoria Hotel in New York City.

★　★　★

Three's Company star, fitness guru, and cookbook author **Suzanne Somers** and manager-husband **Alan Hamel** have owned the majestic Spanish-style home located at 385 Alta Vista Road (off Ridge Road) for almost twenty-five years. It's where they commiserated after Somers was ousted from the show she helped to make famous, where she developed the Thighmaster, and wrote half a dozen books. This charming, bougainvillea-fringed, two-story house with the pale pink walls and green shutters, encased by wrought-iron railings and tiled verandahs, is a relic of a bygone age, much of it lost to history.

This was the era of the first desert boom, when movie stars, gangsters, and business tycoons played together. The home has quite a history. Its first owner was **Wright S. Ludington**, the artistic, handsome scion of a wealthy Philadelphia family, whose father was vice president of Curtis Publishing, owners of *The Saturday Evening Post*. Ludington was a prominent collector of contemporary art and classical antiquities in his youth, buying works by Picasso, Braque, and Derian, and was the single-most-generous benefactor of the Santa Barbara Museum of Art.

Ludington owned three glorious estates: Val Verde, a seventeen-acre Moroccan-style palace designed by Bertram Goodhue, architect of the Los Angeles Public Library; the Mediterranean-themed Hesperides House overlooking the Pacific Ocean; and the Renaissance-style October Hill in the picturesque coastal city of Santa Barbara where he lived for most of his adult life. In 1938, this introspective gentleman who appreciated beauty, whether natural or man-made, came to the desert where he began construction of a five-bedroom, four-bathroom home in what was then called Palm Canyon Mesa. The two-story building, set on a granite foundation, was constructed of steel and concrete. Its initial cost: $15,000.

Burros and laborers dragged building materials up the steep terrain. Later, a small crane was installed to lift lumber and other bulky items, which was in turn replaced by a funicular rail system that is still in use today. Upon completion, the home resembled a European villa, with works of art from the owner's collection and a well-stocked wine cellar. Here, Ludington, who was openly homosexual before it was legally or morally acceptable, could entertain his young lovers in complete privacy and indulge his epicurean tastes. He even built an ornate Roman bath (now the swimming pool) at the rear of the property for the sensual enjoyment of his male companions.

Ludington resided at this coveted address through 1946 when he decided to sell the house and return to Santa Barbara, where he remained until his death, age ninety-one, in 1992. Ludington's vast collection of art was willed to the museum he had founded in Santa Barbara in 1941. Its centerpiece, Ludington Court, is named in his honor.

Louis Benoist (pronounced *ben-wa*), the owner of Almaden Santa Clara Wineries and vice president of Meadow Lumber Company, purchased Ludington's former home in 1949. Benoist was a powerful and influential Missouri-born businessman who first came to Palm Springs in 1934 seeking relief for his children's pneumonia. He owned homes in San Francisco and Warm Springs, Virginia, as well as an airplane and a yacht.

In 1941, Benoist divorced his first wife, Geraldine, and married Katharine Bentley, affectionately known as Kay, whose father, Joseph Grace, had a major stake in the California canning industry and controlled Del Monte Foods. He and Benoist were partners in Grace Brothers, a Los Angeles brewery that supplied Brown Derby beer to Safeway stores. Benoist's other business partner was Hernando Courtwright, co-owner of the Beverly Hills Hotel and later, the Beverly Wilshire where he opened Don Hernando's Hideaway.

According to Louis's son, Jay Benoist of Palm Springs, his father was one of the first Southern California winemakers to plant Cabernet grapes, and he helped introduce wine connoisseurs to the delightful taste of Pinot Noir and Chardonnay. In 1950, Benoist commissioned Albert Frey to design a one-room studio (now the guesthouse) above the main house. Fieldstone was used for the exterior and interior walls, while rocks from the side of the mountain passed through the fireplace wall. The roof was made of glass except in the bathroom and had a canvas awning that could be rolled over the top for shade.

For a quarter of a century, the Benoists hosted candlelit dinner parties under the stars. George Brent, Kay Francis, Cesar Romero, Dorothy Lamour and Texas land baron William Boggess, celebrated husband-and-wife acting team Alfred Lunt and Lynne Fontanne, and famed New York stage actress Ina Claire (the ex-wife of actor John Gilbert) with her husband, San Francisco attorney William Wallace Jr., who represented Benoist, were among the invited guests trekking up the steep road in their best finery.

"Louis would stand at the top of the verandah and greet you with a glass of champagne," recalled film and theater producer Paul Gregory, who was at the house the night Benoist died from a heart attack in 1975. The month before, Almaden had delivered twenty cases of wine for a party, but the gate was closed so the heavy boxes were left at the bottom of the road. Son Jay said his father carried the cases all the way up to the house "and that's what probably killed him."

The Hamels bought the stately home for $400,000 from Benoist's widow, Kay Bentley, in 1979. Somers thinks that fate played a large part in her decision to buy the house. "I really believe the home found us," she said. "We were drawn here by something." The ghosts of restless party guests perhaps?

The couple redid the electrical wiring and plumbing and added air-conditioning. They also replaced the existing floor tiles with flagstone, added an arbor that connected the buildings, and turned the old steam room into a separate guest room. Suzanne herself decorated the dining room and main bedroom in a classical Tuscan style and chose the splashes of color—peach, raspberry, boysenberry—that give a warm hue to each living space. The period furniture, she points out, is authentic, the linens are antique, and the art is real.

Somers recently finished remodeling and enlarging the old guesthouse, adding a new bedroom suite, two offices, and a guest wing. Past owners Wright Ludington and Louis Benoist, watching from the verandah, champagne glasses in hand, would no doubt be extremely pleased with her efforts. (Alan, who wanted a faithful renovation, even had a fabricator replicate the building's original steel-framed windows and doors.) Architect Bob Easton designed the new plans, and local contractor Chris Neil supervised the construction.

Things looked better than ever for Somers, who had gone from playing dumb blondes to being voted the Female Entertainer of the Year in Las Vegas. At fifty-four, when most women are feeling the biological effects of aging, Somers still looked like a glowing debutante. People asked, "How does she do it?" They were about to find out. In March 2001, *The National Enquirer* ran a photo of Somers exiting the Lasky Clinic in Beverly Hills where she underwent liposuction treatment to have excess fat removed from her arms, thighs, abdomen, and hips. Somers only admitted to having cosmetic work done on her breasts. Then on March 28, 2001, Somers, dabbing her eyes, told CNN's Larry King that she was battling breast cancer.

At the Mesa's apex, up a narrow dirt road marked "Private Property," is the first of three desert homes that **Edmund Goulding** owned while remaking Howard Hawks's aviation epic *The Dawn Patrol*—the *Top Gun* of its time when first released in 1938. Known as the Little White House, this authentic Spanish Colonial, tucked away in the most northerly corner at 1752 Ridge Road, was originally built and owned by silent screen leading lady **Anita Stewart**, once the sixth-most popular actress in the nation. She retired from acting in 1929, having played plucky heroines in hundreds of "lost" films, where her dark sultry eyes and long sausage curls won her millions of adoring fans, including Louis B. Mayer, who stole her away from Vitagraph to star in his first independent production, *Virtuous Wives*.

Top: Edmund Goulding (Larry Edmunds Bookshop). *Bottom:* Anita Stewart in bed (Larry Edmunds Bookshop).

Stewart, however, was not the goody two-shoes she portrayed on the screen. She was a hardheaded businesswoman with an unrelenting temper. When her brother-in-law, Ralph Ince, who directed Stewart in fifty one- and two-reelers and was married to Anita's older sister Lucille, crippled their actor-brother George Stewart in a drunken brawl, she never forgave him. Shamed, Ince left for England where he worked steadily as a director until he died in a London road accident. In 1924, Ralph's middle brother, Thomas Ince, who directed many large-scale silent screen pageants, notably *Civilization*, mysteriously took ill on William Randolph Hearst's yacht and died amid swirling rumors of infidelity and murder (re-created in Peter Bogdanovich's whodunit, *The Cat's Meow*). Stewart's older brother, John, also an actor, later died from pneumonia.

Tragedy seemed to hang like a widow's veil over Stewart's home, which she sold amid much family dissension in 1931. Four years later, Goulding purchased the property from Mesa developer Edmond Fulford, who unexpectedly died shortly afterwards, leaving many shocked. It was the second blow Goulding had been dealt since he took possession of the unlucky home. On February 3, 1935, his wife, Marjorie Moss, the former partner of Latin ballroom dancer Georges Fontana, who thrilled audiences at New York's Waldorf-Astoria with their erotic tango, succumbed to an incurable lung and throat ailment as her distraught husband, alerted by a doctor's emergency phone call, left the set of his latest film and chartered a plane from Los Angeles to be at his wife's bedside. By the time Goulding arrived at the house, her spirit had departed.

Determined to rid the gloomy place of its omens, the stocky, sandy-haired director embarked on a three-year beautification of the hilltop that Moss adored, cutting back his filmmaking activities to oversee construction of a cluster of homes, resembling a Cornish village, accessible from two separate gateways below and connected on both sides by a little stone bridge stretching across a terraced ravine.

Carole Lombard and Clark Gable on their honeymoon (Backlot Books & Movie Posters).

Actor-architect Tom Douglas, who distinguished himself as the slain German soldier in Ernst Lubitsch's pacifist war drama *Broken Lullaby*, designed and decorated a quartet of guest cottages at numbers 1716, 1718, 1755, and 1765. He painted them white with doors and windows trimmed in turquoise blue. Noted landscape artist Paul Avery, whose lush plantings enhanced homes in Rancho Sante Fe, supplemented the natural vegetation with imported olive trees that he set along the banks of a man-made lake where Goulding's Hollywood friends and colleagues drank champagne and took moonlight swims.

These included the director's star pupil and close friend, David Niven, whose first lead role had been in the 1936 film *Palm Springs*, Greta Garbo (sans clothes) and her photographer-lover, Mercedes D'Acosta, the Duke of Warwick and Viscountess Castlerosse, Her Royal Highness the Maharini of Indore, Countess Dorothy di Frasso, tobacco heiress Doris Duke, society hostess Elsa Maxwell, actress Mary Pickford, and Metropolitan opera star Grace Moore.

In 1940, Barbara Hutton and fiancé Cary Grant had afternoon tea with Goulding and his mother in this idyllic setting where, the previous year, Oscar-winning groom Clark Gable and his zany bride, Carole Lombard, stopped to see Goulding on a motoring trip from Kingman, Arizona, where they had been secretly married—although no official mention was ever made of their desert interlude.

In 1952, **Henry J. Emard**, the founder of Emard Packing Company, once the largest salmon cannery in Anchorage, Alaska, purchased Goulding's home and the surrounding guest cottages. When he died, Emard, who also owned a gold mine, willed the factory to his employees.

Today, these stories of past happenings are still the favored topics of conversation by knowing guests of the home's current owner, **B. Donald "Bud" Grant**, the retired president of CBS Entertainment and a thirty-year broadcasting veteran of daytime programming. Grant began his career at NBC where he is credited with launching the serial *Days*

Of Our Lives. After moving to CBS, he developed *The Young and the Restless* and hired Bob Barker to host *The Price Is Right.* Grant's reign also extended to *Lou Grant, Newhart, Dallas,* and *Knots Landing.*

★   ★   ★

King Camp Gillette, inventor of the patented double-edged safety razor that replaced the straight-edged men's shaving blade (often called a cut-throat razor), is said to have built the vintage California-Spanish estate at 277 West Crestview Drive (324 West Overlook Road), which was the razor king's winter residence from 1923 until his death, age seventy-seven, in 1932.

There are actually two houses—a large three-bedroom residence and a smaller one-bedroom cottage. Because the large property sits on a knoll directly across the street from Sonny Bono's former estate, they are often confused. Don't be mistaken: The Gillette house is surrounded on both sides by a white stucco wall with two large orange coach lamps mounted on each side of the original driveway. The current owner, Henry Fernandez, paid $442,000 for both properties in 1987.

The main house has seen better days, judging by its weatherbeaten appearance. However, it has many interesting design features, including a thirteen-hundred-square-foot reception room, and stone fireplaces in each of the bedrooms. Because Gillette was a tall man (six feet, four inches) and weighed 250 pounds, the master bath contained an oversized tub mounted on gold-clasped feet for his easy access. Hollywood stuntman Buster Wiles, who doubled Errol Flynn in a half-dozen films, recalled meeting Gillette on a visit to Palm Springs at the height of the Great Depression when Wiles was unemployed and looking for a job.

"Coming to a huge estate, I walked inside the gates and up the winding road," he said. "Before me was a mansion, and off to one side was a glassed-in breakfast room. I noticed a bearded man was eyeing me curiously.... Then it hit me like a ton of bricks. He was the guy who manufactured Gillette razor blades: his picture was printed on each box!"

★   ★   ★

Hollywood's eternal prince charming, **Robert Wagner,** and his doe-eyed princess, **Natalie Wood**, were once publicized as "Hollywood's dream couple." At one time they lived year-round in this glorious old stone castle at 303 West Crestview Drive (123 Overlook Glen). Wagner purchased the approximately three-quarter-acre property while starring as expert safecracker Alexander Mundy in the hit TV series *It Takes a Thief* in 1968 and honeymooned here with Wood when they remarried amid much media hoopla in 1972.

According to biographer Warren G. Harris, "The house had five bedrooms plus a

Top: Natalie Wood watches Robert Wagner tee off (Courtesy of Palm Springs Historical Society). *Bottom:* Natalie Wood memorialized (Howard Johns Collection).

three-bedroom guest house adjoining the swimming pool." At the time of their unexpected reunion, Wagner and Wood, who first wed in 1957, were on the rebound from other marriages: "R.J." to 20th Century-Fox starlet Marion Marshall, the ex-wife of musical comedy director Stanley Donen; and "Nat" from producer Richard Gregson, the younger brother of British cinema star Michael Craig, with whom she played a lot of tennis.

The Wagners secretly reconciled at his home for three months in the spring of '72 with their two small children, Kate and Natasha, stepping out together for the first time in a decade to the delight of millions of viewers at that year's Academy Awards. Following their storybook reunion, the husband and wife costarred in the made-for-TV movie, *The Affair*, and traveled to England to appear in a London stage production of *Cat On a Hot Tin Roof*. But the couple's petty jealousies and rumored infidelity, which had soured their first marriage, soon resurfaced, despite the birth of another daughter named Courtney.

In the meantime, Wagner's career prospered with two prime-time series, *Switch* and *Hart to Hart*, while Wood's petered out in big-screen flops like *Meteor* and *The Last Married Couple in America*. On Thanksgiving weekend, 1981, while on hiatus from production of the sci-fi thriller *Brainstorm*, an intoxicated Wood mysteriously drowned off Santa Catalina Island after reportedly quarreling with her husband aboard their fifty-foot cabin cruiser, *Splendour*, over her affections for costar Christopher Walken.

Louis Hayward and Evelyn Keyes (Wayne Knight Collection).

Ten years later, Wagner, who has never publicly discussed the details of his wife's death, married comely actress Jill St. John. Coincidentally, best-selling author **Herman Wouk**, whose coming-of-age saga *Marjorie Morningstar* was filmed in 1958 starring Natalie Wood, later purchased Wagner's former home for $800,000. A scholar and naval historian, Wouk wrote the Pulitzer Prize-winning novel *The Caine Mutiny*, as well as *Youngblood Hawke*, *The Winds of War*, and its sequel, *War and Remembrance*— all of which have been filmed. His books have been translated into thirty languages.

★　★　★

Handsome South African-born actor **Louis Hayward**, who made his cinematic mark as identical twins in the 1939 swashbuckler *The Man In the Iron Mask* (remade in 1997 with Leonardo DiCaprio) and performed similar feats of derring-do in *The Son of Monte Cristo*, lived for sixteen years at 235 West El Portal, surrounded by his collection of antique firearms and German beer steins and mugs.

During World War II, Hayward enlisted in the U.S. Marine Corps where he was assigned to a special photographic unit documenting the dangerous beach assault on Tarawa, a small coral atoll occupied by the Japanese in the South Pacific. The fierce week-long battle resulted in nearly thirty-five hundred American casualties and almost forty-seven hundred Japanese deaths before the defenders were subdued.

Upon his return, Captain Hayward was awarded a Bronze Star for his remarkable filmed account of that bloody conflict titled *With the Marines at Tarawa* and which has been described as "the finest and most startling record of combat ever obtained." It won the Oscar for Best Documentary of 1944. The following year, Hayward divorced his first wife, actress Ida Lupino, and married wealthy socialite Peggy Morrow Field. He resumed acting in *The Return of Monte Cristo*, *Lady in the Iron Mask*, and *Captain Pirate*, but had difficulty memorizing his lines because of his recurring nightmares about the atrocities of war.

In 1963, Hayward received widespread praise when he toured as King Arthur in Lerner and Loewe's *Camelot*. He then retired. "His last year had been spent battling lung cancer, after having smoked three packs of cigarettes a day for half a century," said biographer William Donati. After Hayward died in 1985, his third wife, model June Blanchard, stayed on in the two-bedroom house, jogging up and down the street every morning and feeding groups of stray cats, until her death in 1998. The following year, Hayward's modest home sold for $95,000.

Next time you visit one of thirteen thousand ATMs or forty-five hundred branches nationwide of Bank of America and wonder, as you stand in line waiting to deposit or withdraw money, who started it all—wonder no more. It was Amadeo Peter Giannini, a first-generation American born of Italian descent in San Jose, California. This big, robust man who founded Bank of Italy in 1904, which later became Bank of America, made his name and reputation by loaning money to victims of the devastating San Francisco earthquake and fire of 1906.

Throughout the bank's formative years, its most-valued customers were working-class people: farmers, merchants, and salaried employees. In addition to loaning money for agriculture, garment manufacture, and trucking, Bank of America took a special interest in moviemaking. Giannini's younger brother, Attilio, nicknamed "Doc," initiated the now-common practice of advancing money to producers and holding their film negatives as collateral. Bank of America advanced $1 million for Samuel Goldwyn's *The Kid From Spain* and loaned Warner Brothers $500,000 for its grandiose musical *42nd Street*, which grossed $3,000,000. The bank also bankrolled Walt Disney's first animated feature, *Snow White and the Seven Dwarfs*.

In 1936, **Lawrence Mario Giannini** (who went by Mario) succeeded his father as bank president, a position he held for the next sixteen years. Lawrence Giannini was prevented from participating in many physical activities because of hemophilia, which required painful blood transfusions. Nevertheless, he continued to develop allied business interests such as Transamerica Corporation, and he was named one of the United States' top fifty businessmen by *Forbes* magazine.

In 1946, L. M. Giannini built the five-bedroom house at 246 West Camino Alturas, where he and his wife, Mercedes, stayed each winter. When A. P. Giannini died two weeks after his seventy-ninth birthday in 1949, his son was appointed to fill his father's unexpired term as chairman. During the firm's expansion, bank deposits surpassed $5 billion, and it invested in freeways, schools, subdivisions, and electric power plants. By 1953, Bank of America had financed more than five hundred films.

Mario planned to retire when he turned sixty in 1954, which, he noted with a twinge of nostalgia, was the bank's fiftieth anniversary. But he never made it. According to Giannini's daughter, Anne McWilliams, her father had just driven down to Palm Springs in early 1952 when he suddenly took ill. He was flown back to San Francisco on a chartered plane and admitted to a hospital where doctors performed a delicate operation for hemorrhoids. As Giannini languished in bed, his body was assaulted by an onslaught of viral infections, including influenza, pneumonia, and finally pleurisy, which did irreparable damage to his heart. He died on August 19, 1952, at fifty-seven.

For a man who was entrusted with billions of dollars and had devoted his life to helping others accumulate vast sums of wealth, Giannini died relatively poor. His estate was valued at $461,331, which he left in trust to his wife and two daughters, Anne and Virginia. It is a mark of L. M. Giannini's honesty and integrity that he did not surrender to the strong temptation to line his own pockets.

In the first month of 1988, the **Reverend Jim Bakker** rented the four-bedroom house called "Le Petit Oasis" at 366 Camino Alturas (corner of Camino Monte). Bakker, later indicted and found guilty on twenty-four counts of mail fraud, wire fraud, and conspiracy for bilking 116,000 Praise the Lord supporters of $158 million they contributed for shares in Heritage USA, shamelessly tried to launch a garish Palm Springs version of his beleaguered South Carolina christian vacation resort.

Bakker had the gall to tell reporters he had the support of local government officials and that financing was already in place for the $2-billion project when, in fact, he had neither. Holding court under a poolside umbrella, a map on his lap, this unabashed religious charlatan outlined plans for Heritage Springs, a full-size re-creation of the Holy Land, to be built near Indio. The preacher's eyes narrowed in the midday sun as the telephone's shrill ring went unanswered, and his wife, Tammy, who self-consciously described herself as the maid, scurried back and forth across the patio carrying piles of dirty laundry followed by their yapping Yorkshire terrier, Tuppins.

Bakker spoke of his admiration for the desert like a true believer. "It is a peaceful place, where people are nonjudgmental and content to live and let live. Very seldom do we meet mean people here." Then he unfurled the map and pitched his dream of a self-contained religious city. Bakker's nutty proposal included a one-thousand-room hotel, as well as a twenty-thousand-seat amphitheater and Disneyland-style amusement park depicting scenes from the life of Christ, including the crucifixion and resurrection, where worshipers could applaud God's second coming while presumably giving monetary donations. Leaving no stone unturned, he even suggested there would be a life-size replica of the Wailing Wall for non-Christians, i.e. Jews, who could pay their respects by Visa or MasterCard. Lord, have mercy!

In 1989, Bakker was sentenced to forty-five years in prison plus a $500,000 fine. His term was later reduced to eighteen years, and he served five years and two months before his release on December 1, 1994.

Pandro S. Berman, the benign, wrinkle-browed producer of some of Hollywood's most-exquisite costume dramas and historical epics, first teamed Ginger Rogers with Fred Astaire and helped promote his one-time lover Lucille Ball from extra player to leading actress. Berman lived at 259 Camino Alturas in 1951.

Known as "Pan," Berman's first-class treatment of a broad range of subjects, spanning five decades, resulted in some of the last century's most-replayed films—first at RKO where some of the films he supervised were *The Gay Divorcee*, *Top Hat*, and *The Hunchback of Notre Dame*, then at MGM with such top-flight productions as *Ziegfeld Girl*, *National Velvet*, *The Picture of Dorian Gray*, *The Three Musketeers*, *The Blackboard Jungle*, and *Butterfield 8*. He moved on to independently produce *A Patch of Blue*, *Justine*, and, finally, the "mod" social satire *Move*.

While residing in his Mesa home, Berman, who died of congestive heart failure at ninety-one on July 13, 1996, engaged in preproduction on two of his most-expensively mounted films, the medieval tale of *Ivanhoe* and a glossy remake of *The Prisoner of Zenda*, both of them directed by the sure hand of fellow villager Richard Thorpe.

Beady-eyed comedic actor **Bill Goodwin**, whose buttery voice introduced *The Burns and Allen Show* to CBS radio listeners each week: "[Applause] . . . and here they are, George Burns and Gracie Allen!" purchased Berman's house in 1956. Another of Goodwin's opening lines: "Uh-uh-uh. Don't touch that dial. It's time for … *Blondie!*" became famous. He also played disarming milquetoasts in *Bathing Beauty*, *The Jolson Story*, and *Bundle of Joy*, and presented the first prime-time network cartoon series, *Gerald McBoing Boing*.

On May 9, 1958, Goodwin, who owned and managed the Nooks Hotel, died from a suspected heart attack under peculiar circumstances. A policeman, driving north along Highway 111 at 5 o'clock in the morning, found the actor's body slumped over the steering wheel of his Ford Thunderbird, which was idling in a roadside ditch. When alerted by police, Goodwin's sleepy actress-wife, Phillipa Hilber, mentioned that she had earlier found a note on the kitchen table written by her husband, who had complained of not feeling well, indicating he had gone for a midnight drive. Was it an accident, murder, or suicide? Because of a lack of evidence or any witnesses, Goodwin's death remains an unsolved mystery.

Cue spooky music. Start the smoke machine. Fade in on trench-coated octogenarian host. Monotone TV star **Robert Stack**, who performed fearless heroics in *Eagle Squadron*, *The Bullfighter and the Lady*, and *The High and the Mighty*, visited his mother, Elizabeth Modini's home at 244 Camino Buena Vista in 1955.

Four years later, Stack clinched the role of a lifetime as FBI special agent Eliot Ness in *The Untouchables*, bringing justice to Prohibition gangsters Frank Nitti and Al Capone, for five bullet-riddled seasons. After a quarter of a century playing roles in such films as *Airplane*, Stack was back probing cases of the peculiar and the paranormal on *Unsolved Mysteries*, which first aired in 1988 and was still going strong eleven years later. Stack died in 2003.

★   ★   ★

Sonny Bono purchased his first desert home when he and second wife **Cher** were starring in the campy *Sonny and Cher Comedy Hour* on CBS from 1971 until 1974. The shaggy-haired entertainer purchased this remodeled tile-and-stucco house at 256 Camino Buena Vista from interior designer Stephen Chase.

Known for his self-deprecating humor, Salvatore Philip Bono married eighteen-year-old Cherilyn Sarkisian from El Centro in 1964, the same year they recorded their first song, "Baby Don't Go." The singing duo's first number one hit single was "I Got You, Babe" in 1965.

Top: Sonny and Cher's home at 256 Camino Buena Vista (Photo by Howard Johns). *Bottom:* Sonny and Cher (Steve Kiefer Collection).

Bono cooked delicious pasta dinners and watched television here on weekends with Cher and daughter Chastity until the couple's divorce in 1975. He then stayed on alone, and Cher rented different houses, where she tanned herself prior to starting long concert tours. After a second series, *The Sonny and Cher Show*, was canceled in 1977, Bono found himself without a partner or a full-time job. But it didn't stop him enjoying the creature comforts of this secluded house with a succession of beautiful young women, one of whom became a star in her own right.

"Although a small home, it was a lovely retreat," remembered *Home & Garden* TV host Susie Coelho, the singer's third wife, who was introduced to him on a blind date arranged by Bono's press agent, Jay Bernstein, "and we spent a lot of time there." During this period, Sonny guest-starred on TV's *Fantasy Island*, *The Love Boat*, *Murder She Wrote*, and *The Golden Girls*. He sold the wicker-furnished home after he divorced Coelho and married Mary Whitaker in 1986. Versatile entertainer and radio talk-show host **Joey**

English, who appeared on the Dinah Shore and Merv Griffin variety shows, owns the home next door at 272 Camino Buena Vista.

★ ★ ★

Stylish San Francisco investor **John Gallois** and his elegant wife, Eliza McMullin, heir to the White House Department Store fortune, lived in the opulent two-story, six-bedroom home with hardwood floors and wall-to-wall built-ins at 1995 South Camino Monte. Completed in 1937, this streamlined *moderne* masterpiece—christened "Ship of the Desert" because its glinting profile resembles the deck of an ocean liner, right down to its circular porthole windows—was designed by architects Adrian Wilson and Earle Webster for U.S. Army Colonel (later Brigadier General) Howard Davidson, who commanded the 10th Air Force in India during World War II and received the Distinguished Flying Cross and the Air Medal.

Lou Costello practices his golf swing (Courtesy of Palm Springs Historical Society).

The second of four owners was Warner Brothers studio chief Jack L. Warner, who entertained family and friends here in 1945, after Warner, who served as a major in the Second World War, had left the Army Signal Corps with the rank of colonel. Warner and his wife, Ann Boyar, liked to play tennis and host costume parties. Joining them was son Jack Jr. and stepdaughter Joy Page from Ann's first marriage to actor Don Alvarado.

This majestic house lost much of its original charm after the succeeding owners, John and Eliza Gallois, departed the local social scene, and in the coming decades some Mesa houses were either abandoned or boarded up. In 1998, Los Angeles fashion photographer Jonathan Skow and sportswear designer Trina Turk purchased the vacant home, which was gutted by a suspicious fire shortly afterward, necessitating extensive rebuilding of its charred interior. They finished restoring the house in June 2001.

★ ★ ★

Lou Costello, the shorter, funnier half of the movie comedy team Abbott and Costello, reportedly drank and gambled, minus his conniving partner Bud Abbott, in this cottage at 1810 Mesa Drive in 1948—the same year the bickering team made the smash-hit horror comedy *Abbott & Costello Meet Frankenstein*. Because of his fascination with underworld types, Costello was the subject of FBI surveillance for his "friendly" association with mobster Frank Costello (no relation) and mob-connected actor George Raft, with whom Costello's company produced the now-forgotten TV series *I Am the Law*.

After their acrimonious breakup in 1957, Bud slapped his ex-partner with a $222,465 breach of contract suit, alleging Lou failed to make good on his promise to fully pay him his 50-percent share of profits from the sale of their groundbreaking TV sitcom, *The*

Abbott and Costello Show. Bud said he was only paid $167,524.81 when he should have received around $390,000. They never reconciled. Costello died in 1959, Abbott in 1974.

★ ★ ★

Ruby's Dune's owner **Irwin Rubenstein**, whose smoky bar catered to large numbers of criminal and showbiz types, presided over by Ruby's best friend, Frank Sinatra, had many late nights and quite a few hangovers, which he cured with a homemade bromide, in the house with the inscription "Villa Nirvana West" carved on the front posts at 1885 Mesa Drive. When Rubenstein died in 1978, Sinatra mourned his friend's loss for a week.

★ ★ ★

Clockwise from top: Joseph Cotten's home at 1993 Mesa Drive (Photo by Howard Johns). Joseph Cotten in his garden (Backlot Books & Movie Posters). Johnny Mercer does the highland fling (Larry Edmunds Bookshop).

Eloquent stage and film actor **Joseph Cotten** wrote his self-deprecating autobiography, *Vanity Will Get You Somewhere*, while living on this rolling estate called White Gables (since remodeled) at 1993 Mesa Drive, with his second wife, actress **Patricia Medina**. Cotten, who first visited the desert as a croquet partner and house-guest of Darryl Zanuck, for whose studio he starred in *Niagara* and *Tora! Tora! Tora!*, moved here in 1985 while recuperating from a stroke he suffered four years earlier. (Medina chauffeured her ailing husband twice a week for therapy at the Palm Springs Stroke Activity Center.) Cotten first received widespread attention in Orson Welles' *Citizen Kane* and went on to showcase his gentlemanly ways in such major films as *The Magnificent Ambersons*, *Journey Into Fear*, and *The Third Man*. Pat and Joe Cotten loved the desert air and sunshine, but he was less effusive about life after losing best friend Welles to a heart attack. Cotten was eighty-eight when he succumbed to pneumonia in 1994.

★ ★ ★

Smiling, gap-toothed lyricist **Johnny Mercer** garnered four Oscar wins for the Judy Garland show-stopper "On the Atchison, Topeka and the Sante Fe" from *The Harvey Girls*; "In the Cool, Cool, Cool of the Evening" sung by Ray Milland and Jane Wyman in *Here Comes the Groom*; "Moon River" with composer Henry Mancini from *Breakfast at Tiffany's*; and the title song of *Days of Wine and Roses*, again with Mancini. Mercer lived with his dancer-wife, Ginger Meehan, and their two children, Mandy and Jeff, at 282 Camino Carmelita, which sold for $500,000 in 1997.

When Mercer, who also wrote the words for "Satin Doll," "Autumn Leaves," and "That Old Black Magic," died in 1976, his widow gave their neighbor, Barry Manilow, a stack of her husband's unpublished lyrics. One of them was a dreamy romantic ballad titled "When October Goes." Manilow was so inspired after reading it, he said, that he sat down at the piano that same morning and wrote the melody—in thirty minutes.

In 1999, the Johnny Mercer Box Office at the McCallum Theatre in Palm Desert was dedicated by his daughter on the ninetieth anniversary of her father's birth.

★   ★   ★

Pipe-smoking, alcoholic, crime master **Raymond Chandler**, creator of cynical private eye Philip Marlowe who cheated death time and again in *The Big Sleep*, *The Long Goodbye*, and *Farewell My Lovely*, was a steady desert visitor throughout his working life, usually staying at small hotels or private homes. In December 1957, Chandler was a houseguest of Jessie Baumgardner at 230 West Lilliana Drive, which he borrowed as the setting of Marlowe's rented home in his unfinished last novel *Poodle Springs*—so titled, he explained, because of the small dog's popularity among valley residents.

Chandler described the modern décor in considerable detail. "The front wall, for example, is made of Japanese glass with butterflies in between the two sections. Every room has a door to the outside and a glass wall. There is an interior glass-walled patio which has an almost full-sized palm tree in it, a lot of tropical shrubs, and some pieces of desert rock which probably cost somebody nothing but some petrol, and probably cost her $200 a rock." After completing the first few chapters, Chandler put the novel aside to take a trip to England. He died in 1959 without finishing the book.

★   ★   ★

Three-time Academy Award nominee **Fay Bainter** and her husband, U.S. Navy Lieutenant Commander Reginald Venable, who at different times owned two homes on this street as well as another home in Palos Verdes Tract and the Vaughn Arms Apartments downtown, lived quietly at 242 Camino Descanso in 1958. Bainter won a well-deserved Best Supporting Actress for *Jezebel*, the same year the tireless USO wartime entertainer was also nominated as Best Actress in *White Banners*—directed by her Mesa neighbor Edmund Goulding. (The controversy that arose from the double nomination led to changes in the Motion Picture Academy voting rules.) Bainter, whose specialty was playing kindhearted matrons and sympathetic aunts, including three memorable turns as Mickey Rooney's mom in *Young Tom Edison*, *Babes on Broadway*, and *The Human Comedy*, was Oscar nominated a third time for her last film, *The Children's Hour*. She died in 1968 and is buried with her husband in Arlington National Cemetery.

Fay Bainter (right) and Reginald Venable (Courtesy of Palm Springs Historical Society).

★   ★   ★

Ravishing *Gilda* star **Rita Hayworth**, in the early stages of Alzheimer's disease, which eventually killed her at age sixty-eight in 1987, locked herself away in the house with the Chinese Fu dogs on the wall at 301 Camino Descanso, according to former homeowner Craig Corbett.

The home's current owner, Francis Markley, who paid $338,000 for Corbett's house in 1998, said he found a telling cache of souvenirs from Hayworth's career, including horse-breeding books that belonged to her third husband, Prince Aly Khan, two *Life* magazine cover stories, and various sheet music that someone (Corbett perhaps?) had stashed away in the garage of this two-bedroom ranch home, which was built by Fay Bainter in 1945. Unfortunately, everything was lost, Markley said, in an electrical fire that completely destroyed the house in December 2000—eleven months after he finished remodeling it. (The house has been rebuilt.)

Clockwise from top: Frank Lloyd (right) attending daughter Alma's birthday party (Larry Edmunds Bookshop). Jerry Weintraub playing the odds (Larry Edmunds Bookshop). Rita Hayworth looking lost (Backlot Books & Movie Posters).

★   ★   ★

Concert promoter and film packager **Jerry Weintraub**, who booked Elvis Presley, Frank Sinatra, Bob Dylan, Led Zeppelin, and the Beach Boys, made the quirky box office hits *Nashville*, *Diner*, and *The Karate Kid*, and produced big-screen remakes of *The Avengers* and *Ocean's 11*, owned the house at 2145 Camino Barranca in 1975. Married for more than thirty years to vocalist and former client Jane Morgan, who scored a Top Ten hit in 1957 with the song "Fascination," Weintraub, an inveterate gambler, said he bought the house sight unseen in the middle of a poker game with Sinatra, Dean Martin, and George Hamilton. Actually, it was Hamilton's idea to buy the house. "How much?" Weintraub asked without taking his eyes off his cards. "Thirty thousand dollars," said George. "Then buy it," he replied.

★   ★   ★

Producer-director **Frank Lloyd**, one of the founders of the Academy of Motion Picture Arts and Sciences and a master of sea epics who directed 1935's Best Picture winner *Mutiny On the Bounty*, took an early retirement at 2165 Camino Barranca, his preferred piece of terra firma, in 1955. Lloyd was married to feminist writer Virginia Kellogg, a double Oscar nominee for the James Cagney gangster classic *White Heat* and the groundbreaking women's prison film *Caged*, when he died in 1960.

★   ★   ★

Singer-songwriter **Barry Manilow**, who writes the songs the whole world sings, has the best view of the valley from the Spanish hilltop home he shares with good-looking business associate and longtime partner Garry Kief at 2196 South Camino Barranca. (Note: Nobody gets in or out without being photographed by a closed-circuit TV camera.) The estate, comprising eight bedrooms and five bathrooms, which the singer/songwriter purchased for $705,500 in 1995, has "a gigantic swimming pool, a tennis court, and a separate building where I could hide away and write," he says.

On June 3, 2003, Manilow reportedly broke his nose when he got up from bed to get a glass of water in the middle of the night and accidentally walked into a bedroom wall. *Ouch!* The fifty-six-year-old performer, who was knocked unconscious, laughed off the incident when the freak accident made headlines the following day, but it started cynics wondering: Was the Sultan of Schmaltz giving the media a snow job about his upcoming nose job? Whatever you do, Barry, they teased, don't blow!

Given Manilow's talent and love of music—twenty-five consecutive Top Forty hits, fifty-eight million records sold—it's a fitting tribute that the home was once owned by someone else with a musical bent, Hollywood director **Walter Lang**, who turned out Technicolor musical hits like highly polished gemstones: *The Little Princess*, *Moon Over Miami*, *State Fair*, *With a Song In My Heart*, and *Call Me Madam*, among them.

Top: Barry Manilow's hilltop home (Photo by Howard Johns). *Bottom:* Barry Manilow at fifty-six (Howard Johns Collection).

Lang's career was capped by his Oscar nomination as Best Director for *The King and I* starring Yul Brynner. Lang concluded his winning career with the high-kicking Parisian stage romp *Can-Can* then retired in 1961 to this house, which he purchased from Bank of America Vice president Walter Braunschweiger and his artist-wife Helen Raymond.

When he died of kidney failure following vein surgery in 1972, Lang, the husband of actress Madeline Fields, was nearly forgotten by newer film fans untutored in classical love songs and Viennese waltzes. Thankfully, that opinion has been changed by frequent TV airings and DVD releases of those films. His son, Richard Lang, who trained as an assistant director at his father's old studio working on *Doctor Dolittle* and *The Sound of Music*, went on to direct episodes of some of TV's top shows—*Charlie's Angels*, *Beverly Hills 90210*, and *Melrose Place*.

★   ★   ★

World operatic superstar **Lily Pons**, who mesmerized audiences from London's Covent Garden to the Teatro Colon in Buenos Aires with her unsurpassed coloratura and bel canto roles, marveled at the view from "Toujours Eblouissante," which the French-born soprano shared with husband-conductor Andre Kostelanetz at 13 Cahuilla Hills Drive in 1956.

A firm believer in the power of numerology, Pons chose this particular address because she had a fascination with the number thirteen. She always made important decisions on that date, including the signing of contracts, and her car's license plate was LP-13. That same year Pons, who enjoyed a fleeting Hollywood acting career in *I Dream Too Much* and *That Girl From Paris*, celebrated her twenty-fifth season with the Metropolitan Opera House where, during the lean years of the Great Depression, "the Little Nightingale" as she was called, helped save the gilded institution from near-bankruptcy with her standing-room-only performances. (Pons's concert at the Hollywood Bowl holds the record for the highest number of paid admissions: 26,410.)

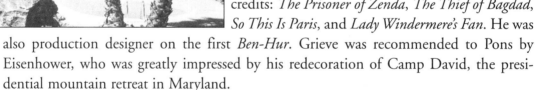

During World War II, when Pons entertained thousands of shell-shocked army troops, no less a person than General Dwight Eisenhower was so smitten with her porcelain skin, doll-like figure, and angelic voice that he sent "Darling Lily" a handwritten note, prompting a lifelong friendship and kindling rumors of a secret love affair.

Desert life attracted even more admirers to her custom-built home with its red and gold Chinese interiors by Harold Grieve, previously a 1920's Hollywood art director with impressive credits: *The Prisoner of Zenda*, *The Thief of Bagdad*, *So This Is Paris*, and *Lady Windermere's Fan*. He was

Top: Lily Pons (Wayne Knight Collection). *Bottom:* Lily Pons's home at 13 Cahuilla Hills Drive (Courtesy of Palm Springs Historical Society).

also production designer on the first *Ben-Hur*. Grieve was recommended to Pons by Eisenhower, who was greatly impressed by his redecoration of Camp David, the presidential mountain retreat in Maryland.

Clifton Webb, Lucille Ball, and Danny Kaye were among the privileged invitees who attended Pons's housewarming party, where the mountainside reverberated until sunrise with the sound of champagne corks and arias. And it was here, unseen behind a bamboo curtain and waterfall, that her daily routine consisted of burning incense, drinking green tea, and meditating cross-legged in the presence of a stone Buddha. In 1958, Pons and Kostelanetz, who had both performed at President Eisenhower's first and second inaugural balls, ended their twenty-year marriage, and she retired shortly thereafter. Pons's last public performance was on stage at the Palm Springs High School Auditorium in 1973. She died, age seventy-seven, on February 13, 1976. Her former residence sold for $500,000 in 1995.

★　　★　　★

Jolie Gabor, the Hungarian family matriarch, held frequent bridge parties with her third husband, Edmund de Szigethy, at 17 Cahuilla Hills Drive for four decades until her death at age 102, when the home was sold for $175,000. Gabor's daughter Zsa Zsa, meanwhile, resided next door at 19 Cahuilla Hills Road between marriages in 1960. (Completely remodeled, this home fetched an astounding $495,000 when it was offered for sale in 2002.) The story of how an indomitable woman like Jolie Gabor came to be living in the desert is a saga in itself.

The Gabor sisters (clockwise): Magda, Zsa Zsa, Eva, and their mother Jolie (Larry Edmunds Bookshop).

One summer evening at Gabor's Ridgefield, Connecticut, home, while her husband was preparing to barbecue some steaks, Jolie, on her way to the pool, tripped and fell down the stairs, breaking her leg. After being hospitalized, she had a stroke that left her paralyzed. The doctors held little hope for her. Then out of Edmund's mouth came the encouraging words, "I will take her to Palm Springs."

Gabor was overjoyed, her recovery was swift, and in appreciation for this unexpected good fortune, she opened the doors to her new house, laying out expensive banquets. Thus, began a longstanding social tradition. The de Szigethy-Gabor home "with its kidney-shaped swimming pool cut from rock and its spectacular view of the San Jacinto Mountains was always ablaze with Hungarian friends like actor Paul Lukas, international friends like Prince Youka Troubezkoi, and Mrs. Felizia Vanderbilt," remembered Jolie Gabor, along with "show business friends like composer Frederick Loewe and Lily Pons," who, Gabor insisted, walked down the hillside carrying a knife and a lantern for protection against nighttime predators.

Not content to stop there, the inexhaustible society maven, who gave Maria Callas's mother a $50-a-week job in her New York jewelry store, opened Jolie Gabor's Pearl Salon, an extension of her Madison Avenue boutique, on South Palm Canyon Drive. She listed such custom-made beauty products as Crème Gabor (luscious pink cream containing Hungarian chamomile), Gabor Foundation Cream, Madame Jolie Gabor Makeup Base, and the *pièce de résistance:* Pearl de Jolie perfume covered with cultured pearls for $12.50 per ounce. Her clientele included Governor Edmund "Pat" Brown and Mamie Eisenhower, whom Jolie honored with a special luncheon at the Cahuilla Hills Drive home, resplendently decorated with tables of scented candles, red and pink carnation centerpieces, and pineapple boats filled with exotic fruit. At these special occasions, Gabor herself serenaded guests with two of her favorite songs, "Never On Sunday" and "Que Sera Sera."

The largest party ever held at the home was for Jolie and Edmund's twenty-fifth wedding anniversary in 1982, according to biographer Peter H. Brown, noting that "while members of old-line families, such as the Hearst's," dominated the traditional social scene, the Gabors were "the leaders of the splashy celebrity set."

In much later years, Jolie Gabor slowed down, but she never lost her spirit or her sense of humor. Approaching ninety, the doyen of etiquette and beauty, who freely admitted to having had several facelifts (unlike her vanity-conscious daughters) implored the Lord, "Please, God, not now," whenever she was in the bathtub, joking, "I don't have on my makeup."

Shortly after Jolie died on April Fools' Day, 1997, Magda was admitted to Eisenhower Medical Center with a kidney infection. She died on June 11 of the same year. Jolie and Magda—but not Eva—are buried side by side at Desert Memorial Park in Cathedral City. (Note: The letters "Z-Z" on the gateposts of 2285 Cahuilla Hills Road are the initials of former owners Donald and Shelley Zamborelli—not Zsa Zsa Gabor as is often claimed.)

Fabulous Palm Springs Follies theatrical impresario and master of ceremonies **Rifael "Riff" Markowitz**, who produced HBO's cult anthology series *The Hitchhiker*, built the peculiar house, which one observer has likened to a Quonset hut, at 2401 Cahuilla Hills Drive—one hilltop away from Barry Manilow's home.

After spending ten years in the Philippines where he contracted a mysterious tropical malady while producing and starring in the low-budget action films. *The Steel Claw, Samar,* and *Hell of Borneo*, **George Montgomery** returned to the desert and roughed it while constructing a new home at 2429 Cahuilla Hills Drive in 1974.

Chapter 10

Call of the Canyons

outh Palm Springs spans the southernmost portion of the city
to the outlying Indian Canyons. It includes the highly desir-
able Canyon Country Club and exclusive Smoke Tree Ranch,
which former White House chief of protocol Joseph Verner Reed,
recalling his frequent visits there, called "the Hobe Sound of the
West." In 1957, the Alexander Company, run by father-and-son
contractors George and Robert Alexander (who earlier built
Ocotillo Lodge) began building sixty tract homes in Twin Palm
Estates. The modest, solid, post-and-beam construction was
designed by architects William Krisel and Daniel Palmer, who
favored a simple, horizontal design with such recognizable features
as splayed "butterfly" roofs, flagstone walls, and clerestory windows.

★   ★   ★

Sonja Henie skating
on thin ice (Larry
Edmunds Bookshop).

For fifty years, people have insisted that **Sonja Henie**, dubbed the Queen of Figure
Skating, winner of ten consecutive world championships and three gold medals at the
1928, 1932, and 1936 Olympics, owned a home in the desert. She didn't. But her handsome, blond-haired brother did. Leif Henie, who idolized his younger sister and designed
the fur-lined, velvet-trimmed costumes she wore on stage and in films, lived at 1829
Navajo Circle, behind Twin Palms Drive.

When Leif Henie and his second wife, Sally Weihle, moved to this brand-new home
in 1957, however, the Norwegian brother and sister were in the middle of a family feud.
Two years earlier, Sonja had sued him to get control of Leif's sixteen-hundred-acre ranch
in San Diego County, which he intended to subdivide into a housing development called
Henie Hills. After a lot of money had been spent in litigation, the lawsuit was settled in
favor of both parties. But it caused a terrible rift. Although the siblings and their respective spouses were not on speaking terms, it didn't stop Sonja and her third husband, Niels

Onstad, from visiting her brother's Twin Palms home and accosting them. Apparently, Sonja would stand outside and ring the doorbell, shouting, "Let us in!" Leif's wife would refuse to open the door, saying, "Go away!"

Another time, Onstad tried to climb over the back wall. Finally, a private detective was hired to watch the house. When Sonja and her husband came back, the detective told them *no trespassing allowed*. Henie continued skating at different venues until her death from leukemia in 1969. Leif passed away in 1984.

Robert Buckner, a highly respected writer and novelist who penned the screenplays for *Jezebel*, *Yankee Doodle Dandy*, and *Love Me Tender*, Elvis Presley's screen debut, owned the house with French-Italian décor and landscaping by ex-actor Tom Neal at 1841 Navajo Circle. Buckner's talents were not limited to writing. He also produced *Gentleman Jim*, *Mission to Moscow*, and *Confidential Agent*.

Edward Dmytryk, the imaginative director of *Murder, My Sweet*, *Crossfire*, and *The Caine Mutiny*, occupied the Alexander-built house at 1852 Apache Circle. Dmytryk moved here in 1957 with actress-wife Jean Porter, who had a featured role in her husband's story of atonement, *The Left Hand of God*. A card-carrying member of the Communist Party, Dmytryk had been blacklisted in 1951 for being one of the uncooperative Hollywood Ten and served six months in jail.

After he recanted, amid the angry cries of Communist Party members that he was a "fink," the chastened filmmaker resumed his directing career with *Raintree County*, *The Young Lions*, *The Carpetbaggers*, and *Alvarez Kelly*, starring Palm Springs neighbors Elizabeth Taylor, Dean Martin, Alan Ladd, and William Holden. Dmytryk was ninety when he died in 1999. He had left the desert, never to return, he said, because he felt snubbed.

Producer **Irving Allen**, who won an Oscar for his two-reel short subject *Climbing the Matterhorn* and was a business partner of Albert R. Broccoli in twenty British-made adventure films that starred American actors Alan Ladd, José Ferrer, Victor Mature, Robert Mitchum, and Robert Taylor at less than their best, bought the home at 1840 South Caliente Road in 1957. Broccoli and Allen (not to be confused with Irwin Allen, the master of disaster) dissolved their partnership, and Allen doggedly continued alone, missing out on the James Bond windfall that befell his former partner, though Allen did manage a small coup of his own: producing all four Matt Helm spy movies that bore more than a passing resemblance to Broccoli's oversexed secret agent.

Fifties curly-haired singing rave **Eddie Fisher** had a string of number one hits with "I'm Walking Behind You," "Oh My Papa," and "I Need You Now." His melodic voice and forceful style put him in the same class as Perry Como and Dean Martin, and he was tipped (incorrectly) to take over from Frank Sinatra. Fisher's immense popularity with American teenagers, who called the cocky youngster "the Coca-Cola Kid," took him from the Catskills to Carnegie Hall and made him the idol of millions of pubescent girls.

At the height of his fame, Fisher and first wife Debbie Reynolds melted into each other's arms in this Alexander-built home at 955 La Jolla Road (off South Camino Real), which they purchased after they were married in 1955.

"Eddie and I would drive down to our little house in Palm Springs on the weekends," remembered Reynolds. "Eddie could play golf with his buddies, and I could visit with friends." In 1956, the same year their daughter, Carrie, was born, "America's Sweethearts" as the press called them, costarred in *Bundle of Joy*, a box-office dud that signaled the beginning of the end of their marriage—but not their popularity. Reynolds made *Tammy and the Bachelor* the following year, and Fisher, who divorced her in 1959, continued working in television and nightclubs. Fisher gave Reynolds $40,000 a year in alimony and child support, and let her keep the Palm Springs house where their son, Todd, who was born in 1958, recuperated after undergoing a hernia operation.

★　★　★

Kindly actor **Donald Woods**, who played Tammy's dad in the spin-off TV series that starred Debbie Watson, along with the movie version *Tammy and the Millionaire*, lived at 985 La Jolla Road in 1966. Woods also played fatherly supporting roles in William Castle's spook-filled, three-dimensional *13 Ghosts* (remade in 2001) and the trite Elvis Presley hillbilly farce *Kissin' Cousins*. His last film was *True Grit*, which won a Best Actor Oscar for its paunchy star, John Wayne.

★　★　★

Fantasy man **Ray Bradbury**, who authored the compelling allegorical tales *Fahrenheit 451*, *The Illustrated Man*, and *The Martian Chronicles* and from whose brain were hatched the alien prophecies *It Came From Outer Space* and *The Beast from 20,000 Fathoms*, lets his imagination run wild down the street at 1837 South Caliente Drive, where he has lived since 1981. Bradbury, who adapted the screenplay for John Huston's film version of that whale of a tale, *Moby Dick*, seems to defy the rule that no man is an island—he doesn't own a computer or a driver's license, for example, and skirts social convention in

Top: Eddie Fisher with Debbie Reynolds (Larry Edmunds Bookshop). *Bottom:* Science fiction writer Ray Bradbury (Larry Edmunds Bookshop).

almost every form. "This man, who sent people on exploratory flights to the distant stars," observed Huston of Bradbury's eccentricities, "was terrified of planes. You could hardly coax him into a car."

★   ★   ★

Scriptwriter **Larry Gelbart**, an apprentice to Bob Hope and Sid Caesar in his youth, gave unsuspecting Broadway theatergoers and jaded critics a much-needed kick in the pants when he unveiled his ribald, sidesplitting, Tony Award-winning farce, *A Funny Thing Happened On the Way to the Forum*, and blew war its loudest raspberry when he wrote and produced the award-winning TV series *M*A*S*H* for its first four seasons. Gelbart proved after thirty years of writing jokes that he was full of comic surprises when he received two well-deserved Best Screenplay Oscar nominations for *Oh, God!*, and the cross-dressing *Tootsie*, which he typed in his Canyon South condominium with the green hedge at 1907 South Caliente Drive.

★   ★   ★

There was nothing funny about what happened to one of Gelbart's neighbors, however. On October 24, 1963, **Beverly Wills**, the look-alike actress-daughter of comedienne Joan Davis, for whom Larry Gelbart had once contributed radio scripts, perished with her two young sons and their grandmother in a house fire started by a burning cigarette at 1983 Yucca Place (off Marion Way).

Because of Wills's close resemblance to Davis, whom she had impersonated as a child in her mother's film *George White's Scandals*, it was thought only natural that she be recruited to play her mom's sister in the madcap sitcom *I Married Joan*—"what a girl, what a whirl, what a life!" But it was Wills's scene-stealing turn as Dolores, the tipsy all-girl band member, whose joke about the one-legged jockey gives drag-wearing Jack Lemmon the hiccups in Billy Wilder's riotous gangster spoof, *Some Like It Hot*, that gave the promising twenty-nine-year-old her best reviews.

On the day of the fire, the next-door neighbor, Canadian artist O. E. L. Graves, who was renowned for his colorful portraits of the Sarcee Indian tribe, had seen smoke and raised the alarm, but was unable to rescue the trapped victims because of the flames. The only thing Graves and his wife, Violet, could do was to shake their heads.

★   ★   ★

Don Fedderson, the talented producer of *My Three Sons*, *Family Affair*, and *To Rome With Love*, entertained stars Fred MacMurray, Brian Keith, and John Forsythe at 1877 Navajo Drive, where he lived with his second wife, actress Yvonne Lime. Lime played Michael Landon's girlfriend in *I Was a Teenage Werewolf* and later cofounded Childhelp USA.

★   ★   ★

Gravel-voiced comedy actress **Jean Carson**, who costarred on *The Betty Hutton Show* and played the recurring role of Daphne, the good-time girl who raised Don Knott's temperature on *The Andy Griffith Show*, can be found at 190 Sahara Road in Sahara Park, a collection of senior mobile homes on streets named Cairo, Nile, Suez, and Tobruk, complete with a life-size Camel mascot in front of the park's main entrance at 1955 South Camino Real (opposite Tiki Spa).

Actor **Peter Thompson**, a fellow Sahara Park resident of 203 Aladdin Road, was a familiar cowboy screen presence on TV's *The Lone Ranger* and *Death Valley Days*, as well as many film Westerns, notably as one of Randolph Scott's trigger-happy brothers in *Santa Fe* and an army lieutenant fighting Apaches alongside George Montgomery in *Indian Uprising*. Thompson was killed at age eighty in a local traffic accident on October 9, 2001.

Jean Carson smooches Don Knotts (Steve Kiefer Collection).

Regardless of her many professional setbacks and a raft of personal troubles that began when she replaced Judy Garland in the 1950 film version of Ethel Merman's stage triumph, *Annie Get Your Gun* and ended when, bereft of moral support, she turned her back on Hollywood, **Betty Hutton** still has plenty of fans who derive tremendous enjoyment from seeing her whoop it up in such entertaining films as *The Miracle of Morgan's Creek*, *Incendiary Blonde*, and *The Perils of Pauline*, in addition to listening to her recordings of such popular songs as "It Had To Be You"—the first of eleven Billboard hits, which have been reissued on compact disc.

Hutton, who recently celebrated her eighty-first birthday, rarely goes out in public these days, but she's still full of voice, despite lingering health woes. The once-jubilant singer-actress was diagnosed with Epstein-Barr syndrome in 1993 and takes medication to counter the effects of lethargy. Now that she's grown accustomed to the outpouring of love she has received from people all over the world, let's hope that Hutton, who currently resides in a small apartment in Canyon Villas at 2080 South Camino Real, a stone's throw from her one-time costar Jean Carson, can finally relax knowing that she hasn't been forgotten.

Rory Calhoun's tempestuous ex-wife **Lita Baron**, who played spicy señoritas in *Savage Drums*, *Red Sundown* (opposite her then-husband), and *The Broken Star*, currently lives in a three-bedroom Canyon Vista Estates home at 1508 South La Verne Way. Baron's neighbor, the unpredictable comedian **Shecky Greene**, who left nightclub audiences in stitch-

Top: Horse riders at Smoke Tree Ranch (Courtesy of Palm Springs Historical Society). *Bottom:* Cartoon King Walt Disney (Larry Edmunds Bookshop).

es with his off-the-wall humor and proved his acting dexterity in *Tony Rome*, *The Love Machine*, and Mel Brooks's *History of the World: Part I*, is still telling jokes but isn't drinking anymore at 1642 South La Verne Way.

★　★　★

And in 1980, Canadian-born comedy writer **John Aylesworth**, who created the TV variety show *Hee Haw* with partner Frank Peppiatt, lived at 1549 East Twin Palms Drive.

★　★　★

Smoke Tree Ranch at 1800 South Sunrise Way, which derives its name from the blue-tinged trees that adorn the property, contains some eighty wood-framed homes where residents, called "colonists," gather for chuck wagon breakfasts and communal dinners in the log cabin-style clubhouse. Begun in 1930 by Charles Doyle, who started Deep Well, it was acquired five years later by Fred Markham as an authentic Western-style resort for city slickers, complete with square dances, riding and roping demonstrations, badminton, and shuffleboard. The majority of Smoke Tree residents are descended from old Washington and Oregon manufacturing families. Homes are passed from generation to generation (there are no outside sales).

In 1938, actor Jerome Cowan, who played the slain detective Miles Archer in John Huston's *The Maltese Falcon*, was a ranch guest. Los Angeles real estate developer Paul Trousdale maintained a home there in 1951, as did multimillionaire sports enthusiast Paul Helms, the founder of Helms Bakeries. His home was dubbed "the Western White House" after newly elected President Dwight D. Eisenhower stayed there for one week in 1954. Another resident was Milo Bekins, heir to one of the world's largest moving and storage companies. William Clay Ford Jr. the chairman of Ford Motor Company, currently owns a home there.

★　★　★

The ranch's most-famous homeowner of this or any other time is undoubtedly the much-celebrated animation-pioneer **Walt Disney**, who owned two houses there; the first in 1948 and a second one that he had constructed in 1957.

"Walt had built the desert home so he could go bowling, his latest athletic passion, or play golf with Bob Hope and Ed Sullivan, whenever either happened to be in town," said biographer Marc Eliot.

Walt Disney Hall, the ranch's dining room, complete with his famous "loop-the-loop" signature, is dedicated to its illustrious former resident, who was awarded more Oscars than any other individual: a staggering twenty-six. He received his first statuette for creating Mickey Mouse, followed by a regulation Oscar plus seven miniature ones for the first full-length cartoon, *Snow White and the Seven Dwarfs*. A decade later, Disney's fascinating true-life adventure *The Living Desert*, which depicted a wide selection of Palm Springs flora and fauna, was the first feature-length documentary to win an Oscar. Disney's career was capped with thirteen nominations and five wins for the magical *Mary Poppins*.

A lifelong smoker and drinker, Disney shirked the importance of good health in favor of running a profitable corporation, building a theme park, and hosting a weekly TV show, allowing himself and his employees few respites. A rare exception was Thanksgiving Day, which he celebrated with his wife, Lillian Bounds, at daughter Diane Disney's home in Los Angeles for the last time in 1966. Afterward, Disney drove to the desert where he collapsed at his ranch and had to be resuscitated by paramedics. He was taken by private ambulance to St. Joseph's Hospital in Burbank for cobalt treatment for lung cancer, which had earlier resulted in the removal of his left lung. Two weeks later, the man who had miraculously changed *Pinocchio* from a wooden puppet into a boy, made *Peter Pan* fly, and revived *Sleeping Beauty* with a princely kiss, stopped breathing at the age of sixty-five. No doctor or animator could bring him back to life.

Hollywood song-and-dance man George Murphy (Backlot Books & Movie Posters).

However, the claim that Disney was the only big-name celebrity to live at the ranch is misleading. California Republican Senator **George Murphy**, a former stage and film hoofer who danced with Eleanor Powell in *Broadway Melody of 1938*, Shirley Temple in *Little Miss Broadway*, and Judy Garland in *Little Nellie Kelly*, also resided there.

In 1950, Murphy received a special Oscar. Formerly the Vice president of Desilu Studios and Technicolor Corporation, he was elected to the U.S. Senate in 1964, defeating incumbent Pierre Salinger. Walt's brother, Roy Disney, a frequent ranch guest and close friend of George Murphy, gave the GOP a large financial contribution, including $5,000-worth of Disney stock, toward Richard Nixon's successful presidential campaign in 1968. Murphy served one term and returned to private life in 1971. He died, age eighty-nine, in 1992.

Chicago builder Roy Fey, who first came to the desert in 1955, constructed the majority of homes in this placid mini-neighborhood of **Canyon Estates**. The father of local realtor Robert Fey, he was among the first Palm Springs builders to enter a long-term land lease with Agua Caliente Tribal Indians, eventually constructing more than twelve hundred homes, among them Mesquite Canyon Estates and Caballeros Estates.

★   ★   ★

Formula One racing-car driver **Kevin Cogan**, whose professional twelve-year career saw more speedway crashes than actual wins, though his earnings amounted to more than $1 million, lived with his parents at 1910 Toledo Avenue when he was a Palm Springs High School student in 1972. Cogan's bad luck included crashing his car into Mario Andretti at the start of the 1982 Indianapolis 500. ("It wasn't my fault," he protested.) Cogan later suffered a broken right arm, forearm, and right thigh, requiring extensive rehabilitation, when his car hit a wall at the 1991 Indy race. It was his third crash in eleven years.

★   ★   ★

Screenwriter **James R. Webb**, who re-created the Wild West in *The Charge at Feather River*, *The Big Country*, and *Cheyenne Autumn*, owned the house at 1967 Ledo Circle (off Toledo Avenue) at the time of his death in 1974. A master storyteller, Webb wrote three of Burt Lancaster's best films: *Apache*, *Vera Cruz*, and *Trapeze*. He also adapted the taut psychological thriller *Cape Fear* (remade in 1991). Webb's monumental script, spanning several generations of pioneers for *How the West Was Won*, received an Oscar for Best Screenplay in 1963. The Writers Guild of America established the James R. Webb Memorial Library in his honor in 1984.

★   ★   ★

Costume designer Charles LeMaire posing with statuettes (Backlot Books & Movie Posters).

Songwriter **Mack David**, who grabbed eight Best Song Oscar nominations for such various film scores as *Hush . . . Hush, Sweet Charlotte* with Frank DeVol, *Cat Ballou* with Jerry Livingston, and *Hawaii* with Elmer Bernstein, lived one block away at 1575 Toledo Circle in 1976. Those were the days when TV viewers sung along to David's corny lyrics, though few of them knew who wrote the words to *Casper the Friendly Ghost* or "the soft island breeze … strange melodies" that accompanied the ukulele theme from *Hawaiian Eye* or the harmonizing vocals of *77 Sunset Strip* with its ear-catching "Click! Click!" Well, now you know.

★   ★   ★

20th Century-Fox costume designer **Charles LeMaire**, a three-time Oscar winner for his exquisitely tailored creations in *All About Eve*, *The Robe*, and *Love Is a Many-Splendored Thing*, lived at 2272 Toledo Avenue until his death, age eighty-eight, in 1985. LeMaire, who was nominated for the gold statuette a total of seventeen times, took over as head of Fox's wardrobe department in 1943, where over a ten-year period, he fitted Tyrone Power's codpiece in *Captain from Castile*, pinned Marilyn Monroe's billowing skirt in *The Seven Year Itch*, and measured Gregory Peck's inseam for *The Man In the Gray Flannel Suit*.

In his youth, LeMaire had toiled behind the scenes making headdresses and feather boas for Florenz Ziegfeld, the Shubert Theatre, and even the Ringling Brothers Barnum & Bailey Circus, outfitting everyone from clowns to chimpanzees—which qualified him, he laughingly felt, for a career in Hollywood.

★ ★ ★

Fess Parker, who defended the Alamo and was king of the wild frontier in two top-rated TV shows, *Davy Crockett* and *Daniel Boone*, felt right at home with his wife, Marcella Rinehart, at 2514 South Toledo Avenue, next to Smoke Tree Stables (2500 Toledo Avenue). Unfortunately, when Parker, a fifteen-year resident, complained about the constant smell of horse manure, the city told him it was just a load of hay, so he packed his bags and moved to Santa Barbara in 1990 where he now runs a successful hotel and winery. Not only is Parker treated with more respect there, he's in great demand for his excellent Chardonnay, Pinot Noir, and Riesling, one hundred cases of which were uncorked for the opening of the Ronald Reagan Presidential Library and Elizabeth Taylor's wedding to her eighth husband Larry Fortensky.

★ ★ ★

Latin composer-arranger **Hugo Montenegro**, whose grunt-filled recording of the theme from Clint Eastwood's *The Good, the Bad and the Ugly* became a surprising number two hit in mid-1968, spiced things up in his Canyon Estates home, near the clubhouse, at 2347 South Madrona Drive. Montenegro, who also scored the groovy music that accompanied the animated titles for TV's *I Dream of Jeannie* and worked his same magic on *The Partridge Family*, died there of emphysema in 1981.

★ ★ ★

Top: Helen Rose (right) and daughter Jody holding costume sketches (Courtesy of Academy of Motion Picture Arts and Sciences). *Bottom:* Fess Parker holding his breath (Larry Edmunds Bookshop).

MGM costume designer **Helen Rose**, an eight-time Oscar nominee for her fabulous ball gowns, beaded bodices, full skirts, and evening dresses trimmed in red lace, black velvet, and blue chiffon that adorned some of Hollywood's best figures and won Rose the gold statuette for *The Bad and the Beautiful* and *I'll Cry Tomorrow*, moved to 1380 Malaga Circle (off Paseo Del Rey) in 1978. Among the proudest accomplishments of Rose, who also suggested the idea for the Oscar-winning script of *Designing Woman*, based on her life, was creating Doris Day's $40,000 wardrobe for *Love Me Or Leave Me* and designing the antique wedding gown, crinoline skirt, and pearl headpiece for Grace Kelly's wedding to Prince Rainer III of Monaco. Rose died in 1985.

★ ★ ★

Eleanor Parker (Steve Kiefer Collection).

Ravishing redhead **Eleanor Parker**, a three-time Oscar nominee for her tour-de-force roles as a battered prisoner in *Caged*, the forlorn wife of policeman Kirk Douglas in *Detective Story*, and crippled Australian opera star Marjorie Lawrence in *Interrupted Melody*, has lived at 2195 South La Paz Way since 1977. Whether the role was sexy or slovenly, Parker always displayed a slow-burning temperament with a *mah*-velous voice to match her expressive hazel eyes, making it difficult to pick the best film from so many good ones. She was Paul Henried's lover in *Of Human Bondage*, Humphrey Bogart's girlfriend in *Chain Lightning*, and William Holden's charge in *Escape From Fort Bravo*. Charlton Heston rescued Parker from killer ants in *The Naked Jungle*. Frank Sinatra wooed her twice in *The Man With the Golden Arm* and *A Hole In the Head*, and she matched wits with Clark Gable in *The King and Four Queens*. Later, as the tea-sipping baroness, the stately actress welcomed Christopher Plummer and Julie Andrews to her Austrian chateau in *The Sound of Music*.

The most atypical home for this district is the pink-colored Spanish façade of 1333 East Via Estrella. On the corner, at 1255 East Via Estrella, is the plain, contemporary-style building with double-door entry in the shape of a makeup compact, designed in 1974 for **Jerome Factor**, then the president of Max Factor cosmetics, whose company invented "flexible greasepaint" liquid foundation, false eyelashes, lip gloss, and eyebrow pencils. If you're a diehard movie fan, then you'll want to take South Caliente Drive to Sierra Way and turn left. This is the northern entrance of **Canyon Country Club**, a curving ribbon of Florida-style fairway homes and meandering golf carts that are preferred by scores of entertainers.

Ralph Young, one half of the pink-scalloped dress shirt, blue tuxedoed, Brylcreemed singing team Sandler and Young, lives at 1099 East Sierra Way. Young's first hit song "Dominique" with partner Tony Sandler went platinum. Their first long-playing record, *Side By Side*, lasted nineteen weeks on Billboard's LP chart. Eleven albums and hundreds of sellout concerts followed, including numerous guest shots on *The Ed Sullivan Show* and *The Tonight Show* starring Johnny Carson.

There isn't much that British writer-director-producer **Val Guest** hasn't done or hasn't done it with. He played practical jokes on Alfred Hitchcock, befriended Beatrice Lillie, loaned money to Errol Flynn, discovered Jean Simmons, entertained Dirk Bogarde in the Spanish Pyrenees, offered Michael Caine a much-needed job, was turned down by Audrey

Hepburn, ate a memorable dinner with Woody Allen, and chatted with David Niven over drinks in Beirut. Oh—and he made a lot of movies, too.

Best known for his tongue-in-cheek comedies and thought-provoking social dramas, Guest and his American-born actress-wife, **Yolande Donlan**, who starred as Billie Dawn in *Born Yesterday* on London's West End and played dizzy blondes in several of her husband's quirky films, including *Miss Pilgrim's Progress*, *The Body Said No!*, and *Mr. Drake's Duck*, now enjoy the good life at 1033 East Sierra Way, with the house plaque "La Closerie."

A former newspaper reporter, Guest began writing screenplays in the 1930s for the Crazy Gang comedies, starring revered London music hall entertainers Arthur Askey, Will Hay, and the song-and-dance team of Bud Flanagan and Chesney Allen, who camped it up in *The Frozen Limits*, *Gasbags*, and *The Ghost Train*. They were so popular, Val was promoted to the director's chair for two Margaret Lockwood musical dramas, *Give Us the Moon* and *I'll Be Your Sweetheart*.

In between making films, Guest married Donlan, a twice-published author, whose friendships with Noel Coward, Laurence Olivier, Vivien Leigh, and Douglas Fairbanks Jr. undoubtedly led to one of her books, *Shake the Stars Down*. In 2001, Guest, still spry at age ninety, published his amusingly titled autobiography *So You Want to Be In Pictures*, in which he recounted his extensive career, spanning eight decades and such further cinematic classics as *Expresso Bongo* and *The Day the Earth Caught Fire*, which won the British Academy of Film and Television Arts (BAFTA) award for Best Screenplay. He also directed the James Bond spoof *Casino Royale* and the prehistoric fable *When Dinosaurs Ruled the Earth*—an Oscar nominee for Best Visual Effects.

Top: Val Guest and Yolande Donlan (Courtesy of Val Guest). *Bottom:* David Janssen sipping a beer (Courtesy of *Palm Springs Life*).

The Guests' home is adorned with rare movie posters and signed photographs of these and other films. But the couple's frenetic days are now a thing of the past. They much prefer to meander about the living room and enjoy home-cooked meals with their small circle of friends. "There we can sometimes glance out the window," Guest indicated, "and watch history in the making as ex-President Gerald Ford tries to putt his ball into the fourteenth hole."

★　　★　　★

David Janssen, the worried star of TV's *The Fugitive*, could relax with his first wife, Ellie Graham, in this stylish flagstone-walled, wrought-iron-gated home built by Chuck Dwight with interiors designed by Noel Birns at 2220 Yosemite Drive. Janssen purchased the house after finishing his four-year run from the law as Dr. Richard Kimble in 1967.

A former child actor who appeared in more than seventy films, Janssen had little time to enjoy this new home. He was soon back in front of the movie cameras in *The Green Berets*, *The Shoes of the Fisherman*, and *Marooned*, as well as two TV detective series that demanded his full attention, *O'Hara, U.S. Treasury* and *Harry O*, followed by twenty made-for-TV movies. After Janssen died from a heart attack caused by the stress of overwork in 1980, the house was bought and sold by several people, including Keely Smith, who owned it in 1997.

★   ★   ★

William Demarest wearing his toupee (Larry Edmunds Bookshop).

Preppy actor **Richard Krisher**, a graduate of 20th Century-Fox's talent school, who played second leads in the gritty urban police thrillers, *The St. Valentine's Day Massacre*, *Tony Rome*, *The Detective*, and *The Boston Strangler*, and later became a successful Palm Springs realtor, owned this sandstone-colored house with the abstract wall sculpture at 2250 Yosemite Drive. He died there from a heart attack, age sixty-one, in 2000.

★   ★   ★

Cranky-faced **William Demarest**, best remembered as stew-stirring Uncle Charley in the Fred MacMurray TV sitcom *My Three Sons*, always had a smile for young fans who knocked on his front door at 2290 Yosemite Drive. (Note: You can't miss the house, it's painted brick red.) Demarest's crumpled features and rusty voice were a mainstay of hundreds of movies since 1927's *The Jazz Singer*. Twenty years later, he was nominated for an Oscar as the singing cantor's best friend in *The Jolson Story*.

This reliable "old ham," who talked tough but, when prodded, showed a softer side, was at his best dispensing sage advice to the younger generation, especially in the social satires of writer-director Preston Sturges, such as *Sullivan's Travels*, *Hail the Conquering Hero* and, most memorably, as unwed mother Betty Hutton's uptight father, Constable Kockenlocker, in *The Miracle of Morgan's Creek*. For more than a decade, Demarest, wearing his favorite sports cap and assisted by his wife, Lucille Thayer, hosted their annual golf tournament at Canyon Country Club, raising money for Variety Clubs International, until his death from pneumonia in 1983 at age ninety-one.

★   ★   ★

Take Sequoia Place west to Alhambra Drive, where Canyon Country Club estates builder Boris Gertzen and designer Harry Kelso sold customized fairway homes starting at $35,000 in 1962. The original model is located at 2355 Alhambra Drive.

★   ★   ★

Gene Barry, the dandified TV star of *Bat Masterson* and *Burke's Law*, owned the home at 2370 Alhambra Drive in 1975. The unpredictable Barry, who traded quips with Mae West in her saucy play, *Catherine Was Great*, fought space aliens in *The War of the Worlds*, and kissed a man in Broadway's *La Cage aux Folles*, later moved to Rancho Mirage.

★ ★ ★

In 1968, actor **Teddy Hart**, the younger brother of eminent Broadway lyricist Lorenz Hart, who cowrote the Broadway musicals *Jumbo*, *On Your Toes*, *Babes in Arms*, and *Pal Joey* with composer Richard Rogers, used the 70-percent share of income from his brother's songs to pay the rent at 2410 Alhambra Drive. Lorenz died in 1943, Teddy in 1971. (Dorothy Hart, Teddy's widow, moved to 2627 West Kings Road.) Thirty years later, his former home sold for $510,000.

★ ★ ★

Return to Sierra Way and continue in a westerly direction to South Calle Palo Fierro.

★ ★ ★

Monty Hall, the congenial host of *Let's Make a Deal*, the popular TV game show that has run in various incarnations for forty years, previously lived at 457 San Jose Road (Canyon View Estates).

★ ★ ★

Big band singer **Beryl Davis** started out warbling "Don't Sit Under the Apple Tree" and "I'll Be Seeing You" with the Glenn Miller Orchestra in England before coming to America with Bob Hope. She was chosen by Frank Sinatra to be his lead vocalist on *Your Hit Parade*, launching Davis on a half-century career as a guest performer with the likes of Benny Goodman, Vaughn Monroe, and Mel Torme. She curled up for ten years with her husband-manager, Charles "Buck" Stapleton, at 2240 South Calle Palo Fierro in Number 12. Davis's Canyon Country Club Colony home, which she bought in 1992 and sold in 2003, was formerly owned by orchestra conductor-arranger **Percy Faith**, who had a number one hit with the musical theme from *A Summer Place* and also wrote the Oscar-nominated film score for *Love Me or Leave Me*. Faith lived here from 1968 until his death in 1976.

Top: Gene Barry turning gray (Howard Johns Collection). *Bottom:* Beryl Davis in her heyday (Wayne Knight Collection).

★ ★ ★

Boisterous Chicago Cubs broadcaster **Harry Caray**, whose excited *"Hol-ly Cow!"* enlivened thousands of baseball games during his sixty-year career, spent the winters at 2352 South Calle Palo Fierro. A twenty-year desert resident, Caray, who wore thick Mr.

Magoo eyeglasses and constantly chewed on a cigar, was eighty-three when he collapsed from a heart attack at the Basin Street West nightclub in Rancho Mirage after leading the jam-packed audience in a boozy chorus of his favorite song, "Take Me Out to the Ball Game" on the second night of Tony Martin's live appearance there on Valentine's Day, 1998. Caray slipped into a coma and died four days later.

★   ★   ★

Dave Chasen ran one of Hollywood's busiest restaurants. The white-and-green-canopied landmark, where big shots elbowed each other for the best table, stood on Beverly Boulevard in Beverly Hills for almost sixty years. Chasen's was world-famous for its hot chili and blood-rare hobo steaks, its Flame of Love cocktail and congeniality. Its classical décor, red leather booths and white linen tablecloths, made it an easy place to meet for lunch and dinner, which appealed to working actors as well as Hollywood's elite.

Top: Ronald Reagan, Bob Hope, and Nancy Reagan exit Chasen's (Steve Kiefer Collection). *Bottom:* Fred Williamson in vigilante mood (Backlot Books & Movie Posters).

Every night at Chasen's was like a Hollywood premiere. James Cagney, Gary Cooper, William Powell, W.C. Fields, Groucho Marx, Jack Benny, Milton Berle, Bob Hope, Clark Gable, Errol Flynn, Joan Crawford, Elizabeth Taylor, Marilyn Monroe, Barbara Stanwyck, Alan Ladd, Gregory Peck, Kirk Douglas, and Frank Sinatra were regulars.

One night, Humphrey Bogart and Peter Lorre got loaded on Scotch and tried to steal the restaurant's safe. Another time, Orson Welles threw a flaming can of Sterno at producer John Houseman, ending their partnership. Jimmy Stewart held his bachelor party there. Ronald Reagan proposed to weepy-eyed actress Nancy Davis in booth number two. Tony Martin and Cyd Charisse had their first date at Chasen's.

After Dave Chasen's death in 1973, his wife of thirty-one years, **Maude Martin**, a resident of 2622 South Calle Palo Fierro, continued fronting the restaurant until it was sold in 1995. Mrs. Chasen was ninety-seven when she died in 2001.

★   ★   ★

"Blaxploitation" actor/producer/director **Fred Williamson**, whose arresting film titles, *Black Caesar*, *Hell Up In Harlem*, and *The Big Score* sound a lot better than they really are, currently resides at 2672 South Calle Palo Fierro with producer-wife Linda Radovan. Given that these films are strictly for late-night insomniacs and lovers of low camp, it's surprising and somewhat gratifying that Williamson's take-no-prisoners acting style is still in demand after all these years although not in top-draw films with the minor exception of 1996's *Original Gangstas*.

Known for his brute strength as "the Hammer," Williamson is a former Oakland Raiders and Kansas City Chiefs football player. He played in the Super Bowl and coanchored *Monday Night Football* with Howard Cosell for one season. But his days of kicking a ball are over. He now prefers to act in his own vanity films and play golf. Movie lovers be warned, however: You'll mostly see Fred beating the crap out of some poor slob in a straight-to-video movie, e.g. *Foxtrap, Down 'n Dirty*, buried on the back shelf of your local video store. No refunds!

★　　★　　★

Go east along Avenida Granada.

★　　★　　★

Harper Goff, the imaginative Disneyland art director who designed exhibits for the Epcot Center and the World Showcase, moved to 2333 South Via Lazo in 1978. It's an unusual house, with double entry wrought-iron gates leading to a Roman-style circular courtyard and swimming pool more befitting a toga party than a music recital. However, it was here that Goff, a member of the Dixieland jazz band, Firehouse Five Plus Two, with Mickey Mouse's late animator Ward Kimball, strummed the banjo on weekends.

In addition to working for Disney, Goff was production designer on Kirk Douglas's epic *The Vikings*, for which he constructed three full-size sailing ships. He also created the multicolored confectionary sets on which Gene Wilder's mysterious candy man cavorted, surrounded by shiny foil-wrapped candy bars and orange-faced Oompa Loompas, in *Willy Wonka and the Chocolate Factory*. Goff, whose symbolic designs await rediscovery, died, age eighty-one, in 1993.

★　　★　　★

Continue until you reach Camino Real.

★　　★　　★

Would you believe . . . ? **Don Adams**, who played Maxwell Smart, the bumbling secret agent from CONTROL that battled the evil plans of KAOS on TV's *Get Smart*, owned the house at 2548 South Camino Real. "I find that hard to believe . . ." Well, Adams, who won three Emmy Awards for his comical performance and later was the voice of the bionically articulated *Inspector Gadget*, moved to this ranch-style home in 1977. His home sold for $225,000 in 1995.

Get Smart star Don Adams with his two sons (Backlot Books & Movie Posters).

★　　★　　★

Western tough guy **Chuck Connors**—who became a household name to a generation of baby boomers as steely-eyed cowpoke Lucas McCain on TV's *The Rifleman*—constructed this fairway home with the black wrought-iron front gate at 2585 South Camino Real. The six-foot, five-inch Connors started out playing basketball for the Boston Celtics, then

he rebounded to baseball's Chicago Cubs and L.A. Dodgers. He and his second wife, actress Kamala Devi, who costarred with him in 1962's *Geronimo*, occupied the home from 1963 to 1972. Connors, the proud owner of a yellow Manx dune buggy, which he kept in his garage, also starred in the TV show *Branded*, and hosted the weekly adventure series *Thrill Seekers* while living here. He died from lung cancer in 1992, leaving behind four sons, Mike, Jeff, Steve, and Kevin Jr.

★　★　★

Director **Sidney Lanfield**, a master of whimsy who went from handling intractable Basil Rathbone and a ferocious Great Dane in the definitive Sherlock Holmes film mystery, *The Hound of the Baskervilles*, to cutting a lot of ice with three-time Olympic skating champion Sonja Henie in *One In a Million*, watching Fred Astaire and Rita Hayworth glide across the dance floor in *You'll Never Get Rich*, and guffawing at Bob Hope and a talented penguin in *My Favorite Blonde* (one of six screwy comedies Lanfield and Hope made together), resided in this midcentury modern home at

Clockwise from top:
Chuck Connors's home at 2585 South Camino Real (Photo by John Waggaman). Chuck Connors in cowboy attire (Cinema Collectors). William Bendix acting dumb (Steve Kiefer Collection).

2617 South Camino Real with actress-wife Shirley Mason until his death in 1972. Although Lanfield's desert talent roster included Hope, Loretta Young, Jack Benny, and Betty Hutton, precious few of them attended his funeral.

★　★　★

In 1963, farcical *Life of Riley* TV star **William Bendix**, who was Alan Ladd's put-upon costar in six films and his real-life best friend for twenty years, moved to the home with two white stone lions out front at 2744 South Camino Real—one year prior to his death, age fifty-eight, from pneumonia. Bendix died eleven months after Ladd, whose baffling suicide left Bendix, who was absent at the time, inconsolable and filled with guilt.

★　★　★

When his last animated film *The Jungle Book*, featuring the growling voices of the desert's Phil Harris, Louis Prima, and George Sanders, was released in 1967, **Walt Disney** was still the owner of this house at 2688 South Camino Real—even though he had died the previous year. Widow Lillian Disney, a former inker and painter, who was married to her husband for forty-five years and survived him by thirty more until she suffered a fatal stroke, age ninety-eight, in 1997, occupied the home during that time.

Music publisher and self-trained composer **Irving Mills**, who wrote the lyrics for Duke Ellington's "Sophisticated Lady," "Mood Indigo" and the be-bop classic "It Don't Mean a Thing If It Ain't Got That Swing," promoted Cab Calloway's breakthrough hit "Minnie the Moocher," and assembled the all-star black cast for the 1943 musical play-on-film *Stormy Weather*, lived at 1570 Murray Canyon Drive until his death at the age of ninety-one in 1985.

Call it three times unlucky! On April 4, 1994, singer **Ginny Simms**, confined to a wheel-chair, collapsed and died from a massive heart attack in the bedroom of her fairway home at 1578 Murray Canyon Drive. The following year, Conrad Von Dehn, Simms's record producer-son from her marriage to hotelier Hyatt Von Dehn, who had lived there, sud-denly died. Then, in 1999, Simms's developer-husband, Donald Eastvold, CEO of Travelbridge, Air, Land, and Sea, also died in this home.

Directly south are the sanctified Indian canyons—Andreas, Murray, and Palm—that are studded with two thousand California fan palms, some of them hundreds of years old. The Indians ceremoniously burned the tree trunks to honor their dead and promote the growth of edible berries. Eons ago much bloodshed ensued when two tribes fought a ter-ritorial war, and the severed heads of defeated chieftains were brought to this spot and smashed against the rocks. This consecrated place is now a favorite weekend spot of pic-nickers, whose rubber soles clamber up well-worn hiking trails where barefoot Indians once hunted rabbits and quail, their slow passage observed by the watchful eyes of the desert.

Former child actress **Betsy Duncan**, who costarred with Bob Hope in *I'll Take Sweden*, owns a two-story Vista Canyon condominium at 2851 Andalucia Court. Her late hus-band was Ever Hammes, founder of the In-Sink-Erator Manufacturing Company, whose name graces the surgical building at Desert Regional Medical Center.

Openly gay film director **John Schlesinger** never shied away from the harsh realities of life whether they were mods and rockers in swinging London or street hustlers in New York's Times Square. One of the original angry young men of British new wave cinema, Schlesinger made stars out of Alan Bates in *A Kind of Loving*, Tom Courtenay in *Billy Liar*,

Director John Schlesinger (Backlot Books & Movie Posters).

Julie Christie in *Darling* (winner of three Oscars, including Best Actress), and Terence Stamp in *Far From the Madding Crowd*.

Schlesinger then shocked America with his X-rated study of vagrancy and male prostitution in *Midnight Cowboy*, which was nominated for seven Oscars and won three for Best Director, Picture, and Adapted Screenplay. Two years later, the stocky, bald filmmaker was nominated a third time as Best Director for *Sunday, Bloody Sunday*, a bisexual love triangle that featured the screen's first passionate kiss between two men. However, he would never again reach the heights of his earlier career in spite of some brave tries with *The Day of the Locust*, *Marathon Man*, *The Falcon and the Snowman*, *Pacific Heights*, and *Cold Comfort Farm*.

His last film was *The Next Best Thing* about the joys of gay parenthood. The stress of working with the film's two stars, Madonna and Rupert Everett, said a friend, caused the director to experience serious health problems, and in 2000 he underwent quadruple bypass heart surgery. Doctors ordered him to have complete rest following the surgery, so Schlesinger moved to a contemporary-style three-bedroom home at 300 East Bogert Trail, where he suffered a stroke that impaired his speech a mere two weeks before Alan Bates was due to present him with a special award at the 2001 Palm Springs International Film Festival.

Instead, Bates commiserated with his longtime friend at the director's home. They sat and held hands, and when Bates bid him farewell, Schlesinger reportedly broke down and cried. For a man who was accustomed to the hustle and bustle of a big city, Schlesinger must have felt like a fish out of water in this unforgiving desert wasteland. Yet he didn't complain. In 2002, he was honored with a British Academy of Film and Television Arts lifetime achievement award at a star-studded ceremony in Los Angeles, but the director was too ill to attend. Time, like the last reel of one of his many movies, was running out.

On July 21, 2003, Schlesinger was admitted to Desert Regional Medical Center with severe breathing difficulties. He was placed in intensive care and given life support. Four days later, his breathing stilled, the machine was turned off, and he slipped away. With Schlesinger until the very end was the man he had loved for thirty-six years, photographer **Michael Childers**, whose sensual portraits of male sex symbols, including Mel Gibson, Clint Eastwood, Al Pacino, Warren Beatty, John Travolta, Richard Gere, and Arnold Schwarzenegger have adorned more than two hundred magazine covers.

Widely recognized for his skill with texture and light, Childers created innovative poster art for one hundred films, as well as photographing such gay icons as Mae West, Tennessee Williams, Andy Warhol, Joe Dallesandro, David Hockney, and Rock Hudson. Childers forged a strong personal and professional relationship with Schlesinger, working as a coproducer and second unit director on half-a-dozen films.

★   ★   ★

Top: The cast of *Gilligan's Island* (Larry Edmunds Bookshop). *Bottom:* Andrew Neiderman and wife Diane showing off (Courtesy of Melissa Neiderman).

Sherwood Schwartz, who created the classic sitcoms *Gilligan's Island* and *The Brady Bunch* and wrote the lyrics to each theme song—"Just sit right back and you'll hear a tale…" sung by The Wellingtons, and "Here's the story of a lovely lady…" performed by the Brady Bunch Kids—lived at 38-556 Bogert Trail in 1978. Although both shows are now more popular than ever because of innumerable reruns, *Gilligan's Island* was abruptly canceled in its third season by CBS President Bill Paley so that the castaways were never rescued. Several lame movie-length sequels tried to fix the problem, but didn't live up (or down) to the idiosyncratic humor.

The Brady Bunch, meanwhile, spawned two successful feature films. In 2000, the producer's younger brother, Elroy Schwartz of Palm Springs, who wrote the pilot episode of *Gilligan's Island*, sued his sibling in Los Angeles Superior Court claiming he had been cheated out of millions of dollars in unpaid royalties. Naturally, his allegations were refuted, which begs the question: Why did Elroy Schwartz, age seventy-nine, wait thirty-five years to press charges? It all sounds like a tropical storm in a coconut shell.

★　★　★

Andrew Neiderman, the bearded author of *The Devil's Advocate*, which was made into a hugely successful 1997 film starring Al Pacino and Keanu Reeves, wrote this hair-raising best-seller, as well as many supernatural tales filled with creepy characters and mind-bending plots, on his computer at 64-894 Saragossa Drive in Parc Andreas. Neiderman, a part-owner of Palm Springs Brewery, lived there with Diane Wilson, his wife of thirty-nine years. Son Erik runs their beer-making business. Daughter Melissa is a teacher at Palm Valley School in Rancho Mirage.

However, it's unlikely that you'll see Andrew, whose quiet manner belies his overactive imagination, carousing at his tavern. He's busily ghostwriting gothic horror stories for the estate of V. C. Andrews, the wheelchair-bound author of *Flowers in the Attic* and *Petals on the Wind*, who died in 1986. So far Neiderman has completed twenty full-length anthology Andrews novels, plus fifteen similarly themed minibooks that are intended for younger readers. *Willow*, the latest of these spectral tales, was published in 2002—the same year the Neidermans moved to a new house at 1034 Andreas Palms Drive. The prolific author churns out scary books under his own name, including *The Dark*, *In Double Jeopardy*, *Curse*, *Amnesia*, and *Dead Time*. His latest novel *The Baby Squad* was published in 2003.

★　★　★

Emmy-winning TV director **Jerry Thorpe**, who made memorable contributions to such prime-time institutions as *Hawaii Five-O*, *Kung Fu*, and *Falcon Crest*, lives at 38-365 Maracaibo Circle West. Among Thorpe's plethora of credits, he was one of the regular directors of *The Man From U.N.C.L.E.* and later brought his talent for intrigue to *Harry O*. Son Richard Thorpe (named after his grandfather) proved he has the same stuff as his dad when he directed various episodes of the medical drama *E.R.*

★   ★   ★

Marlene Dietrich's daughter and protective heir, **Maria Riva**, played her promiscuous, switch-hitting mother as a child in 1934's *The Scarlet Empress* and later wrote the best-selling biography, *Marlene*, which traced the extraordinary life of the husky-voiced Berlin chanteuse-turned-international star. Most recently, she edited a photographic tribute in commemoration of her mother's one-hundredth birthday. Riva lives at 38-430 Maracaibo Circle West, where she moved in 1993—one year after Dietrich's death at ninety in a darkened Paris apartment.

Maria's father, Rudolf Sieber, died in 1976. Her husband, William Riva, an NBC television art director, later made a name for himself in industrial design. Riva's sons are third-generation showbiz. Michael is a Hollywood production designer, who was nominated for an Oscar for Best Art Direction on *The Color Purple*. Peter Riva is a New York literary agent. David is a documentary filmmaker who produced *Marlene Dietrich: Her Own Song*. And John-Paul works as a Hollywood production assistant.

★   ★   ★

Controversial producer-director **George Englund**, who painted a bleak picture of Armageddon in *The World, the Flesh and the Devil*, showed the hypocrisy of politics in *The Ugly American*, and uncovered the inner workings of the Vatican in *The Shoes of the Fisherman*, leads a more-conventional lifestyle at 3415 Andreas Hills Drive in Andreas Hills, which he purchased for $180,000 in 1997.

Producer George Englund (Larry Edmunds Bookshop).

Chapter 11
Southridge Scandals

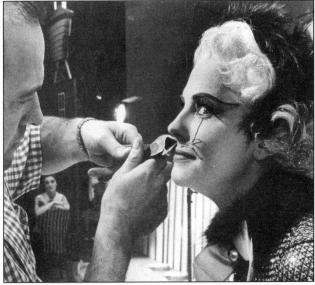

outhridge, the small, gated community of approximately twenty custom-built homes, which resembles a giant eagle's nest when viewed from Highway 111, is perched high on the side of Smoke Tree Mountain and manned by twenty-four-hour armed security guards. The only public access is a three-mile walking path, Araby Trail, that takes hikers up the southwestern mountainside from **Araby Tract**, a low-lying neighborhood named after Saudi Arabia.

Makeup artist Ben Lane applies cat whiskers to *Guys and Dolls* costar Vivian Blaine (Courtesy of Ben Lane).

Ben Lane, hailed as one of Hollywood's finest makeup artists, applied pancake, eyeliner, and rouge to dozens of famous faces—from Elizabeth Taylor and Frank Sinatra to Cary Grant and Barbra Streisand—in nearly one hundred TV and film productions. He retired to the Garden Villas at 1861 Sandcliff Road (off Barona Road) in 1982.

Lane's diverse list of credits runs from *National Velvet* to *Annie*. He also designed the scary makeup effects for William Castle's *13 Ghosts*, *Homicidal*, and *Strait Jacket*. He was director of makeup for Columbia Pictures, Screen Gems, and Warner Brothers, and received an Emmy nomination for his frightening suburban vampires in *Salem's Lot*.

★   ★   ★

Three Oscars for Best Set Decoration/Art Direction were awarded for *Cavalcade*, *The Song of Bernadette*, and *Anna and the King of Siam* to veteran 20th Century-Fox art director **William S. Darling** a twenty-year resident of 1990 Barona Road. A skilled painter and graphic artist, Darling joined Fox's art department in 1933, where he supervised scores of period films set in Western and Colonial times, many of them for directors John Ford and Henry King. Among Darling's outstanding efforts were five Will Rogers comedies, typified by *A Connecticut Yankee*; eight Shirley Temple musicals, including *The Little Colonel*; and five Tyrone Power adventures. Twenty years after his retirement, Darling still kept an easel and brushes close at hand so he could capture the glorious desert sunsets on canvas. He died one day after celebrating his eighty-second birthday in 1964.

Nicolai Remisoff, who was art director and production designer on thirty-one feature films and four TV series, retired to 2088 Barona Road in 1965. Remisoff worked frequently with director Lewis Milestone, starting with the 1939 classic, *Of Mice and Men*.

Remisoff's first recognition came as a newspaper cartoonist and stage designer in his native Russia until political revolution forced him to flee his country. After immigrating to the U.S. in 1923, he worked as a cover illustrator for *Vanity Fair*, *House & Garden*, and *Vogue*. Known as "Remy," he designed Marshall Field catalogs, brochures for Cadillac, and created the Elizabeth Arden beauty salons in New York, Chicago, San Francisco, and Hollywood. Remisoff, whose collection of paintings, drawings, and letters was donated to the University of Southern California, New York Public Library, and the Art Institute of Chicago, lived in this house for ten years until his death in 1975 at ninety-one. His son, Leonid Remisoff, was also a Palm Springs resident.

Proof of the insatiable hunger for celebrity gossip is the case of **Grace Vanderbilt**, who purportedly resided at 2630 Anza Trail. Vanderbilt's name is synonymous with the crème de la crème of American society. Grace was the beguiling daughter of New York millionaire inventor Cornelius Vanderbilt III, a descendant of the famous banking family. Cornelius Vanderbilt's fortune crumbled when he lost $8 million in the 1929 stock market crash, and the family was forced to sell its Fifth Avenue mansion. Grace later married the grandson of West Virginia coal baron Senator Henry Davis. She died in 1964—a mere twenty years after she inherited part of a $4-million fortune from her talented father, who suffered a fatal cerebral hemorrhage in 1942.

Women's fashion designer Gloria Vanderbilt, her cousin, was the most-famous heiress of the era, dubbed "Little Gloria" by the tabloids and the subject of a bitter custody battle at age ten. The much-married socialite was a regular lunch patron at La Cote Basque, the New York French restaurant profiled by Truman Capote in his bitchy social exposé that was published in *Esquire*.

A Vanderbilt in Palm Springs! The social butterflies must have fluttered their wings in collective excitement at the good news. But it was a case of mistaken identity. The Grace Vanderbilt (1910-1996) who lived here wasn't a rich heiress at all. She was a registered nurse.

In 1956, *Perry Mason*'s creator **Erle Stanley Gardner**, who authored 127 courtroom novels, could be found pounding away on his typewriter at 2714 Anza Trail. Gardner, a professional attorney for twenty-two years before he embarked on a full-time writing career, turned down an offer of $1 million to sell the TV rights to his fictional legal eagle—though he eventually relented while living here, thus paving the way for Raymond Burr's successful TV career.

The rebuff was typical of Gardner, who disliked the noisy interruption of telephones. He would only communicate with his publisher and agent via mail. Six secretaries were on hand at all times to take his daily dictation. A keen amateur explorer, criminologist, and fanatically opposed to gambling, Gardner also owned homes in San Francisco, Oceanside, and Yucca Valley, as well as a date farm near Indio.

In 1937, he built Rancho del Paisano, a twenty-seven building compound on three thousand acres in Temecula, California, where he raised horses, dogs, and cattle. It was there that Gardner, age eighty, died in 1970. *Perry Mason*, incidentally, spawned six feature films, 271 TV episodes, 3,000 radio programs, and 20 made-for-TV movies with its trumpet-blowing musical theme by Fred Steiner. (Somewhat eerily, Hedda Hopper's actor-son William Hopper, who played Burr's investigator Paul Drake, died in Desert Hospital from a stroke on March 6, 1970—the same year of Gardner's death. Hopper was the third actor from the series to die, preceded by William Talman and Ray Collins.)

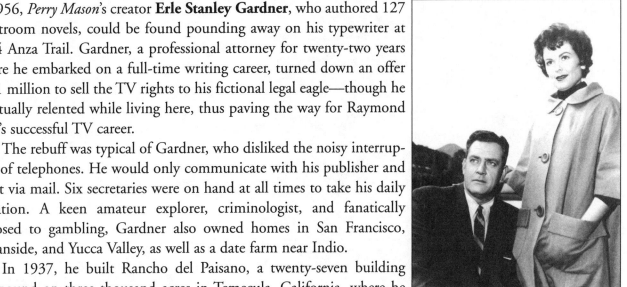

Erle Stanley Gardner's *Perry Mason* was tailor-made for Raymond Burr (Howard Johns Collection).

Marlene Dietrich's youngest grandson, **John-Paul Riva**, who followed his three brothers Michael, Peter, and David into the fine arts, currently resides a short distance away at 2742 Jacaranda Road. "Growing up, I was sheltered by my parents. We were a big family," said Michael Riva, who is married to Tin Pan Alley songwriter Harry Warren's granddaughter, Julia Warren.

The Rivas are a multitalented brood, and Paul is no exception. His actress-wife, Marilee Warner, is the founder and artistic director of the Playwrights' Circle, which promotes the performing arts.

Scott Holden, the youngest son of Southridge's William Holden, maintained a cordial relationship with his frequently absent dad. The two worked together in *The Revengers* and *Breezy*. The younger Holden lived at 2390 South Araby Drive until 1993.

Top: Architect John Lautner designed "Sunburst" at 2175 Southridge Drive (Photo by Nick Springett). *Bottom:* Sean Connery defends himself against two female attackers in a scene from *Diamonds Are Forever* (Larry Edmunds Bookshop).

Southridge Estates, the chosen address for a privileged few of Palm Springs's highest social echelon, was first subdivided and built on land sold by realtor Russell Wade to developers Alan Petty and Richard Rahn in 1963.

Palm Springs interior designer **Arthur Elrod**, who decorated many movie star homes, lived with his partner, Harold Broderick, in the futuristic, circular house that resembles a giant parasol at 2175 Southridge Drive. Built in 1968, this striking poured-concrete-and-glass edifice, named Sunburst, was designed by visionary Los Angeles architect John Lautner, who considered himself an artist rather than an architect.

Proof of his artistic brilliance can be found in the home's polished roof: a conical concrete dome with clerestories radiating from the center like a desert flower. The intention, Lautner said, was to make the home's location seem as natural as possible—"not a style stuck on a rock." If the house looks familiar, that's because you saw it in the seventh James Bond movie, *Diamonds Are Forever*, as Blofeld's desert fortress where Sean Connery is ambushed by a pair of karate-chopping gymnasts named Bambi and Thumper. The two girls pummel Bond until he finally subdues them in Elrod's pool, which seems poised on the edge of space.

Builder and concrete expert Wally Niewiadomski, who worked on several of Frank Lloyd Wright's houses, dug eight feet into the ground and constructed the sixty-foot black-slate living room floor around existing rocks and boulders. The main entrance consisted of a large pivoting copper gate with a roof garden above the bedroom and carport. Elrod chose the art and furnishings and was "tickled to death" by the widespread attention his home received on movie screens in 1971.

Tragedy struck three years later. On the morning of February 18, 1974, while en route to his uptown office, forty-six-year-old Elrod and New York designer William Raiser were fatally injured when a speeding motorist ran a stoplight and hit their blue Fiat at the intersection of Farrell Drive and Ramon Road. Elrod was thrown from the wrecked vehicle, which skidded ninety feet, trapping Raiser behind the wheel. They were the city's first road fatalities that year. At the time, Elrod, whose work had been featured on twenty-five magazine covers, had reportedly been commissioned to redesign the interior of Air Force One.

Supermarket retail king **Ron Burkle** the Vice president of Food-4-Less Supermarkets and Ralph's Grocery Co., paid $1.8 million for Elrod's former home in 1996. Burkle's Yucaipa Companies, for whom former President Bill Clinton worked as a paid consultant after leaving the White House, controls 70 percent of Golden State Foods, the lucky supplier of beef patties and hamburger buns to McDonald's.

★　★　★

Steve McQueen—the King of Cool—liked to race dirt bikes and rode a half-track Land Rover along the mountainside below the two-story house he shared with Oscar-nominated *Love Story* actress **Ali MacGraw** at 2203 Southridge Drive. If you look closely, say neighbors, you can still see the tire tracks he left behind. Architect Hugh Kaptur designed this four-bedroom home in 1964 for Edwin H. Morris, one of the world's largest music publishers. E. H. Morris, who moved here from the Movie Colony (where he previously lived at 650 North Via Miraleste), owned the copyrights to hundreds of well-known songs—from "Glow Little Glow Worm" and "The Christmas Song" to "Ghost Riders in the Sky" and "Tenderly." Ex-Beatle Paul McCartney purchased Morris's entire song library, making him the world's biggest music publisher.

McQueen bought the house from Morris during the record-breaking run of *Bullitt* in 1969. "Since Steve had become a giant star, it had become necessary to isolate our homes from the general public," said the actor's first wife, Neile Adams, who was married to him at the time. To prevent anyone from building too close to them, McQueen bought the lot next door—an indication of his mushrooming fame and drug-fueled paranoia. Terrified of being stalked, he carried a loaded .38 automatic handgun at all times.

McQueen hired Peter Shore to decorate the house and gave Neile $100,000 to spend on furnishings. Their family spent the Easter weekend here, as well as Christmas 1970. John Sturges, who directed McQueen in three films, visited him at home to discuss the actor's pet project, *Le Mans*. After McQueen and Adams divorced in 1972, Steve continued to live here with MacGraw, his costar in *The Getaway*, whom he married at the height of his box-office popularity in 1973. Because of McQueen's insistence that his wife not make any more films, even though he appeared to good advantage in *Papillon* and *The Towering Inferno*, they became estranged, and he sold the house in 1976.

"When Steve and I finally dissolved our marriage, he got our house and everything

Top: Ali MacGraw gets some air (Larry Edmunds Bookshop). *Bottom:* Steve McQueen (right) takes New York columnist Ed Sullivan for a joyride in his dune buggy (Steve Kiefer Collection).

in it, right down to the frying pan and salad servers," said MacGraw, who had signed a prenuptial agreement—*oops!* But during the time they spent together, the couple enjoyed life to its fullest here and in Malibu. Incidentally, McQueen was refused admission to the opening of Melvyn's Restaurant at the Ingleside Inn after owner Mel Haber mistook the scruffy-looking actor for a dangerous Hell's Angel and turned him away. McQueen died from a heart attack while undergoing surgery for chest cancer in Juarez, Mexico in 1980. He was fifty.

Chicago-based *Jet* publisher, *Ebony* founder, and owner of the world's largest black publishing company **John H. Johnson** and his wife, Eunice Walker, own the luxury home at 2379 Southridge Drive. Their daughter, Linda, is currently president of the company; photographer-son John Jr., died in 1981. A self-made multimillionaire, generous philanthropist, and member of the Forbes 400, Johnson (author of the inspiring autobiography, *Succeeding Against the Odds*) has had dinner at the White House under seven presidents—a sterling achievement in a rags-to-riches life tinged with sadness, but filled with great accomplishment.

Architect **Edward Giddings**, who created authentic native thatched *palapas* for exclusive hotels in the Mexican beach resorts of Puerto Vallarta and Cabo San Lucas, where millions of American tourists stretch out on the golden sand each year, designed the incredible two-and-a-quarter acre stone estate "La Piedra," sculpted from six hundred tons of Idaho quartzite, with imported granite and marble interiors by the late Gerrold Jerome, at 2399 Southridge Drive.

Bob Hope, tagged as California's biggest land baron for his extensive real estate holdings (valued between $500 and $700 million) must have heaved a sigh of relief when he finally moved into this gigantic cone-shaped concrete fortress dubbed "the House of Hope" at 2466 Southridge Drive in 1979. The partially completed, two-story house, instantly recognizable by its distinctive circular roof, mysteriously caught fire and burned to the ground on a hot summer's day in 1973. Rumors flew like wildfire that arson or maybe an ancient Indian curse caused the incendiary destruction—provoked, it was suggested, by Hope's reputation of being tightfisted. (Some claim the cheapskate comedian either got the land for free or paid $1 an acre.)

Neither suggestion is true. The fire started, said the home's architect John Lautner, "when welders' sparks ignited and burned the wood sheathing off the steel frame" that encased the roof, necessitating some design changes. Most noticeably, a skylight over the massive three- to four-story entertainment court was omitted and a sixty-foot diameter opening left in its place.

Firefighters extinguish the blaze that destroyed Hope's Southridge house (Photo by Steve Kiefer).

Hope's home after it was completely rebuilt (Courtesy of Palm Springs Historical Society).

Christened by wags "the Flying Saucer" and sometimes compared unfairly to the TWA Terminal at New York's Kennedy Airport and the Houston Astrodome because of its cavernous twenty-five thousand square feet, this architectural monument is one of the most awe-inspiring landmarks in Southern California.

Upstairs are two master bedrooms (one for him, one for her), a kitchen, and dining room. Downstairs consists of a huge entertaining area, billiard and trophy room, two guest suites, service quarters, plus another kitchen and dining area. There are two swimming pools—one of them the size of a small lake. Hope, though, was nonplussed when he first saw a model of the space-age house.

Bob Hope was still getting laughs at ninety-five (Courtesy of Ward Grant).

"Well, at least when they come down from Mars, they'll know where to go," he wisecracked. (Lautner's reaction to this comment went unrecorded.) The six-bedroom, nine-bathroom party home was built for Hope, says a friend, by a grateful Chrysler Corporation, the company that advertised on his regular TV variety show and still sponsors his Palm Springs golf tournament, held every year, rain or shine, since 1965. During the festivities, golf carts bused guests from the street below up to the house, where they strolled inside, their voices echoing off the one-hundred-foot wide arched openings, while a band played Dixieland music on the lawn and waiters served drinks and appetizers.

"The house has been the scene of many great moments," said Dolores Hope. "The classic Italian parties continued—only on a larger scale. Our holidays, which were always special became even more so because we now had the room to house our expanded family, which by then included grandchildren!"

Hope celebrated his ninety-fifth birthday here, opening the house for invited media and posing for photographs. But his advanced age was clearly evident despite a daily regimen of golf, vitamins, and an afternoon massage. He appeared slow and stooped, unable to hear and see, though he still signed autographs. Unlike rivals Jack Benny and Milton Berle, Hope made it to one hundred—he died from pneumonia two months later on July 27, 2003, at his Toluca Lake home in Los Angeles County with Dolores and their extended family at his bedside. Hope's Southridge home, which cost in excess of $3.5 million to build (twice) more than twenty-five years ago, is now worth an estimated $20 million.

The comedian's longtime friend and Toluca Lake neighbor **William Holden** lived a few doors down from Hope's house at 2433 Southridge Drive. The two had been buddies since meeting on Paramount's back lot in 1941 when they would visit each other's dressing rooms, tell stories, and swap jokes. Holden and Hope both welcomed the company of pretty ladies and enjoyed an ice-cold "tipple" at the end of each day's filming.

When Holden's art collection outgrew his Deepwell bachelor pad, he had plans drawn up for a place large enough to display the various primitive tribal paintings and sculptures he had found in his world travels. In 1972, he bought four acres of rock-encrusted land near the top of the hill and commissioned desert architect Hugh Kaptur to design a brand-new house that was part contemporary home and part museum—sort of a living memorial to the actor.

When he grew too old and tired, Holden planned to pull up the drawbridge on his life that had seen love affairs with Audrey Hepburn and Capucine, undercover trips to Communist countries, and safaris to Africa, and sit back and watch the world go by.

Drawing inspiration from European architectural muse Ludwig Mies van der Rohe, whose dictum "less is more" seems to have had a profound effect on the actor's outlook, Holden specified that the two-bedroom seven-thousand-square-foot home should have a flat roof, so it wouldn't obstruct the profile of the mountain; floor-to-ceiling glass windows for a perfect aerial view of the canyons; and an innovative gravity-fed "infinity" swimming pool—believed to be the first of its kind built in the desert.

"Bill wanted something very contemporary and clean looking," explained Kaptur, who was contacted after Holden rejected a design by Stewart Williams as "too expensive." Together, Holden and Kaptur came up with a simpler, less-costly approach using split-face concrete-block walls, vaulted wood-beamed ceil-

Left: Stefanie Powers and William Holden enjoy the desert sunshine at his Southridge home (Courtesy of Stefanie Powers). *Right:* William Holden's death made worldwide headlines (Howard Johns Collection).

ings, and a cantilevered sundeck with gaslit fire pit and giant Jacuzzi. They added wood paneling and wall-to-wall carpeting in the interior rooms for a softer look.

Kaptur's flexibility stimulated Holden's imagination, and they often solved problems through improvisation. "Ever since I was a kid," grinned Holden, pointing at the blueprint, "I always wanted a secret door." Kaptur took a pencil eraser and made the downstairs utility room into a museum. A set of temple doors, which Holden had retrieved on a visit to Zanzibar, was installed in his office where he displayed native masks, spears, and a big map of Africa on the wall.

The builder was William Foster, a general contractor and former city mayor, who had the difficult task of turning Holden's long-cherished dream into a reality, drilling through solid bedrock to lay the home's steel foundations. Designer James Callahan chose rich earth colors, silk-grass wall coverings, and pewter metal treatments for the home's interiors.

When Holden, nearing sixty, moved here at the beginning of 1977, his film career had tapered off. He increasingly concentrated his energies on wildlife conservation, spent less time traveling, and more time relaxing at home. At night, he turned on the stereo sound system, poured himself a drink, and gazed out at the city lights twinkling below. The paradox is that few people, even those closest to the unassuming actor, were invited into Holden's showplace with its bronze double-door entry where he kept his polished Oscar, surrounded by a vast library of leather-bound volumes of history, Toulouse-Lautrec lithographs, Chinese silk tapestries, and handwoven rugs.

What gave Holden his greatest joy and made him laugh out loud, however, was Bertie, an enormous Burmese python that would slither around his neck or curl up and go to sleep in his lap. Yet he could still pour on the charm when needed, cracking a smile at the Shell station attendant so he wouldn't have to wait in line during the days of gas rationing or making idle chatter at the supermarket checkout. Neighbors still talk about the time that Holden's girlfriend, Stefanie Powers, accidentally crashed one of his motorcycles while joyriding along the bottom of the mountain, and he was so concerned for the actress' safety that he held her in his arms. They also talk about the day that Holden gallantly led a bucket brigade up the hill in an effort to save his neighbor Hope's house from being consumed by fire in 1973.

Regrettably, Holden did not live to see the resurgence and growth of Palm Springs as a world-class tourist resort. Holden's death in November 1981, when he tripped on a throw rug in a drunken fall in his Santa Monica beachfront condominium, cut his head on a coffee table, and bled to death, caused an outpouring of sorrow and grief for this intensely proud and solitary man. (Eighteen months later, Michigan attorney Stanley Schwartz paid more than $2 million for Holden's home.) Still, Holden's legacy in life and in art lives on. In 1982, attempting to fill the void left by Holden's passing, Powers established the William Holden Wildlife Education Center in Kanyuki, Kenya, as part of the William Holden Wildlife Foundation, which the couple started in 1973.

Looking up at this towering hill of Paramount stars from her tiny living room at 186 Vega Street in Horizon Mobile Home Village (entrance: 3575 East Palm Canyon Drive) was **Lillian Roth**, Broadway's brightest young star until alcoholism destroyed her career and she attempted suicide. Roth had once headlined at the same studio as Holden and Hope in *The Love Parade*, *The Vagabond King*, and *Animal Crackers*. But she went from star to fall-down drunk with a bottle-a-day habit, enduring years of degradation until *I'll Cry Tomorrow*, her unapologetic autobiography, hit the best-seller lists and she was portrayed on film by Susan Hayward. After regaining sobriety, Roth could finally afford to live a normal life, and in 1970 she bought a prefabricated metal cottage here—her modest home for the next five years. She died in 1980.

Take Highway 111 east for one quarter of a mile.

Golfer-turned-developer **Johnny Dawson**, who went from selling Spalding sporting goods to winning amateur tournaments in a ten-year streak, defeating George Maston, Frank Hixon, and Bruce McCormick, earned the title "Golf's Uncrowned King." He designed and built **Seven Lakes Country Club** (entrance: 4100 Seven Lakes Drive), a planned community of approximately 350 homes, where he lived at 12 Desert Lakes Drive in 1966.

Dawson cemented his reputation with this challenging eighteen-hole course, his fourth since constructing the fairways of Thunderbird, El Dorado, and La Quinta. His wife, Velma Dawson, decorated the clubhouse, which was designed by William Cody. Mrs. Dawson also created the freckle-faced TV puppet *Howdy Dowdy*, whose handmade doll is now worth an estimated $50,000. Dawson was paid a mere $300, she said, to sculpt the small redhead figure that entertained millions of boys and girls on NBC's long-running kiddies' show.

In 1968, seventy-eight-year-old Dwight Eisenhower hit his first and only hole-in-one on the club's thirteenth green. Ike's triumph was the talk of the nation. But Ike had little time to savor his accomplishment. He died from congestive heart failure the following year.

Jolly radio announcer and sometime actor **Don Wilson** became a popular local TV chat show host after the demise of *The Jack Benny Program*, on which his hearty laugh and sponsor's pitch for Jell-O, "Mmmmm . . . six delicious flavors," made him the most-recognizable voice on radio. Wilson lived at 168 Desert Lakes Drive in 1977. One year later, he drove Benny's old Maxwell touring sedan to the opening of the Bank of Indio, where he got lots of laughs.

Philippines-born beauty **Brenda Marshall**, who was Errol Flynn's prim and proper leading lady in two films, *The Sea Hawk* and *Footsteps In the Dark*, moved to 171 Desert Lakes Drive in 1973 after divorcing her actor-husband of thirty years, William Holden, with whom she had two sons, Scott and Peter—both named after prominent pioneer families from the actor's hometown, O'Fallon, Illinois. A heavy smoker, Ardis, as she was known by her ex-husband and close friends, died from throat cancer in 1992.

On July 1, 2002, film editor **Harry Gerstad**, a two-time Oscar winner for the boxing saga *Champion* and 1952's Western classic *High Noon*, whose expert cutting helped José Ferrer win Best Actor by a long nose for *Cyrano de Bergerac*, made George Reeves appear to leap from tall buildings in a single bound in *The Adventures of Superman*, and superimposed the exclamations *Pow! Biff! Wham!* over the fight scenes of 1966's *Batman* movie, died at 193 Desert Lakes Drive, where he had lived since his retirement in 1973. He was ninety-three. Gerstad edited fifty films, including five for director Edward Dmytryk and seven for producer Stanley Kramer.

Singer **Carmene Ennis**, the widow of Bob Hope's lanky radio show bandleader Skinnay Ennis, lived alone at 195 Desert Lakes Drive in 1975—twelve years after her soft-spoken husband, who appeared in the film musicals *College Swing*, *Follow the Band*, and *Sleepytime Gal*, choked to death on a bone at a Beverly Hills restaurant in 1963.

Fourteen years after the death of rumple-faced actor **William Demarest**, who appeared in 150 films from 1927's *The Jazz Singer* to *Won Ton Ton, The Dog Who Saved Hollywood*, his widow, Lucille Demarest, moved to 300 Desert Lakes Drive in 1997.

Meanwhile, a slow putt from Tahquitz Creek Resort (formerly Palm Springs Municipal Golf Course), where streets are affectionately named Bob-O-Link, Lakeside, and Pebble Beach, **Scott Ellsworth**, the basso-profundo deejay of Cathedral City radio station KWXY, who earned the reverence of music buffs as creator and host of the long-running Los Angeles KFI-AM jazz program "Scott's Place," resides at 6117 Arroyo Road in Mountain Shadows.

TV Producer **Jo Swerling Jr.**, who assembled some of Stephen J. Cannell's biggest prime-time hits, including *Baretta*, *The A-Team*, *Hunter*, *21 Jump Street*, and *The Commish*, blending humor and hard-hitting action, lived at 6176 Arroyo Road (off Golf Club Drive and Montecito Drive) in 1981. His father, Jo Swerling, wrote the screenplays for *The Westerner* and *The Pride of the Yankees* starring Gary Cooper, as well as Alfred Hitchcock's waterlogged *Lifeboat*.

Turning west on Highway 111, past Rimrock Shopping Center, **Robert Kline**, the respected producer of William F. Buckley Jr.'s *Firing Line*, as well as the Oscar-nominated 1981 documentary *Being Different* and Oliver Stone's Vietnam romance *Heaven & Earth*, lives nearby with his two sons, Adam and Joshua, in a Canyon Sands condominium at 2277 North Gene Autry Trail.

In 1961, **Gene Autry** bought the Holiday Inn at 4200 East Palm Canyon Drive. Country singer Gene Austin crooned "My Blue Heaven" and other songs to a packed audience when the hotel officially reopened as Melody Ranch in 1965, and Autry tossed his white Stetson into the air yelling, "Drinks are on the house!" The hotel, packed from top to bottom with fancy-dressed señoritas, became the preferred hangout of the singing cowboy's buddies Pat Buttram and Smiley Burnette, where they indulged each other during happy hour in the Red Cantina Lounge.

Whenever he was sleepy-eyed or hungover, Autry stayed overnight at the Western-style ponderosa, which he subsequently renamed the Gene Autry Hotel, regaling appreciative diners with songs and stories every Easter, Thanksgiving, and Christmas for three unforgettable decades until its sale in 1994. At that time, the sixteen-acre establishment closed its doors and underwent a complete makeover. One wonders what members of Autry's baseball team, the Angels, who used to hit the hay there during spring training, would have thought when the hotel reopened the following year as a gaudy facsimile of the Trianon Palace in Versailles, offering the latest hairstyles, facial masks, and body waxings under the supervision of French fashion designer Hubert de Givenchy and his trained staff.

Robert Downey Jr. after he was arrested and booked at Palm Springs Police Department (Courtesy of KMIR-TV).

A fourth name change later, under the aegis of shape-shifting band singer, talk show host, and game show inventor **Merv Griffin**, the hotel became Merv Griffin's Resort & Givenchy Spa in 1998, a favorite stopover for luminaries such as Gregory Peck, Lauren Bacall, and John Travolta during the city's winter film festival.

Although it's been said that Griffin, a high-profile La Quinta resident, runs a tight ship, encouraging that only "the best of the best" stayed in his French Regency rooms, a careless slip by an unidentified employee cost the hotel its five-star reputation. On November 25, 2000, an anonymous 911 call brought two police cars to a screeching halt outside the hotel's polished marble lobby. Minutes later, four armed police officers raided the $600-a-night room of actor **Robert Downey Jr.**, who the previous evening had been sitting down alone to a traditional Thanksgiving turkey dinner.

Who blew the whistle on him? It could have been anyone: a nervous bellhop, a pissed-off waiter, or a nosy maid with a passkey to room 311. Red-eyed and perspiring, Downey allowed the police to search his lodgings. They found a bag containing cocaine and Valium. The Oscar-nominated *Chaplin* star was handcuffed and taken to Palm Springs police station where he was charged with possession of a controlled substance and violating parole for an earlier offense. After spending the night locked up with drunks and other offenders, the humiliated thirty-five-year-old was released on $15,000 bail and ordered to appear for sentencing in Indio Municipal Court.

Downey returned to work on Fox TV's *Ally McBeal*, from which he would soon be fired, but his legal troubles were far from over. Meanwhile Griffin, facing the prospect of empty rooms, quietly sold the hotel in the summer of 2002. One year later, its name was changed to Le Parker Meridien.

What caused this unforgivable lapse in judgment that resulted in the mass defection of so many desert celebrities? To find the answer we have to journey back in time to the desert's salad days when Hollywood lived in fear of having its dirty secrets splashed across the front pages of scandal sheets that preyed on movie stars' fears and phobias. Actors of both sexes risked suspension if they were caught with their pants down. They didn't dare go someplace that was prohibited, like a speakeasy or a brothel, in case it ended up in the next day's news. The threat of unemployment was enough to keep the boldest performers out of trouble—but not all of them towed the line.

When Robert Mitchum was buttonholed by members of the press who wanted him to describe life behind bars after spending sixty days in the slammer in 1949 for possession of marijuana, the sleepy-eyed actor sarcastically replied that prison was "like Palm Springs, without the riffraff."

Mitchum wasn't talking about hooligans; he was speaking about Hollywood's upper crust, which he never could tolerate, then or later. Unfortunately, his words fell on deaf ears. Increasing numbers of actors found themselves getting into more trouble than a Greyhound bus full of fun seekers south of the Mexican border. Despite agents' repeated assurances of their clients' repentance, the numbers of celebrity wrongdoers continued rising until they reached endemic levels.

There were many reasons for this: more superstars, higher salaries, and bigger egos. The problem this posed for Palm Springs was a lessening of moral standards, a loosening up and letting go of long-held social traditions and etiquette, for example, no more dress codes and dinner reservations. Dine-in became take-out. To stay or go became the big question. But go where?

The burgeoning global tourism industry whisked annual vacationers, including many Hollywood stars, out of the country on crowded jet airliners bound for Europe and Asia. This mass defection curtailed cross-country road trips and put Palm Springs on the back burner. The ensuing energy crisis, gas rationing, and power shortages didn't help either. The final nail in the coffin, so to speak, was the culture clash of two Hollywoods, one old and the other new, that were like oil and water. Younger stars had neither the time nor the temperament to take up golf and tennis. They preferred car racing instead.

Palm Springs found itself in a quandary. What to do? Business leaders did not anticipate the falloff in hotel bookings, and restaurant and nightclub patronage, which had been the desert's bread and butter since the days of the double feature. The same thing happened in Las Vegas, which struggled with a severe economic downturn. But Palm

Springs was hit harder. It didn't have permitted gambling—like it does today.

The city fathers should have been beating the drums like Gene Krupa looking for better business opportunities, but they opted to turn off the lights and save electricity. The stars that did remain did their best to keep the party going. But nobody wants to be the last person to leave in the morning. So inevitably, as the sun came up, they left. But it wasn't all gloom and doom. The For Rent signs gave a small ray of hope. At least demolition teams hadn't started tearing the place down, saving many historical buildings from the wrecker's ball. The wistful song "As Time Goes By" perfectly described the city's heartbreaking dilemma.

When recent mayor William Kleindienst first arrived in the desert, he said it was still parochial by today's standards, but with a cosmopolitan spin to it. Much of the credit for turning things around has been attributed to Kleindienst, who served two consecutive terms in office (he was defeated at the polls by openly gay African-American candidate Ron Oden in November 2003) along with his predecessor Sonny Bono, who brought the golf and tennis resort constant media attention via his frequent appearances on *Good Morning America* and *The Late Show with David Letterman*. They lobbied the state capital, as well as Congress, imploring government and corporate investors to pump money into the stagnating local economy.

Like the misty village of Brigadoon, to which this fragile paradise has been likened, disappearing then reappearing every one hundred years, the viability of Palm Springs as a metaphorical gold mine of tourism has, up until now, been entirely dependant on the whims of high society. Entrepreneurs frequently missed this finer point, pandering only to obstinate bluebloods instead of a broader clientele. The lone exception was the Agua Caliente Band of Cahuilla Indians, whose push into legalized gaming after so many years of red tape has so far provided more than two thousand jobs and approximately $33 million in revenue. Who would have thought that these descendants of Indian chieftains would bring future economic prosperity to the same city that ostracized their ancestors.

Regardless, it has taken the city nearly fifty years to repeal archaic laws and endorse much-needed development. Progressive change in the desert has never come easily. Draconian policies almost strangled the moribund city to death—at a time when it needed every dollar it could lay its hands on to repair the damage that had been done to its commercial infrastructure.

The slow but inevitable shift to more upscale marketing of the city's natural and man-made attributes, encompassing wildlife education and architectural preservation to hotel management and business administration, has defined the city and given its political leaders and constituents a renewed sense of purpose. This unwavering self-determination, striving to overcome environmental and economic adversity, was never more apparent than during the last six years after more than a decade of severe fiscal drought, when new generations of enthusiastic homebuyers, architectural scholars, and dedicated film buffs rediscovered the city's finer points—from crumbling Spanish-Colonial palaces and faded art-deco hotels to forlorn midcentury modern masterpieces.

These latter-day angels with a passion for brick and mortar have breathed needed life back into the city's neglected post-and-beam structures when the only alternative for most of them was the onset of a rumbling bulldozer. This welcome metamorphosis followed a similar revitalization of West Hollywood, California and South Beach, Florida, when tens of thousands of motivated young people, many of them gays and lesbians, began buying up property, painstakingly restoring and refurbishing the teetering structures. The significance of this new architectural movement cannot be denied even if the results sometimes run counter to tradition.

What cannot be argued is the seemingly limitless choice and variety of individual expression that has proliferated throughout the desert region like tiny wildflowers bursting forth after a heavy rainstorm. In December 2002, the Agua Caliente Band of Indians, who control sixty-seven hundred acres of valuable land in and around Palm Springs, broke ground on a new $95-million casino project in the business district. Eleven months later, the newly-opened Spa Resort Casino with 1,000 slots, 40 table games, a 300-seat buffet, and 150-seat cocktail lounge, opened its doors to the public. It is hoped that this contemporary, Las Vegas-style configuration of swaying palms, granite boulders, and blue-tiled turrets, which signifies the sovereign tribe's affinity with water, will take the desert empire into a new cultural phase heralding the city's belated entry into the twenty-first century.

Tribal chairman Richard Milanovich, who has galvanized the local Indians in their fight for financial independence, proclaimed the casino's official unveiling a grand day. Supporters of the tribe's three hundred members might call it sweet revenge. If the tribe's members have learned one important lesson from their Hollywood invaders, who made Palm Springs the Playground of the Stars, it is, Build It and They Will Come.

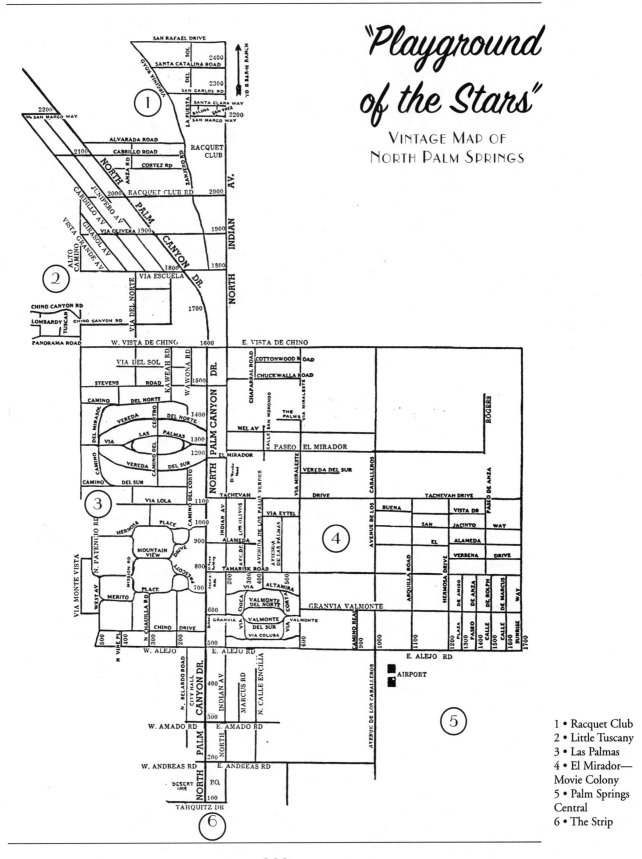

"Playground of the Stars"

VINTAGE MAP OF
NORTH PALM SPRINGS

1 • Racquet Club
2 • Little Tuscany
3 • Las Palmas
4 • El Mirador—
Movie Colony
5 • Palm Springs
Central
6 • The Strip

VINTAGE MAP OF
SOUTH PALM SPRINGS

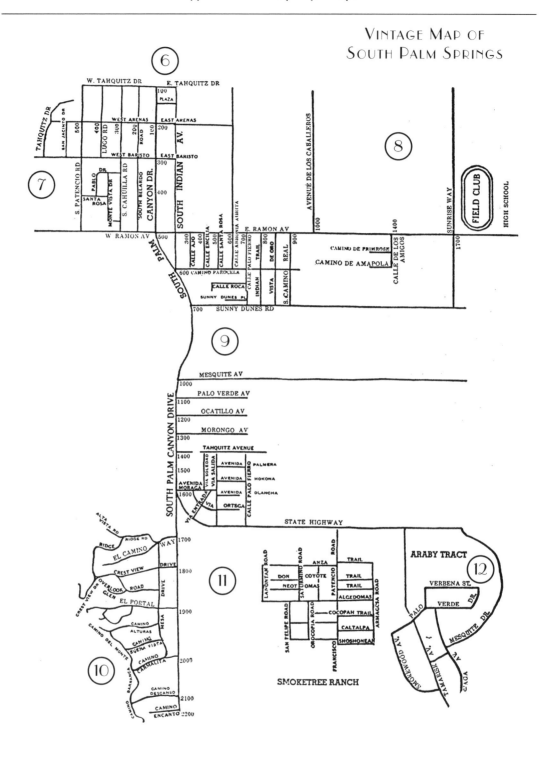

6 • The Strip
7 • Tennis Club
8 • Palm Springs
Central
9 • Greater Deepwell
10 • Mesa
11 • South Palm
Springs
12 • Araby—
Southridge

Bibliography

The following books and magazine articles were either referenced or quoted by the author in the preceding text:

Ainsworth, Katherine. *The McCallum Saga*. Palm Springs Public Library, Palm Springs, CA, 1996.

Albrecht, Donald. *Designing Dreams: Modern Architecture in the Movies*. Harper & Row, New York, 1986.

Amburn, Ellis. *The Sexiest Man Alive: A Biography of Warren Beatty*. Harper Entertainment, New York, 2002.

Amory, Cleveland. *The Last Resorts*. Harper & Brothers, New York, 1952.

Bach, Steven. *Dazzler: The Life and Times of Moss Hart*. Alfred A. Knopf, New York, 2001.

Barson, Michael. *The Illustrated Who's Who of Hollywood Directors*. The Noonday Press, New York, 1995.

Bellamy, Ralph. *When The Smoke Hit The Fan*. Doubleday & Co, New York, 1979.

Benny, Jack and Joan Benny. *Sunday Nights At Seven*. Warner Books, New York, 1990.

Berg, A. Scott. *Goldwyn*. Alfred A. Knopf, New York, 1989.

Black, Shirley Temple. *Child Star*. McGraw-Hill Publishing Co, New York, 1988.

Blackwell, Mr. with Vernon Patterson. *From Rags to Bitches*. General Publishing Group, Los Angeles, 1995.

Bogert, Frank M. *Palm Springs: First Hundred Years*. Palm Springs Heritage Associates, 1987.

Bono, Sonny. *And The Beat Goes On*. Pocket Books, New York, 1991.

Boynton, Margaret, as told by Chief Francisco Patencio. *Stories and Legends of the Palm Springs Indians*. Times-Mirror, Los Angeles, 1939.

Brady, Kathleen. *Lucille: The Life of Lucille Ball*. Hyperion, New York, 1994.

Brown, Peter H. *Such Devoted Sisters: Those Fabulous Gabors*. St. Martin's Press, New York, 1985.

—————. *Kim Novak: Reluctant Goddess*. St. Martin's Press, New York, 1986.

Cahn, Sammy. *I Should Care*. Arbor House, New York, 1974.

Callinicos, Constantine with Ray Robinson. *The Mario Lanza Story*. Coward-McCann, New York, 1960.

Cassiday, Bruce. *Dinah!* Franklin Watts, New York, 1979.

Cher as told to Jeff Coplon. *The First Time*. Simon & Schuster, New York, 1998.

Clarke, Gerald. *Capote: A Biography*. Simon & Schuster, New York 1988.

Colacello, Bob. "Palm Springs Weekends." *Vanity Fair*, June 1999.

Collier, Peter and David Horowitz. *The Rockefellers: An American Dynasty*. Holt, Rinehart and Winston, New York, 1976.

Cooper, Jackie with Dick Kleiner. *Please Don't Shoot My Dog*. William Morrow & Co, New York, 1981.

Cotten, Joseph. *Vanity Will Get You Somewhere*. Mercury House, San Francisco, 1987.

Crane, Cheryl with Cliff Jahr. *Detour*. Arbor House/William Morrow, New York, 1988.

Curtis, James. *James Whale: A New World of Gods and Monsters*. Faber and Faber, Boston-London, 1998.

Curtis, Tony with Barry Paris. *Tony Curtis: The Autobiography*. William Morrow & Co, New York, 1993.

Cygelman, Adele. *Palm Springs Modern*. Rizzoli, New York, 1999.

Dardis, Tom. *Harold Lloyd: The Man On The Clock*. Viking Press, New York, 1983.

Darin, Dodd and Maxine Paetro. *Dreamlovers*. Warner Books, New York, 1994.

Davidson, Bill. *Spencer Tracy: Tragic Idol*. E.P. Dutton, New York, 1987.

Davis, Ronald L. *Van Johnson: MGM's Golden Boy*. University Press of Mississippi, Jackson, 2001.

Donati, William. *Ida Lupino: A Biography*. University Press of Kentucky, Lexington, 1996.

Douglas, Kirk. *The Ragman's Son*. Simon & Schuster, New York, 1988.

—————. *Climbing the Mountain: My Search for Meaning*. Simon & Schuster, New York, 1997.

Drake, James A. and Kristin Beall Ludecke, editors. *Lily Pons: A Centennial Portrait*. Amadeus Press, Portland, Oregon, 1999.

Eells, George. *Hedda and Louella*. G.P. Putnam's Sons, New York, 1972.

Eliot, Marc. *Walt Disney: Hollywood's Dark Prince*. Birch Lane Press, New York, 1993.

Escher, Frank, editor. *John Lautner, Architect*. Artemis, London, 1994.

Evans, Robert. *The Kid Stays in The Picture*. Hyperion, New York, 1994.

Fisher, Eddie with David Fisher. *Been There, Done That*. St. Martin's Press, New York, 1999.

Francisco, Charles. *Gentleman: The William Powell Story*. St. Martin's Press, New York, 1985.

Gabor, Jolie as told to Cindy Adams. *Jolie Gabor*. Mason/Charter, New York, 1975.

Gardner, Ava. *Ava: My Story*. Bantam Books, New York, 1990.

Gelbart, Larry. *Laughing Matters*. Random House, New York, 1998.

Gil-Montero, Martha. *Brazilian Bombshell: The Biography of Carmen Miranda*. Donald I. Fine, New York, 1989.

Goldman, Herbert G. *Jolson: The Legend Comes to Life*. Oxford University Press, New York, 1988.

Graham, Sheilah. *The Garden of Allah*. Crown Publishers, New York, 1970.

Guest, Val. *So You Want To Be in Pictures*. Reynolds & Hearn, London, 2001.

Guiles, Fred Lawrence. *Marion Davies*. McGraw-Hill Book Company, New York, 1972.

—————. *Tyrone Power: The Last Idol*. Doubleday & Company, New York, 1979.

Haber, Mel. *Bedtime Stories of the Ingleside Inn*. Lord John Press, Northridge, CA, 1988.

Hack, Richard. *Hughes: The Private Diaries, Memos and Letters*. New Millennium Press, Beverly Hills, 2001.

Harris, Marlys J. *The Zanucks of Hollywood*. Crown Publishers, New York, 1989.

Harris, Warren G. *Natalie & R.J.: Hollywood's Star-Crossed Lovers*. Doubleday & Co, New York, 1988.

Hart, Kitty Carlisle. *Kitty: An Autobiography*. Doubleday & Co, New York, 1988.

Haskins, James with Kathleen Benson. *Lena: A Personal and Professional Biography of Lena Horne*. Stein and Day, New York, 1984.

Herman, Jan. *A Talent for Trouble: The Life of Hollywood's Most Acclaimed Director, William Wyler*. G.P. Putnam's Sons, New York, 1995.

Herman, Jerry with Marilyn Stasio. *Showtune*. Donald I. Fine Books, New York, 1996.

Hess, Alan and Andrew Danish. *Palm Springs Weekend*. Chronicle Books, San Francisco, 2001.

Heymann, C. David. *Liz*. Birch Lane Press, New York, 1995.

Higham, Charles. *Merchant of Dreams: Louis B. Mayer, MGM and the Secret Hollywood*. Donald I. Fine, Inc., New York, 1993.

Hudson, Karen E. *Paul R. Williams, Architect*. Rizzoli, New York, 1993.

Huston, John. *An Open Book*. Alfred A. Knopf, New York, 1980.

James, Marquis and Bessie Rowland James. *Biography of a Bank*. Harper and Brothers, New York, 1954.

Johns, Howard. "A Most Happy Fella." *Palm Springs Life*, August 1999.

—————. "And the Winners Are." *Palm Springs Life*, March 2001.

—————. "Bob & Dolores: A Love Story." *Palm Springs Life*, January 1999.

—————. "Celebrity Home Tour." *Palm Springs Life*, September 1999.

—————. "The Great and the Beautiful." *Palm Springs Life*, June 1999.

—————. "His Kind of Town." *Palm Springs Life*, February 1999.

—————. "Many Splendored Things." *Palm Springs Life*, August 1997.

—————. "The Suzanne Somers Guide to Desert Life." *Palm Springs Life*, July 1999.

—————. "Too Much of a Good Thing is Wonderful." *Palm Springs Life*, April 1998.

Johnston, Moira. *Roller Coaster*. Ticknor and Fields, New York, 1990.

Keith, Slim with Annette Tapert. *Slim: Memories of a Rich and Imperfect Life*. Simon and Schuster, New York, 1990.

Kelley, Kitty. *His Way: The Unauthorized Biography of Frank Sinatra*. Bantam Books, New York, 1986.

King, Greg. *Sharon Tate and the Manson Murders*. Barricade Books, New York, 2000.

Kloss, Sherry. *Jascha Heifetz Through My Eyes*. Kloss Classics, Muncie, Indiana, 2000.

Kramer, Stanley with Thomas M. Coffey. *A Mad, Mad, Mad, Mad World: A Life in Hollywood*. Harcourt Brace & Company, New York, 1997.

Lamour, Dorothy as told to Dick McInnes. *My Side Of The Road*. Prentice-Hall, Inc., New Jersey, 1980.

Lamparski, Richard. *Whatever Became Of?* Crown Publishers, Inc., New York, 1968.

Lawford, May, Lady and Buddy Galon. *Bitch: The Autobiography of Lady Lawford*. Branden Publishing Co., Brookline Village, MA, 1986.

Lazar, Irving. *Swifty: My Life and Good Times*. Simon & Schuster, New York, 1995.

Lees, Gene. *Inventing Champagne: The Worlds Of Lerner and Loewe*. St. Martin's Press, New York, 1990.

Leigh, Janet. *There Really Was a Hollywood*. Doubleday & Co., Garden City, New York, 1984.

LeRoy, Mervyn and Dick Kleiner. *Mervyn LeRoy: Take One*. Hawthorn Books, New York, 1974.

Lewis, Jerry and Herb Gluck. *Jerry Lewis: In Person*. Atheneum, New York, 1982.

Liberace. *The Wonderful Private World of Liberace*. Harper & Row, New York, 1986.

Linet, Beverly. *Ladd: The Life, The Legend, The Legacy of Alan Ladd*. Arbor House, New York, 1979.

Lurie, Rod. *Once Upon a Time In Hollywood*. Pantheon Books, New York, 1995.

MacGraw, Ali. *Moving Pictures*. Bantam Books, New York, 1991.

Macnee, Patrick and Marie Cameron. *Blind In One Ear*. Mercury House, San Francisco, 1989.

MacShane, Frank. *The Life of Raymond Chandler*. E.P. Dutton, New York, 1976.

Manilow, Barry. *Sweet Life: Adventures on the Way to Paradise*. McGraw-Hill, New York, 1987.

Mann, William J. *Behind the Screen: How Gays and Lesbians Shaped Hollywood*. Viking, New York, 2001.

————. *Wisecracker: The Life and Times of William Haines, Hollywood's First Openly Gay Star*. Viking, New York, 1998.

Martin, Tony and Cyd Charisse. *The Two of Us*. Mason/Charter Publishers, New York, 1976.

Marx, Arthur. *The Secret Life of Bob Hope*. Barricade Books, New York, 1993.

McCarthy, Todd. *Howard Hawks: The Grey Fox of Hollywood*. Grove Press, New York, 1997.

McDougal, Dennis. *The Last Mogul: Lew Wasserman, MCA and the Hidden History of Hollywood*. Crown Publishers, New York, 1998.

Messner, Tammy Faye. *Tammy: Telling It My Way*. Villard Books, New York, 1996.

Meyers, Jeffrey. *Inherited Risk*. Simon & Schuster, New York, 2002.

Moldea, Dan E. *Dark Victory: Ronald Reagan, MCA and the Mob*. Viking, New York, 1986.

Mungo, Ray. *Palm Springs Babylon*. St. Martin's Press, New York, 1993.

Neff, Wallace Jr. *Wallace Neff: Architect of California's Golden Age*. Capra Press, Santa Barbara, 1986.

Nelson, Nancy. *Evenings With Cary Grant*. William Morrow & Co, New York, 1991.

Niven, David. *The Moon's a Balloon*. G.P. Putnam's Sons, New York, 1972.

————. *Bring On the Empty Horses*. G.P. Putnam's Sons, New York, 1975.

Paley, William S. *As It Happened: A Memoir*. Doubleday, Garden City, NY, 1979.

Peretz, Evgenia. "La Dolce Capri." *Vanity Fair*, May 2001.

Pizzo, Stephen, Mary Fricker and Paul Muolo. *Inside Job: The Looting of America's Savings and Loans*. McGraw-Hill, New York, 1989.

Presley, Priscilla Beaulieu with Sandra Harmon. *Elvis and Me*. G.P. Putnam's Sons, New York, 1985.

Pyron, Darden Asbury. *Liberace: An American Boy*. University of Chicago Press, IL, 2000.

Reynolds, Debbie with David Patrick Columbia. *Debbie: My Life*. William Morrow, New York, 1988.

Rippingale, Sally Presley. *The History of the Racquet Club of Palm Springs*. U.S. Business Specialties, Yucaipa, California, 1985.

Rogers, Ginger. *Ginger. My Story*. HarperCollins Publishers, New York, 1991.

Rosa, Joseph. *Albert Frey, Architect*. Rizzoli, New York, 1990.

Rose, Frank. *The Agency: William Morris and the Hidden History of Show Business*. HarperBusiness, New York, 1995.

Schoell, William. *Martini Man: The Life of Dean Martin*. Taylor Publishing, Dallas, Texas, 1999.

Scully, Frank. *In Armour Bright*. Chilton Books, Philadelphia and New York, 1963.

Serraino, Pierluigi and Julius Shulman. *Modernism Rediscovered*. Taschen, Cologne, 2000.

Sherman, Vincent. *Studio Affairs*. University Press of Kentucky, Lexington, 1996.

Shipman, David. *Judy Garland: The Secret Life of an American Legend*. Hyperion, New York, 1992.

Shore, Sammy. *The Warm-Up*. William Morrow & Co., New York, 1984.

Smith, Sally Bedell. *In All His Glory*. Simon & Schuster, New York, 1990.

Somers, Suzanne. *After the Fall*. Crown Publishers, New York, 1998.

Sperling, Cass Warner and Cork Millner. *Hollywood Be Thy Name*. Prima Publishing, Rocklin, CA, 1994.

Stenn, David. *Clara Bow: Runnin' Wild*. Doubleday, New York, 1988.

Stine, Whitney. *Stars & Star Handlers*. Roundtable Publishing, Santa Monica, 1985.

Strait, Raymond. *Queen of Ice, Queen of Shadows*. Stein and Day, New York, 1985.

Swanson, Gloria. *Swanson on Swanson*. Random House, New York, 1980.

Thomas, Bob. *Building a Company: Roy O. Disney and the Creation of an Entertainment Empire*. Hyperion, New York, 1998.

————. *Golden Boy: The Untold Story of William Holden*. St. Martin's Press, New York, 1983.

————. *Liberace: The True Story*. St. Martin's Press, New York, 1987.

Thomson, David. *Showman: The Life of David O. Selznick*. Alfred A. Knopf, New York, 1992.

Toffel, Neile McQueen. *My Husband, My Friend*. Atheneum, New York, 1986.

Turk, Edward Baron. *Hollywood Diva: A Biography of Jeanette MacDonald*. University of California Press, Berkeley and Los Angeles, 1998.

Turner, Lana. *Lana*. E.P. Dutton, New York, 1982.

Vanderbeets, Richard. *George Sanders: An Exhausted Life*. Madison Books, Latham, Maryland, 1990.

Vanderbilt II, Arthur T. *Fortune's Children: The Fall of the House of Vanderbilt*. William Morrow & Co., New York, 1989.

Vellenga, Dirk with Mick Farren. *Elvis And The Colonel*. Delacorte Press, New York, 1988.

Welk, Lawrence with Bernice McGeehan. *Wunnerful, Wunnerful*. Prentice-Hall, New Jersey, 1971.

Wiles, Buster. *My Days With Errol Flynn*. Roundtable Publishing Inc., Santa Monica, CA, 1988.

Wynn, Ned. *We Will Always Live in Beverly Hills*. William Morrow & Co., New York, 1990.

Index

White, Cornelia, 119, 123
Whiteman, Paul, 63
Whittinghill, Dick, 155
Whorf, Richard, 209
Wilcoxon, Henry, 197
Wilding, Michael, 92, 166
Willard, Stephen, xvii
Williams, Cindy, 56
Williams, E. Stewart, architect, ix, 42, 111, 123, 144, 180, 182, 275
Williams, Esther, 170, 189
Williams, Harry, architect, 118
Williams, Paul R. architect, 127, 138, 175, 176
Williamson, Fred, 258-259

Willows Historic Inn, 124
Wills, Beverly, 248
Wilson, Adrian, architect, 237
Wilson, Don, 277
Winninger, Charles, 208-209
Wood, Natalie, 7, 84, 110, 231-232
Woods, Donald, ix, 178, 247
Wouk, Herman, 232
Wrather, Jack, Jr., 219-220
Wright, Frank Lloyd, architect, 47, 80, 117, 126, 270
Wright, Lloyd, architect, 117
Wyler, William, xvi, 3, 90, 91, 202-203, 220
Wynn, Eve, 180
Wynn, Keenan, 180

Wynn, Rosalie. *See* Hearst, Rosalie
Wyman, Jane, 11, 88, 146, 210, 238

Young, Hugh, 183
Young, Loretta, 89, 91, 117, 137, 152, 154, 197, 213-214, 260
Young, Ralph, 254

Zanuck, Darryl F., xvi, 9, 102, 161-163, 164, 165, 195, 238
Zanuck, Richard, 163
Zanuck, Susan, 163, 195
Zanuck, Virginia, 162, 163-164
Zane, Frank, 169
Zimbalist, Sam, 204